Tales That Touch

Interdisciplinary German Cultural Studies

Edited by
Irene Kacandes

Volume 33

Tales That Touch

Migration, Translation, and Temporality in Twentieth- and Twenty-First-Century German Literature and Culture

Edited by
Bettina Brandt and Yasemin Yildiz

DE GRUYTER

ISBN 978-3-11-153457-2
e-ISBN (PDF) 978-3-11-077892-2
e-ISBN (EPUB) 978-3-11-077905-9
ISSN 1861-8030

Library of Congress Control Number: 2022933875

Bibliographic information published by the Deutsche Nationalbibliothek
The Deutsche Nationalbibliothek lists this publication in the Deutsche Nationalbibliografie;
detailed bibliographic data are available on the internet at http://dnb.dnb.de.

© 2024 Walter de Gruyter GmbH, Berlin/Boston
This volume is text- and page-identical with the hardback published in 2022.
Cover image: FotoMak/iStock/Getty Images Plus
Typesetting: Integra Software Services Pvt.

www.degruyter.com

For Leslie A. Adelson, who continues to unlock doors and scholarly imaginations for so many

Acknowledgments

The editors would like to thank Yoko Tawada and Zafer Şenocak for their literary contributions and their colleagues in this volume for their essays. They also acknowledge with gratitude Irene Kacandes, our series editor, for her enthusiasm and stewardship of this project. We are equally indebted to Myrto Aspioti and Stella Diedrich at De Gruyter for their expert assistance. Bettina Brandt is grateful to Daniel Purdy for his involvement and continuous care, and thanks Chrisann Zuerner for her practical assistance with many manuscript-related issues. Yasemin Yildiz would like to thank Michael Rothberg for his helpful input and support during the preparation of this volume.

Contents

Acknowledgments —— VII

Bettina Brandt and Yasemin Yildiz
Introduction: Tales that Touch —— 1

Prelude

Yoko Tawada
Der Name und die Zeit —— 25
The Name and the Time —— 27

Reframing Time and Exile

Jamie H. Trnka
Suspended Time, Exile, and the Literature of Transnational Antifascism: Parentheses and Postscripts —— 31

Anna M. Parkinson
Untimely Tales: Psychoanalysis as Spectral Modernism in Hans Keilson's Novel, *The Death of the Adversary* —— 53

B. Venkat Mani
Future Sense and Refugee Time: Reading Anita Desai's *Baumgartner's Bombay* as a Global Novel —— 73

Multilingualism, Translation, Transfer

Ulrike Vedder and Erik Porath
Gaps and Tatting: Reading, Translating, Collecting (Anna O., Bertha Pappenheim, Uljana Wolf) —— 95

John Namjun Kim
A Betweenness that Beckons: Rhythm and Rhyme in Tawada's Poetic Time —— 119

Deniz Göktürk
Beyond Fidelity and Treason: On the Ironic Poetics of Translation —— 139

Yuliya Komska
Jews, Animals, Migration: H. A. Rey's Commercial and Non-Commercial Nature Drawings in Brazil —— 165

Narratological Itineraries

Claudia Breger
Belonging in the Folds of Fact and Fabulation: Fictionality, Narration, and *Heimat* in Saša Stanišić's *Herkunft* —— 191

Paul Michael Lützeler
Intertextuality in Peter Schneider's Narrative Fiction from *Lenz* to *Couplings*: An Essay —— 217

Katrina L. Nousek
(Re)constructing *Heimat*: Intermedial Archives in Saša Stanišić's *Vor dem Fest* and Alexandra Saemmer's "Böhmische Dörfer" —— 233

Communities / Constellations of the Aftermath

Barbara Mennel
Private Precarity and Public Theory in Irene von Alberti's *The Long Summer of Theory* —— 257

Brett de Bary
Unnatural Disaster as Chronotope: "Lines" of Connection and Language as the "Flesh" of Time in Yoko Tawada's *The Emissary* —— 279

Gizem Arslan
Writing *Heimat*: José F. A. Oliver at *Heim* with Paul Celan —— 297

Damani J. Partridge
Comparison Limits – "Touching Tales" of Atrocity: An Anthropologist's Reflections —— 323

Envoi

Zafer Şenocak
Ausreisen oder Reißaus nehmen —— 335
To Exit or To Escape —— 337

Notes on Authors —— 339

Index —— 345

Bettina Brandt and Yasemin Yildiz
Introduction: Tales that Touch

This volume sketches contemporary transnational German Studies, a field in no small part furthered and shaped by the scholarship, translational activity, and mentorship of Leslie A. Adelson. What unites the following contributions – essays on a wide variety of cultural texts from the twentieth and twenty-first century – is the surefooted opening up of what is German Studies today in transnational, multilingual, and intermedial, ways. Adelson's mentorship of many of the contributors to this volume – as well as many beyond it – has produced a generation of scholars who approach German Studies by "opposing oppositions" and instead exploring "tales" that "touch." That is to say, the chapters in this volume, like Adelson's work, all steer away from limited notions of national frames, languages, and archives, staid self-other binaries, and taken-for-granted notions of reference and instead are open with curiosity towards objects that may not even have been recognized as belonging to the field not too long ago.

Transnational German Studies has been on the rise since the 2000s. Yet this term means different things to different people.[1] Contemporary transnational German Cultural Studies can be described as a field which studies cultural objects and practices (including texts and languages) that have been crisscrossing in and out of German-speaking lands from the eighteenth through the twenty-first century. Thus, scholars of transnational German Studies foreground long but often interrupted and then again forgotten histories of contact and exchange, displacement, multilingualism, and translation. They also bring into focus, though from unexpected angles, the geopolitical events that provoked and/or followed these dislocations, and the new ethnic constellations that developed as a result. Finally, transnational German Studies scholars working across the boundaries of nation states, cultures, literature, and other media bring into view unexpected and creative responses to a multitude of entanglements, undoing ethno-nationalisms in the process.

---

1 For an account disentangling some of the terminology and stakes in the context of reconceiving German literary history, see David D. Kim and Urs Büttner, eds., *Globalgeschichten der deutschen Literatur. Methoden. Ansätze. Probleme* (Stuttgart: J. B. Metzler, 2021).

https://doi.org/10.1515/9783110778922-001

"Touching tales" revisited

The title of this volume borrows, with some modification, one of Adelson's signature concepts. With characteristic precision and insistence on specificity, Adelson introduced "touching tales" as an alternative to the cultural fable of "between two worlds" in the context of her reconceptualization of German literature of Turkish migration.[2] It is worth briefly stepping back to the context from which Adelson's intervention arose.

In the 1990s, Adelson took a strong stance against the prevalent approaches to the literature coming out of migration.[3] She argued equally against, on the one hand, quasi-sociological readings, and, on the other hand, intercultural hermeneutics, the then-dominant forms of thinking about migration literature in *Germanistik*. Instead of reading texts as documenting migrant life-worlds, as in sociological approaches, she argued for reading them as creative literary acts. Instead of taking the "self-other" binary as foundational, and all texts of this literature only conceivable in terms of cross-cultural understanding between these predetermined poles, as so much of the intercultural scholarship did, Adelson argued that scholars should "oppose oppositions" by opening up to the possibility that other stories may be told at the site of this literature.[4] In her subsequent manifesto "Against Between," she identifies the image of a "bridge" "between two worlds" – over and over repeated in many cultural depictions as well as in scholarship on migrants – as the crucial trope underwriting this binary discourse.[5] As

---

[2] Leslie A. Adelson, *The Turkish Turn in Contemporary German Literature: Toward a New Critical Grammar of Migration* (New York: Palgrave Macmillan, 2005), 20.
[3] The literature in question had come first into view in the 1970s as "Gastarbeiterliteratur," was then generalized in the 1980s as "Ausländerliteratur," and in the 1990s subsumed variously under "Migrantenliteratur" and "Interkulturelle Literatur." Literature coming out of Turkish migration also gradually began to be seen as a corpus in its own right, though more so in Anglophone German Studies than in German academia. For critical accounts of the changing labels and their significance, see Adelson, *Turkish Turn*, 23 and B. Venkat Mani, *Cosmopolitical Claims: Turkish-German Literatures from Nadolny to Pamuk* (Iowa City: University of Iowa Press, 2007). Both Adelson and Mani take an expansive view of the literature of Turkish migration as not limited to texts written by authors who migrated from Turkey to Germany.
[4] Leslie A. Adelson, "Opposing Oppositions: Turkish-German Questions in Contemporary German Studies," *German Studies Review* 17.2 (May 1994): 305–330.
[5] Leslie A. Adelson, "Against Between: A Manifesto," in *Unpacking Europe: Towards a Critical Reading*, eds. Salah Hassan and Iftikhar Dadi (Rotterdam, Netherlands: NAi Publishers, 2001), 244–255. Framing her intervention as a "manifesto" indicates Adelson's sense of urgency and her call for dramatic reorientation. On manifestos as a genre see Martin Puchner, *Poetry of the Revolution. Marx, Manifestos, and the Avant-Gardes* (Princeton: Princeton University Press, 2005).

she forcefully demonstrates, the notion of "betweenness" as the dominant way of conceiving the cultural presence of Turkish migrants in Germany, serves to conjure up incommensurable "worlds" marked as either "Turkish" or "German," and migrants themselves as forever suspended in that betweenness, condemned to passivity, immobility, and muteness.[6] This fable, Adelson shows, leads to readings of "things Turkish" as something with clear, knowable contours that corresponds only to well-known stories.[7]

Adelson counters this positivistic conception by questioning the very premises of the discourse and asks instead: "To what exactly is reference made when one speaks of the Turkish presence in German culture today?"[8] With regard to the literature and other cultural texts, this likewise means a shift in framing the inquiry: "The question is not What or whom do these texts represent? but rather What do they do in any given instance? What cultural labor do they actually perform?"[9] In other words, she calls for assumptions of representational stability to give way to open-ended inquiry and attention to the works' particular imaginative interventions. In this approach, "relevant frameworks" are not a given, but the very analytical lenses that need to be probed and reimagined.[10]

As these questions begin to suggest, Adelson's own intervention into the field comes out of close attention to referentiality – understood as the open, dynamic question of the relationship between literary figuration and historical

---

6 See also Adelson, *Turkish Turn*, 3–6. While "betweenness" could potentially also connote a productive space (see John Namjun Kim's rich discussion in this volume), the *dazwischen* that has been most often operative in postwar West German discourse on cultural difference has been primarily disabling. Besides "between two worlds," the German idiom "zwischen den Stühlen" (between the chairs), another frequent trope in this context, makes this particularly clear. In contrast to any malleable notion of betweenness, this idiom exclusively envisions lack and paralysis for those without seats while intelligibility and agency are attributed only to those who have one. The structure that this fable describes has since also been identified by other scholars across disciplines. See for instance, historian and critical race theorist Fatima El-Tayeb, *European Others: Queering Ethnicity in Postnational Europe* (Minneapolis: University of Minnesota Press, 2011) and education scholar Rosa Fava, *Die Neuausrichtung der "Erziehung nach Auschwitz," in der Einwanderungsgesellschaft: Eine rassismuskritische Diskursanalyse* (Berlin: Metropol Verlag, 2015).
7 Adelson, *Turkish Turn*, 22.
8 Leslie A. Adelson, "Back to the Future: Turkish Remembrances of the GDR and Other Phantom Pasts," in *The Cultural After-Life of East Germany: Transnational Perspectives*, ed. Leslie A. Adelson, AICGS Humanities 13 (2002): 93–109, here 93.
9 Adelson, "Back to the Future," 93.
10 Adelson, *Turkish Turn*, 9.

matter – and treating it as a "riddle" rather than a foregone conclusion.[11] *Making Bodies, Making History: Feminism and German Identity*, her award-winning second book, already takes up issues of referentiality, albeit under different terms, while the concept quite explicitly propels Adelson's reading of experimental writer, filmmaker, and social theorist Alexander Kluge in her most recent book, *Cosmic Miniatures and the Future Sense: Alexander Kluge's 21st-Century Literary Experiments in German Culture and Narrative Form*.[12] Whether in direct ways or more obliquely, lessons learned from Adelson's mobilization of referentiality to open up discourse into unexpected realms inform many of the contributions in this volume, as readers will see.

In her scholarship leading up to and including *The Turkish Turn in Contemporary German Literature*, and underwritten by referentiality as a riddle to be explored, Adelson proposes "touching tales" as a counter-fable to rigid betweenness. With "touch" she seeks to identify a mode of contact that does not necessarily impose notions of closed off entities ("worlds") coming together, but rather conjures up and traces non-reified, non-hierarchical, unpredictable proximity, and friction producing variable affects.[13] In literary works, she further argues, this "touch" does not so much occur on a thematic level or through the encounter of discrete figures but pulsates through the text in various formal elements, requiring close attention to narratives' makeup. Adelson rereads Emine Sevgi Özdamar's "tongue stories," for instance, as "imaginative engagement with abstract patterns and literary conceits of halving, dividing, coupling," which link them to "multiple vectors of remembrance."[14]

Through this radical reorientation away from "betweenness" towards "touching tales," Adelson's readings in *The Turkish Turn* unearth the ways in which 1990s German literature of Turkish migration frequently engages in "things" generally conceived of as "German." She thus argues that much of this literature

---

[11] Fittingly, *Turkish Turn* begins with an anecdote that incorporates a riddle and its unexpected resolution: "If it looks like a duck, walks like a duck, and talks like a duck, it could be a grebe," *Turkish Turn*, 1. Adelson introduced the notion of a riddle in her 2000 essay, "Touching Tales of Turks, Jews, and Germans: Cultural Alterity, Historical Narrative, and Literary Riddles for the 1990s," *New German Critique* 80 (2000): 93–124.

[12] Leslie A. Adelson, *Making Bodies, Making History: Feminism and German Identity* (Lincoln and London: University of Nebraska Press, 1993); Leslie A. Adelson, *Cosmic Miniatures and the Future Sense: Alexander Kluge's 21st-Century Literary Experiments in German Culture and Narrative Form* (Berlin and Boston: De Gruyter, 2017).

[13] See Partridge in this volume for Adelson's use of "touch" as a helpful heuristic for making sense of anthropological observations of cultural contact in different contexts.

[14] Adelson, "Back to the Future," 98, 96. For the relevant stories "Mutterzunge" and "Großvaterzunge," see Emine Sevgi Özdamar, *Mutterzunge: Erzählungen* (Berlin: Rotbuch, 1990).

"involves a *preponderance* of interventions into and beyond national archives of twentieth-century German culture."[15] Her specific readings lead her to make palpable, among other things, new ways in which migration, Holocaust memory, the Cold War, and the Armenian Genocide are meeting in these literary texts in unexpected affective shapes.[16] Far from constituting celebratory moments of coming together, she shows, moreover, that "touching tales of Turks, Jews, and Germans" – one of the recurring preoccupations in this literature – "are infused with the stuff of taboo."[17]

"Touching tales," then, is about probing imaginations of a world of commingling of the unexpected, shadowed by complex affects and varied historical phantasms, all brought to bear in particular dimensions of aesthetic innovation through (non-)figural and narrative means. Tales that touch are, in other words, not something given but something to be explored with the tools of literary and interdisciplinary cultural scholarship. It is in this sense that we draw on and generalize her fable for the present volume.

---

[15] Emphasis in original. Adelson, *Turkish Turn*, 12. As this careful formulation indicates, Adelson does not make a methodological claim for the exclusivity or primacy of the German archive in general but about the specific texts and her readings of them in particular. Since then, much scholarship in Turkish-German studies has indeed turned to the exploration of the "Turkish archive" and its transnational meaning. This is not a regression, however, as it was only in the wake of Adelson's analysis that the turn to Turkish has been reframed from a merely positivistic gesture to a much more complex investigation of referentiality. What is different in these recent readings from earlier, essentializing assumptions of "Turkish culture" as a presumed reference point, is that in these present explorations "the Turkish archive" itself is conceived of and interrogated as a heterogenous, historical formation. For examples drawing on and reconceiving such expanded archives, see Göktürk's reading of Şenocak's Turkish-language novels in the present volume as well as Ela Gezen, *Brecht, Turkish Theater, and Turkish-German Literature: Reception, Adaptation, and Innovation after 1960* (Rochester: Camden House, 2018) and Kristin Dickinson, *DisOrientations: German-Turkish Cultural Contact in Translation, 1811–1946* (University Park, PA: The Pennsylvania State University Press, 2021).

[16] Adelson was one of the first scholars to register this phenomenon, exemplified particularly by Zafer Şenocak's conjunction of the echoes of the Holocaust and the Armenian genocide in his 1998 novel *Gefährliche Verwandtschaft / Perilous Kinship*, trans. Tom Cheesman (Swansea: Hafan Books, 2009). For further explorations and elaborations of the entanglements coming out of migration and Holocaust memory, see Kader Konuk, "Taking on Turkish and German History: Emine Sevgi Özdamar's *Seltsame Sterne*," *Gegenwartsliteratur* 6 (2007): 232–256 and Konuk, "Genozid als transnationales historisches Erbe? Literatur im Kontext türkischer und deutscher Geschichte," in *Gegenwart schreiben: Zur deutschsprachigen Literatur 2000–2015*, eds. Corinna Caduff and Ulrike Vedder (Munich: Wilhelm Fink, 2016), 163–175 as well as Michael Rothberg and Yasemin Yildiz, "Memory Citizenship: Migrant Archives of Holocaust Remembrance," *Parallax* 17.4 (2011): 32–48.

[17] Adelson, *Turkish Turn*, 81.

If Adelson's reconceptualization of German literature of Turkish migration was propelled by the need to free the literature from tired frames and explore it from new angles, her scholarship since dives further into the specificity of the contemporary literary imagination, as she asks, "What new cultural functions accrue to the literary imagination at the turn of the twenty-first century?"[18] Drawing on anthropologist Arjun Appadurai's emphasis on the critical role of imagination in today's social life while turning to the specific role of *literary* imagination, Adelson explores the latter's productive capacities to "engage or even alter the dimensionality of contemporary experience."[19] In scholarship inspired particularly by the literary works of Yoko Tawada, Zafer Şenocak (and his sometime-collaborator Berkan Karpat), and, above all, Alexander Kluge, she identifies time as the dimension of experience that contemporary literature engages in novel ways. In contrast to the longstanding examination of the past, however, she points to the significance of futurity as a concern that comes to the foreground now.[20] In fact, in *Cosmic Miniatures*, her study of Kluge's twenty-first century short prose narratives, characteristically marked by their recurring conjunction of catastrophe and counterfactual hope, Adelson argues that Kluge develops "a new sensorium of time."[21] Weaving together postclassical narratology, critical theory, and philosophy, she identifies a "future sense" that his miniatures render accessible to human experience qua narrative form. This preoccupation with temporality as a crucial intervention of the literary imagination in touching tales is also legible in many of the contributions to this volume that turn on readings of literary configurations of time.

---

18 Leslie A. Adelson, "Experiment Mars, Turkish Migration, and the Future of Europe: Imaginative Ethnoscapes in Contemporary German Literature," in *Ethnic Europe: Mobility, Identity, and Conflict in a Globalizing World*, ed. Roland Hsu (Stanford: Stanford University Press, 2010), 191–211, here 197.
19 Leslie A. Adelson, "Literary Imagination and the Future of Literary Studies," *Deutsche Vierteljahrschrift für Literaturwissenschaft und Geistesgeschichte* 89 (2015): 675–683, here 677. See also Arjun Appadurai, *Modernity at Large: Cultural Dimensions of Globalization* (Minneapolis: University of Minnesota Press, 1996) and Arjun Appadurai, *The Future as Cultural Fact: Essays on the Global Condition* (London: Verso, 2013).
20 See the special issue "Futurity Now" that Adelson guest-edited together with Devin Fore, "Futurity Now," eds. Leslie A. Adelson and Devin Fore, *Germanic Review* 88.3 (2013). See also Amir Eshel, *Futurity: Contemporary Literature and the Quest for the Past* (Chicago: University of Chicago Press, 2012), who defines futurity quite differently, however.
21 Adelson, *Cosmic Miniatures*, 21.

Contemporary German literature pluralized

The opening up of literary scholarship that Adelson enables through her reframing of referentiality may be even more necessary today, at a moment when contemporary German literature is diversifying to an unprecedented degree and thus challenges scholarship to keep up. After all, today's literary and cultural landscape in Germany can no longer be viewed through a lens that only registers Turkish-German and German-Jewish voices as constituting diversity. In fact, both of these literatures themselves are undergoing change as well as being embedded in a larger context of a much greater diversity of voices. Just think of Cemile Şahin's *Alle Hunde sterben* [All Dogs Die, 2020], a Germanlanguage novel archiving the distinctly *Kurdish* experience of violence and forced migration within Turkey in a stripped down poetics of torture.[22] Or consider the multilingual volume *Baghdad, Haifa, Berlin* (2019) of Mati Shemoelof, a Berlin-based Israeli poet of Arab-Jewish background triangulating languages, places, and memories.[23] Neither of these texts fits neatly into the categories of "Turkish-German" or "German-Jewish" as they had come to be imagined in the last few decades.[24]

New voices, new archives, new touching tales abound elsewhere in this contemporary German literary landscape as well, potentially remaking its "identitti."[25] 2016 Bachmann-prize-winner Sharon Dodua Otoo's novel *Adas Raum* [*Ada's Realm*] exemplifies further the times and places that German literature is going and the connections it is making in the current moment.[26] *Adas Raum* tells the stories of four different women named Ada across four different historical

---

[22] Cemile Şahin, *Alle Hunde sterben* (Berlin: Aufbau, 2020).
[23] Mati Shemoelof, *Baghdad, Haifa, Berlin. Gedichte* (Berlin: Aphorisma Verlag, 2019). On Shemoelof, see Sharon Zelnick, "Reading Mati Shemoelof's Mizrahi Israeli Postmonolingual Poetics in Germany as Protest," unpublished seminar paper, UCLA, 2021.
[24] For a reconceptualization of German-Jewish Studies, see also Leslie Morris, *The Translated Jew: German Jewish Culture outside the Margins* (Evanston, IL: Northwestern University Press, 2018).
[25] The word is taken from the title of Mithu Sanyal's satirical novel, *Identitti* (2021) about investments in racial identity and refractions of orientation in a digital age. In the novel, "Identitti" is the blogger name of protagonist Nivedita, a Düsseldorf-based doctoral student who finds out that her admired professor of Postcolonial Studies has merely been passing as non-white.
[26] Sharon Dodua Otoo, *Adas Raum* (Frankfurt am Main: Fischer, 2021). The novel is currently being translated into English as *Ada's Realm* by Jon Cho-Polizzi. Otoo, who had previously published in English, won the Bachmann Prize for her first story written in German, "Herr Gröttrup setzt sich hin." A trilingual version has been released in limited edition, with translations into British and American English, respectively. *Herr Gröttrup setzt sich hin/Herr Gröttrup Takes a Seat/ Herr Gröttrup Sits Down*, trans. into British English by Katy Derbyshire, trans. into American English by Patrick Ploschnitzki and Judith Menzl (Berlin: Vice Versa,

moments and contexts: from fifteenth-century Ghana to nineteenth-century London, to a German concentration camp in the 1940s, and finally to contemporary Berlin. Crucially, the novel moves through a plethora of inanimate-object narrators (a broom, a doorknob, etc.) that also generate a peculiar relationship to temporality, connecting posthumanism and Afrofuturism.[27] More than mere thematic expansion, literary imaginations evolve, drawing on new archives, making new contacts, establishing new literary and cultural relations. What we can observe increasingly and to what this present volume also testifies, then, is that this pluralization is reaching a new threshold.[28]

Scholarship thus also has to respond to these pluralizations of histories, memories, multilingualisms, and not the least, formal innovations. New fields, such as Asian-German Studies, do indeed respond to this development in innovative ways.[29] Taking into account the central role of Yoko Tawada in propelling

---

2020). Otoo's multilingualism underscores how central language crossings have become to contemporary German literature.

[27] Priscilla Layne identifies the connection between Afrofuturism and Posthumanism already in "Herr Gröttrup." On Afrofuturism as one of the noticeable dimensions of and as a framework for reading recent Black German writing, see further Layne, "Space is the Place: Afrofuturism in Olivia Wenzel's *Mais in Deutschland und anderen Galaxien* (2015)," *German Life and Letters* 71.4 (2018): 511–528.

[28] In this context, we can read even irritated critics as confirming the growing sense of this new pluralization. See Moritz Baßler, "Der neue Midcult," *Pop. Kultur und Kritik* 18 (2021): 132–149, https://pop-zeitschrift.de/2021/06/28/der-neue-midcultautorvon-moritz-bassler-autordatum28-6-2021-datum/, 21 July 2021. Eagerly picked up in German-language *Feuilletons*, Baßler laments that there is too much attention paid to particular identities in contemporary German literature and that this attention lowers literary quality, perpetuating a long tradition of dismissing authors and texts that tell stories from non-majoritarian perspectives under the guise of aesthetic criteria. He specifically singles out Olivia Wenzel's novel *1000 serpentinen angst* [*1000 Coils of Fear*, 2020] whose protagonist, like the author, is a queer Black East German woman, for "intersectional overkill." Completely ignoring the fact that the novel is told through a questioning dialogue of shifting, non-character-bound narrators, he goes on to attack Wenzel for an alleged authoritarian mode of narration because in one scene the novel does not switch perspectives to empathize with the young Neonazis that the protagonist encounters as a terrifying presence at a Brandenburg lake. For Baßler, it seems, not centering white men is a literary crime. Contemporary German literature appears to be committing this crime more often than ever before.

[29] For more about this rapidly expanding field see, for instance, Mita Banerjee, "Bollywood meets the Beatles: Towards an Asian German Studies of German popular culture," *South Asian Popular Culture* 4.1 (April 2006): 19–34; Veronika Füchtner and Mary Rhiel, eds., *Imagining Germany, Imagining Asia. Essays in Asian-German Studies* (Rochester: Camden House, 2013); Bettina Brandt and Daniel L. Purdy, eds., *China in the German Enlightenment* (Toronto: University of Toronto Press, 2016); Joanne Miyang Cho, Eric Kurlander and Doug McGetchin eds., *Transcultural Encounters Between Germany and India in the 19th and 20th Century: Kindred*

this emerging field, Bettina Brandt has argued that Tawada's writings may particularly resonate with Asian-German Studies because her geopolitically triangulated, multilingual narratives can add to larger scale networks that both fragment and transform straightforward narratives about nation states, ethnic or racial identities while, for instance, bringing into view trade and slave routes. In the process, texts such as those of Tawada and others writing new Asian-German narratives, dissolve both sides of the "Asian German" moniker, often by placing them in specific historical settings, to address differences within "Asian" and "German" speaking worlds.[30]

Adelson has been instrumental in what we might call the first diversification, making Turkish-German literature for instance much more central, but she also has provided and continues to generate concepts helpful in addressing this evolving literary-cultural field and the type of scholarship that could respond to its challenges. As a scholar who has consistently sought out authors and materials that "defy easy categorization," as Jamie Trnka reminds us in this volume, she has much to offer for this pluralizing moment. From the beginning, she has resisted identity-based readings and categories and has been more interested in "touching tales" precisely as a mode of inquiry that is open to the unexpected constellations and imagination. With her, instead of asking "who or what does a text represent," we can pose the question "what cultural labor does this text do?" and "what are the relevant frameworks in which this literature resonates most deeply?" It is through close attention to textual detail that we may see the multiple frames into which texts incorporate themselves. Adelson demonstrates this attention to the work of literary imagination in a recent essay on Emine Sevgi Özdamar and Michael Götting via her attention to

---

Spirits (New York: Routledge, 2014); Joanne Miyang Cho, Lee M. Roberts and Christian W. Spang, eds., *Transnational Encounters Between Germany and Japan* (London: Palgrave MacMillan: Palgrave Series in Asian German Studies, 2017); Joanne Miyang Cho and Doug McGetchin, eds., *Gendered Encounters Between Germany and Asia. Transnational Perspectives since 1800* (Palgrave MacMillan: Palgrave Series in Asian German Studies, 2017); Joanne Miyang Cho and L. M. Roberts, eds., *Transnational Encounters Between Germany and Korea* (London: Palgrave MacMillan, 2017); Chunjie Zhang, ed., *Composing Modernist Connections in China and Europe* (New York: Routledge, 2018).
30 See Bettina Brandt, "Asia, Fantasia, Germasia" in "What is Asian German Studies," *The German Quarterly* 93.1 (2020): 106–141, here 120–123. Other contributors to this *German Quarterly* forum on Asian-German Studies are Chunjie Zhang, Doug McGetchin, Stefan Keppler-Tasaki, Thomas Pekar, Caroline Rupprecht, Johanna Schuster-Craig, Joanne Miyang Cho, Qinna Shen, and Veronika Füchtner.

the literary configurations of temporality.[31] Neither denying the specificities of Turkish-German and Black German writing, nor essentializing them, she instead pursues ways in which both texts under consideration open up "future narrative."[32]

Taking Adelson's concepts as a point of departure, this volume argues that neither the objects of analysis nor the scholarly inquiries follow clear-cut groupings and binaries. Instead, we see a new type of pluralization that allows for and thrives on cross-cutting inspiration.[33]

Migration, translation, and temporality reframed

The three key terms of our volume – migration, translation, and temporality – succinctly point both to arenas into which Adelson's scholarship intervenes, as well as to threads that are woven throughout this volume and are crucial dimensions of contemporary transnational German Studies. Each of these concepts appears in different constellations across the volume as a whole, at times in the foreground and at times in the background.

Of these, the nature of the presence of "migration" may be particularly noteworthy: in many of the contributions, migrations are not necessarily the primary object of analysis. Instead, they are a crucial, unavoidable backdrop and underlying dynamic inflecting German culture and approaches to it. It is notable, for instance, how often *Heimat* discourse – a concept conventionally associated with one, however imaginary, place rather than with movement – is explicitly taken up in this volume compared to explicit thematizations of migration. *Heimat*, of course, is a resurgent, if contested, concept in contemporary German discourse.[34] Two manifestations may suggest the spectrum of its reemergence in abbreviated fashion: on the one hand, the federal interior ministry was renamed in 2018 as "Ministry of the Interior and of *Heimat*," hoisting

---

[31] Leslie A. Adelson, "Future Narrative as Contested Ground: Emine Sevgi Özdamar's 'Bahnfahrt' and Michael Götting's Contrapunctus," *Gegenwartsliteratur* 17 (2018): 41–67.

[32] For an interrogation of futurity from the vantage point of racialized communities in Europe, see also Fatima El-Tayeb, "Time Travelers and Queer Heterotopias: Narratives from the Muslim Underground," *The Germanic Review*, Special Issue "Futurity Now," eds. Leslie A. Adelson and Devin Fore 88.3 (2013): 305–319.

[33] Thus, Claudia Breger takes inspiration from "Afro-fabulations" by Tavia Nyong'o and "critical fabulation" by Saidiya Hartman in order to read Saša Stanišić's *Herkunft*.

[34] See the essays by Breger, Nousek, and Arslan in this volume for detailed accounts of the contemporary turn.

the term onto a highly visible cabinet level presence. On the other hand, Fatma Aydemir and Hengameh Yaghoobifarah's much-cited 2019 edited volume featuring essays by a wide range of authors "with a migration background" declared programmatically and provocatively *Eure Heimat ist unser Alptraum* [*Your Homeland is Our Nightmare*].[35] Whether *Heimat* is embraced or rejected, however, the essays by Breger, Nousek, and Arslan in the present volume underscore that it is situated unavoidably in a context marked by migration.

In German Studies, migration has principally come into view in the wake of postwar labor recruitment and the cultural transformations it has brought. While significant, however, this focus on labor recruitment that has provided the main narrative for Turkish migration, to take one example, has also obscured numerous other concurrent but separate migrations of a political, artistic, or personal nature, that have reverberated largely unrecognized in postwar German culture.[36] In recent years, there have also been calls to expand the purview of the field through a longer historical lens, establishing how much migration has already been a factor in what came to be known as "German" culture before the twentieth century.[37] While such a historical perspective also relies on and includes a broadened understanding of migration(s), a major paradigm shift with regard to which (im)mobilities come into view appears to be shaping up in the wake of the so-called refugee *crises* of the 2010s. Instead of denoting voluntary, legal moves across borders leading to settlement,[38] migration is increasingly conceived in relationship to forced moves and especially the production of refugees, raising distinct questions and also registering differently in literature and culture as objects of scholarship in transnational German Studies.[39]

---

[35] Fatma Aydemir and Hengameh Yaghoobifarah, eds., *Eure Heimat ist unser Alptraum* (Berlin: Ullstein, 2019). A selection of the essays from that volume has been published in English translation in *TRANSIT* 12.2 (2020), https://transit.berkeley.edu/volume-12-2/.
[36] Gezen's study of the moves of Turkish theater practitioners (such as Aras Ören, Vasif Öngören, and Emine Sevgi Özdamar), in particular, strikingly reveals the multiplicity of migrations between Turkey and Germany in the postwar period and their heretofore obscured impact. See *Brecht, Turkish Theater, and Turkish-German Literature*.
[37] See for example, Brent O. Peterson, "*Peter Schlemihl*, the Chamisso Prize, and the Much Longer History of German Migration Narratives," *German Studies Review* 41.1 (2018): 81–98.
[38] In this regard, Tom Cheesman's formulation of Turkish-German literature of "settlement" rather than "migration" is quite apt. See Cheesman, *Novels of Turkish German Settlement: Cosmopolite Fictions* (New York: Camden House, 2007).
[39] Bulgarian-Austrian author Dimitré Dinev's 2004 two-page essay "In der Fremde schreiben" [Writing in a Foreign Land] draws striking attention to the distinct material preconditions of writing for a refugee. As he puts it, "So in order to write in a foreign land, you have to first negotiate with many traffickers and choose the right ones," Dinev, "In der Fremde schreiben," *der Standard* 24 (January 2004).

This shift of attention also reframes exile, as closely connected to refugeedom, in new ways. We therefore argue that German Studies has to have a broadened notion of migrations.

Consequently, migration appears in many different forms across this volume. Yuliya Komska takes us on a journey tracing the multiple moves of Hans August Reyersbach who became famous as H.A. Rey, the co-creator, together with his wife Margaret Rey, of Curious George. Taking as a starting point the line drawings of animals in Rey's archive, which date to his time in early 1930s Brazil where he worked as a commercial illustrator, Komska moves back and forth between the multiple migrations of Rey from Hamburg to São Paulo and the United States. While illuminating the changing styles of his animal drawings and their aesthetic and commercial dimension via Jewish Animal Studies and Brazilian modernism, Komska also provides a different tale of Jewish migrations, with particular attention to the settler colonial dimension of moving to Brazil.[40]

Just as migration is not a subject limited to some essays but fundamentally structures many of them, translation and multilingualism are integral to numerous primary sources as well as to the scholarly approaches that readers will encounter here.[41] This prevalence is in part the result of the varied migrations noted above that lead to new linguistic constellations. Several of the writers in our volume work with translation as both part of their daily experience and as a literary technique for their formal poetic experimentations.[42] In the case of

---

40 For growing research into German-Brazilian entanglements, see for example Anke Finger, Gabi Kathöfer, and Christopher Larkosh, eds., *KulturConfusão: On German-Brazilian Interculturalities* (Berlin and Boston: De Gruyter, 2015). There is also a growing call in North American German Studies to address the field's relationship to settler colonialism, especially as an ongoing structure of the present rather than of the past, through a decolonial perspective. On decolonization as an activist practice that seeks to respond to settler colonialism and white supremacy and thus is quite distinct from postcolonial studies, see for instance Regine Criser and Ervin Malakaj, eds., *Diversity and Decolonization in German Studies* (New York: Palgrave MacMillan, 2020).
41 We are using "translation" in our volume as a shorthand to also include multilingualism, although these two modes of bringing languages together are quite distinct. See Yildiz, "Response," Forum on Translation and Migration, *Translation Studies* 6.1 (January 2013): 103–107. Adelson's own contribution to that forum raises the same issue as a question. See Adelson, "Response," *Translation Studies* 5.1 (August 2012): 361–364.
42 This is particularly true of Yoko Tawada and Uljana Wolf. For a direct connection between these two multilingual authors see for instance Yoko Tawada, "A Laudatio for Uljana Wolf. Erlanger Literary Prize for Poetry as Translation 2016," trans. Bettina Brandt, in *Tawada Yoko. Writing and Rewriting*, ed. Doug Slaymaker (Washington, D.C.: Lexington Books, 2019), 139–146. For the poetic role that translation plays in Tawada's writings see Bettina Brandt, "The Bones of Translation: Tawada's Translational Poetics," in *Challenging the Myth of*

others, only multilingual scholarship beyond German can unlock texts and contexts in new ways. As Jamie Trnka's discussion in this volume of the scholarship on Carlos Cerda's translated literature shows, what seems obvious now – to consider the translational dimension of an exiled author's work and not simply read him as if he had written in German – was barely a parenthetical note in the past. That is, translation and multilingualism are not features of particular works only, but in contemporary transnational German Studies suffuse the field as a whole. As the contributions to this volume underscore, then, German Studies cannot be monolingual.[43]

Temporality, to take our third element, comes into view in contemporary transnational German Studies in varied ways too. In the study of the cultural productions of postwar years, time has figured primarily in relationship to "the past," which itself has almost always meant National Socialism, the Holocaust, and World War II. After the overarching centrality of engagements with *Vergangenheitsbewältigung* (the dominant expression for "coming to terms with the past") for studies of postwar German literature, however, an increased turn to an exploration of figurations of the future has been evident in the last two decades.[44] This focus on new imaginative engagements with future-making, historically tied to the last fin de siècle, does not imply an absolute break with concerns about the past, however, but it does recast these, when they appear. In this volume, too, we see time and temporality appear in various ways as both thematic and analytical lenses. In the first section, specific work on the different functions of time in periods of exile is prevalent while the last section concerns "aftermaths" of fascism and other human-made catastrophes. In the analyses across chapters, temporality may highlight non-synchronicity in the writing, translation, publication, and reception of literary works and explore the implication of this non-synchronicity (Trnka, Parkinson), while, at other times, the treatment of time within texts comes to the fore (Trnka, Mani, de Bary).

Monolingualism, eds. Liesbeth Minnaard and Till Dembeck (Amsterdam and New York: Rodopi, 2014), 183–196.

[43] On multilingual practices in twentieth-century German literature as well as the particular role played by earlier German thinkers in establishing monolingualism as a structuring paradigm of modernity, see Yildiz, *Beyond the Mother Tongue: The Postmonolingual Condition* (New York: Fordham University Press, 2012) and David Gramling, *The Invention of Monolingualism* (New York and London: Bloomsbury, 2014).

[44] See Adelson and Fore, eds. *Futurity Now*.

Chapters

The contributions in the first section of our volume take up writing about exile and refuge in different constellations and literary modes. In each case, however, the vantage point of refuge and exile strikingly turns to temporality, intimating the particular significance of "time" for this state of being, thrust outside the calendrical time of the nation yet also put under pressure by it. The literary works under discussion each reconstellate past, present, and future in distinctive ways that open up quite different "touching tales," as contributors show.

Jamie Trnka opens the section by making a strong case for considering the writings of Carlos Cerda, a Chilean exile in the GDR, who began his writing career there. With texts produced in the GDR in Spanish but for a long time only accessible in their German translation, Cerda's stories, like so much other exile writing, require a rethinking of the frames in which they are read, and point to the need for conceptualizing "an expanded German archive." Meanwhile, as Trnka shows, Cerda's persistent attention to and reworking of time in his stories has a distinctly political dimension. Bringing together in stylistically intricate ways the violences of Chilean and German fascism as well as resistance to it, Trnka identifies in Cerda's employment of "suspended time" the contours of a transnational antifascist literature as a new frame.

Anna Parkinson turns to German-Jewish writer and psychoanalyst Hans Keilson, who survived the Nazi regime hiding in the Netherlands and then settled in that country. Akin to Cerda's, Keilson's publication history provides important insights into the altered temporality of writing in exile. Detailing the complex and nonlinear order of his publications and their reception across languages and literary markets – with a central focus on his 1959 novel *Der Tod des Widersachers* (published in English in 2010 as *The Death of the Adversary*) – Parkinson highlights how especially "untimely" his writings were for a postwar (West-) German reading public. This untimeliness, she demonstrates, is connected to Keilson's "spectral modernism" and the psychoanalytically inflected stories he tells about the victim-aggressor relationship and his daring narrative probing of the affective structure of hatred.

As for **B. Venkat Mani**, he draws explicitly on Adelson's concept of "future sense" in order to provide a reading of "refugee time" in Anita Desai's 1988 novel *Baumgartner's Bombay*. The novel tells the story of a German-Jewish refugee from the Nazis who escapes and then settles in India, experiencing both the last years of British rule (partly in an internment camp) and the aftermath of Independence, which was accompanied by partition instantly producing millions of refugees. Guided by Adelson's "examination of the temporal with the sensory" at the site of literary imagination, Mani makes a case for centering the figure of the refugee in literary studies as registering frames hitherto invisible and thereby recasting the global novel.

Each of the chapters in the first section develops its argument to a significant degree through attention to translations (Trnka, Parkinson) and multilingualism (Mani), demonstrating how much these two dimensions are necessary and productive parts of understanding writings that crisscross frames and languages. The second section features chapters that reflect directly on these linguistic dimensions.

Ulrike Vedder and Erik Porath (trans. Bettina Brandt) revisit Anna O. a.k.a Bertha Pappenheim's story, along with contemporary poet Uljana Wolf's poetic take on it. One of the most famous case studies of early psychoanalysis, Anna O.'s symptoms strikingly included language conversions: she could temporarily only speak, read, and translate English, French, and Italian, but not any German. Instead of understanding this as language loss, Vedder and Porath, together with Wolf, suggest we read these symptoms as a multiplication of languages. Vedder and Porath knit their reading of Anna O.'s multilingualism together with Pappenheim's subsequent story as German-Jewish woman, activist, writer, and collector of lace at the turn of the nineteenth to twentieth century. The motifs of gaps and the indeterminacy of referentiality are reframed by Wolf, Vedder and Porath, multilingually and intertextually, as openings to new touching tales in pluralized expression.

Two poems by Yoko Tawada, one originally in German, one in Japanese, provide the poetic material through which **John Namjun Kim** revisits Adelson's discussion of betweenness. Probing which figurations of betweenness foreclose new knowledge and which can open it up, Kim's intricate readings of this bilingual author suggest that possibility lies not necessarily at the referential level of language at all, but in the mobilization of languages' sonic materiality. Kim thus contributes to a reading of bilingual writing untethered from straightforward cultural, national, or ethnic referentiality and instead offers up close attention to the material of language(s) as the site of poetic illumination.

Like other chapters, **Deniz Göktürk**'s essay takes on both translation and multilingualism, in this case through the writings of Zafer Şenocak. Rejecting the stereotypical pairings of fidelity and treason, so often employed in conceptualizing translation, Göktürk instead draws attention to irony as a literary means of undoing such close referentiality. She demonstrates its significance in particular for Şenocak's poetics across his career. By considering his recent novels in Turkish, she also expands our understanding of the evolving nature of Turkish-German literature and its multifaceted interventions. Göktürk, herself a translator of novels by Aras Ören and Bilge Karasu, also pays tribute to Adelson's critical work as a translator.[45]

In **Yuliya Komska**'s chapter on H. A. Rey's line drawings, mentioned earlier, translation comes into view not so much as a linguistic issue of the source material as of the importance of access to multilingual archives and the need for multilingual research competence in transnational German Studies. German Studies gains better understanding of unexpected creative paths and aesthetic resonance by broadening its purview linguistically and medially.

The third section highlights narratological approaches to contemporary German literature. In striking contrast to trends towards "distant reading," Adelson's recent work continues to advocate and turn on attention to detail in "microscopic" readings.[46] As all the contributions to this volume demonstrate, along with new methodologies such as those developed in digital humanities, close reading continues to be a productive and vigorous mode of interpretation.[47] In this section, the readings specifically draw on narratological categories and inquiries, which they push in new directions. As Adelson has shown with the narratological dimension of "touching tales," such inquiries can yield new conceptions of different scales of imaginative "worlds."

Like Adelson, **Claudia Breger** is interested in the creative and ethical potential of literary imagination. In the present volume, she revisits fictionality itself through a reading of Saša Stanišić's award-winning 2019 book *Herkunft*, which is part memoir taking up pieces of the family's experience in and loss of home in the former Yugoslavia, and part poetological reflection on autofiction. Developing a new conceptualization of referentiality, Breger demonstrates the ways that fact and fictionality are folded together in the making of literary worlds and ultimately argues for the reparative potential of fabulation. To this end, Breger draws on Adelson as well as African-American cultural theorists Saidiya Hartman and Tavia Nyong'o, productively and responsibly crossing disciplinary boundaries.

---

[45] Adelson's introduction to and selection and translation of Şenocak's essays has been pivotal in the author's visibility in Anglophone German Studies. See Zafer Şenocak, *Atlas of a Tropical Germany. Essays on Politics and Culture, 1990–1998*, trans. and ed. Leslie A. Adelson (Lincoln and London: University of Nebraska Press, 2000).

[46] Adelson, *Cosmic Miniatures*, 21.

[47] For an example of digital humanities that productively merges the technological possibilities of digital tools with critical humanities-based inquiry, see Todd Presner, "The Ethics of the Algorithm: Close and Distant Listening to the Shoah Foundation Visual Archive," in *Probing the Ethics of Holocaust Culture*, eds. Claudio Fugo, Wulf Kansteiner, and Todd Presner (Cambridge, MA: Harvard University Press, 2015), 175–202.

Where Stanišić's *Herkunft* meditated on *Heimat* in indirect ways, his novel *Vor dem Fest* explicitly participates in and rewrites the genre of *Heimatliteratur*. **Katrina L. Nousek** who also focuses on Saša Stanišić through a narratological lens, zeroes in on this novel as well as its accompanying website, thereby extending the consideration of *Heimat* to its contemporary refraction in "intermedial archives." Contrasting Stanišić's project with that of Alexandra Saemmer's "born-digital" memory project around the lost *Heimat* of German expellees renders further insights.

The work of intertextuality figures repeatedly in this volume, such as in the readings of Vedder and Porrath, and of Göktürk, where it is an important means of loosening and rearranging referentiality. **Paul Michael Lützeler**'s essay (trans. Bettina Brandt) focuses on the critical role of intertexts that Goethe's *Werther* and Büchner's *Lenz* have for Peter Schneider's 1970s student-movement inspired writings. In these texts, Lützeler argues, Schneider reframes and repurposes the earlier *Sturm und Drang* texts by highlighting the intense subjectivity and intergenerational political conflicts that both historical moments shared while rejecting the self-destructive hopelessness of pre-Revolutionary rebels in favor of an insistence on the possibility of achieving real political change. Lützeler's contribution also reminds us of the key role of the 1970s in German Studies' attention to contemporary literature, which he helped inaugurate and to which Adelson, his doctoral student, was one of the first generation of scholars to dedicate themselves.[48]

The final section explores constellations of communities of the "aftermath." In Adelson's reading of Kluge, futurity emerges from the conjunction of catastrophic destruction and counterfactual hope. In this section, different constellations of the aftermath of catastrophe and hope are at stake.

Continuing the turn to media other than print literature, **Barbara Mennel** analyzes Irene von Alberti's 2015 essay film *The Long Summer of Theory* (2017). Following three young, white, middle-class female German artists in Berlin in the minimal frame narrative, the film explores Left theory coming out of 1968 and the legacy of its utopian imaginings of solidarity from the vantage point of

---

[48] See Adelson's autobiographical reflections on her own evolution in the field, where contemporary literature was not deemed worthy of serious attention until the late 1970s, "From Erfahrungshunger to Realitätshunger: Futurity, Migration, and Difference," in *Transatlantic German Studies: Testimonials to the Profession*, eds. Paul Michael Lützeler and Peter Hoeyng (Rochester, NY: Camden House, 2018). Her own dissertation and subsequent first book on the 1970s prose of Botho Strauss was part of this new direction. See Adelson, *Crisis of Subjectivity. Botho Strauss's Challenge to West German Prose of the 1970s* (Amsterdam: Amsterdamer Publikationen zur Sprache und Literatur, Rodopi, 1984).

the neoliberal present and its production of precarity. Throughout the film, its fictional main protagonist interviews real theorists, intellectuals, and artists and engages in dialogues explicating poststructuralist and post-Marxist theories. As Mennel shows, the film does not take a nostalgic look back but instead searches for collective visions of the future. Yet, as she further demonstrates, this search is underwritten by an unquestioned whiteness, which constitutes a key blind spot worth pondering.

With **Brett de Bary**, scholar of Japanese literature, we return to Tawada once more, this time to her novel *The Emissary* (originally published in Japanese in 2014, and in an award-winning English translation by Margaret Mitsutani in 2018). Set in a future Japan utterly changed by unnamed "natural" and "unnatural" disasters, the novel combines Tawada's signature linguistic play and whimsy with imaginative explorations of the contours of life after catastrophe. In her reading, de Bary zeroes in on the "riddle of referentiality" evident throughout the text as articulating formally both the elusive "absent cause" of the disaster and the literary resource of defying reification that the authoritarian state in the novel seeks to enforce. The aftermath in the novel becomes thus multiply legible, de Bary suggests, as both an account of "post-disaster" and of "post-fascism," in which hope can still be envisioned, albeit via transformed bodies and uncharted routes.

The final two contributions consider the conjunctions of the aftermath of the Holocaust, on the one hand, and of postwar migrations, on the other hand, as constitutive elements of the contemporary. They do so in quite different disciplinary modes and emphases. Literary scholar **Gizem Arslan** explores how contemporary authors who write "under the sign of migration and translation," such as Zafer Şenocak and José F.A. Oliver, draw on mid-century post-Holocaust German-Jewish poets like Rose Ausländer and Paul Celan to articulate a complex notion of belonging. Long before the current resurgence of *Heimat* discourse that Breger and Nousek also explore in their respective chapters, Oliver had been engaged in poetologically refracting notions of "HEIMATT" (the title of his 1989 poetry volume) in poems that bring together Alemannic and Andalusian reference points and linguistic echoes, exploring the tension between multiple national, regional, and local scales. In the present essay, Arslan hones in on Oliver's intertextual homages to Ausländer and Celan in poems such as "Czernowitz," following his visit to the Jewish poets' lost hometown. Through her reading – like Kim's earlier one attuned to the materiality of poetic language – we see how *Heimat* itself turns into a touching tale speaking to unrootedness, displacement, and, not the least, mediation, rather than being a fixed place and sole resource of nationalist and xenophobic forces.

In a quite different register and mode of writing, anthropologist **Damani J. Partridge** mobilizes Adelson's "touching tales" in the context of his own discipline for a series of reflections. These reflections take us from Berlin-based Palestinian and Turkish/Turkish-German youth visiting Auschwitz, to the lifeless body of Syrian refugee child Alan Kurdi on the shores of the Mediterranean, finally to the stories of Palestinians and African Americans in Detroit. For Partridge, Adelson's "touching tales" strike a chord and become a method that allows him to ask how ethnography's practitioners might "reconfigure processes of collaboration" in order to develop a decolonial practice as part of their research.[49] An analysis based on "touch," Partridge further proposes, constitutes a more productive mode than comparison as it "helps us better understand experiences that might be relatable if not equivalent." This final contribution underscores the interdisciplinary impact of Adelson's work along unexpected paths.

Tales that Touch is bracketed by two literary tributes. Among the numerous contemporary authors Adelson has written about over the years – from Botho Strauss to Anne Duden, Sten Nadolny to Aras Ören, Jeanette Lander to Feridun Zaimoglu, Emine Sevgi Özdamar to Michael Götting, and most recently to Alexander Kluge – two authors stand out for their recurring place in her scholarship from the 1990s to the present. In trenchant essays as well as through her translational activity, Adelson has played a major role in articulating the significance of Zafer Şenocak as a leading writer and public intellectual of post-1989 Germany. It was in part his writing that led her to pose the "riddle of referentiality" and elaborate her concept of "touching tales." Similarly, Yoko Tawada's writing has been a touchstone for Adelson's thinking about translations, thresholds, and futurity. It is thus only fitting that we enter and leave this volume through these author's literary tributes for her. Tawada's "Der Name und die Zeit" (translated by Bettina Brandt as "The Name and the Time") offers a "tawadaesque" reading of the honoree's own name, while Şenocak's poem "Ausreisen oder Reißaus nehmen" ("To Exit or To Escape," likewise translated by Bettina Brandt), finally, plays on the indeterminate nature of departure – a fitting way to close a volume dedicated to exploring unexpected itineraries of languages, literatures, and imaginations.

---

49 Besides his contribution in this volume, see also Damani Partridge, "What would it mean to decolonize Detroit? How does anthropology figure?," *HAU: Journal of Ethnographic Theory* 11.1 (2021): 299–308, where he also invokes "touching tales."

Works cited

Adelson, Leslie A. *Crisis of Subjectivity. Botho Strauss's Challenge to West German Prose of the 1970s* (Amsterdam: Rodopi, 1984).
Adelson, Leslie A. *Making Bodies, Making History: Feminism and German Identity* (Lincoln: University of Nebraska Press, 1993).
Adelson, Leslie A. "Opposing Oppositions: Turkish-German Questions in Contemporary German Studies," *German Studies Review* 17.2 (May 1994): 305–330.
Adelson, Leslie A. "Touching Tales of Turks, Jews, and Germans: Cultural Alterity, Historical Narrative, and Literary Riddles for the 1990s," *New German Critique* 80 (2000): 93–124.
Adelson, Leslie A. "Against Between: A Manifesto," in *Unpacking Europe: Towards a Critical Reading*. Eds. Salah Hassan and Iftikhar Dadi (Rotterdam, Netherlands: NAi Publishers, 2001). 244–255.
Adelson, Leslie A. *The Turkish Turn in Contemporary German Literature: Toward a New Critical Grammar of Migration* (New York: Palgrave Macmillan, 2005).
Adelson, Leslie A. "Back to the Future: Turkish Remembrances of the GDR and Other Phantom Pasts" in *The Cultural After-Life of East Germany: Transnational Perspectives*. Ed. Leslie A. Adelson, AICGS Humanities 13 (2002): 93–109.
Adelson, Leslie A. "Experiment Mars: Contemporary German Literature, Imaginative Ethnoscapes and the New Futurism," in *Leseprobe. Über Gegenwartsliteratur. Interpretationen und Interventionen. Festschrift für Paul Michael Lützeler zum 65. Geburtstag von ehemaligen StudentInnen/About Contemporary Literature. Interpretations and Interventions. A Festschrift for Paul Michael Lützeler on his 65th Birthday from former Students*. Ed. Mark W. Rectanus (Bielefeld: Aisthesis Verlag, 2008), 23–50.
Adelson, Leslie A. "Experiment Mars, Turkish Migration, and the Future of Europe: Imaginative Ethnoscapes in Contemporary German Literature," in *Ethnic Europe: Mobility, Identity, and Conflict in a Globalizing World*. Ed. Roland Hsu (Stanford: Stanford University Press, 2010), 191–211.
Adelson, Leslie A. "The Future of Futurity: Alexander Kluge and Yoko Tawada," *The Germanic Review* 86 (2011): 153–184.
Adelson, Leslie A. "Response," *Translation Studies* 5.1 (August 2012): 361–364.
Adelson, Leslie A. "Literary Imagination and the Future of Literary Studies," *Deutsche Vierteljahresschrift* 89.4 (2015): 675–683.
Adelson, Leslie A. *Cosmic Miniatures and the Future Sense: Alexander Kluge's 21st-Century Literary Experiments in German Culture and Narrative Form* (Berlin and Boston: De Gruyter, 2017).
Adelson, Leslie A. "Future Narrative as Contested Ground: Emine Sevgi Özdamar's 'Bahnfahrt' and Michael Götting's *Contrapunctus*," *Gegenwartsliteratur* 17 (2018): 41–67.
Adelson, Leslie A. "From Erfahrungshunger to Realitätshunger: Futurity, Migration, and Difference," in *Transatlantic German Studies: Testimonials to the Profession*. Eds. Paul Michael Lützeler and Peter Hoeyng (Rochester, NY: Camden House, 2018). 5–22.
Appadurai, Arjun. *Modernity at Large. Cultural Dimensions of Globalization* (Minneapolis: University of Minnesota Press, 1996).
Appadurai, Arjun. *The Future as Cultural Fact. Essays on the Global Condition* (London: Verso, 2013).

Aydemir, Fatma and Hengameh Yaghoobifarah, eds. *Eure Heimat ist unser Alptraum* (Berlin: Ullstein, 2019).
Banerjee, Mita. "Bollywood meets the Beatles: Towards and Asian German Studies of German popular culture," *South Asian Popular Culture* 4.1 (April 2006): 19–34.
Baßler, Moritz. "Der neue Midcult," *Pop. Kultur und Kritik* 18 (2021): 132–149.
Brandt, Bettina. "The Bones of Translation: Tawada's Translational Poetics," in *Challenging the Myth of Monolingualism*. Eds. Liesbeth Minnaard and Till Dembeck (Amsterdam and New York: Rodopi, 2014), 183–196.
Brandt, Bettina. "Asia, Fantasia, Germasia," in "What is Asian German Studies," *The German Quarterly* 93.1 (2020): 106–114.
Brandt, Bettina and Daniel L. Purdy, eds. *China in the German Enlightenment* (Toronto: University of Toronto Press, 2016).
Cheesman, Tom. *Novels of Turkish German Settlement: Cosmopolite Fictions* (New York: Camden House, 2007).
Cho, Joanne Miyang, Eric Kurlander, and Doug McGetchin, eds. *Transcultural Encounters Between Germany and India in the 19th and 20th Century: Kindred Spirits* (New York: Routledge, 2014).
Cho, Joanne Miyang, Eric Kurlander, Doug McGetchin, Lee M. Roberts, and Christian W. Spang, eds. *Transnational Encounters Between Germany and Japan* (London: Palgrave MacMillan, 2017).
Cho, Joanne Miyang, Eric Kurlander, and Doug McGetchin, eds. *Gendered Encounters Between Germany and Asia. Transnational Perspectives since 1800* (London: Palgrave MacMillan, 2017).
Cho, Joanne Miyang, Eric Kurlander, Doug McGetchin, and Lee. M. Roberts, eds. *Transnational Encounters Between Germany and Korea* (London: Palgrave MacMillan, 2017).
Criser, Regine and Ervin Malakaj, eds. *Diversity and Decolonization in German Studies* (New York: Palgrave MacMillan, 2020).
Dickinson, Kristin. *DisOrientations. German-Turkish Cultural Contact in Translation, 1811–1946* (University Park, PA: The Pennsylvania State University Press, 2021).
Dinev, Dimitré. "In der Fremde schreiben," *Der Standard* 24 (January 2004): A4.
El-Tayeb, Fatima. *European Others. Queering Ethnicity in Postnational Europe* (Minneapolis, MN: University of Minnesota Press, 2011).
El-Tayeb, Fatima. "Time Travelers and Queer Heterotopias: Narratives from the Muslim Underground," *The Germanic Review*, Special Issue "Futurity Now." Eds. Leslie A. Adelson and Devin Fore 88.3 (2013): 305–319.
Eshel, Amir. *Futurity: Contemporary Literature and the Quest for the Past* (Chicago: University of Chicago Press, 2012).
Fava, Rosa. *Die Neuausrichtung der "Erziehung nach Auschwitz" in der Einwanderungsgesellschaft: Eine rassismuskritische Diskursanalyse* (Berlin: Metropol Verlag, 2015).
Finger, Anke, Gabi Kathöfer, and Christopher Larkosh, eds. *KulturConfusão: On German-Brazilian Interculturalities* (Berlin and Boston: De Gruyter, 2015).
Füchtner, Veronika and Mary Rhiel, eds. *Imagining Germany, Imagining Asia. Essays in Asian-German Studies* (Rochester: Camden House, 2013).
Gezen, Ela. *Brecht, Turkish Theater, and Turkish-German Literature: Reception, Adaptation, and Innovation after 1960* (Rochester: Camden House, 2018).
Gramling, David. *The Invention of Monolingualism* (New York and London: Bloomsbury, 2014).

Kim, David D. and Urs Büttner, eds. *Globalgeschichten der deutschen Literatur. Methoden. Ansätze. Probleme* (Stuttgart: J. B. Metzler, 2021).

Konuk, Kader. "Taking on Turkish and German History: Emine Sevgi Özdamar's *Seltsame Sterne*," *Gegenwartsliteratur* 6 (2007): 232–256.

Konuk, Kader. "Genozid als transnationales historisches Erbe? Literatur im Kontext türkischer und deutscher Geschichte," in *Gegenwart schreiben: Zur deutschsprachigen Literatur 2000–2015*. Eds. Corinna Caduff and Ulrike Vedder (Munich: Wilhelm Fink, 2016), 163–175.

Layne, Priscilla. "Space is the Place: Afrofuturism in Olivia Wenzel's *Mais in Deutschland und anderen Galaxien* (2015)," *German Life and Letters* 71.4 (2018): 511–528.

Mani, B. Venkat. *Cosmopolitical Claims: Turkish-German Literatures from Nadolny to Pamuk*. (Iowa City: University of Iowa Press, 2007).

Morris, Leslie. *The Translated Jew: German Jewish Culture outside the Margins* (Evanston, IL: Northwestern University Press, 2018).

Otoo, Sharon Dodua. *Adas Raum* (Frankfurt am Main: Fischer, 2021).

Otoo, Sharon Dodua. *Herr Gröttrup setzt sich hin/Herr Gröttrup Takes a Seat/ Herr Gröttrup Sits Down*. Trans. into British English by Katy Derbyshire, trans. into American English by Patrick Ploschnitzki and Judith Menzl (Berlin: Vice Versa, 2020).

Özdamar, Emine Sevgi. *Mutterzunge: Erzählungen* (Berlin: Rotbuch, 1990).

Partridge, Damani J. "What would it mean to decolonize Detroit? How does anthropology figure?" *HAU: Journal of Ethnographic Theory* 11.1 (2021): 299–308.

Peterson, Brent O. "*Peter Schlemihl*, the Chamisso Prize, and the Much Longer History of German Migration Narratives," *German Studies Review* 41.1 (2018): 81–98.

Presner, Todd. "The Ethics of the Algorithm: Close and Distant Listening to the Shoah Foundation Visual Archive," in *Probing the Ethics of Holocaust Culture*. Eds. Claudio Fugo, Wulf Kansteiner, and Todd Presner (Cambridge, MA: Harvard University Press, 2015), 175–202.

Puchner, Martin. *Poetry of the Revolution. Marx, Manifestos, and the Avant-Gardes* (Princeton: Princeton University Press, 2005).

Rothberg, Michael and Yasemin Yildiz. "Memory Citizenship: Migrant Archives of Holocaust Remembrance," *Parallax* 17.4 (2011): 32–48.

Şahin, Cemile. *Alle Hunde sterben* (Berlin: Aufbau, 2020).

Şenocak, Zafer. *Gefährliche Verwandtschaft* (Berlin: Babel, 1998).

Şenocak, Zafer. *Perilous Kinship*. Trans. Tom Cheesman (Swansea: Hafan Books, 2009).

Şenocak, Zafer. *Atlas of a Tropical Germany. Essays on Politics and Culture, 1990–1998*. Trans. and ed. Leslie A. Adelson (Lincoln and London: University of Nebraska Press, 2000).

Shemoelof, Mati. *Baghdad, Haifa, Berlin. Gedichte* (Berlin: Aphorisma Verlag, 2019).

Slaymaker, Doug, ed. *Tawada Yoko. Writing and Rewriting* (Lexington, KY: Lexington Books, 2019).

Tawada, Yoko. "A Laudatio for Uljana Wolf. Erlanger Literary Prize for Poetry as Translation 2016." Trans. Bettina Brandt. In *Tawada Yoko. Writing and Rewriting*. Ed. Doug Slaymaker (Washington, D.C.: Lexington Books, 2019), 139–146.

Yildiz, Yasemin. *Beyond the Mother Tongue: The Postmonolingual Condition* (New York: Fordham University Press, 2012).

Yildiz, Yasemin. "Response," Forum on Translation and Migration, *Translation Studies* 6.1 (January 2013): 103–107.

Zhang, Chunjie, ed. *Composing Modernist Connections in China and Europe* (New York: Routledge, 2018).

Prelude

Yoko Tawada
Der Name und die Zeit

Ich habe den Namen „Leslie Adelson" auseinandergenommen und analysiert. Diese Operation verlief in der Sprache, in der ich mich mit ihr immer unterhalten habe: Deutsch.

Dieser Text kann schwer übersetzbar sein, weil er mit Buchstaben spielt. Sollte der Autor ein schlechtes Gewissen haben, wenn er so einen Text schreibt? Nein. Die Unübersetzbarkeit fördert manchmal die Kreativität des Übersetzers.

Übrigens, ich benutze in diesem deutschen Text ausschließlich die männlichen Formen der Wörter „Autor" und „Übersetzer", weil die Unterscheidung zwischen „Autorin" und „Autor" in der englischen Übersetzung sowieso verschwindet. Das erleichtert mich und ich atme aus in der kurzen Pause vom Gender-Krieg der Grammatik. Im Deutschen müsste man heutzutage „Autor*innen" und „Übersetzer*innen" schreiben. Ich habe nichts gegen diese Schreibweise, aber sie hat für mich einen kleinen Haken: Wegen der kurzen Pause mitten im Wort (zwischen „Autor" und „innen" oder zwischen „Übersetzer" und „innen") wird der Wortteil „innen" unfreiwillig stark betont. Ich bekomme dann den Drang, „außen!" zu rufen, denn so viel Innerlichkeit kann ich nicht immer gut ertragen. Innen, innen, innen, außen! Eine Innenantenne ist wichtig, aber ohne die Außenantenne kann man keine fremdsprachige Sendung empfangen. Die Innenbeleuchtung ist wichtig für ein helles Wohnen, aber die Außenbeleuchtung ist genauso wichtig, damit auf der Straße keine einsame Seele vom teuflischen Schatten befallen wird. Das Wort „innen" wird wiederholt, um die Frauen in der Sprache präsent zu machen. Aber eine Frau ist nicht gleich eine Frau. Zwei Frauen können so unterschiedlich sein wie eine Frau und ein Mann. Wenn man die Gender-Vielfalt wirklich berücksichtigen will, müsste man lesbische, asexuelle, pansexuelle, schwule und weitere Formen für jede Berufsbezeichnung erfinden.

Zurück zur Analyse des Namens. Der Vorname „Leslie" beginnt mit dem Buchstaben L, der zwölfte Apostel im Alphabet. Der Buchstabe L leuchtet blumig in Lilien und Lavendel. Hier muss der Übersetzer schon gemerkt haben, dass der Autor aus Rücksicht extra solche deutschen Wörter ausgewählt hat, die im Englischen auch mit L beginnen. Der Autor sollte sich dafür schämen, denn er soll sich beim Schreiben keine Gedanken darüber machen, wie der Text übersetzt wird. Ein Künstler soll die Übersetzung nicht manipulieren. Geschäftsleute sollen die Zukunft kalkulieren, auf Sinken oder Steigen der kommenden Zeit spekulieren. Politiker sollen die Zukunft planen, lenken und gestalten. Die

Übersetzung ist eine Zukunft des Textes und vielleicht ist diese Zukunft am besten mitgedacht, wenn der Autor nicht explizit darüber nachdenkt.

Zurück zu den Buchstaben: Mir scheint, dass sich die Form des Buchstabens „E" nach rechts wendet. Auch der Buchstabe „s" blickt nach rechts. Das kann man deutlich sehen, wenn man ihn als eine Schlange betrachtet. Das Wort „Es" schreitet nach rechts, wo die Wörter stehen, die als nächstes gelesen werden.

Auch der große Buchstabe „L" und der kleine Buchstabe „e" blicken nach rechts, während die kleinen Buchstaben „l" und „i" wie zwei Zedern zum Himmel wachsen.

Es ist nicht so, dass ein Satz von links nach rechts laufen würde. Sätze setzen sich auf einen Platz und bewegen sich nicht. Sie laufen nicht. Es ist der Leser, der die gelesenen Buchstaben mit seinem Blick immer nach hinten, das heißt nach links, schickt. Ist nun die linke Seite die Zukunft oder die rechte?

Wahrscheinlich fällt nicht jedem Betrachter auf, dass das Wort „es" im Namen „Leslie" enthalten ist, genau wie im Wort „Leser".

Endlich habe ich die Analyse der ersten Hälfte des Vornamens absolviert und beginne mit der zweiten Hälfte. Was kann man zu den drei Buchstaben „lie" sagen? Das Wort „Liebe" beginnt mit „lie". Kaum ein Wort hat so viele Komposita erzeugt wie „Liebe". Ich denke an Wörter wie „Liebesknochen", „Liebeszauber", „Liebestrank". Ein Name, der auf „lie" endet, hat ein offenes Ende.

Der Vorname stammt von den Vorfahren, während der Nachname oft an den Nachkommen weitergegeben wird. Es gibt in Skandinavien Familiennamen wie Erikson oder Peterson, und so weit wie ich weiß, bedeuten sie „der Sohn von Erik" oder „der Sohn von Peter". Beim Namen „Adelson" fiel mir spontan die Bedeutung „der Sohn des Adligen" ein. Der Adel ist edel, und edel zu sein ist nicht identisch mit aristokratisch zu sein. „Adel" ist ein altes Wort, so alt, dass man vom „Gotischen" sprechen kann. Ich analysiere nicht etymologisch, sondern oberflächlich. Ich analysiere die Buchstaben, die greifbar sind. Ich nehme sie ernst, so wie sie sind, selbst wenn das die Folge einer Verschiebung oder eines Übertragungsfehlers sein sollte. Aus dem Grund erlaube ich mir manchmal, die Namen rückwärts zu lesen. In „Nosleda" ist jene mythologische Figur Leda enthalten. Zeus fühlte sich von ihr angezogen und näherte sich in Gestalt eines Schwans. „Nos" bedeutet „Nase" auf Russisch, eine wunderbare Erzählung von Nikolai Gogol. „Nos" kann auch „No's" bedeuten, etwas vom Nô-Theater. Nun kann es sein, dass die griechische Leda in einem Nô-Theaterstück spricht und tanzt, das von Gogol verfasst wurde. Sie wird rückwärts sprechen und tanzen, aus einer ferneren Zukunft in die nähere.

The Name and the Time

I dismantled the name "Leslie Adelson" and analyzed it. This procedure took place in the language in which I have always conversed with her: German.

This text might be difficult to translate because it plays with the letters of the alphabet. Should the author have a bad conscience when he is writing such a text? No. Untranslatability sometimes challenges the creativity of the translator.

By the way, while I am writing this German text, I am only using the masculine form of the author ("der Autor") and the translator ("der Übersetzer") because the difference that exists in the German language between a male author ("der Autor") and a female author ("die Autorin") ceases to exist when translated into English anyway. That's a relief, and I exhale during the short break in the gender wars of grammar. To be gender-inclusive in present-day German you would write "Autor*innen" and "Übersetzer*innen." I have nothing against this writing practice but there is a small catch: because of the short pause in the middle of these words (between "Autor" and "innen," or "Übersetzer" and "innen,") the last part of these nouns, the "innen" (meaning "inside" in German) is inadvertently stressed. Then, I get the intense urge to shout "outside" because there is only so much inwardness that I can bear. Inside, inside, inside, outside! An indoor antenna is important but without an outdoor antenna you can't receive a broadcast in a foreign language. Interior lighting is important for a bright living space, but exterior lighting is equally important so that no lonely soul is assaulted by a demonic shadow. The word part "innen" is repeated to make women visible in language. But a woman doesn't equal a woman. Two women can be as dissimilar as a man and a woman. If you really want to take gender diversity into account, you would have to create lesbian, asexual, pansexual, gay and other grammatical forms for each job title.

Back to the analysis of the name. The first name "Leslie" begins with the letter L, the twelfth apostle of the alphabet. The letter L blossoms luminously in lilies and lavender. Here, the translator undoubtedly already noticed that the author, out of consideration for the translator, chose German words that in English translation also start with the letter L. The author should be ashamed of this because he should not worry about how the text will be translated when he writes it. An artist should not manipulate the translation. Entrepreneurs should calculate the future, speculate on the ebbs and flows of the time to come. Politicians are supposed to plan, direct and shape the future. The translation is a future of the text and perhaps this future is best conjured up, when the author is not explicitly thinking about it.

Back to the letters: It seems to me that the shape of the letter "E" turns to the right. The letter "s" also looks to the right. You can see this clearly if you think of it as a snake. The word "es" advances to the right where the words that will be read next are located.

The capital letter "L" and the small letter "e" also look to the right while the small letters "l" and "i" grow towards the sky like two cedars.

Of course, a sentence does not actually move forward from the left to the right. Sentences sit down in one place and then do not budge. They do not run. It is the reader's gaze that sends the read letters to the back, that is to say, to the left. So, is the future to the left or to the right?

Probably not everyone notices that the German word "es" (it) is included in the name Leslie just like in the German word "Leser" or reader.

At last, I have completed the analysis of the first half of the first name and now will begin with the second half. What can one say about the three letters "lie"? The German word for love, "Liebe," begins with "lie." Few German words have generated as many composite words as the word "Liebe." I think of the words like "Liebesknochen" (éclair), "Liebeszauber" (love spell) and "Liebestrank" (love potion.) A name that ends in "lie" is open-ended.

The first name comes from the ancestors, while the last name is often passed on to the descendants. In Scandinavia there are family names like Erikson or Peterson, and, as far as I know, these names mean the "son of Erik," and the "son of Peter." When reflecting in German about the name "Adelson" ("Adel" means nobility in German), I spontaneously thought of the meaning "son of a noble man." The nobility is noble but being noble is not the same as being an aristocrat. The word "Adel" is an old word, it's so old that one could call it "gothic." I am not translating etymologically in this case but am offering a surface translation. I analyze the letters that are tangible. I take them seriously, just as they are, even if they are the result of a shift or an error in transcription. For that reason, I sometimes allow myself to read names backwards. The word "Nosleda" includes the mythological figure named Leda. Zeus was attracted to her and approached her in the form of a swan. "Nos" means nose in Russian, a fabulous tale by Nikolai Gogol. "Nos" can also mean "Nō's", something from the Nō theater. That's how a Greek Leda can be speaking and dancing in a Japanese Nō play written by Gogol. She will speak and dance backwards, from a distant future to a nearer one.

Translation Bettina Brandt

Reframing Time and Exile

Jamie H. Trnka
Suspended Time, Exile, and the Literature of Transnational Antifascism: Parentheses and Postscripts

The motivations for our parentheticals are legion. Sometimes we can't bear to leave out what seems extraneous but feels noteworthy, wish to qualify or amplify an idea, or simply hold a place for labors deferred. Midway through their bibliographic essay on Chilean exile literature published by Aufbau Verlag, Christel Dobenecker and Horst Theweleit write: "Parenthetically, it should be noted here that it is the fate of various contributions and even entire books that they are available only in German editions, as translations."[1] It should be noted *here, parenthetically* – but not literally in parentheses. Even in their choice of punctuation, this parenthetical invites more than encloses. What was an aside in 1987 has come to occupy the critical attentions of scholars of translation and of the circulation of authors and texts internationally. Retrieving exiled texts for new audiences and times, we can challenge the resignation of antifascist literature to a parenthetical. Leslie A. Adelson's work, along with that of the many students and colleagues she has touched, has been vital to these changes in the critical landscape of interdisciplinary German cultural studies. Her attention to the parenthetical, to the overlooked details of multilingual encounters, provides keys, creative images, associations, and constellations that open onto new possibilities of knowing.

This essay emerges in the space held open by the parentheses of East German translators, anthologists, and publishers under the signs of proximity, solidarity, and translation delayed. Carlos Cerda (1942–2001) was one of some 2,000 Chilean exiles in East Germany after the 1973 coup. Already an accomplished journalist in Chile and editor of the Communist Party daily *El Siglo* since 1971, Cerda's first published experiments with literary writing were intimately tied

---

[1] Christel Dobenecker and Horst Theweleit, "Chilenische Exilliteratur im Aufbauverlag. 1976–1987," *Weimarer Beiträge* 14.3 (1988): 1563. Dobenecker was a translator of several of Cerda's stories, including "The Poster," on which my reading turns in this essay. "Das Plakat," trans. Christel Dobenecker, in *Erkundungen II. 22 Chilenische Autoren*, eds. Joachim Meinert and Salvattori Coppola (Berlin: Verlag Volk und Welt, 1976): 129–137. All translations are my own unless otherwise noted.

https://doi.org/10.1515/9783110778922-003

to the experience of exile.[2] Cerda's earliest work in East Germany was for the Chilean theater company in exile Teatro lautaro in Rostock. Radio plays and a socialist realist novel that drew heavily on interviews with Luis Corvalán's family round out his generic explorations in a first, wide-ranging phase of literary production.[3] Having explored Cerda's collaborative work and the complex interplay of histories literary and political in his post-exile novels elsewhere, I devote my attention here to the importance of literary exile – by which I mean to denote not only exile from a political state, but from a community of readers – and global memory cultures to the elaboration of a literature of transnational antifascism.[4]

Along the way, I maintain that new impulses from transcultural materialisms (Hector Hoyos) and world literary inquiries into exile, translation, and circulation require us to consider how some exiled authors – including Cerda – selectively appropriated multiple literary and historical traditions and conceived of their work as part of an international project. This is not the place to rehearse the expansive debates for, against, and around world literature; suffice it to say for now that my attention to the worldliness of texts is meant to highlight rather than elide the translational practice that inheres in Cerda's 1970s short stories – and, crucially, facilitate their becoming contemporary resources for antifascist reflection and action in our time.

With Galin Tihanov, I contend that exile must be de-romanticized and understood not just as an expression of individual alienation and detachment within a framework of liberal cosmopolitanism, but as a complex, intersubjective

---

[2] Antonio Skármeta indicates that Cerda wrote from a much younger age, but I have been unable to find any record of published literary work prior to 1975. Skármeta, "Prólogo," Carlos Cerda, *Escrito con L* (Santiago de Chile: Alfaguara, 2001), 14–15.

[3] *The Night of the Soldier* [Die Nacht des Soldaten] premiered in 1975 in Rostock. For an exhaustive list of Chilean radio plays, including all three of Cerda's, see Waltraud Jähnchen, "Dem Furchtbaren mit Hoffnung begegnen. Chile im Hörspiel der DDR," in *DDR-Literatur '84 im Gespräch* (Berlin and Weimar: Aufbau Verlag, 1985), 89–108. *Weihnachtsbrot* [Christmas Bread] is dedicated to Corvalán, Secretary General of the Chilean Communist Party. A well-known figure internationally, his family spent time in Rostock prior to his release from Chilean detention. Cerda describes their conversations and his aims to bridge testimonial and realist forms in an afterward to the novel. Trans. Volker Ebersbach (Berlin: Aufbau Verlag, 1978).

[4] On Cerda's collaboration with DEFA, see "Melodramatic Realism: Shared Time and Temporality in Gunther Scholz's and Carlos Cerda's *Ein April hat 30 Tage*," *German Studies Review* 43.1 (2020): 87–105. Motherhood has slowed this work, but I remain grateful to the many thoughtful comments I have received in attending to his post-exile novels, especially from colleagues at Pennsylvania State University and the Institute for World Literature in Lisbon, both in 2015. Published separately between 1993 and 1999, the novels, conventionally treated as a trilogy, subsequently appeared in a single volume after the author's death: *Tres novelas*, (Santiago de Chile: Alfaguara, 2003).

relationship to multiple places, times, languages, and literatures.[5] Ultimately, attention to exile as a mode of literary circulation challenges still dominant, national literary-historical paradigms that privilege linear narratives of successive, formal innovations within linguistic and regional traditions. At the levels of production, reception, and narrative movement, historiographic impulses complement attention to circulation in world literary scholarship and support accounts of asynchronous literary practices of reception and translation. Here I have in mind both recent attempts to address how, when, and in what language ideas emerge as relevant, and longer standing inquiries into theory's travels.[6] We do well to recall that Cerda understood the work of storytelling as best analogous to philosophy. Drawing on Hegel's apocryphal explanation to his coachman that ideas are things that take root in our heads, he suggests that stories are worlds rooted in our heads, unreal until they emerge onto the page and assume the form of reality.[7] Reading the circuitous paths of exile and return (or, per Mario Bendetti, dis-exile) charted by author and text alike requires attention to exile in temporal terms that exceed the cosmopolitan.[8]

Beginning with "Das Plakat" ["The Poster"] and extending the length of his career, Cerda cannily crafted connections among his discrete textual and historical way stations. It is in part the instability of exile itself – that is, exile not as a state, but as a process in which even the notion of "after exile registers perpetuation in change" – that contributes to the effervescent instability of Cerda's referents and allusions, allowing him to appropriate and recast German texts

---

[5] Galin Tihanov, "De-Romanticizing Exile," in *Critique of Cosmopolitan Reason. Timing and Spacing the Concept of World Citizenship*, eds. Rebecka Lettevell and Kristian Petrov (Oxford: Peter Lang, 2014), 215–238.

[6] Here, too, Tihanov offers a compelling account of the role of Eastern and Central European thought in re-assessing the history and relevance of literary theory, and the prominent place and time of multilingual, interwar exiles in its genesis: Galin Tihanov, *The Birth and Death of Literary Theory. Regimes of Relevance in Russia and Beyond* (Stanford: Stanford UP, 2019). Edward Said's iconic essays couple theory and exile and remain key touchstones for scholars in a remarkable range of disciplines: "Traveling Theory," in *The World, the Text and the Critic* (Cambridge, MA: Harvard University Press, 1983), 226–247 and "Traveling Theory Reconsidered," in *Reflections on Exile and Other Essays* (Cambridge, MA: Harvard University Press, 2003), 436–452. Jonathan Culler makes the case for *The Literary in Theory* (Stanford: Stanford University Press, 2007).

[7] Carlos Cerda, "Nachwort," *Begegnung mit der Zeit*, trans. Achim Gebauer and Rolf Trogisch, afterward trans. Christel Dobenecker (Berlin: Aufbau Verlag, 1976), 150.

[8] Mario Bendetti, *El desexilio y otras conjeturas* (Madrid: Ediciones El País, 1984).

and histories for his own purposes.⁹ The processual nature of exile cannot but bear on literature's production and reception, on how stories and their worlds circulate and are interrupted or suspended temporally. How and when we come by Cerda's insights, the conditions under which they were shaped, may help us understand how to leverage his creative work in our contemporary antifascist engagements.

Banished from time, consigned to memory

Cerda described the experience of exile as a banishment from time itself, an exile to a present with neither roots in the past nor plans for the future: "With the stroke of a pen our world was transformed into memory."[10] His literary experiments with time leverage the exile's memory to reconstruct both – his pen against the *junta*'s. "The Poster" turns on a Chilean exile's encounter with an indeterminate (anti)fascist past. The narrator's imaginative memory of exile and clandestine activism unfolds in a single day in East Germany, but the actions and memories of actions she narrates could as easily take place in Pinochet's Chile as in Nazi Germany. Raising critical questions about time, memory, and antifascist solidarities through deliberately ambivalent structures and referents, Cerda reminds us that exile must be understood in temporal as well as spatial terms. His writings provide one example of the importance of literary thinking and creative modes of cultural translation to the elaboration of multidirectional, antifascist memory since the 1970s.

In order to highlight the importance Cerda places on the role of literature in articulating the temporality of exile, and especially on the interplay of temporal and physical distance, I situate "The Poster" relative to his other, roughly contemporary short stories, translated and published as *Encounter with Time. Stories*.[11]

---

9 Amy Kaminsky, *After Exile* (Minneapolis: University of Minnesota Press, 1999), xvii. Mario Lillo's reading of *To Die in Berlin* attends especially to references to Kafka's *The Castle* [Das Schloss]: "Cartas en/desde Berlín: *Morir en Berlín* de Carlos Cerda y *El desierto* de Carlos Franz," *Acta Literaria* 39.11 (2009): 77–79. I trace additional references to Thomas Mann's *Death in Venice [Der Tod in Venedig]*, E.T.A. Hoffman's *The Deserted House* [*Das öde Haus*], and Goethe's *Faust* and *Egmont* in another article in progress.
10 Cerda, "Nachwort," 150.
11 Carlos Cerda, *Begegnung mit der Zeit*, trans. Achim Gebauer und Rolf Trogisch (Berlin: Aufbau Verlag, 1976). My translations of Cerda are from the German editions. I consult the posthumously published Spanish, but treat the first, East German publications as "originals" for the purposes of an analysis predicated on attention to the site of writing and conception and

Cerda understood them as an expression of poetry's potential "protest against time" in the most desolate places and moments, employing repetition, disorientation, and delay.¹² The collection itself might be viewed through the lens of delayed and deferred encounters with international reading publics, published, as it initially was, in a German translation that was long without a corresponding Spanish original. (More careful archival and genetic work is required to determine whether differences in editions are a result of translation or of Cerda's editorial changes to an extant original prior to the eventual Spanish-language publication.)

The stories not only deploy an antifascist temporality to suspend narrative time, but were themselves suspended, unpublished in Spanish until after Cerda's death and never again published in the same collected arrangement. Cerda's interest in *Encounter with Time* – unlike "The Poster" – is less in history per se than in time, in the capacity of elements of the old to prevail upon the present: as an elderly German antiquarian puts it in one of the stories, "In my work it's not what's old that plays a role, but above all what was in a position to defeat time."¹³ I argue that the written word's capacity to intervene into the experience of times personal and collective in Cerda's writings in exile is a hallmark not only of his particular aesthetic, but of antifascist writing more generally. Antifascist writing is pointedly not the writing of speed or ahistoricism most commonly associated with fascism.¹⁴ If fascism marks both a reactionary return to a mythic and eternal origin and a teleology of rapid progress, Cerda's antifascist temporality is one of temporal deceleration, disorientation, and a preference for historical indeterminacy that privileges connection over telos.

Encounter with Time opens with "Balconies with Flags" ["Balkons mit Fahnen"], written as Cerda was about to embark on his twelve-year exile but long unavailable in Spanish. In the intervening years, the 1976 Aufbau translation was the only accessible version.¹⁵ In "Balconies with Flags," time seems to

---

the language of circulation – in this case, within the expanded (East) German national archive and a broader antifascist archive of imagination.
12 Cerda, *Begegnung mit der Zeit*, 118.
13 Cerda, *Begegnung mit der Zeit*, 139.
14 Fernando Esposito and Sven Reichardt, "Revolution and Eternity. Introductory Remarks on Fascist Temporalities," *Journal of Modern European History* 13.1 Fascist Temporalities (2015): 24–43.
15 A portion of the story appeared in 1976 in French translation, along with other largely unedited works by Chilean exiles, as "Le bombardement a commencé" in a special issue of *Europe*: "Chili. Une culture, un combat." Jens Häseler, "Literatura del exilio chileno antes y después del retorno a la democracia: el caso de Carlos Cerda," in *Coloquio Internacional Migración y Literatura en el Mundo Hispánico*, ed. Irene Andres-Suárez (Madrid: Editorial Verbum, 2004), 314. Not until 2001 was the full Spanish text published with a critical afterward by Paulina Wendt: Carlos Cerda, *Balcones con banderas* (Santiago de Chile: LOM Ediciones, 2001).

stand still for its central character, a woman with pronounced fascist sympathies who nonetheless puts herself in grave danger by agreeing to hide her estranged nephew during the first days of the coup in Chile. She is drowning in what Cerda describes as a "constant, endless present."[16] In their silent circuits around and past one another, the two come to resemble a clockwork, gears interlacing once each hour in front of the radio and its unceasing repetition of names of the dead and the missing.

Other stories in the volume attest to the range of our encounters with time across spaces and places. "The Poet's Trip to the Heart of Time" ["Reise des Dichters zum Herzen der Zeit"] can be read not only in a tradition of Latin American short stories that project pastness and slowed time onto the rural countryside, but as a critical engagement with the role of literature in the chronopolitics of development, going so far as to suggest that literature could contribute to the repair of a time disrupted and ill-measured. "Dialectic of the Persecuted" ["Dialektik des Verfolgten"] explores the perverse effects of torture on the experience of time. "Manola" recounts the excruciating effects of delayed communication and attempts to return to a past no longer accessible to its protagonists. Finally, "The Student in Leipzig" ["Der Student in Leipzig"] contests the regularity of clocks, repeatedly describing temporal disturbances and selectively identifying the narrator with the (mis)measure of time.

Taken as a whole, the collection relies on time and tempo as techniques and tropes of antifascist resistance. Cerda makes the connection explicit in his afterward: "If fascism is an irrational power because it turns back the wheel of time, there, where it mounts its origins, it not only abstracts history, but forces upon humanity a life it believed itself already to have overcome."[17] The manifest presence of an abstracted historical past in the present-day experience of the exile forces an authorial posture of resistance to time itself. The groundwork carefully developed in *Encounter* and its afterward, Cerda extends his attention to time to a more explicit encounter with history in "The Poster." There Cerda resists fascist temporality with recourse to new resources offered by historical solidarities and so restores concrete, embodied histories to the narrative present through connection with an internationalist past. To his techniques of delay, disruption, disorientation, and irregularity, he adds historical superimposition and indeterminate, multidirectional points of historical reference.[18]

---

16 Cerda, *Begegnung mit der Zeit*, 15.
17 Cerda, "Nachwort," 152.
18 Michael Rothberg, *Multidirectional Memory. Remembering the Holocaust in the Age of Decolonization* (Stanford: Stanford University Press, 2009).

Central to my argument, then, is that "The Poster" should be understood as part of this larger body of work concerned explicitly with time as a resource to be harnessed by literary means. "The Poster" appeared the same year as *Encounter* in the second of two anthologies of stories by Chilean exiles published in short succession by the East German Verlag Volk und Welt to promote solidarity.[19] Shortly after his death in 2001, "The Poster" joined two stories from *Encounter* for the first time in any language – this time organized not around the theme of time, but of East German exile.[20] The Spanish volume *Written with L* ["Escrito con L"] marks the recovery of "The Poster" from the anthology *Explorations II*, where it was neglected entirely by critics. To the extent that any of his short stories have received scholarly attention, most has been descriptive rather than interpretive or analytic; regardless of critical approach, it's clear that "The Poster" is very much of a piece with other stories in *Encounter*.[21] I speculate that Cerda's decision to include it instead in an antifascist anthology published the same year may well signal his own sense of the story's critical purchase for the shared labor and richly layered experience of antifascism.

"The Poster" begins with a series of characters, each defined in relation to a precise time and a recurring event: "On a Saturday morning in September, at six fifty-three, Luis watches the reflection of a cold sun through the window of the streetcar and thinks that this time he will arrive on time." Other Chileans are introduced in short succession, each with a specific time and on the way to participate in a voluntary work brigade in Leipzig. From its first sentence the story's timing, September, evokes the Pinochet coup and the concern of brigade members to act or re-act in a timely manner *this time* – implicitly reminding the

---

19 Also in the *Erkundungen* series were volumes devoted to Argentina, Brazil, Mexico, Central America, and Venezuela. Chile and Cuba each had two volumes. The volumes ranged in size, containing twenty to fifty authors per anthology.

20 Carlos Cerda, "El afiche," in *Escrito con L* (Santiago de Chile: Alfaguara, 2001), 99–112. The restoration of "The Poster" to a constellation that includes two *Encounter* texts – "Manola," "The Student in Leipzig" – in the 2001 Alfaguara collection calls for a critical reexamination of the work these stories accomplish in relation, but that is a task that I cannot attend to here – another parentheses to retrieve at a future date.

21 Häseler discusses "Balconies with Flags" but makes no mention of *Encounter* as a whole in his survey of Cerda's exile and post-exile writing: "Literatura del exilio chileno antes y después del retorno a la democracia: el caso de Carlos Cerda." Marina Polster summarizes the stories in her 2001 study, but omits to include "The Poster" entirely from her bibliography of primary literature: *Chilenische Exilliteratur in der DDR* (Marburg: Tectum Verlag, 2001), 40–49, 87. Despite the lack of critical attention to anthologized texts of the era, Cerda viewed the work of anthologies as foundational to revolutionary struggle, as he notes in the afterward to *Weihnachtsbrot*: "Nachbemerkung," 170.

reader of the immediate failure of antifascist resistance and the urgency of continued resistance in exile as well as past failures refracted through the narrative day. And so begins "the play of synchronicity" and historical slippage that suspends time in Cerda's story of continuous antifascist resistance, begun at one time and ending at another as the thread is lost and found: "For Bruno and Eva this Saturday morning is the continuation of another, long past, shaped by fear and hate. [. . . T]his voluntary work morning may have been predestined for as long as anyone can remember, just like that other Saturday morning, so that a story long since started could eventually find its end."[22]

The brigade is tasked with the demolition of a series of houses to clear the way for a factory. The complex matrix of associations with houses and homes remained a central element in Cerda's work until his death in 2001 and achieved special prominence in his novel *An Empty House* [*Una casa vacía*]. The destruction of the house is granted a primarily therapeutic status in "The Poster" and serves as a nexus of memory, imagination, and discontent.[23] The smell of damp grass in the street lined with old houses evokes a jumble of memories in the volunteers, from "my Temuco" to "something long ago" to empty houses and hand to hand combat in old World War II films.[24] The destruction marks both progress – the new factory – and regression, as its sounds trigger memories of destructive acts committed by fascists in Chile: "The sound of breaking panes awakes in the woman a deep discontent, it strikes her like a resounding slap in the face [. . .] she knows that the discontent is really memory."[25] As the memories of the principle character, Eva, become increasingly dense, so, too, do they become indistinguishable from German histories. Paragraph breaks no longer separate narrative strands; Eva and her husband Bruno may or may not be consistently identical with the man/husband and woman/wife who once occupied the Leipzig house; even at the sentence level, it is no longer clear who is where or when as the story hovers between histories, memories, and present-day events. Violent house-to-house searches and the frantic destruction and concealment of compromising political materials precipitated by the fear of impending searches are difficult to place. Leftists frequently buried or burned books, papers, and propaganda in both contexts.

---

[22] "*Spiel der Gleichzeitigkeit.*" Cerda, "Das Plakat," 129, 130. "Bruno" is "Matías" in the 2001 Spanish edition.
[23] Volunteer and psychiatrist Prof. Oteíza jokes even as he makes the therapeutic nature of the work explicit. Cerda, "Das Plakat," 130.
[24] Cerda, "Das Plakat," 130.
[25] Cerda, "Das Plakat," 131.

At the story's climax, the Chileans locate a cache of 1932 KPD electoral posters concealed in the rafters of the house they are dismantling. Eva and Bruno, like the unnamed man and woman who presumably lived in the house in the 1930s, had once concealed posters in their own home, narrowly evading arrest by Chilean fascists referred to as "plain clothes Nazis."[26] While their posters are no longer within reach, the Chileans' joy and astonishment at the recovery of the German posters is palpable as they distribute them amongst themselves and make their way home from a long day's work, planning where – and when – they will hang them.

Cerda was not the only Chilean exile to relate his experience of antifascist exile in the 1970s and 1980s to the experiences of German antifascists in the 1930s and 1940s. Indeed, Salvattori Coppola's afterward to the anthology explicitly compared contemporary Chilean fascism to "Hitler fascism."[27] The comparison was reinforced by (but did not depend exclusively on) the Chilean government's antisemitic rhetoric, which authors sometimes referenced alongside their descriptions of how Chilean fascists appropriated Nazi symbols.[28] More frequently, the comparison was constructed generically via a common understanding of fascism as a modern ideology and political practice that intervenes violently into the social order to enforce new behavioral and juridical norms.[29]

Like some of his West German contemporaries, whose work I analyzed in my study *Revolutionary Subjects*, Cerda's literary presentation of intersecting histories of fascisms and antifascist exiles might be read with accounts of Germany's role in global imaginations of justice.[30] A story that explores the unforeseeable recovery of its eponymous object, "The Poster" generates an encounter with the past. It models and rewards a new and constructive form of antifascist reading as generative and multidirectional remembrance that circulates still: Cerda's publications were not contemporary with his own national audience, but in using the narrative space of the story to make his own timeliness, he invites us to do the same. We can draw on his inventive practice and imagination

---

26 Cerda, "Das Plakat," 132.
27 See Coppola, "Nachwort," in *Erkundungen II. 22 Chilenische Autoren*, eds. Joachim Meinert and Salvattori Coppola (Berlin: Verlag Volk und Welt, 1976), esp. 285–287. He also references Franco's Spain.
28 In Cerda's case, these references are most frequent in *Weihnachtsbrot*.
29 See Esposito and Reichhardt, "Revolution and Eternity," 25.
30 Trnka, *Revolutionary Subjects. German Literatures and the Limits of Aesthetic Solidarity with Latin America* (Berlin and Boston: De Gruyter, 2015), 90. These prominently include Rothberg's *Multidirectional Memory*.

as we seek individual and collective resources to respond to resurgent fascisms and populisms afoot in Europe, the US, and Latin America.³¹

Attention to antifascist memory can add another dimension to comparative memory studies centered frequently on or underwritten by studies of the Holocaust. Historian Federico Finchelstein, for instance, argues persuasively that: "Despite the prevalence of sources, transnational approaches that integrate fascism with the Holocaust experience are not easily found in Holocaust and fascist historiography."³² His work attests to how deeply time and history are inscribed in fascist violence and self-presentation globally. This is perhaps nowhere more evident than in his discussion of the deliberate production of temporal disorientation in Argentina's post-Nazi fascist concentration camps, and about the explicit attempts of perpetrators to weaponize remembrance and reenactment of the Holocaust, producing in Jewish prisoners a traumatic "temporal schizophrenia [. . .] The victims could not tell the difference between past and present."³³ The conflation of past and present traumas produced new violences in fascist Argentina.³⁴

It would be inaccurate to suggest that antisemitism in 1970s Chile was experienced or enacted in the same way; indeed, historians note differences in regional antisemitisms in the Southern Cone dating to the late nineteenth century.³⁵ No figures are marked as Jews in Cerda's stories. They nonetheless linger

---

31 On the emergence and circulation of Latin American and European populisms, where new populisms have returned to embrace violence and other features that its earliest, postfascist formations rejected, see Federico Finchelstein, "Populism without Borders. Notes on a Global History," *Constellations* 26 (2019): 418–429.

32 Federico Finchelstein, "From Holocaust Trauma to the Dirty War," *Historical Reflections/Réflexions Historiques* 41.3 (Winter 2015): 51.

33 Finchelstein, "From Holocaust Trauma to the Dirty War," 48, 53–55. The temporal disorientation of torture in a Chilean rather than Argentine context registers most explicitly in "Dialectic of the Persecuted," briefly discussed above.

34 Finchelstein, "From Holocaust Trauma to the Dirty War," 48.

35 See for example Sandra McGee Deutsch, *Las Derechas: The extreme Right in Argentina, Brazil and Chile, 1880–1939* (Stanford: Stanford University Press, 1999), esp. 9, 17–21. Differences between Argentine and Chilean experiences aside, nationalist and fascist ideologies throughout the twentieth century in Chile consistently embraced antisemitism, and many Jewish Chileans were tortured and detained under Pinochet. Close connections to Nazism have been exhaustively documented by Víctor Farías, *Los Nazis en Chile* (Barcelona: Editorial Seix Barral, 2000); for a concise overview of the shift from the National Socialist Movement in Chile to post-World War II, see Jean Grugel, "Nationalist Movements and Fascist Ideology in Chile," *Bulletin of Latin American Research* 4.2 (1985): 109–122. Picking up after Grugel leaves off, Gustavo Guzmán explores the increased prominence of Chilean antisemite Miguel Serrano on contemporary right-extremism globally. "Miguel Serrano's Antisemitism and Its Impact on the

on the production of temporal disorientation as an experience of fascist dictatorship and torture that prompt us to consider the experience of a post- and anti-fascist time more broadly; readers of German were bound proleptically to read the 1932 election posters in relation to both fascism and genocide, layering their own experience of time and history with those of the author and his characters. Cerda's "The Poster" produces a countertemporality of new hope by retrieving and convoking transcontextual antifascist resistance in the face of violence in fascist Chile.

To layer complex experiences and histories of fascism and the Holocaust is not to mistake their collapse or accede to what Lea David has termed the standardization of memories of mass crimes internationally under our current human rights regime.[36] David argues that Holocaust memorialization has become the standard against which memory and its efficacy are judged. Reading Cerda out of time and with an eye to her remarks on the contemporaneity of the *Historikerstreit* with Latin American explorations of how to deal with history and memory of fascist dictatorships, we find both resolutely plural ways to remember the past and the promise of multidirectional memories of (anti)fascism to forge new sources of hope in the present.[37]

"The Poster" resists standardization not only in its transnational and transcontextual historical conceits, but also and prominently through its articulation of antifascist memories around hidden and recovered objects.[38] No preservationist

---

Twenty-first Century Countercultural Rightists," *Analysis of Current Trends in Antisemitism* 40.1 (2019). https:// doi.org/1515/actap-2019-0001.

36 Lea David, "Against Standardization of Memory," *Human Rights Quarterly* 39 (2017): 296–318.

37 David, "Against Standardization of Memory," 302. An anthropologist, she is especially critical of the prescriptive standardization of universalized assumptions about trauma and mourning. See esp. 310–314. In a related vein, Carolyn J. Dean explores the complex relationship between an impulse toward universalization and attentiveness to difference in representations and responses to mass violence: *The Moral Witness: Trials and Testimony after Genocide* (Ithaca: Cornell University Press, 2019).

38 I am grateful to the editors for noting the proximity of this line of analysis to Marianne Hirsch's and Leo Spitzer's "Testimonial Objects: Memory, Gender and Transmission," *Poetics Today* 27.2 (Summer 2006): 353–383. Inspired by Roland Barthes's *punctum*, they describe how testimonial objects function as "points of memory." The process orientation of their concept, in which testimonial objects are created, exchanged, and bequeathed, and their careful attention to the objects as both useful for and generative of remembrance, linking personal and cultural memory, require further exploration in the context of comparative antifascist memory work. In particular, attention to how points of memory might be said to function in the case of mass produced ephemera and acts of salvage or recovery rather than intentional preservation and transfer of unique objects suggest productive differences as well as affinities with Cerda's "Poster," – and perhaps other texts engaged in amplifying material objects' generative

impulses here, no plans for salvage: "Don't worry about anything, you can tear it all down. No need to be careful with any of it, says the youngest German."[39] The house cannot be repaired, restored, or recovered. If the global "memory boom" places special weight on the idea that memory is foundational to the construction of collective and personal identity, what should we make of this two-pronged gesture: the demolition of an edifice and the recovery, pointedly, of ephemera?[40] What emerges is an act of co-memory without memorialization, the intermingling of memories of resistance to oppression, erasure, and concealment. Cerda crafts a narrative world in which objects – particular in their very materiality – create historically specifiable but portable junctures for shared or proximate memories that are anything but prescriptive or universal.[41]

Cerda's focus is not on the memory of traumatic violence in and of itself; as the title and trajectory of the story make clear, the posters are bearers of multidirectional, antifascist memory that engenders hope and connection. The brigade members don't respond to the posters as markers of an antifascism defeated in its moment. (Indeed, clearer in the Spanish than the German, the notion of nursing olds wounds or dwelling on past defeats is swiftly and ironically dismissed in the figure of a brigadier licking a minor, clumsily self-inflicted wound as he looks on excitedly.)[42]

The concealment and recovery of the posters in the ruined house punctuate moments of fear and retreat vividly recalled by Eva/the woman and become an emblem of a recovery yet-to-come in Chile. Far from the "fascist rebellion against the disenchanted temporality of modernity" with its cult of speed, Cerda uses the

---

potential through historical and cultural comparison. The narrative indeterminacy of what is being remembered by whom in "Das Plakat" troubles the distinction between memory and postmemory to the extent that the relation of specific testimonial objects to points of memory to which they cannot be said to testify in any indexical fashion would open an expansive field of texts and objects for analysis indeed.

39 Cerda, "Das Plakat," 130.
40 David, "Against Standardization of Memory," esp. 303–304.
41 The editors kindly drew my attention to the resonance of "co-memory" with Irene Kacandes's concept of "cowitnessing": "Die Ungnade der späten Geburt: Challenges in the Twenty-First Century for Central Europeans: German Studies Association Presidential Address 2016," *German Studies Review* 40.2 (May 2017): 389–405. The act of co-memory in Cerda is internal to the fictional text as much as it is constituted between a contemporary reader/cowitness and the text, adding the need for further layers of "transhistorical-transcultural cowitnessing" (396) to any analysis. To be sure, my reading of Cerda's text as timely shares in Kacandes's commitment to active postremembering and the moral imperative to develop a repertoire of resistance in the face of contemporary violence and suffering.
42 In the German, he licks the blood from his hand ("Das Plakat," 136); in the Spanish, he more evocatively licks his wound ("El Afiche," 111).

posters as a trope whose literary effect is the suspension of time in the service of antifascism, a catalyst for generating an encounter with the past.[43]

In addition to this temporal effect, the posters are a historical-material reference: they are what Hoyos calls "things with a history," and as such, invite transcultural materialist analysis from the vantage of the present. Leaning on Hoyos's welcome call for a reinvigorated Marxist Humanism in place of New Materialisms that obscure history and thereby human agency, we can identify in "The Poster" – the story and the object – a material artifact that bears witness to and connects (but does not collapse) lifetimes, changed party, national, and global politics, and human resistance in the face of fascist violence.[44] The significance of printed material in the context of East German-Chilean solidarity recalls specific, historical acts that extend beyond the political commonplaces that might be evoked by Communist poster art, or even the specific institutional commitment to the preservation and display of Chilean poster art.[45] Years before the success of the Unidad Popular (UP) and, eventually, Allende's diplomatic recognition of East Germany, technologies of print reproduction were key to establishing a network of political, economic, and cultural relationships between the two states. Inga Emmerling has documented the central role of East German technical and material assistance to the Chilean Communist Party beginning in 1960 with their interest in East German printing presses. East German support can be connected to the successful mass production of propaganda that ultimately led to a UP victory; Chilean workers' delegations received technical training in East Germany and were among those already safely abroad at the time of the coup or with well-established contacts that enabled them to escape.[46] As an editor of *El Siglo*, a paper printed with resources provided under East Germany's solidarity efforts, Cerda no doubt knew of the important resonance printed material had in the context of antifascist internationalism. At least one of the

---

43 Roger Griffin, "Fixing Solutions: Fascist Temporalities as Remedies for Liquid Modernity," *Journal of Modern European History* 13.1 (2015): 23.
44 Hector Hoyos, *Things with a History. Transcultural Materialism and the Literatures of Extraction in Contemporary Latin America* (New York: Columbia University Press, 2019). Here I have in mind especially his "Introduction: A Tale of Two Materialisms." Baumbach et al. provide concise contextualization of New Materialism in the broader theoretical landscape of the humanities: "For a Political Critique of Culture," *Social Text* 127.34 (June 2016): 1–20.
45 Jens Kirsten's exceptional bibliography includes numerous poster exhibits from Chile and elsewhere in Latin America in the 1970s and 1980s. Of special note here is *Chile im Herzen. Internationale Solidarität im Spiegel des Plakats* (Berlin: Solidaritätskommittee der DDR, 1981).
46 Inga Emmerling, *Die DDR und Chile. Außenpolitik, Außenhandel und Solidarität* (Berlin: Ch. Links, 2013), 362–367.

brigadiers in "The Poster" plans to hang his 1932 KPD poster next to a poster of Allende, reinforcing medial and historic connections.

Cerda's use of the aesthetic to bolster rather than to displace the material thus serves a deep commitment to the construction of an internationalist culture of aesthetic solidarity. Connecting the archives of educational and labor exchange initiatives, cultural diplomacy, and political exile, Cerda's imaginative recovery of the posters activates the kind of associative thinking identified by Bettina Brandt and Valentina Glajar in their work on the politics of archives: "Archived materials tend to bring out connections and allow for the imaginative associations that may destabilize existing homogeneous narratives. In touching archival materials and bringing them back to life, we allow the past to break through into our present, as we critically rethink the immediacy of the latter."[47] As they go on to note, citing historian Peter Fritzsche, the expansion and transnational pull of archives has made clear that "'German history no longer belong[s] to Germans alone,'" – if it ever did.[48] With Cerda, and in our own moment, we can claim antifascist histories and stories as part of a reactivated archive.

Cerda's movement – personal and textual – through and with literatures and histories is elaborate, but not anomalous. As Kaminsky and other scholars of exile literature have noted, exilic identity is tied to national identity, and so to national literature.[49] But it profoundly unsettles both. World literary perspectives – prominently including translation studies – help to capture this dynamic by allowing us to locate exiled authors and their works both within and beyond nationally based literary histories. Andrés Avellaneda affirms, "[f]orced geographical relocation produces fractures and disalignments in literary projects" whose analysis brooks an expanded understanding of the national.[50] Such productive disalignments in Cerda's short stories open onto figures that are both identifiably German and simultaneously stripped of national specificity as nameless Man and Woman, figures who experience fear, hope, and resistance in international and transtemporal contexts.

The suspension of time that Cerda's writing effects generates solidarities that we might productively read alongside Ernst Bloch's notion of a synchronicity of the nonsynchronous, or even a temporal pendant to Paolo Bartolini's

---

[47] Bettina Brandt and Valentina Glajar, "Introduction: The Politics of Archives," *Seminar* 53.3 (September 2017): 193.
[48] Brandt and Glajar, "The Politics of Archives," 198.
[49] Kaminsky, *After Exile*, 22.
[50] Cited in Kaminsky, *After Exile*, 37.

notion of linguistic inclusion via techniques of superimposition, modes of writing that withhold points of textual orientation by layering texts,

> occlude[ing] what is already known [and] preclude[ing] the full and unimpeded visibility of the unknown. The act of superimposition, because of its very nature of uncategorical and non-narrative inclusion, introduces another language that speaks the unspeakable and that communicates the very negativity of language. It is not that translation and exile leave us without language, or identity, or clarity, or orientation. Rather, they leave us with a further language that can say what the other two cannot, that can expose and communicate their limitations.[51]

At the interstices of historical and cultural/linguistic translation, it is the encounter with time (in the story proper and for its readers) that calls for attention to the ways in which antifascist resistance is both radically contingent on its historical moment and transferable (in the shape of objects, affects, and dispositions such as hope).

Cerda leverages the visible limits of national memories of (anti)fascism, reorienting our views of each through a comparative impulse that geographic and temporal superimposition invites. The sense of connection and historical perspective that he achieves relies both on the translation of events and objects and the translation and anthologization that enabled his story to find an audience. Without confusing the historical and generic specificity that inheres in Rebecca Walkowitz's study of the novel in world literature, we might productively ask how Cerda's work, too, is "born translated" in the sense that translation is "neither secondary nor incidental to [his] works. It is a condition of their production."[52] Certainly, it is a condition for their publication and reception that extended well beyond the duration of his physical exile. (East) German translations of Cerda's stories, resolutely concerned with time and history at the level of theme, narrative, and form, are deeply connected to questions of time and timeliness, to the pasts and futures of the translated text. Walkowitz's born-translated novels may have little in common with translations born of exile and in solidarity-inflected publishing programs in East Germany. Nonetheless, elements of her approach ring true and clear, and resonate with key questions about the stories' circulation and temporality of reception – in other words, with the very conditions under which "The Poster" becomes contemporary

---

51 Paulo Bartolini, *On the Cultures of Exile, Translation, and Writing* (West Lafayette: Purdue University Press, 2008), 89.
52 Rebecca Walkowitz, *Born Translated. The Contemporary Novel in an Age of World Literature* (New York: Columbia University Press, 2015), 4.

(again) here and now: "Once literary works begin in several places, they no longer conform to the logic of national representation."[53]

Where might Cerda's 1970s short stories be said to begin? And in what sense? In Chile, in Spanish, in exile in the GDR, in German translation? The play and suspension of time extends beyond the text proper to the life of the text and its reception across places, times, and languages. Just as importantly, and even more difficult to specify, I wonder: where might they be said to end?

From temporal dislocation to becoming contemporary

In her 2004 study *The Dialectics of Exile*, Sophia McLennan coined the term *destiempo* in analogy to *destierro* to describe deprivation or expulsion from one's time with the paradoxical effect that "the exile lived in two times simultaneously, in the present and the past."[54] In "The Poster," Cerda mobilizes the very history from which he saw himself banished to offer a counterpoint to fascist narratives of overcoming time itself to make and control history. Radicalizing McLennan's assertion, Cerda's time is not geographically localizable; the past is not Santiago, the present not Leipzig. He lays claim to multiple times and places, superimposing and destabilizing multiple histories. Cerda's antifascist aesthetic treats history and time as resources, sources of strength and connection within an increasingly global literary field demarcated by the politics of exile, international publishing, and translation as a condition for publication. In "The Poster," exilic writing is not linked primarily to the circulation of discrete national, linguistic, or political subjects, but, in this case, to the cultivation of novel and asynchronous internationalist collectives whose interpretation requires the similar cultivation of comparative and historical reading practices. Its antifascist temporality resides neither in the imaginative resurrection of past antifascist collectives, nor in supraindividual victory of an antifascist collective over time itself. Rather, it rests on the recovery of discrete, historical objects, ideas, and missives that engender connection and hope derived from struggle. It rests in the repetition of everyday acts of defiance, hope, concealment, and recovery that themselves engender belonging to – and not transcendence of – history.

---

[53] Rebecca Walkowitz, *Born Translated*, 30.
[54] Sophia McLennan, cited in Bartolini, *On the Cultures of Exile, Translation, and Writing*, 100.

Cerda's story invites us to reflect on the past that we might imagine now and in the future.⁵⁵

In the afterward to *Encounter with Time*, Cerda elaborates on the extreme situation of the exiled author, connecting his expulsion from the "house of language" to both his expulsion from the past and subjection to a present that is neither rooted in the past nor contiguous with what might have been a future. The exile is condemned to inhabit memory, and so participates in a complex layering of times and places. As Cerda links the becoming concrete of worlds to the becoming timely of hope in the act of narration, so, too, does he affirm the responsibility of the exiled author to produce distance and disorientation in the reader.⁵⁶ In "The Poster," he troubles the metaphor of the house profoundly, moving fluidly from the destruction of one house by fascist police to the (positively valorized) destruction of another house underwriting an act of antifascist recovery, solidarity, and (re)construction. The "house of language" from which the author was excluded gives way to the translated house, the "relational language of translation and exile."⁵⁷ Where time is a trap in the pro-Pinochet domestic space of "Balconies with Flags," extending in a painful expression of the myth of the eternity of the nation localized to a single apartment, for the protagonists of "The Poster" time becomes an ally.

Exilic writing can be seen in the figure of the house to participate in the destabilization of narrative worlds and their times. The work of concealment and excavation are inseparable in the story, underscoring the inherent ambiguity of "home" without contesting its affective pull. As two houses, two stories are superimposed on one another, so are two sets of posters – those hidden in Chile and those hidden and recovered in Germany. The enduring purchase of a revolutionary, antifascist writing figured in the eponymous poster could be seen to imply a universal or timeless antifascist aesthetic as a counterpoint to fascism's own universals. As I read Cerda, the superimposition of once distinct texts and languages achieves something else entirely: it takes advantage of the suspension of time to repurpose or re-inhabit times past and times yet-to-come through history, rather than retreat into the eternity of a reactionary, ahistorical fascist temporality.

---

55 According to Griffin, "The premise of all fascist movements and regimes is that history can be made." For a concise overview of regeneration, resurrection, and immortality as "the affective heart of generic fascism," see Griffin, "Fixing Solutions: Fascist Temporalities as Remedies for Liquid Modernity," 15–18.
56 Cerda, "Nachwort," esp. 150, 156.
57 Bartolini's, *On the Cultures of Exile, Translation, and Writing*, 89.

Cerda's literary writing, then, offers a window not only into the layering and multidirectionality of memories of antifascist exile, but in fact intervenes into the dominant understanding of exile itself. Bartoloni has described exile as a "topography of individuals," building on long-held, Romantic concepts of the exile in liberalist terms.[58] Galin Tihanov, whose work I referred to above, calls upon us to reinscribe the individual into the collective experiences of displacement and exile that have motivated our interest in exile since the twentieth century, yet remain curiously excluded from our consideration so long as we fail to interrogate the nineteenth-century underpinnings of our discussions. Cerda's attention in "The Poster" to individuals as part of collectives (in the form of the voluntary work brigade) meets that challenge in surprising ways, integrating German and Chilean histories. The construction of a multidirectional antifascist memory, like Maria's gaze as it falls on the poster at the close of the 2001 Spanish version, is interminable. But it is also restless, as the 1976 German version would have it.[59] What might emerge in the movement of Cerda's texts across languages and audiences, with editions a quarter century apart, is still unfurling, like a tightly rolled poster.

Postscript: Translative reading for the past-present age

Anyone fortunate enough to have been in one of Leslie Adelson's seminars knows that they nearly always began – in her own temporal twist – with a postscript. Meticulously and densely handwritten on lined loose-leaf paper, her notes recapitulated and extended the previous seminar, drawing together strands of conversation and outstanding conclusions, and preparing the ground for a fresh and focused start. Mine will reach further back, to connect to one of my first lessons from Adelson in the form of her introduction to *Making Bodies, Making History*.[60] My twenty-year-old self had never heard of Agnes Heller, never thought about how history was multiple in ways that extended beyond the historiographic to a philosophy of history as distinct from a theory of history, how the past, present, and future might themselves include multiple levels (which Adelson sums up

---

[58] Bartolini, *On the Cultures of Exile, Translation, and Writing*, 103; Tihanov, "De-Romanticizing Exile," esp. 216–217.
[59] Cerda, "El Afiche," 112; "Das Plakat," 137.
[60] Leslie A. Adelson, *Making Bodies, Making History. Feminism and German Identity* (Lincoln and London: University of Nebraska Press, 1993), 23–27.

as flow, structure, and meaning). With all deference to her literary readings, it was the deft summary and framing that most captured my attention and piqued my interest. I read those four pages more times than I can recall and underlined nearly every word. If, with Adelson's Heller, we choose our histories, which we choose matters a great deal. In the past-present age, we confront "the historical past as it activates our hopes and fears, through symbols to which we ascribe meaning."[61] Cerda's textual construction of resistance across continents and times "no longer alternative in character" is one I meet with hope, a past-present age that has become meaningful to me 'beyond [my] power to alter it.'[62] I find in it an artifact of history and specifically of literary history, a text both suspended and circulated in translation and exile, and an antifascist resource oriented toward multiple futures.

As Rebecca Walkowitz reminds us, the temporality of translation, too, is always close to hand: "it is contemporary, above all, because it is historical. In translation, literature has a past as well as a future."[63] Sketching a reading along the axes of the exilic/spatial and the temporal/archeological, I have tried to capture the value of attending to Cerda's translation multiply (that is, to translation as transfer across language, time, and audience, as well as in the generation of transcontextual and multidirectional historical comparisons).[64] I am positioned to read Cerda's literary text as I do and with colleagues who acknowledge his value within the discipline of German Studies because of the ground Adelson's work has prepared. Narrating the movement of his protagonists across distinct but superimposed times and places of internationalist, antifascist praxis, Cerda is one of many authors who defy easy categorization in any national literary tradition and require that we attend more carefully to cultural logics of circulation and dis-placement at work in German literature as world literature today. Comparative work on the global reach of an expanded German archive benefits from Adelson's keen insights into the intermingling of the social and the literary and attention to the imaginative power of literary forms that gesture toward the future even as they belong to our pasts. Reading Cerda's exilic literature for the past-present moment, it seems, is also a re-reading of the layers of Adelson's contributions to a field.

---

61 Adelson, *Making Bodies*, 26.
62 Heller cited in Adelson, *Making Bodies*, 24.
63 Walkowitz, *Born Translated*, 6.
64 For more detailed discussion of these key dimensions of translation in Chilean exile writing, see my "Choreographing Exile: Lothar Warneke's and Omar Saavedra Santis's *Blonder Tango*," *The German Quarterly* 84.3 (Fall 2011).

This was surely the case, too, with respect to the interpersonal connections she has enabled and that I consider again as I write now: As I worked to trace the becoming contemporary of 1970s antifascism in Carlos Cerda's "The Poster," to peel back the layers of debris in the house his characters set out to demolish, clearing the way for newer foundations of material production, and discovering the immaterial but precious stuff of history and hope, this essay felt more urgent in 2021 than when I first spoke on his short stories five years ago. Then, at a two-day colloquium on *Dis-Placements, Refuges and Other Cultural Belongings* co-convened by a former student of Adelson's at SUNY Binghamton (Carl Gelderloos), featuring a key note and workshop by another of her students (Yasemin Yildiz), and with talks by myself and two other former Adelson students (Gizem Arslan and Katrina Nousek), conversations of the AfD's showings in the 2016 German state elections already weighed heavy on the participants. I return to read and hope again with Cerda and with others who have learned from and with Adelson to attend to the details and to find purchase in forms from futures past and yet to come. Like the belatedness of Cerda's Spanish original, like his characters' belated recovery of antifascist posters, his story arrives – for us – just in time.

Works cited

Adelson, Leslie A. *Making Bodies, Making History. Feminism and German Identity* (Lincoln and London: University of Nebraska Press, 1993).
Bartolini, Paulo. *On the Cultures of Exile, Translation, and Writing* (West Lafayette: Purdue University Press, 2008).
Baumbach, Nico, Damon R. Young, and Genevieve Yue. "Introduction. For a Political Critique of Culture," *Social Text 127* 34.2 (June 2016): 1–20.
Bendetti, Mario. *El desexilio y otras conjeturas* (Madrid: Ediciones El País, 1984).
Brandt, Bettina and Valentina Glajar. "Introduction: The Politics of Archives," *Seminar* 53.3 (September 2017): 193–201.
Cerda, Carlos. *Balcones con banderas* (Santiago de Chile: LOM Ediciones, 2001).
Cerda, Carlos. *Begegnung mit der Zeit*. Trans. Achim Gebauer and Rolf Trogisch. Afterward trans. Christel Dobenecker (Berlin: Aufbau Verlag, 1976).
Cerda, Carlos. *Escrito con L* (Santiago de Chile: Alfaguara, 2001).
Cerda, Carlos. "Nachbemerkung," in *Weihnachtsbrot*. Trans. Volker Ebersbach (Berlin: Aufbau Verlag, 1978): 169–175.
Cerda, Carlos. "Nachwort," in *Begegnung mit der Zeit*. Trans. Achim Gebauer and Rolf Trogisch. Afterward trans. Christel Dobenecker (Berlin: Aufbau Verlag, 1976).
Cerda, Carlos. "Das Plakat," Trans. Christel Dobenecker. In *Erkundungen II. 22 Chilenische Autoren*. Eds. Joachim Meinert and Salvattori Coppola (Berlin: Verlag Volk und Welt, 1976): 129–137.

Cerda, Carlos. *Tres novelas* (Santiago de Chile: Alfaguara, 2003).
Cerda, Carlos. *Weihnachtsbrot*. Trans. Volker Ebersbach (Berlin: Aufbau Verlag, 1978).
Coppola, Salvattori. "Nachwort," in *Erkundungen II. 22 chilenische Autoren*. Eds. Joachim Meinert and Salvattori Coppola (Berlin: Verlag Volk und Welt, 1976): 285–293.
David, Lea. "Against Standardization of Memory," *Human Rights Quarterly* 39 (2017): 296–318.
Dean, Carolyn J. *The Moral Witness: Trials and Testimony after Genocide* (Ithaca: Cornell University Press, 2019).
Dobenecker, Christel and Horst Theweleit. "Chilenische Exilliteratur im Aufbauverlag. 1976–1987," *Weimarer Beiträge* 14.9 (1988): 1561–1564.
Emmerling, Inga. *Die DDR und Chile. Außenpolitik, Außenhandel und Solidarität* (Berlin: Ch. Links, 2013).
Esposito, Fernando and Sven Reichardt. "Revolution and Eternity. Introductory Remarks on Fascist Temporalities," *Journal of Modern European History* 13.1 Fascist Temporalities (2015): 24–43.
Farías, Víctor. *Los Nazis en Chile* (Barcelona: Editorial Seix Barral, 2000).
Finchelstein, Federico. "From Holocaust Trauma to the Dirty War," *Historical Reflections/ Réflexions Historiques* 41.3 (Winter 2015): 47–58.
Finchelstein, Federico. "Populism without Borders. Notes on a Global History," *Constellations* 26 (2019): 418–429.
Griffin, Roger. "Fixing Solutions: Fascist Temporalities as Remedies for Liquid Modernity," *Journal of Modern European History* 13.1 Fascist Temporalities (2015): 5–23.
Grugel, Jean. "Nationalist Movements and Fascist Ideology in Chile," *Bulletin of Latin American Research* 4.2 (1985): 109–122.
Guzmán, Gustavo. "Miguel Serrano's Antisemitism and Its Impact on the Twenty-first Century Countercultural Rightists," *Analysis of Current Trends in Antisemitism* 40.1 (2019). doi: 10.1515/actap-2019-0001.
Häseler, Jens. "Literatura del exilio chileno antes y después del retorno a la democracia: el caso de Carlos Cerda," in *Coloquio Internacional Migración y Literatura en el Mundo Hispánico*. Ed. Irene Andres-Suárez (Madrid: Editorial Verbum, 2004): 313–325.
Hirsch, Marianne and Leo Spitzer. "Testimonial Objects: Memory, Gender and Transmission," *Poetics Today* 27.2 (Summer 2006): 353–383.
Hoyos, Hector. *Things with a History. Transcultural Materialism and the Literatures of Extraction in Contemporary Latin America* (New York: Columbia University Press, 2019).
Jähnchen, Waltraud. "Dem Furchtbaren mit Hoffnung begegnen. Chile im Hörspiel der DDR," in *DDR-Literatur '84 im Gespräch* (Berlin and Weimar: Aufbau Verlag, 1985): 89–108.
Kacandes, Irene. "Die Ungnade der späten Geburt: Challenges in the Twenty-First Century for Central Europeans: German Studies Association Presidential Address 2016," *German Studies Review* 40.2 (May 2017): 389–405.
Kirsten, Jens. *Lateinamerikanische Literatur in der DDR. Publikations- und Wirkungsgeschichte* (Berlin: Ch. Links, 2004).
Lillo, Mario. "Cartas en/desde Berlín: *Morir en Berlín* de Carlos Cerda y *El desierto* de Carlos Franz," *Acta Literaria* 39.11 (2009): 69–89.
McGee Deutsch, Sandra. *Las Derechas: The Extreme Right in Argentina, Brazil and Chile, 1980–1939* (Stanford: Stanford University Press, 1999).
Polster, Martina. *Chilenische Exilliteratur in der DDR* (Marburg: Tectum Verlag, 2001).

Rothberg, Michael. *Multidirectional Memory. Remembering the Holocaust in the Age of Decolonization* (Stanford: Stanford University Press, 2009).

Said, Edward. "Traveling Theory," in Edward Said, *The World, the Text, and the Critic* (Cambridge, MA: Harvard University Press, 1983), 226–247.

Said, Edward. "Traveling Theory Reconsidered," in Edward Said, *Reflections on Exile and Other Essays* (Cambridge, MA: Harvard University Press, 2003), 436–452.

Skármeta, Antonio. "Prólogo," in Carlos Cerda, *Escrito con L* (Santiago de Chile: Alfaguara, 2001), 13–22.

Tihanov, Galin. "De-Romanticizing Exile," in *Critique of Cosmopolitan Reason. Timing and Spacing the Concept of World Citizenship*. Eds. Rebecka Lettevell and Kristian Petrov (Oxford: Peter Lang, 2014), 215–238.

Trnka, Jamie H. "Choreographing Exile: Lothar Warneke's and Omar Saavedra Santis's *Blonder Tango*," *The German Quarterly* 84.3 (Fall 2011): 309–327.

Trnka, Jamie H. "Melodramatic Realism: Shared Time and Temporality in Gunther Scholz's and Carlos Cerda's *Ein April hat 30 Tage*," *German Studies Review* 43.1 (2020): 87–105.

Trnka, Jamie H. *Revolutionary Subjects. German Literatures and the Limits of Aesthetic Solidarity with Latin America* (Berlin and Boston: De Gruyter, 2015).

Walkowitz, Rebecca. *Born Translated. The Contemporary Novel in an Age of World Literature* (New York: Columbia University Press, 2015).

Anna M. Parkinson
Untimely Tales: Psychoanalysis as Spectral Modernism in Hans Keilson's Novel, *The Death of the Adversary*

Beginnings: Time out of joint

> The ghost is not simply a dead or a missing person, but a social figure, and investigating it can lead to that dense site where history and subjectivity make social life. [. . .] Being haunted draws us affectively, sometimes against our will and always a bit magically, into the structure of feeling of a reality we come to experience, not as cold knowledge, but as a transformative recognition.[1]
>
> Avery F. Gordon, *Ghostly Matters*

The life and work of Jewish-German psychoanalyst, Holocaust survivor, poet, and modernist fiction author Hans Keilson, whose life bridged more than a century, from his birth in Germany in 1909 to his death in 2011 at the age of 101 in the Netherlands, is replete with the quality of untimeliness. In the opening lines of his final autobiographical German publication titled *There My House Stands*, Keilson states: "Whoever has lived and survived as a Jew and a persecuted person on the run in the middle of Europe, is offered, in retrospect, only one single, unbroken continuity as the background of his existence: that of the calendar with its monotonous, recurring numbers of weeks and months, weekdays, Sundays, and holidays, printed in red ink and valid all over the world."[2] In this statement Keilson captures a heightened variation of what Walter Benjamin referred to as the "homogeneous, empty time" of modernity.[3] To those in hiding, time stands still; it is monotonous, repetitive, all-encompassing. The conceit of calendrical time provides a backdrop for punctual acts of untimeliness, providing the temporal relief against which the present becomes legible. The hypervigilant phenomenology of anxious wartime waiting expands time

---

1 Avery F. Gordon, *Ghostly Matters: Haunting and the Sociological Imagination* (Minneapolis: University of Minnesota Press, 2008), 8.
2 My translation [AP]. "Wer als Jude und Verfolgter auf der Flucht mitten in Europa gelebt und überlebt hat, dem bietet sich im Rückblick als Hintergrund seines Daseins nur eine einzige, ungebrochene Kontinuität an: die des Kalenders mit seinen eintönig, wiederkehrenden Zahlen der Wochen und Monate, Wochen- und Sonn- und Festtagen, mit roter Farbe gedruckt und gültig in aller Welt." Hans Keilson, *Da steht mein Haus: Erinnerungen*, ed. Heinrich Detering (Frankfurt am Main: Fischer, 2011), 9.
3 Walter Benjamin, "Theses on the Philosophy of History," in *Illuminations*, ed. and intro. Hannah Arendt, trans. Harry Zohn (New York: Schocken Books, 1968), 253–264.

https://doi.org/10.1515/9783110778922-004

into endlessness, interrupted at best by good news (or no news at all), and at worst by violence.

Keilson's choice of the word "house" for his memoir's title, rather than the more familiar "home," warrants closer examination, not least due to the ambivalent proximity Freud charted between the German word for home ("*Heim*" and "*heimlich*") and its strange etymological proximity to the German word for uncanny ("*das Unheimliche*"), which translates literally as "the unhomely." We will return later to the question of how to inhabit a haunted house, a locus characterized first and foremost as untimely. But for now, the publication history of Keilson's three novels alone provides a study in untimeliness: his first novel, *Life Goes On* [*Das Leben geht weiter*], a melancholy account of the inexorable toll of the unrest of the Weimar Republic on a Jewish merchant family, was published by the prestigious Fischer publishing house in 1933.[4] This book was the last book debut by a Jewish author published by Fischer before the National Socialists came to power, and by 1934 it was already banned.[5] On recounting how he found a copy of his first novel in a public library in the Netherlands in 1936, shortly after emigrating there with his future wife, Gertrud Manz, Keilson, too, puzzled at the novel's uncanny untimeliness, stating: "Did it [Keilson's novel] rush ahead of me, or has it caught up with me again?"[6]

In 1942, after his emigration to the Netherlands, Keilson started writing what was to be published as his third book, *The Death of the Adversary* [*Der Tod des Widersachers*]. This manuscript went underground – quite literally – when for reasons of safety it was buried in a garden in Delft after the Nazi Occupation of the Netherlands forced Keilson into hiding for the remainder of the war. Housing a tale of hiding in the Netherlands under Nazi occupation, Keilson's second published book, *Comedy in a Minor Key* [*Komödie in Moll. Eine Erzähung*], was published in German in 1947 by Amsterdam's Querido Press, an important publishing company for German-language writers in exile during the Nazi regime. After sending the manuscript of his novel *The Death of the Adversary* for consideration to numerous German publishing houses between 1951 and 1958, Keilson finally found a German publisher for his book in 1959. With the Georg Westermann Press in Braunschweig, which specialized in postwar textbooks and pedagogical texts, Keilson's novel found its (first) home.

---

4 For a full account of the book's history, see: Hans Keilson, "Das Leben geht weiter – nach fünfzig Jahren," in *Kein Plädoyer für eine Luftschaukel. Essays, Reden, Gespräche*, ed. Heinrich Detering (Frankfurt am Main: Fischer, 2011), 43–48.
5 Hans Keilson, "Zeittafel," in *Kein Plädoyer für eine Luftschaukel*, 157–160.
6 Translation AP. "War er mir vorausgeeilt, oder hatte er mich wieder eingeholt?" "Das Leben geht weiter," 48.

The German publication in 1959 of *The Death of the Adversary* appeared to be out of synch with the *Zeitgeist* of postwar, Cold War society, at least in West Germany. This may in part be due to the quirky ambivalence, darkly ironic style, and self-imposed naiveté of the novel's unnamed Jewish protagonist's account of his projected intimate relationship with Hitler during the latter's rise to power and his refusal to look danger in the eye until it is too late, themes that appeared to be as outrageous as they were close to home. This narrative strategy of perverse projective identification, combined with the darkly humorous and, nonetheless, deadly earnest tone of the book made it difficult to categorize and – no doubt – sat uneasily with its postwar readers, some of whom may well have wanted to forget the German nation's love affair with Hitler.

Keilson directly addresses this untimeliness in an interview in 1999 with Ulrich Walberer, where he speculates on his potential reading public in the postwar period:

> The book definitely was published too early; the issues addressed in the book were in a manner of speaking not yet viable (*lebensfähig*), not even in Israel. Grief, suffering, rage, the wish for vengeance had elicited affects and emotions that defined people's lives at the time of the book's publication. Anyone who attempted to reflect on this, all of these historical events, including the brutality, was rejected.[7]

The term "nicht lebensfähig," which can be translated as not viable, is also medical term indicating the condition of a fetus as previable, or not sufficiently developed to survive outside of the womb.[8] By rendering his book premature for the then existing German readership, and acknowledging the "grief, suffering,

---

[7] "Das Buch ist wohl zu früh erschienen, die darin behandelte Problematik war damals sozusagen noch nicht lebensfähig, sogar in Israel nicht. Trauer, Schmerz, Wut, der Wunsch nach Rache hatten Affekte und Emotionen ausgelöst, die das Leben der Menschen zur Zeit des Erscheinens dieses Buches bestimmt haben. Jemand, der versucht hat, dieses zu reflektieren, ein ganzes historisches Geschehen, auch in seiner Grausamkeit zu reflektieren, der wurde abgelehnt." Hans Keilson, "Ich brauche kein Mahnmahl für meine Trauer," interview with Ulrich Walberer, *Neue Rundschau* no. 4 (1999): 77–88, here 83. The translation is my own.

[8] It is important to acknowledge the (perhaps unintentional) proximity of Keilson's phrase "nicht lebensfähig" to describe the nature of his readership's brusque unwillingness to engage with the difficult topics he broached in his book to the harsh Nazi euphemism "lebensunwertes Leben" (life unworthy of life). The latter was used by the Nazi regime to categorize undesirable segments of the population that they thought had no right to be alive, for example, seriously ill, intellectually impaired or even behaviorally disturbed individuals, most of whom were housed in institutions. It should be noted, however, that Keilson's book was untimely in the sense that it "couldn't yet" be engaged with – thus wasn't able to come into its own, whereas, the reverse was the case with the individuals targeted by the Nazis for death, who were alive – but for whom untimely early deaths had been planned.

rage, and the wish for vengeance" in the potential Israeli readership, Keilson in effect also addresses the potential challenge of frank and difficult fiction such as his (and other exiled writers struggling to publish their fiction) for the German readership of the time.

It would be remiss to claim that *The Death of the Adversary* did not receive some critical attention in Germany on its publication in 1959.[9] However, the reception of the English translation published in 1962 was, by comparison, positively panegyric. The novel was recognized by the magazine *Time* as one of the year's ten best books, along with texts by Vladimir Nabokov and Jorge Luis Borges.[10] In 2005, the S. Fischer Verlag published Keilson's collected works, spanning poetry, psychoanalytic and literary essays, and his published prose fiction.[11] Cleaving to Keilson's work's history of untimeliness, in a 2010 review in the *New York Times Book Review*, Francine Prose serendipitously (and seemingly singlehandedly) resurrected *The Death of the Adversary* for an English language readership. The review discusses the novel (then out of print in English), although it was occasioned by Keilson's *Comedy in a Minor Key*, which had just been published as an English-language translation for the first time in 2010.[12] Nothing short of eulogy, the first sentence of Prose's review declares both novels "masterpieces" and Hans Keilson "a genius," thus securing a significant amount of international interest in *Death of the Adversary* for the first time since 1962 (and a stunning, if not extremely belated debut for the English translation of *Comedy in a Minor Key*).[13] Hans Keilson's novels were finally reaping the engaged readership that he had sought for his fiction in the immediate postwar period.

---

9 For the reception history of Keilson's *Death of the Adversary* in response to its initial publication in Germany in 1959, see Anna M. Parkinson, "Zwischen Nirgendwo und Immer Wieder: Das Unzeitgemäße in Hans Keilsons Romanen und die nicht ganz verpasste Begegnung mit dem *Tod des Widersachers*," in *Im Abseits der Gruppe 47 – Albert Vigoleis Thelen und andere "Unzeitgemäße" im Literaturbetrieb der 1950er und 60er Jahre*, eds. Hans Eickmanns, Werner Jung, and Jürgen Pütz (Duisburg: Universitätsverlag Rhein-Ruhr, 2019), 111–124.
10 "The Year's Ten Best," *Time*, 4 January 1963, 8–10.
11 Hans Keilson, *Werke in Zwei Bänden*, eds. Heinrich Detering and Gerhard Kurz (Frankfurt am Main: S. Fischer Verlag, 2005).
12 Hans Keilson, *Comedy in a Minor Key*, trans. Damion Searls (New York: Farrar, Straus and Giroux, 2010).
13 Francine Prose, "As Darkness Falls," *New York Times Book Review*, 8 August 2010, 1–2, https://www-proquest-com.turing.library.northwestern.edu/docview/747992986/fulltextPDF/DE1D53933EDE4979PQ/20?accountid=12861, last accessed 4 December 2020.

Canny reminders: Corpses and the literary corpus

Many different factors are at play in the social and academic fields through which literary norms are established and sustained. One indication of these norms and taboos over time is the constitution of literary canons. Over the past few decades, postwar writings by German-Jewish authors such as Keilson and Jewish Holocaust survivor, historian and prose author H.G. Adler have emerged from the debris of literary history.[14] The fiction of these exiled authors draws in part on formal techniques of interwar modernism, such as stream-of-consciousness narration, abstraction, and a decidedly fragmented or nonchronological sense of narrative time. Once published, a novel that is not reviewed and widely read easily can fall between the cracks of institutional and individual memory. The belated (and labored) publication of work by these authors, as well as their ex-territoriality from the German language literary scene and publishing houses, only partly accounts for their postwar neglect and subsequent exile from the contemporary formation of the postwar West German literary canon. As regards the Holocaust literary canon more broadly speaking, I won't rehearse here the discussions about the limits of Holocaust representation in literature and memoir – the question of whether the representation of traumatic events is either desirable or possible – that have been explored in detail elsewhere.[15] Suffice it to say that some genres appear to have been considered more appropriate than others for representing the Shoah. In particular, historical and autobiographical fiction written for the most part in a realist style, such

---

14 Stephan Braese, *Die andere Erinnerung: Jüdische Autoren in der westdeutschen Nachkriegsliteratur* (Berlin: Philo, 2001). On H.G. Adler's work see: Helen Finch and Lynn Wolff, eds., *Witnessing, Memory, Poetics: H.G. Adler & W.G. Sebald* (Rochester, NY: Camden House, 2014).

15 See, among others Lawrence L. Langer, *Preempting the Holocaust* (New Haven: Yale University Press, 1998); Lawrence L. Langer, *Holocaust Testimonies: The Ruins of Memory* (New Haven: Yale University Press, 1991); Berel Lang, ed., *Writing and the Holocaust* (New York: Holmes & Meyer, 1988); Elie Wiesel, *Against Silence: The Voice and Vision of Elie Wiesel*, ed. Irving Abrahamson (New York: Holocaust Library, 1985). The following volume of essays offers an excellent overview of various positions taken by historians and literary and cultural theorists on representation of the Holocaust: Saul Friedlander, ed., *Probing the Limits of Representation: Nazism and the "Final Solution"* (Cambridge, MA: Harvard University Press, 1992). For a selection of excerpted readings and a summary of the intellectual positions, interpretations and confusion in (not only) the German context regarding Adorno's so-called dictum about writing poetry after Auschwitz, see Petra Kiedaisch, ed., *Lyrik nach Auschwitz? Adorno und die Dichter* (Stuttgart: Reclam, 1995).

as Elie Wiesel's canonical work, is seen as authentic, accessible, and hence appropriate for inclusion in the canon of Holocaust Studies.[16]

Some Jewish-German authors and survivors living in exile during the war and in the postwar period were already deeply engaged in creating representations of their experiences in poetry, autobiography, and fiction. For these authors the question seems to have been less if the Holocaust should or could be represented, than how to find a receptive publisher and an engaged readership for their fiction. There appears to have been a hesitancy on the part of larger publishing houses in the postwar period to take on fiction or memoirs by survivors of the Shoah whose writing was considered formally or thematically difficult, confrontational or morally ambivalent. Exemplary of this lingering tendency is the case of the delayed publication in Germany of Jewish survivor and German-language author Edgar Hilsenrath's satirical novel *The Nazi and the Barber* (1977).[17] Drawing on the picaresque tradition, his novel's plot is driven by the grotesque behavior of the first-person narrator-protagonist, a former SS Officer, who assumes the identity of his Jewish childhood friend, one of his many murdered Jewish victims, and goes to the extreme of emigrating to Palestine when given the chance. An earlier, but lesser-known example is H.G. Adler's disturbing novel *The Journey* [*Eine Reise*], which details in fragmented and at times challengingly surreal terms the deportation, persistent dehumanization, and murder of members of the Lustig family in the (never-named, but nonetheless evident) context of the Nazi "concentrationary universe."[18] Completed around 1951, Adler's novel took a further eleven years to reach a readership; it was finally published in 1962, similar to Keilson's, by a small publishing house, Bibliotheca Christiana.[19]

To offer a point of contrast, in the immediate postwar years, former conservative revolutionary and interwar right-wing agitator Ernst von Salomon had no trouble reconnecting with Ernst Rowohlt, his former publisher, to secure the publication in 1951 of his vituperative magnum opus, a memoir of sorts, fully eight hundred pages in length, entitled *The Questionnaire* [*Der Fragebogen*]. This nationalistic (Prussian) postwar bestseller took the form of an exhaustively

---

[16] For a thorough summary of the arguments rehearsed about genre and Holocaust representation, see Michael Rothberg, *Traumatic Realism: The Demands of Holocaust Representation* (Minneapolis: University of Minnesota Press, 2000).

[17] Erin McGlothlin, "Narrative Transgression in Edgar Hilsenrath's *Der Nazi und der Friseur* and the Rhetoric of the Sacred in Holocaust Discourse," *The German Quarterly* 80.2 (Spring 2007): 220–240.

[18] H. G. Adler, *Eine Reise* (Bonn: Bibliotheca Christiana, 1962).

[19] Peter Filkins, *H. G. Adler. A Life in Many Worlds* (Oxford: Oxford University Press, 2019), 316–318.

resentful response to the postwar Allied questionnaire that all Germans were required to complete as part of the denazification process, initially used to assess the extent of their culpability during the Third Reich.[20] Perhaps an autobiographical text written by a former radical right-wing interwar agitator, driven by toxic spite towards the Allied occupying forces was considered a safer literary investment, better attuned to the postwar German *Zeitgeist*, and far less disturbing and challenging than autobiographically-inflected writing by his contemporary German-Jewish authors giving literary form to their recent experiences of persecution under the Nazi regime.

Returning to Keilson's novels: just what might it have been that unsettled the postwar editors who rejected his book? His first postwar publication in 1947 with Querido, the German-language exile publishing house in Amsterdam, was titled *Comedy in a Minor Key*. The terse, omniscient narrator gives an account of the dilemma faced by a Dutch couple forced to dispose of the body of the Jewish man they had been hiding in their house during the war. At first blush, the narrator appears to deliver the story in a rational, even-handed tone, that is, until closer scrutiny reveals subtle stylistic shifts. The narrative voice undercuts its own observations through its ironic tone and the disparaging distance taken from the protagonists of the story, a young Dutch couple. Their proudly defiant act of hiding a Jewish man in their house culminates in their sudden and unexpected need to dispose of his corpse after his premature death from natural causes. The ironic tone of the narrator belies the ethical and everyday costs of hiding the persecuted, when the inexperienced Dutch couple find themselves in the titular, darkly comedic, yet dangerous position of having to secretly remove the corpse from their house. This turns out to be no laughing matter. In an ironic reversal, they themselves are threatened with persecution and must go into hiding when they neglect to remove an identificatory laundry tag from the dead man's pajamas before depositing his corpse on a bench in a local park. The novella dramatizes the abovementioned distorted temporality of persecution and hiding by way of a poetics of the uncanny; what could be closer to a haunting than a novella about the fate of a Jewish man who dies in hiding in an attic in the Netherlands during the German occupation?

In what might be called a forensic vein, in her consideration of Keilson's *Comedy in a Minor Key*, Leslie A. Adelson interprets the "illegal corpse," "the dead

---

[20] I have written elsewhere about the highly negative affective charge produced in the wake of Ernst von Salomon's book in the immediate postwar period in West German culture. See Anna Parkinson, "*Ressentiment*: Democratic Sentiments and the Affective Structure of Postwar West Germany," in *An Emotional State. The Politics of Emotion in Postwar West German Culture* (Ann Arbor: University of Michigan Press, 2015), 67–112.

physical remnants of [the hidden Jewish man's] life," not only as a problem for the Dutch couple, but also as the locus of a "secret knowledge" that demands interpretation and exposes the couple to the ongoing threat of danger from Nazi occupiers and Dutch collaborators.[21] It is precisely this morbid uncanny remainder at the level of plot, this "secret," that characterizes Keilson's prose, albeit in different ways, in his postwar novels. For, if *Comedy in a Minor Key* confronts readers with a morbid epistemological challenge, a series of dark, ambivalent episodes in *Death of the Adversary* leads to an ontological uncertainty that portends less a farce than a tragedy worthy of Hamlet.

Uncanny remainders: Between the living and the dead

Recently deceased feminist literary scholar and Jewish-Austrian Holocaust survivor Ruth Klüger did not suffer lightly what Gillian Rose elsewhere called "Holocaust piety,"[22] or what she herself variously referred to as "*KZ*-sentimentality" or "-kitsch."[23] She offered a critique in no uncertain terms of normative or moralizing interpretations that portray the Holocaust as "ineffable" in secular-theological frameworks. According to Klüger, these responses are, at best, a reaction to the overwhelming nature of the events and, at worst, the advancement of a moral or political agenda. Klüger's writing, specifically the German version of her autobiographical memoir *weiter leben. Eine Jugend* [*Still Alive: A Holocaust Girlhood Remembered*] is a frank and courageous reckoning with her childhood under the growing threat of Nazism in Austria, the survival of her childhood years in Auschwitz, and her postwar immigration to the United States. At the same time, it is an exposure and formidable critique of some of the many taboos surrounding Holocaust representation and memory in the discourses that frame and

---

[21] Leslie A. Adelson, "Minor Chords? Migration, Murder, and Multiculturalism," in *Wendezeiten, Zeitenwenden: Positionsbestimmungen zur deutschsprachigen Literatur, 1945–1995*, eds. Robert Weninger and Brigitte Rossbacher (Tübingen: Stauffenburg, 1997), 119.
[22] Based on the premise of what cannot be represented or the "ineffable," Gillian Rose names this critical stance as one of "Holocaust piety," that acts "to mystify something we dare not understand, because we fear that it may be all too understandable, all too continuous with what we are – human, all too human." Gillian Rose, "Beginnings of the Day – Fascism and Representation," in *Mourning Becomes the Law. Philosophy and Representation* (Cambridge: Cambridge University Press, 1996), 41–62.
[23] Ruth Klüger, *weiter leben. Eine Jugend* (Munich: Deutscher Taschenbuch Verlag, 2005), 75–80.

regulate discussions of the Holocaust, ostensibly in the name of propriety or authenticity, in academic, museological, and literary arenas.

In an earlier publication anticipating the topoi of *weiter leben*, Klüger identified and challenged the moralism that at times regulates literary representations of the Shoah, saying: "But what if an entire literature or even a corpus of works emerges that is at odds with good taste?"[24] Klüger gives, by way of example, the uncompromising stories of the Polish writer Tadeusz Borowski, adding: "If I had to write a work of fiction on the topic of the Jewish catastrophe, I wouldn't choose a realistic framework. I would invent a ghost story, for a ghost is something unresolved, especially a violated taboo, an unprocessed crime."[25] This statement touches on the spectral or uncanny qualities at the heart of Keilson's final novel: namely, the challenges faced in representing in fiction events based on experiences of an individual's anticipated psychological and physical annihilation, the destruction of a society's moral substance, and the planned extinction of particular demographic targets under the Nazi regime. In other words, just as the experiential extremes faced by the persecuted were in excess of quotidian social reality, so too might authors thereafter find it necessary to draw on representational forms that render the extremity of these experiences. It is in this sense that Keilson's *The Death of the Adversary* can be read as a story of psychoanalytic possession. I propose that this entails engaging the spectral aesthetics of the uncanny to give form to extreme experiences – in this case, by exploring the intersubjective emotional dynamics of hatred, a theme Keilson returned to repeatedly in his writing.[26]

Perhaps unsurprisingly, since Keilson was an avid reader of Sigmund Freud's work in the Weimar period and went on to qualify as a psychoanalyst in the Netherlands, where he remained in the postwar era, the ontological destabilization evinced in his fiction often arises from a dynamic dialectical movement between opposing psychological forces constitutive of the narrative (conscious/unconscious or the pleasure principle/the death drive). Arguably the darkest and most

---

24 Klüger asks: "Wie aber, wenn eine ganze Literatur oder doch ein Korpus von Werken entsteht, die gegen den guten Geschmack verstoßen?" Ruth Klüger, "Dichten über die Shoah. Zum Problem des literarischen Umgangs mit dem Massenmord," in *Spuren der Verfolgung. Seelische Auswirkungen des Holocaust auf die Opfer und ihre Kinder*, ed. Gertrud Hardtmann (Gerlingen: Bleicher Verlag, 1992), 205.
25 "Wenn ich eine frei erfundene Geschichte zum Thema der jüdischen Katastrophe schreiben müßte, so würde ich keine realistischen Rahmen wählen. Ich würde eine Gespenstergeschichte erfinden, denn ein Gespenst ist etwas Ungelöstes, besonders ein verletztes Tabu, ein unverarbeitetes Verbrechen." Klüger, "Dichten über die Shoah," 220.
26 See, for example: Hans Keilson, "Die Faszination des Hasses" (1996–1997), in *Kein Plädoyer für eine Luftschaukel*, 95–118.

complex of Keilson's novels, *The Death of the Adversary* is an object lesson in the ambivalence structuring intersubjective relationships under duress and persecution. The novel sets the stage with a brief frame narrative describing a meeting in the Netherlands shortly after World War II. A Dutch lawyer, whose motivations remain unclear, gives an anonymous manuscript written in German to an unnamed first-person narrator to read. The lawyer mysteriously describes the author of the manuscript as "a victim of persecution," and clumsily frames the manuscript as its author's attempt "to come to terms with some very personal problems of his life."[27] This statement belies the story's complexity, which gives an account of a young Jewish-German protagonist, written in hiding in the Netherlands during the Occupation, concerning his life in Berlin in the dusking of the Weimar Germany and the ascension of the Nazi Party, traumatically punctuated by the young man's account of his parents' deportation to Auschwitz.

The protagonist of the central, framed, or nested story is clearly Jewish, but is never directly named as such; in fact, he attempts to camouflage both his as well as his "adversary's" identity, who is simply referred to as "B." (a substitute for Hitler's name). Surely among the most intricate postwar literary explorations of the structure of the victim-aggressor relationship, the novel is a daring Freudian-inflected presentation of hatred, exposing the affective structure and constitutive emotions of antisemitism by way of a Jewish protagonist feeling his way into the position of his adversary, Hitler. The perversely confident protagonist believes that he can deflect his adversary's defamations and threats and convince him of the error of his (unnamed, but clearly antisemitic) prejudice. The narrative conceit in the protagonist's extended imaginary dialogue with Hitler/B. revolves around the protagonist's disavowal of the looming threat of persecution that would otherwise force him into a victim position and consequently demand from him a slew of negative feelings. Instead, in an attempt to neutralize the threat Hitler represents, he initially identifies with him as an opponent to be won over, rather than a hostile, potentially deadly Other. The "camouflaging" of the protagonist and his adversary through their anonymity also allows us to read the novel as a parable cautioning against the dangers of prejudice that structure all victim-perpetrator relationships.

---

27 Hans Keilson, *The Death of the Adversary*, trans. Ivo Jarosy (New York: Farrar, Straus and Giroux, 2010), 5–6.

"Doing in the dead": Uncanny reminders of that which is yet to be

If the "illegal corpse" and its secret in *Comedy in a Minor Key* make ongoing epistemological demands on the living, I would argue that *Death of the Adversary* provokes a state of ontological instability through its depiction of a series of disturbing encounters perhaps none more aggressive than the lengthy episode devoted to a young Nazi's account of his group's nocturnal desecration of a Jewish cemetery. When the unnamed Jewish-German narrator is visiting a young German woman, from whom he conceals his Jewish identity, their evening is interrupted by the arrival of her older brother and a group of his grim antisemitic friends. The youngest and least mature of the group is goaded by the taunts of the others into giving an ambivalent account of how he and a motley crew of like-minded young men, "organized" to desecrate a Jewish burial ground, had "crept along [. . .] like a funeral possession that carries off a secret corpse in the dead of night."[28] Forty pages in length and constituting twenty percent of the novel, this chapter is uncharacteristically long and sets up a complex array of perspectives through the intersubjective dynamics described in the episode of the grave desecration and focalized through the Jewish narrator. The youngest boy in the group is verbally cajoled, encouraged, and bullied into recounting his nocturnal activities by the three older boys. Through his description of the interactions between his fellow desecrators, readers are introduced to their oscillating reactions of shame, fear, and triumph as they prepare themselves for what lies ahead; they alternate between relativizing and justifying their destructive acts of symbolic violence, which provides a vivid dress rehearsal for future acts of violence inflicted on the living members of the Jewish community. Speaking of a fellow perpetrator, the young Hitler enthusiast admits to their initial apprehension on arriving at the cemetery walls:

> 'Yes, it must be done,' he repeated after me in a frightened voice, 'and I'll do it.' I was sorry for him, he sounded so pitiful, as though he had been ordered to commit a murder – and, after all, wasn't it a kind of murder we were preparing to commit there? Only it wasn't live human beings who fight back when they're attacked and scream, but their remains, bones and ashes. We'd come to do in the dead. And if you ask me, as one who has taken part in it and am proud of having been allowed to do so, I tell you that it's much more difficult to do in the dead than the living.[29]

---

28 Keilson, *Death of the Adversary*, 149. All quotation marks cited are included in the novel.
29 Keilson, *Death of the Adversary*, 145.

This passage illustrates the ontological instability at the heart of Keilson's account of hatred in the novel. "Doing in the dead" – namely the act of attacking defenseless (because inanimate) human remains as if they were living, struggling human beings – demands the perpetrators' overcoming their respect for and the superstition associated with the dead. The ensuing categorical confusion between the living and the dead is destabilizing. It is with "insane dread" that the narrator and protagonist of the main story senses but does not acknowledge how this frightful symbolic revivification of the dead contains its dialectical inverse: namely, the making dead of the living. For the perpetrators must assign the dead agency in order to justify the ontological struggle as one of self-preservation in the face of "their [the corpses'] nefarious activities." The desecrator continues:

> We raced down the path leading to the smaller tombstones. We saw them standing there, all of them upright, as though they were threatening and defying us. They were arms or legs or heads which the skeletons had pushed out of their holes in the ground, as a sign that they were still a power to be reckoned with, that they had not yet left the earth but had merely withdrawn into her body in order to continue their nefarious activities from there. We ran as though they were driving us through the little pathways. [. . .] There lay the first headstone: we had pushed it over on to the grave and it looked as though the corpse had fallen over and lay with his pale belly on his own grave. Then we got busy on the grave. There's a difference between having a child's grave or an adult's one under one's foot. Perhaps one tramples a little more tenderly on the young brood of death than on the old ones. The next stone was down, and the next, we pushed it over backwards. There it lay, as though the corpse had crawled out of the upper end of his grave and were now lying on his back, helpless in the cool September night.[30]

The boys' symbolic act of apostasy provides the casuistry for their "self-defense" against the Jewish "undead" in the cemetery. This episode shudders from one Gothic trope to the next, from the undead to the uncannily dark graveyard, animating aesthetic codes and conventions invested in ontological uncertainty.

In her book on the transmutations of the poetic form of elegy under the conditions of modernity, *Dying Modern*, Diana Fuss defines a poetic genre she calls the "corpse poem" as "poetry not about the dead but spoken by the dead, lyric utterances not from beyond the grave but from inside it."[31] Pointing to the ontological challenges – and unlikelihood – of this form of poetry in our post-industrial age of mass death and perpetual war, Fuss, writes:

---

30 Keilson, *Death of the Adversary*, 155.
31 Diana Fuss, "Reviving . . . Corpses," in *Dying Modern: A Meditation on Elegy* (Durham: Duke University Press, 2013), 44–77, here 44–45.

the corpse poem poses a series of difficult questions about death, survival, and the animating power of language. Why would a poet wish to experience, prematurely, the state of decomposition, either one's own or someone else's? Why, and when, is a dead voice more appropriate than a live one? What does speaking through the fictional persona of a cadaver allow poets to achieve that writing in their own living voices apparently prohibits?[32]

In this chapter of Keilson's novel the rhetorical act of prosopopoeia is not the revivifying speech act of a poet on behalf of a dead or absent person. Rather, it arises from a complex set of projective narrative frameworks that actively blur the question of origin and agency. First, we have the Jewish narrator/protagonist, who passively, and with shame and self-loathing, relays the scene of fascist desecration described by the aspiring fascist youth. In turn, the boy is an ambivalent figure in all of his pride, fear, superstition, and qualms of conscience. By ventriloquizing the boy's story, the narrator does give voice to the dead, but only circuitously by retelling the boy's disturbing account. To add to this complex of narrative frameworks, the reader, presumably along with the protagonist of the frame narrative to whom the lawyer gave this manuscript to read, is also kept in the dark about the ultimate fate of the narrator: did he survive the storm of fascism or not? We are unable to answer this question until we reach the concluding frame narrative that effectively closes the novel, returning it to the nested narrative structure. In short, through the shifting temporality produced through narrative framing in the novel we remain unsure of the future of the manuscript writer, although the episode of the grave desecration marks the point in the narrative at which the protagonist finally achieves a belated recognition of the danger in which both he and Germans find themselves.

By revivifying human remains and anthropomorphizing tombstones in the Jewish cemetery, the boy neither lends voice to the dead's grievances, nor does he advance a coherent political critique, which Fuss gives as the two criteria for prosopopoeia in her study of elegy. Positing the (un)dead as a "nefarious" force that threatens the living allows the desecrators to project an unnatural power onto the dead and provides the opportunity to rehearse for the subsequent violence that will be brought against the living. This in turn justifies the desecrators' fear and gives, in a false and circular logic, the premise for the "necessity" of their struggle against the Jewish "brood of death" in the first place. In other words, Keilson's grave desecrators create a deadly fantasy in the present moment as a guarantor for the as-yet-unknown future that will be the genocide of the European Jewish population.

---

32 Fuss, *Dying Modern*, 45.

The *locus classicus* for the intersection of psychoanalysis and literature, Sigmund Freud's 1919 essay "The Uncanny" ["Das Unheimliche"] could likewise be read as a short treatise on ontological instability.[33] Freud's recursive reading of the uncanny as "that class of the frightening which leads back to what is known of old and long familiar," is sufficiently capacious to embrace both the epistemological and ontological dimensions of the concept.[34] Referring to a citation from Schelling, Freud emphasizes the pivotal relationship between the known and the unknown constitutive of the uncanny: *"'Unheimlich' is the name for everything that ought to have remained . . . secret and hidden but has come to light."*[35]

Drawing on the work of Ernst Jentsch, Freud indicates another approach to the term "uncanny" that could be called its ontological dimension. Freud states: "Jentsch believes that a particularly favorable condition for awakening uncanny feelings is created when there is intellectual uncertainty whether an object is alive or not, and when an inanimate object becomes too much like an animate one."[36] This sense of "intellectual uncertainty" arises when confronted by objects that may or may not be alive. In other words, it arises from a state of precarious ontological stability even – or perhaps especially – in the case of literature, where, Freud argues, we readily suspend disbelief when called upon by the author to do so as part of the reading experience.[37] However, according to Freud, the same does not happen when the author intends the story to take place in "the world of common reality," as in the case of Keilson's representation of a particular psychological reality in relation to a specific historical context. This is the space in literature where the uncanny becomes detached from epistemic certainty, shifting into the realm of ontological uncertainty.[38] When confronted with death, Freud argues, it is not uncommon for people to feel a sense of the uncanny, although Freud disparagingly refers to this form of the uncanny as "atavistic." For although we "no longer believe in" the ideas of our "primitive forefathers" and have "*surmounted* these modes of thought," we nonetheless "do not feel quite sure of our new beliefs."[39] In other words, the teleology

---

[33] Sigmund Freud, "The Uncanny," in *The Standard Edition of the Complete Psychological Works of Sigmund Freud* vol. XVII (1917–1919). *An Infantile Neurosis and Other Works*, trans. and ed. James Strachey with Anna Freud (London: The Hogarth Press and The Institute for Psycho-analysis, 1955), 218–253.
[34] Freud, "The Uncanny," 220.
[35] Italics in the original. Schelling cited in Freud, "The Uncanny," 224.
[36] Freud, "The Uncanny," 233.
[37] Freud, "The Uncanny," 250.
[38] Freud, "The Uncanny," 250.
[39] Freud, "The Uncanny," 247. Emphasis in original.

of the evolution of our "civilized" beliefs is not unswerving and "the primitive fear of the dead is still so strong within us and always ready to come to the surface on any provocation," where "the dead man becomes the enemy of the survivor."[40] Indeed, according to Freud, "dead bodies," "the return of the dead," and "spirits and ghosts" are common catalysts for a sense of uncanniness.[41]

Thus, the desecrator's account of his experiences in the cemetery belongs to the category of the uncanny in the latter sense. However, this is complicated by the fact that it is only by deserting the field of reality altogether that the desecrators are able to compel themselves into the necessary frenzy of violent destruction. That is, it is only by invoking an imagined ontological instability or shift between the living and the dead by anthropomorphizing human remains and tombstones that the boys are able to fully turn their Jewish fellow citizens into a form of otherness, a recognized precondition for acts of targeted violence. By destabilizing the ontological boundary between the living and the dead, the desecrators in turn cross a threshold that allows them to envisage the living as already dead, or at least inhuman – the Jewish-German acting as the uncanny *Doppelgänger* or ontological negative of the non-Jewish German.

This hair-raising episode is taken to yet another level in the boy's description of one perpetrator's frenzied flight into annihilation:

> He ran like one possessed, it was a fantastic sight, the climax of the whole exhibition, I'll never forget it. He leaped like a black goblin from grave to grave – great big leaps, with his black body twisting and twirling in the air. He held his arms away from his body, moving them backwards and forwards as though he were rowing through the night. His body had an incredible elasticity, even the deep sand of the grave mounds did not affect it, up he came again and on to the next grave. And all the time he was making gurgling sounds that seemed to come from deep inside his guts. I went after him. I saw him trampling down the last mounds by the wall, his legs were moving faster and faster on the same spot. A mad fury seemed to have taken hold of him, he dropped down full-length on the grave, grabbed at the cold, wet earth with both hands and began to scratch and dig. His fingers devoured the soil, deeper and deeper they dug, as though he wanted to scratch the buried bones out of the ground. His face was pressed to the ground and the sand got into his mouth. He spat, gargled, and went on scratching like mad. Then he suddenly stopped, lay there like dead, jumped up again and leaped at the next grave.[42]

Arguably, it is the boy himself who is rendered uncanny, "a fantastic sight," unhuman or animal-like in his frenzied destruction of the graves, he is "like a black goblin." Displaying seemingly preternatural bodily capacities, his movement

---

40 Freud, "The Uncanny," 242.
41 Freud, "The Uncanny," 241.
42 Keilson, *Death of the Adversary*, 159.

is described in terms that place him on the spectrum of the uncanny somewhere between a "gurgling," carnivorous animal and an automaton that "lay there like dead." The passage suggests that if there is a form of the nonhuman present in the Jewish cemetery, then it is not so much embodied by the human remains or the gravestones as by the desecrators themselves.

Returning to corpse poetics, I note that Fuss argues that corpse poems that struggle most to come into existence are those written by poets of the Holocaust, saying: "the Holocaust appears to mark the historical limit beyond which the corpse poem hesitates to venture." She continues: "The point is clear: after the unthinkable event of genocide, no fiction of the living dead can possibly be sustained."[43] However, Keilson and other authors writing about the Holocaust, such as H.G. Adler, would beg to differ with Fuss on this question. In Keilson's novel, the unflinching depiction of the narrator's growing, yet necessarily suppressed horror in listening to an account of the desecration of the burial grounds of his people gives voice to the fascist distortion and negation of both the narrator's and, in turn, Keilson's life world.

Be it through hyberbole, alienation, distortion, or manifestations of the uncanny, Keilson's novel captures the co-existent structures of everyday life along with the violence of being caught in another's logic that is driven by the aim of one's own extinction. That which exceeds the logic of realist representation in Keilson's novel takes place through representational codes that are by definition already excessive. Elsewhere in the novel Modernist strategies for expressing alienation, such as fragmentation and stream-of-consciousness narrative, are deployed to capture formally the dialectical restlessness of the ambivalence characteristic of Keilson's prose and plots. In his novel, Gothic tropes and the psychoanalytic heuristic of the uncanny mark existential thresholds and index the haunting quality of guilt-ridden memory. Whether we categorize Keilson's style in the episode above as a modality of the Gothic, an inverted form of corpse poetics or elegy, or the instantiation of what might be called spectral modernism,[44] designating its peculiar admixture of modernist aesthetics and

---

43 Fuss, *Dying Modern*, 64.
44 I use this term here drawing on what has been loosely called the "spectral turn" in literary and philosophical discourses, including those about Holocaust literature. My pairing of the spectral with the term modernism points towards the question of how to characterize the style of the novel, which is decidedly fragmentary in form, often ironic in tone, and gives access to the narrator at times through passages written in a stream-of-consciousness. Likewise, the psychically divided and ambivalent character of the narrator captured in these pages owes as much to modernist writing as it does to psychoanalysis. On the spectral turn, see, for example Colin Davis, *Haunted Subjects: Deconstruction, Psychoanalysis and the Return of the Dead* (Basingstoke: Palgrave Macmillan, 2007); Andrew Smith and Jeff Wallace, eds.,

elements of the Gothic resonant with psychoanalysis, it exceeds the novel's coexistent realist generic conventions and any straightforward fidelity to the real or testimonial in much Holocaust literature.

Living with the (un)dead

As Klüger suggests, there is an ethical call and response of kinds at stake in the staging of spectral modernism in the context of Holocaust literature. Embedded in a reverse *Bildungsroman* of sorts, extreme or liminal experiences require a readership willing and able to make legible the otherwise unacknowledged social import of hauntings of this kind – the novel's poetic truth, it could be said – as uncomfortable or even hurtful as this experience might be. Avery Gordon in the opening epigraph emphasizes the political and ethical import of a reading that remains attentive to the historical and material perspectives required to decipher social forms of haunting or "that dense site where history and subjectivity make social life."[45] Haunting is a prerequisite for recognizing wrongdoing or the unfinished business of traumatic experiences, after which social rituals of exorcism may become possible. Keilson's final text, the memoir *There my House Stands*, refers not only to the material security of the home (*Heim*), but also gestures towards the *Unheimlichkeit* (or uncanniness) of his coexistence with a century's worth of memories. Keilson's ghosts are both housed in and exorcized through his psychoanalytic work, his essays, poems, and fiction. As with the untimely arrival of a message in a bottle (*Flaschenpost*), these novels have reached their readers belatedly. But might this very asynchrony not be what makes haunted sites legible to the reader in the first place?

Gothic Modernisms: History, Culture and Aesthetics (Basingstoke: Palgrave Macmillan, 2001); María del Pilar Blanco and Esther Peeren, eds., *The Spectralities Reader: Ghosts and Haunting in Contemporary Cultural Theory* (New York: Bloomsbury, 2013); Gabriele Rippl, Philipp Schweighauser, Tina Kirss, Margrit Sutrop, and Therese Steffen, eds., *Haunted Narratives: Life Writing in an Age of Trauma* (Toronto: University of Toronto Press, 2013); Roger Luckhurst, "The Contemporary London Gothic and the Limits of the 'Spectral Turn,'" *Textual Practice* 3.16 (2002): 527–546; Jean Paul Riquelme, "Introduction: Dark Modernity: From Mary Shelley to Samuel Beckett: Gothic History, the Gothic Tradition, and Modernism," in *Gothic and Modernism: Essaying the Dark Literary Modernity*, ed. Jean Paul Riquelme (Baltimore, MD: Johns Hopkins University Press, 2008), 1–23; Zuzanna Dziuban, ed., *The ›Spectral Turn‹: Jewish Ghosts in the Polish Post-Holocaust Imaginaire* (Bielefeld: transcript, 2019).

45 Gordon, *Ghostly Matters*, 8.

Works cited

Adelson, Leslie A. "Minor Chords? Migration, Murder, and Multiculturalism," in *Wendezeiten, Zeitenwenden: Positionsbestimmungen zur deutschsprachigen Literatur, 1945–1995*. Eds. Robert Weninger and Brigitte Rossbacher (Tübingen: Stauffenburg, 1997), 115–129.
Adler, H. G. *Eine Reise* (Bonn: Bibliotheca Christiana, 1962).
Benjamin, Walter. "Theses on the Philosophy of History," in *Illuminations*. Ed. and intro. Hannah Arendt, trans. Harry Zohn (New York: Schocken Books, 1968), 253–264.
Braese, Stephan. *Die andere Erinnerung: Jüdische Autoren in der westdeutschen Nachkriegsliteratur* (Berlin: Philo, 2001).
Davis, Colin. *Haunted Subjects: Deconstruction, Psychoanalysis and the Return of the Dead* (Basingstoke: Palgrave Macmillan, 2007).
Del Pilar Blanco, María and Esther Peeren, eds. *The Spectralities Reader: Ghosts and Haunting in Contemporary Cultural Theory* (New York: Bloomsbury, 2013).
Dziuban, Zuzanna, ed. *The ›Spectral Turn‹: Jewish Ghosts in the Polish Post-Holocaust Imaginaire* (Bielefeld: transcript, 2019).
Filkins, Peter. *H. G. Adler. A Life in Many Worlds* (Oxford: Oxford University Press, 2019).
Finch, Helen and Lynn Wolff, eds. *Witnessing, Memory, Poetics: H.G. Adler & W.G. Sebald* (Rochester, NY: Camden House, 2014).
Freud, Sigmund. "The Uncanny," in *The Standard Edition of the Complete Psychological Works of Sigmund Freud* vol. XVII (1917–1919). *An Infantile Neurosis and Other Works*. Trans. and ed. James Strachey with Anna Freud (London: The Hogarth Press and The Institute for Psycho-analysis, 1955), 218–253.
Friedlander, Saul, ed. *Probing the Limits of Representation: Nazism and the "Final Solution"* (Cambridge, MA: Harvard University Press, 1992).
Fuss, Diana. *Dying Modern: A Meditation on Elegy* (Durham: Duke University Press, 2013).
Gordon, Avery F. *Ghostly Matters: Haunting and the Sociological Imagination* (Minneapolis: University of Minnesota Press, 2008).
Keilson, Hans. "Ich brauche kein Mahnmahl für meine Trauer." Interview by Ulrich Walberer, in *Neue Rundschau* no. 4 (1999): 77–88.
Keilson, Hans. *Werke in Zwei Bänden*. Eds. Heinrich Detering and Gerhard Kurz (Frankfurt am Main: Fischer, 2005).
Keilson, Hans. *Comedy in a Minor Key*. Trans. Damion Searls (New York: Farrar, Straus and Giroux, 2010).
Keilson, Hans. *The Death of the Adversary*. Trans. Ivo Jarosy (New York: Farrar, Straus and Giroux, 2010).
Keilson, Hans. *Kein Plädoyer für eine Luftschaukel. Essays, Reden, Gespräche*. Ed. Heinrich Detering (Frankfurt am Main: Fischer, 2011).
Keilson, Hans. *Da steht mein Haus. Erinnerungen*. Ed. Heinrich Detering (Frankfurt am Main: Fischer, 2011).
Kiedaisch, Petra, ed. *Lyrik nach Auschwitz? Adorno und die Dichter* (Stuttgart: Reclam, 1995).
Klüger, Ruth. "Dichten über die Shoah. Zum Problem des literarischen Umgangs mit dem Massenmord," in *Spuren der Verfolgung. Seelische Auswirkungen des Holocaust auf die Opfer und ihre Kinder*. Ed. Gertrud Hardtmann (Gerlingen: Bleicher Verlag, 1992), 203–221.
Klüger, Ruth. *weiter leben. Eine Jugend* (Munich: Deutscher Taschenbuch Verlag, 2005).

Lang, Berel, ed. *Writing and the Holocaust* (New York: Holmes & Meyer, 1988).
Langer, Lawrence L. *Holocaust Testimonies: The Ruins of Memory* (New Haven: Yale University Press, 1991).
Langer, Lawrence L. *Preempting the Holocaust* (New Haven: Yale University Press, 1998).
Lourie, Richard. "Displaced Minds," in *The New York Times*. 9 January 2009. https://www.nytimes.com/2009/01/11/books/review/Lourie-t.html, 20 December 2020.
Luckhurst, Roger. "The Contemporary London Gothic and the Limits of the 'Spectral Turn'," *Textual Practice* 3.16 (2002): 527–546.
McGlothlin, Erin. "Narrative Transgression in Edgar Hilsenrath's *Der Nazi und der Friseur* and the Rhetoric of the Sacred in Holocaust Discourse," *The German Quarterly* 80.2 (Spring 2007): 220–238.
Parkinson, Anna M. *An Emotional State. The Politics of Emotion in Postwar West German Culture* (Ann Arbor: University of Michigan Press, 2015).
Parkinson, Anna M. "Zwischen Nirgendwo und Immer Wieder: Das Unzeitgemäße in Hans Keilsons Romanen und die nicht ganz verpasste Begegnung mit dem *Tod des Widersachers*," in *Im Abseits der Gruppe 47 – Albert Vigoleis Thelen und andere "Unzeitgemäße" im Literaturbetrieb der 1950er und 60er Jahre*. Eds. Hans Eickmanns, Werner Jung, and Jürgen Pütz (Duisburg: Universitätsverlag Rhein-Ruhr, 2019), 111–124.
Prose, Francine. "As Darkness Falls," in *New York Times Book Review*, 8 August 2010, 1–2. https://www-proquest.comturinglibrarynorthwesternedu/docview/747992986/full textPDF/DE1D53933EDE4979PQ/20?accountid=12861, 20 December 2020.
Rippl, Gabriele, Philipp Schweighauser, Tina Kirss, Margrit Sutrop, and Therese Steffen, eds. *Haunted Narratives: Life Writing in an Age of Trauma* (Toronto: University of Toronto Press, 2013).
Riquelme, Jean Paul. "Introduction: Dark Modernity: From Mary Shelley to Samuel Beckett: Gothic History, the Gothic Tradition, and Modernism," in *Gothic and Modernism: Essaying the Dark Literary Modernity*. Ed. Jean Paul Riquelme (Baltimore, MD: Johns Hopkins University Press, 2008), 1–23.
Rose, Gillian. "Beginnings of the Day – Fascism and Representation," in *Mourning Becomes the Law. Philosophy and Representation* (Cambridge: Cambridge University Press, 1996), 41–62.
Rothberg, Michael. *Traumatic Realism: The Demands of Holocaust Representation* (Minneapolis: University of Minnesota Press, 2000), 25–58.
Smith, Andrew and Jeff Wallace, eds. *Gothic Modernisms: History, Culture and Aesthetics* (Basingstoke: Palgrave Macmillan, 2001).
Time Inc. "The Year's Ten Best," *Time*, 4 January 1963, 8–10.
Wiesel, Elie. *Against Silence: The Voice and Vision of Elie Wiesel*. Ed. Irving Abrahamson (New York: Holocaust Library, 1985).

B. Venkat Mani
Future Sense and Refugee Time: Reading Anita Desai's *Baumgartner's Bombay* as a Global Novel

> We received an inquiry from our Indian sister organization to the effect, whether the Indian Government has signed the agreement 'relating to the issue of a Travel Document to Refugees who are the concern of the Intragovernmental Committee on Refugees.' [. . .] As far as I can gather from your publication, India has not yet assigned this agreement, I would, however, be very grateful to you if you could give me some definite information.
>
> K. Alexander, "Council for the Protection of the Rights and Interests of Jews from Germany"   (London, 1947)

> Stop that whining and show me your passport, will you?' [. . .] 'German, born in Germany,' [. . .], 'Yes, but of Jewish origin, therefore a refugee . . .
>
> Anita Desai, *Baumgartner's Bombay* (1988)

In July 2019, a few months before the global pandemic upended our lives to temporarily replace the discussion of refugees from media and politics, I found myself in Geneva at the United Nations High Commission for Refugees (UNHCR) archives. My goal was humble: to get a *sense* of the history of creation of the term "refugees" in the years leading up to the Geneva Convention and the formation of the UNHCR in 1951. It was a sunny weekday morning in Geneva. The social text of Geneva itself that surrounded me on my walk to the archives had a strong international presence: students, scholars, diplomats, UN workers, visiting dignitaries from various parts of the world, as well as residents from Africa, Asia, and the Middle East running restaurants, barbershops, and cafés.

Buried deep in a file pertaining to the Intergovernmental Committee on Refugees (ICR), precursor institution to the UNHCR, I found a short letter addressed to the ICR office in London. The weight of the documents above and below the letter had flattened out any creases, the paper had slightly yellowed but held together strongly, yet the force of the typewriter keys still made the lettering look embossed, as if to convey the urgency of the inquiry being made. The letterhead used belonged to the "Council for the Protection of the Rights and Interests of Jews from Germany, London" with Rabbi Dr. Leo Baeck listed as the President; it was signed by K. Alexander, the secretary of the Council at the time.

The content of the letter – cited in the opening epigraph of this chapter – may not on the surface seem important, or key to unveiling a major historical

https://doi.org/10.1515/9783110778922-005

puzzle. But to me, the letter appeared as a major document of what is often brushed away as "minor" events in history. The source of significance of the letter lay not merely in the prominence of names associated with it. Dr. Baeck, known for his work as the president of the Reichsvertretung der deutschen Juden (The Reich Representation of German Jews 1939–1943), where he defended the rights of Jewish-Germans after Hitler's ascension to power in 1933, and after whom a major institute for Jewish history is today named in London. Or that the signatory of the letter was K. (Kurth) Alexander, who worked as the secretary and in several organizational leadership capacities with the Reichsvertretung in Berlin and then with the Council in London. What was striking to me, apart from the urgent query in the letter and the request to seek more information in a pre-Internet world, was also the date: 9 June 1947.

As someone who grew up in postcolonial India, it was hard for me to miss that the letter was written and dispatched less than two months before the independence of India from the British Raj on 15 August 1947, a date that also marked the partition of India and Pakistan through the creation of the Radcliff Line. The letter, which already came out of two bloody episodes of European history with a global impact – World War II and the Holocaust – seemed to anticipate another future event that would be equally marred by bloodshed, lead to mass forced displacement of millions of human beings, cost of life and limb through the large-scale creation of refugees on both sides of the subcontinental border. While the main purpose of the letter was clearly to inquire about the political status of Jewish refugees in colonial India, the date also marked the time when a fascist empire, the Third Reich had just collapsed, and the expiry date of the British empire in South Asia was on the horizon. Most importantly, the letter bore the imprint of two German Jewish refugees, forced to move to London, the heart of the British colonial metropolis, who were eager to find out about the fate of many others like them who were stuck in India, a prominent but distant part of the colony.

The letter from the UNHCR archives opens the door to follow the story of German Jews who sought refuge in India during the National Socialist period. The fictional character Hugo Baumgartner, protagonist of the Indian novelist Anita Desai's much celebrated, and equally criticized novel *Baumgartner's Bombay* (1988), from where I take the second epigraph of this essay, belongs to this community of refugees. Born in Germany, with a German passport, and as the citation implies, as a German Jew who tries to explain to a colonial authority figure in India that he is not quite the enemy alien he's suspected to be, indeed a victim of a much larger war, and not the perpetrator. When read with the letter, the novel offers for consideration a subset of inquiries about the figure of a human being deemed to be or understood under the category "refugee" –

albeit caught between two empires, one built on racial purity, and the other on white supremacy.

I begin with the juxtaposition of archival and literary documentation of a major transitional period of human history marked by mass violence, forced displacements, and the creation of refugees for several reasons. First, to draw attention to the global connectivity of pasts, presents, and futures of refugees, drawing on the past, but relevant for the contemporary era of refugees. I want to underline the significance of centralizing the figure of the refugee in literary studies to explore how the refugee figure forms and informs the kind of hidden, under-represented, under-discussed, or often glossed over "minor" events that are nonetheless part of a global catastrophe. Second, I propose that paying attention to the figure of the refugee can assist in understanding a globally oriented aesthetic transformation of the novel, indeed a place to test the scope and limits of the now popular category of a "Global" novel. To this end, I will expand on "refugee time" as a useful concept to think about the aesthetic and political possibilities of a novel's globality. My reading of *Baumgartner's Bombay*, especially its protagonist Hugo Baumgarten will be framed through Leslie A. Adelson's discussion of "future sense" in her groundbreaking study of time, form, and narrativity in *Cosmic Miniatures and Future Sense* (2017). Finally, in reading an Indian novel in English as a "Global" novel which belongs to several literary traditions, including German-Jewish literatures and Refugee literatures, I also want to underscore how accounting for narratives of forced migration into the mainstream of social change can further assist in undoing ethnonationalism of literary fields such as German Studies and help us begin to articulate a "future sense" of productive critical exchanges.

How can following the figure of a refugee caught in the interstices of two hegemonic global powers lead us to understand comparatively under-represented and under-discussed historical experiences and global connections? How can thinking through German Jewish refugees in non-Euro-American nations in the mid-twentieth century add new perspectives to our understanding of the global dispersion and circulation of refugees? How does placing a refugee at the center of our literary historical imagination unsettle unexamined assumptions about categories such as a novel of exile, a refugee novel, a German-Jewish novel? Let me approach these questions with a brief sketch of some of the lines of critique that the novel has been subjected to, following which I will offer my own reading of "refugee time" in the novel with a discussion of "Future Sense" and the "Global Novel."

The Novel and the novelist: Orientalist, antisemitic, Western, or Indian?

When *Baumgartner's Bombay* was first published in the US in 1989, prominent reviewers made sure that the partial German origins of the author were duly mentioned. Paul West of the *New York Times* started with a condescendingly sexist beginning, assuring the readers that Desai "has a subtle mind," then adding that she "grew up in Old Delhi, the daughter of a German mother and an Indian father."[1] In the *New York Review of Books*, Rosemary Dinge read the novel as part of "Exile" literature, framing her reading by splitting Desai's lineage right in the middle: "half-Indian, half-German," to infer with certainty that "many of the characters live with a sense of unease and displacement."[2] It hardly mattered if the protagonist of the novel being reviewed was German-Jewish, who came to India in the shadow of the Third Reich, and categorically presents himself as a refugee. The centuries long history of Jewish presence in India, the special case of German-Jewish refugees in India during the last years of the British Raj, which coincided with the downfall of the Nazi regime, or the place of a German-Jewish refugee in India at the time of creation of millions of refugees during the bloody partition of the subcontinent, were all deemed a subject "new to English fiction."[3]

Given the stature of the novelist and the subject, the novel has garnered immense critical attention among Germanists, Comparatists, experts on Jewish Studies, as well as scholars of postcolonial literatures in English. While the public-sphere evaluation of the novel celebrated it though vocabularies of exoticism and novelty due to the German and Indian heritages of the author, some of the scholarly evaluations of the novel critiqued it precisely on those lines: for a constructed exoticism, a western gaze, an Orientalist portrait of the city of Bombay (now Mumbai), but also appropriation of the Holocaust, and more. Germanists such as Petra Fachinger declare that Desai's "view of India is influenced by her being the daughter of a German."[4] Along similar lines, Australia-based English literature scholar Tony Simoes da Silva (German) accuses Desai of orientalist appropriation, noting that the novel is "about India, but not that

---

[1] Paul West, "The Man Who Didn't Belong," *The New York Times*, 9 April 1989, 3.
[2] Rosemary Dinnage, "Exiles," *The New York Review of Books*, 1 June 1989, 1–9.
[3] Dinnage, "Exiles."
[4] Petra Fachinger, "India/Sri Lanka, the Holocaust, and the European Gaze in Anita Desai's *Baumgartner's Bombay* and Jeannette Lander's *Jahrhundert der Herren*," in *Mapping Channels between Ganges and Rhein: German-Indian Cross-Cultural Relations*, ed. Jörg Esleben et al. (Newcastle: Newcastle Cambridge Scholars Publ., 2008), 136.

of India."⁵ Judie Newman, Britain-based scholar of American Studies reads Baumgartner as living in "an ersatz enclave," whose "image of Germany becomes progressively distanced from reality. Like all colonisers, he finds himself yearning for a motherland which he had never really known . . ."⁶

If Desai's alleged Orientalism is one line of critique, the other goes in the direction of her appropriation of Jewish history, especially the Holocaust. Comparatist Axel Stähler frames his reading through Desai's acceptance speech delivered upon receiving the Harold U. Ribalow Prize (1989) by *Hadassah Magazine*, in which she categorically stated that the conferral of the prize "clears me of an accusation, made by a critic of the book, that I had 'appropriated' material that was not mine."⁷ While the larger goal of Stähler's reading is to redeem Desai of such accusations – "[O]bviously, the Holocaust is a contested phenomenon," Stähler states – he also goes to pronounce that the award and the American editions "seem to reclaim Desai's novel for what appears to be American and more specifically Jewish American sensibilities which are crucially informed by the discourse of Jewish victimhood."⁸ Stähler, too, cannot resist coming back to Desai's German heritage: "The story of Baumgartner finally gave Desai the long-hoped-for opportunity to give voice to this silenced part of her."⁹

Indian scholars were more generous and stayed away from these dual lines of accusations. But central to most of their readings is existentialist and/or identity crises that perturb an exile. Mrinalini Solanki framed her reading of Hugo Baumgartner through strategies of survival to counter "separateness" and "lostness," as an alien in India,¹⁰ whereas Usha Bande highlighted that Desai's textual knowledge and engagement with the Holocaust was not disadvantageous to the narrative because "she paints not the Holocaust but the corroding effect on man and man's finer sensibilities."¹¹ Rekha Kamath, leading Indian Germanist in an essay co-authored with the German scholar

---

5 Tony Simoes Da Silva, "Whose Bombay Is It Anyway?: Anita Desai's 'Baumgartner's Bombay' Tony," *Ariel* 28.3 (1997): 75.
6 Judie Newman, "History and Letters: Anita Desai's Baumgartner's Bombay," *World Literature Written in English* 30.1 (1990): 202.
7 Axel Stähler, "The Holocaust in the Nursery: Anita Desai's Baumgartner's Bombay," *Journal of Postcolonial Writing* 46.1 (2010): 76.
8 Stähler, "The Holocaust in the Nursery," 77.
9 Stähler, "The Holocaust in the Nursery," 78.
10 Mrinalini Solanki, *Anita Desai's Fiction: Patterns of Survival Strategies* (Delhi: Kanishka Publishing House, 1992), 1.
11 Usha Bande, *The Novels of Anita Desai: A Study in Character and Conflict* (New Delhi: Prestige Books, 1988), 133.

and Hindi translator Rainer Lotz focused on the "interculturality" of the text, yet identified "marginality . . . as a result of emigration" the cause of Baumgartner's "complete absence of any self-defined identity, since he does not project himself either in terms of being a German, a Jew, or even a naturalized Indian."[12]

My discussion of the novel is framed less through the lines of critique listed above and grounded more in current socio-political realities. I was reading this novel in 2020, when the news of refugees from Syria, Myanmar, and Venezuela – which dominated political discussions in Europe and the Americas – was suddenly eclipsed by the Coronavirus pandemic. This new experiential reality that quarantined human beings and fractured the sense of calendrical, progressive time for all citizens of the world, while laying bare social inequities and fault lines of race, religion, and class. As someone who considers himself a reader who cannot detach the reading experience from the place and time of reading, it seemed more urgent to think about refugees whose own sense of calendrical time often seems stunted due to long waits for paperwork or acceptance. To frame my lines of inquiry, a discussion of "future sense" in conjunction with the Global novel seems appropriate.

Future sense, futural horizons

Leslie A. Adelson's erudite engagement with the German theorist, experimental writer and film-maker Alexander Kluge begins under the banner of "Hope in Time," directing the reader to a promised exploration of "above and below [. . . as] two vectors of spatial orientation."[13] Perhaps coincidentally so, her exploration begins with Kluge's writing of short stories in the 1950s while watching Fritz Lang's Berlin production of *The Tiger of Eschnapur*, which, as is well known, was not only shot in Berlin, but also in India in the 1950s. Starting with this reference that immediately connects Kluge, even if indirectly, to a non-European space narrated in the film, Adelson's arrival at the term "future sense" happens in various registers of spatial-temporal elaborations.

---

[12] Rainer Lotz and Rekha Kamath, "Interculturality, a View from Below: Anita Desai's Baumgartner's Bombay," in *Jewish Exile in India, 1933–1945*, eds. Anil Bhatti and Johannes H Voight, in association with Max Mueller Bhavan (New Delhi: Manohar Publishing, 1999), 164.
[13] Leslie A. Adelson, *Cosmic Miniatures and the Future Sense: Alexander Kluge's 21st-Century Literary Experiments in German Culture and Narrative Form* (Berlin and Boston: De Gruyter, 2018), 1.

Future sense, first and foremost, is proposed by Adelson as a way of approaching narratives that account for, engage with, and/or are born of a "sheer" and "systematic" magnitude of disaster."[14] She places Kluge's storytelling project at the "crossroads of hope and destruction," adding that her project "draws its breath from relations between the very large and the very small that are easily overlooked whether one prefers to stress the warp of destruction or the hoof of hope in [Kluge]'s prose."[15] As she further argues, an attention to "other relations of scale and perspective – *cosmic, global, and German* – are key to unlocking what operatively binds the strands of hope and narrative form together . . ."[16]

Adelson accords meaning to the term future sense by placing it at the center of this triangulation: cosmic, global, and German, and through a consideration of "imprecise sites of mediation between the real and the possible, between the possible and the impossible, between the known and the unknown."[17] It is in this larger mediatory gesture that Adelson finds in Kluge's writing: "the hope for human survival and unalienated life in the face of catastrophic destruction associated in the main with cruelty, war, genocide, fascism, dictatorship, and capitalist exploitation of life, labor, and time."[18] Adelson's project signals toward "our own cultivation of future sense in reading [Kluge] for our dis-junctive and con-junctive time."[19] Such a cultivation, as I read it, lies in our capacity as readers to connect the very large with the very small through a conceptual animation of "experiential treasure in [. . .] combined social and narrative senses,"[20] "beyond a mere indexing of hopeful possibility or obstinate resistance,"[21] and, following Adelson's reading of the political philosopher Seyla Benhabib, as "a storytelling investment in the real force of contrafactual hope against competing forces of catastrophe and despair."[22]

Admittedly, Adelson's project and her elaborations on future sense cannot simply be dislodged from her investigation of Kluge's works, especially his "cosmic miniatures," or from the larger philosophical and critical tradition, a genealogy of thought that Adelson creates through her own identification of "imprecise sites of mediation." Without intending to do epistemic injustice to

---

14 Adelson, *Cosmic Miniatures and the Future Sense*, 3.
15 Adelson, *Cosmic Miniatures and the Future Sense*, 3.
16 Adelson, *Cosmic Miniatures and the Future Sense*, 3, my emphasis.
17 Adelson, *Cosmic Miniatures and the Future Sense*, 20.
18 Adelson, *Cosmic Miniatures and the Future Sense*, 20.
19 Adelson, *Cosmic Miniatures and the Future Sense*, 22.
20 Adelson, *Cosmic Miniatures and the Future Sense*, 25.
21 Adelson, *Cosmic Miniatures and the Future Sense*, 26.
22 Adelson, *Cosmic Miniatures and the Future Sense*, 29.

the project, and yet at a distance from Kluge, I want to focus on how Adelson's examination of the temporal with the sensory, especially palpable in her formulations cited above open possibilities for new conceptual articulations for thinking through their relationship within the "globality" of refugee narratives, especially in the genre of the novel.

In her illuminating Introduction to "The Global Novel," a special issue of *New Literary History* (2020), Debjani Ganguly tellingly begins by noting that the "conjunction of global with the novel generates considerable heartburn in some quarters about the form's complicity with the forces of globalization, its rampant marketability, its abdication of the social role, and the banal professionalization through creative writing programs."[23] Registering this critique and yet embracing it to inaugurate a sincere consideration of the genre, Ganguly presents several sharp articulations that help one understand the globality of the novel. She registers the global as a "belated marker of sedimented histories, their accrual and remediation embedded in the language of the contemporary,"[24] within which she places the form of long fictional prose with multiple forms it has acquired in different traditions. Beyond the "mimetic exactitude as a mode of cultural equivalence" or the "march of the modern European novel form and its relentless capture of cultural difference across both time and space,"[25] Ganguly presents the global novel as a "vast literary and theoretical corpus"[26] to be unfolded with a plurality of interventional insights, and "scalar issues [that] . . . encompass the temporality, form, and magnitude of human experience that such literary inscription entails across diverse cultural milieu."[27] The introduction ends at a futuristic interrogation. In the context of environmental politics and hegemonic control over and exploitation of natural resources, Ganguly asks, "What happens to the novel form when it encounters a *futural horizon* that is both already written into the earth's stratigraphy and yet impossible to visualize?"[28]

Undoubtedly, the theoretical-analytical context in which Adelson matures her concept of "future sense" and Ganguly references a "futural horizon" are different. The terms cannot be conflated. Sense refers to both the recognition of external stimulus by the body, but also a cognitive faculty of detection and

---

[23] Debjani Ganguly, "The Global Novel: Comparative Perspectives," *New Literary History* 51.2 (2020): v.
[24] Ganguly, "The Global Novel," vi.
[25] Ganguly, "The Global Novel," vii.
[26] Ganguly, "The Global Novel," vii.
[27] Ganguly, "The Global Novel," vii.
[28] Ganguly, "The Global Novel," xvi, my emphasis.

perception of a state, meaning, or a case. Horizon is the circular line on the earth visible from a particular point, where the earth and the sky seem to meet, a point that gets it gets more distanced as one moves toward it. And yet horizon also refers to the limit of one's ability to perceive or know. The addition of the "future" – something that has not yet occurred or not yet been experienced or known, has not yet been stimulated and therefore yet to be detected – is what grants a point of intersection to these two phrases. The awareness of the past, and the uncertainty about that which is yet to be experienced or will move away even further as one moves toward it makes the terms particularly useful in the context of refugee narratives.

First of course is the adumbration to the magnitude of events especially a disaster or catastrophe such as war, genocide, fascism etc. as Adelson points out, or in the case of Ganguly, climate change, that have a forceful impact on the very lives of human beings, and therefore also on the narratives of those lives, whether in miniature forms, as short or long prose. Second, any sense of the future or futural horizon cannot be dissociated from the narrative of history or the past, a thought that is illuminated by Adelson's use of the phrase "experiential treasure" and Ganguly's "magnitude of human experience." For such treasure, despite the disastrous nature of a catastrophe, to be brought to light and shared through a narrative necessitates experience with and of the event. However, this experience cannot be restricted to only privileging firsthand experience and/or reportage or survival testimonial (though neither scholar excludes it either). Which leads to the third and final intersection that I find useful for our discussion: the narration and documentation of the event and the afterlife through creative imagination, through what Adelson calls a "storytelling investment" and Ganguly a "literary inscription."

In other words, instead of packaging and storing an event in the past, burying it deep in some file as a letter in an archive, or in the pages of a novel or a short story, a narrative of disaster relies not on a simple past or a past perfect tense. Instead, narratives of life, stories of times between hope and destruction, between what has already been written and yet is impossible to visualize, must animate the energy of past perfect continuous tense, that "having gone through" or "having had contact with," to indicate future sense or futural horizons.

This specific derivation or recasting of the discussion of future sense by Adelson opens an entry to think through refugee time in the context of a global novel, especially one that registers memory of a Nazi past in a newly independent postcolonial nation-state that has just undergone a bloody partition. Before I turn to *Baumgartner's Bombay*, I want to focus on the globality of a refugee narrative or the refugee novel.

Global novel and refugee time

Precisely because the creation of refugees occurs in the shadow of a catastrophe with impact far beyond and long after the place and time where the said event of magnitude takes place, it would be safe to contend that in refugee literature, novels derive their globality through refugees, and offer a chance to understand the globality of refugees through the novel. But the modes in which this two-way globality manifests itself within the narrative are multiple. The first mode is through the multilingual composition of the novel. By this I do not simply mean the presence of two or three or more languages within the novel, or the actual composition of the novel in one or more scripts. The global novel is multilingual as one language becomes the vessel, the carrier of many other languages. Instead of code-switching, forms of linguistic "code-stitching"[29] register the investment in storytelling. Languages of past places and times come together with languages of present times and past and the present places. The multilingualism is cause and effect of the multi-locational composition of the global novel.[30] Points of departure and arrival, but also points of transit become part of the narrative. Last, but not the least, the refugee novel is multi-temporal in ways that are very different from a *Bildungsroman*, or a novel of (willful) migration, or a historical novel. The temporality, I want to argue, differs not merely in the choice of linear teleology or simply the puncturing of that teleology by switching between the past and the present in long-form storytelling. Here I want to make the case that the connections between time, experience, and narrative form – on which Adelson develops the idea of future sense – can be very helpful to think through the extended waiting time that becomes central to the formation of refugee subjectivity.

Any measure of refugee time must be located between destruction and hope, a sense of a life that has been destroyed through the catastrophe, a sense of the present that often appears as a temporary, "gap" period between the past life and the future life that could actually entail the return to that past, and a sense of the future – either of return, or an acceptance of, if not resignation to, the reality of permanence, however precarious, in that was which was supposed to be temporary. Refugee time, first and foremost, is out of sync with the unifying, homogenizing time, the "steady onward clocking of calendrical time"

---

[29] Jahan Ramazani, "Code-Switching, Code-Stitching: A Macaronic Poetics?" *ARCADE*, http://arcade.stanford.edu/dibur/code-switching-code-stitching-macaronic-poetics-0, 1 September 2017.
[30] B. Venkat Mani, "Multilingual Code-Stitching in Ultraminor World Literatures Reading Abhimanyu Unnuth's *Lāla Pasīnā* (1977) with Amitav Ghosh's *Sea of Poppies* (2008)," *Journal of World Literature* 3.3 (2018): 373–399.

which gives the nation its "sociological solidity."[31] But to claim that refugee time is independent of national time would also be a fallacy. Refugee time is in a de facto relationship with the bureaucratic time of the nation that steadily clocks onward, and is quite dependent on it. From the acceptance of admission, to the processing of asylum, to the granting of permission to work, refugee time is forced to be in sync with national bureaucracy, for the very existence of a refugee as a recognized political subject depends on it. In this way, refugee time is simultaneously part of the national time of the host-nation and the time of global bureaucracy, of the refugee recognition and protection organizations such as the UNHCR, or, as we shall see in *Baumgartner's Bombay*, the time of major world historical events, such as Hitler's coming to power in Germany, the Second World War, the Holocaust, and the time leading up to the moment of decolonization and then partition of India and Pakistan. But the relationship with global time of world historical events assures steady progression to a closure for a refugee. The stalled, stopped, uncertainly progressing, in-transit, and yet deceptively routine-based, normalized time of a refugee camp adds to the multi-temporal existence of the refugee, and consequently also to the refugee narrative encompassed in the global novel. And it is precisely in this waiting time of the refugee that occurs between tangible and intangible, entangled strands of time that the experiential pain translates itself into future sense through hope. In the connections between the very large and the very small emerges a futural horizon, that illuminates both the systemic follies of the past that led to the creation of the refugee, as well as offers a futural horizon, a sense of the future, a futurity of hope that becomes the source of and fortifies human resilience. To illustrate the significance of these thoughts, let me now turn to *Baumgartner's Bombay*. At a distance from previously outlined readings, I am more interested in the story of the German-Jewish refugee Hugo Baumgartner, the German Jew who had to leave Berlin in the 1930s via Hamburg and Venice, and his Bombay, which he calls his home for fifty years until his murder by a young German hippie in the 1980s.

Baumgartner's Bombay: Cosmic, global, German . . .

The novel begins with a woman – whom the readers will soon get to know as Lotte, another German Jew and Baumgartner's closest friend in Bombay – hurriedly entering her apartment clutching on to "bits of paper."[32] Lotte is in a

---

31 Homi K. Bhabha, *The Location of Culture* (New York: Routledge, 1994), 158.
32 Anita Desai, *Baumgartner's Bombay* (New York: Vintage, 1988), 1.

mournful state as she tries to make herself some coffee and opts for Gin. German enters this Indian English novel on the very second page, italicized to mark the difference, as we hear her sob: "Hugo, Hugo, *mein Gott*, Hugo, what's happened, *was ist dann, wie kannst du* . . ."[33] The bits of paper, stuck together with a "writing so spidery, it formed a kind of skein or web, on the yellowed paper" bear the "dates of long ago that Lotte hardly remembered – thirty-nine, forty, forty-one – just as she thought, suspected."[34] The thought, suspicion of Lotte, even in a first reading, is shared through recognition by the reader, for the years in the German context reveal a period of catastrophe which is hard to miss. Lotte finds out that Hugo is addressed in the postcards as "'*Meine kleine Maus*,' '*Mein Häschen*,' '*Liebchen* . . .'," with every letter reassuring him "I am well and do not worry"[35] and signed off "'Mama.' Others 'Mutti.' Some 'Mü.'" Lotte, the narrator tells us, tries to "prevent those words, that language, from entering her, invading her . . . The language she wanted not to hear or speak . . ."[36] And yet, overcome by grief, we hear Lotte now respond in German as she moans, "Nein, nein, nein, Hugo, no,"[37] following which, the bitterness associated with the language through the years mentioned on the post-cards and the years of careful prevention come undone, and "All the marzipan, all the barley sugar, the chocolates and toffees of childhood"[38] return as she drowns in her tears.

This powerful opening scene of the novel immediately sets up a conflicted bi-lingual stage for the rest of the novel: an invocation of a German catastrophe with global impact, a period of material and humanitarian destruction, including that of a human being's connection with a language. The presence of German in this scene, or in the rest of the novel may be marked scripturally through italics, but, as the novel proceeds, the reader will realize that this suturing of German into English, this code-stitching in italics so German can mark its difference on paper, is palpable also within the heart of the Jewish protagonist that the reader will soon be introduced to. Unlike Lotte, who has spent years preventing herself from using the language, Hugo Baumgartner's relationship will be more ambivalent, more tolerant, more in tune with specific situations that he encounters during his half-century stay in India.

Immediately afterwards, the scene shifts to Hugo's dilapidated apartment, to what the readers will find out is one of the last days of his life. Living in

---

33 Desai, *Baumgartner's Bombay*, 2, original emphasis.
34 Desai, *Baumgartner's Bombay*, 3.
35 Desai, *Baumgartner's Bombay*, 3.
36 Desai, *Baumgartner's Bombay*, 4.
37 Desai, *Baumgartner's Bombay*, 5.
38 Desai, *Baumgartner's Bombay*, 5.

penury with several cats whom he rescued and healed, Hugo is talking to them as he gets ready to go to Café de Paris, where he's a customer despite his limited means, as they provide leftover and discarded meat and fish for the cats. If Lotte's German comes back as memories of sweets such as Marzipan and chocolates, Hugo's first appears as lists of a wishful menu to the cats: "*Blutwurst, Leberwurst, Bratwurst – was willst du?*"[39] And as he comes down the stairs of his apartment building, we get a picture of a cosmopolitan Bombay in which people from all regional, linguistic, and religious backgrounds are at home: Sindhis (Hiramani), Parsis (Taraporevala), Portuguese and/or Goan Catholics (Cohelo, da Silva) as well as Marathi and Gujarati (upper caste) Hindus (Barodekar and Patel). This is the spirit of Bombay before it became Mumbai, where a German Jew has created a little home for himself.

Hugo's trip to the Café de Paris continues within this image of Bombay. Its owner Farrokh is a Parsi, belonging to the community of Zoroastrians who came to India as refugees from Persia in the ninth century as the spread of Islam threatened their religious freedom. This is where Hindi enters the novel with the nickname the café staff have given him, Billéwala Pagal – the Madman of Cats – unitalicized, sewn into the scriptural fabric of the page.[40] Farrokh discusses with him a "problem": a drugged out young man, a Hippie back from the Himalayas sleeping in the café, and Farrokh wants Hugo, or Bommgarter Saab as he calls him, to help. The appearance of the young man: "Nordic possibly . . . so pale – if not Teutonic"[41] sets a serious quandary for Hugo, and upon hearing Farrokh greet another Parsi customer with "*Kem cho*" (how are you), Hugo returns home.

Hugo's return to his cats inaugurates the history of his presence in India, through which the racialization of a German Jewish refugee becomes clear: "Accepting – but not accepting; that was the story of his life, the one thread that ran through it all. In Germany he had been dark – his darkness had marked him the Jew, der Jude. In India he was fair – and that marked him the *firanghi* [foreigner]. In both lands, the unacceptable."[42] This realization brings Hugo back to the visit to Café de Paris, and to his own history, first in a refugee camp (as an alien enemy) in British India with other Germans, then to the Hippie, and ultimately to the Germany of his youth:

---

39 Desai, *Baumgartner's Bombay*, 5.
40 Desai, *Baumgartner's Bombay*, 10.
41 Desai, *Baumgartner's Bombay*, 12.
42 Desai, *Baumgartner's Bombay*, 20.

> In the camp, they had looked at each other covertly, and not only was German-ness stamped like a number on each, but further information as well – that one was a Jew, another Aryan . . . That fair hair, that peeled flesh and the flash on the wrist – it was a certain type that Baumgartner had escaped, forgotten. Then why had this boy to come after him, in lederhosen, in marching boots, striding over the mountains to the sound of the *Wandervogels Lied?* The *Lieder* and the campfire. The campfire and the beer. The beer and the yodelling. The yodelling and the marching. The marching and the shooting. The shooting and the killing. The killing and the killing and the killing.[43]

Lotte's mourning on Hugo's death at the beginning of the first chapter of the book is ended with Hugo's trembling with fear. Suturing bits and pieces of German with English, then Hindi and Parsi in the cosmopolitan city of Bombay does not allow escape from the trauma of remembrance of the National Socialist past. In fact, the sequential arrangement of languages, locations, and historical events reveals how the three cannot be separated, how they are intertwined in the memory of a refugee, especially a Jewish refugee in India.

Hugo's reconstruction of his past life, remembering racial marking through skin and eye color – too dark for Germany and too light for India – and leading up to the *Wandervogelslied* are intertwined in the next chapter, set in pre-War Berlin, just before the Nazis take control. Rhythms of a comfortable life in the interwar period are heard along with nursery rhymes in German: "Hoppe, Hoppe, Reiter . . .," "O' Tannenbaum o' Tannenbaum . . .,"[44] "Eiapopeiea . . ."[45] and others, interrupted starkly by antisemitic chants of "Baumgartner, Baum, hat ein Nase wie ein Daum"[46] from fellow students in his school in a Berlin that is becoming increasingly dangerous for its Jewish residents. We learn that Hugo's father was a successful furniture businessman, who ended up in Dachau and then commits suicide. His father's business partner, a German from Hamburg who takes over the shop, arranges for Hugo's travel to India through his business connections, and Hugo arrives, having escaped being sent to a concentration camp just by a stroke of luck.

Through these multilingual, multilocational expressions of patchworks of past and present, readers are led to the first decade of Hugo's stay in India. The middle section of the novel, the back-and-forth narration between historical periods and geo-political locations, carries what Debjani Ganguly refers to as the "accrual and remediation of sedimented histories." However, the remediation happens through what Adelson terms "imprecise sites of mediation,"

---

43 Desai, *Baumgartner's Bombay*, 21.
44 Desai, *Baumgartner's Bombay*, 35.
45 Desai, *Baumgartner's Bombay*, 42.
46 Desai, *Baumgartner's Bombay*, 38.

substantially, and formally. Through these imprecise sites, first in the detention camp as a refugee, and then in the shadow of partition in independent India, the "dis-junctive" and "con-junctive" times of the refugee, are caught in the interstices of two imperial powers: British, and German, one established, the other aspiring. Here as well, a new register between an English that is still developing, a German that must be hidden, including sound-inflections of German accent that surreptitiously cross over to English and make him appear as dangerous for the British, and Bengali (in Calcutta where he moves for a few years) and later the Bombay-Hindi with words from several languages including Marathi, which he understands but cannot quite use – all these elements will form and inform the "experiential treasure" of his waiting time, even if English remains the language of narration of the novel, and the language mostly used by Hugo.

Hugo is in Calcutta in the 1930s, where he receives news of the strengthening of Hitler's power and the organized, systematic forced displacement of Jews and their annihilation. He plans to bring his mother to India, but their letter exchanges come to an end. After the lovely addresses from his mother and the remembrance of nursery rhymes, two words: "Adresse unbekannt"[47] stamped on a letter he sent to his mother reveals the realities of one of the darkest periods of human history. His efforts to connect with her through telegrams are also unsuccessful. And then he is taken into the detention camp, where he desperately tries to convince the British guards and overseeing officers that he is Jewish, and therefore a refugee.[48] A fellow German Jew reminds him: "They don't even know that there are German Jews and there are Nazi Germans and they're not exactly the same."[49]

Soon the conditions in the internment camp become worse, and Hugo's waiting begins for the war to end, for him to come out of the camp, for him to be recognized as a refugee, and for him to be able to start a new life. He wants to be freed of the "constant and oppressive company of his compatriots," while he ponders, "What will he do upon release?"[50] Germany appears as a "dark, monstrous block" to which he can never return. And there are Nazis among the Germans who rejoice at the news of every defeat that England suffers in the war. Here the linearity and detail of the narrative is interrupted with headlines from every single front – in Rangoon, Singapore, and Andaman Islands – that the British lose to Japanese forces. And the Nazis in the camp also bring back

---

47 Desai, *Baumgartner's Bombay*, 94.
48 Desai, *Baumgartner's Bombay*, 105.
49 Desai, *Baumgartner's Bombay*, 106.
50 Desai, *Baumgartner's Bombay*, 109.

German: "Heute gehört uns Deutschland, Morgen gehört uns die ganze Welt."[51] The British authorities, realizing the extent of violence against Jewish inmates, eventually separate them from the Nazi Germans. In a poignant moment that appears right in the middle of the novel, one of the Jewish residents asks, "And what shall we call our new home? . . . Auschwitz or Theresienstadt?"[52] As if placed carefully among the horrible news from the war in Europe and Asia and tensions within the camp, the following fragments appear in the narrative, with the hendiadys alluding to Wagner's *Rheingold* [The Rhinegold], Thomas Mann's *Zauberberg* [The Magic Mountain], as well as the powerful film by Alain Resnais: "*Nacht und Nebel*. Night and Fog. Into which, once cast, there was no return. No return. No return."[53]

Even in the midst of this mass destruction, darkness, night, fog, and completely unforeseeable future, hope is not abandoned. Hope appears in nascent form, first drawing solace in everyday habits of living: "Extraordinary how a cigarette could retrieve a man from the lip of hell and insanity."[54] The inmates play cards and spend their days "talking and talking, incredibly enough, of food, always of food. How was it possible in this situation to think and talk about food?"[55] And yet, the wish for eating *Wienerschnitzel, Leberknödel, Kartoffelpuffer*, and for one inmate "auch Butter"[56] just once before dying becomes part of routine chats, as everyone in the camp tries to alleviate the "burden, the tedium, the emptiness of the waiting days . . . the emptiness of the space into which they had been swallowed."[57] As the inmates try to overcome their fears and fill the present-day tedium – fully aware that what they and the world are going through has been caused by very large forces of history – they remain connected to the very small, the everyday, the mundane, and discover that "some of the prisoners had not only a past but a future too, outside and beyond the camp."[58] The Jewish inmates of the camp feel "thankful for the protection of the British-run camp, however sick with sorrow over the fate of their relations or of Germany, however restless and frustrated and bored by the lifeless monotony of the camp. At least it was a refuge, even if temporary."[59]

---

51 Desai, *Baumgartner's Bombay*, 116.
52 Desai, *Baumgartner's Bombay*, 117.
53 Desai, *Baumgartner's Bombay*, 119.
54 Desai, *Baumgartner's Bombay*, 119.
55 Desai, *Baumgartner's Bombay*, 119.
56 Desai, *Baumgartner's Bombay*, 120.
57 Desai, *Baumgartner's Bombay*, 125.
58 Desai, *Baumgartner's Bombay*, 130.
59 Desai, *Baumgartner's Bombay*, 132.

The temporary refuge comes to an end, as India becomes a permanent home, but not without confronting Hugo with yet another world historical event awaiting in the near future. When Hugo comes out of the jail, he is confronted with the rising religious tensions between Hindus and Muslims. Calcutta of 1945 is very different from Calcutta of 1943 when he was sent to the camp. His acquaintance and friend, a Muslim called Habibullah, hands him some of the last letters from his mother, which end in February 1941.[60] "They are driving us out," Habibullah remarks as he suggests that he'd better leave for Bombay. Hugo, realizing that "Germany when he flourished had not wanted him and Germany destroyed would have no need for him either,"[61] decides to move to Bombay. He "climbs over [Hindu] refugees [from what will become East Pakistan, and then eventually Bangladesh] to get to the train in Bombay."[62] And in a Bombay full of refugees, also from (West) Pakistan, Hugo starts his life anew.

Desai's depiction of life in a detention/refugee camp, especially her astute attention to retention of hope and a future sense in Hugo's life, as well as the life of many prison inmates is remarkably humane, not merely because it stages global and fractured national histories, but because it sutures the very large with the very small with an urgency, which yet succeeds to convey with a strong sense of hope. Hugo acquires an important business position with Mr. Chimanlal, the acquaintance of his father's German business partner from Hamburg when he gets to Bombay. A series of mishaps with Chimanlal's will lead to the end of his job and his last days of abject penury. And yet here too, the company of the cats, friendship with Lotte, and his regular visits to Café de Paris to collect food for his cats keep him busy. And despite his experiences with Germany, with "Aryans," and the anxiety and suspicion initially caused by seeing Kurt passed out in the café, Hugo gives him refuge in his apartment. But Kurt, a drug addict, kills him for his valuables. The novel ends on a somber note. The readers return to the scene of the crime and then to Lotte's apartment, where she has put the postcards in order: "Each one stamped with the number J 673/1. As if they provide her with clues to a puzzle, a meaning to the meaningless."[63] To a reader like me, in the twenty-first century, living in another time of refugees, the ending provides a clue to a different puzzle: the stamping of a painful part of German-Jewish history and the darkness of the Holocaust stamped on the bloody birth certificates of India and Pakistan. The novel ends, inviting a

---

60 Desai, *Baumgartner's Bombay*, 164.
61 Desai, *Baumgartner's Bombay*, 167.
62 Desai, *Baumgartner's Bombay*, 180.
63 Desai, *Baumgartner's Bombay*, 230.

rethinking of the globality of human suffering, reminding the reader of the pain, but also hope and resilience through fractured refugee time: cosmic, global, German, and if I may add, Indian.

Coda

In her envisioning of a future for German Jewish Studies, Leslie Morris powerfully expresses that "[German Jewish Studies should not] simply give us more readings of canonical and marginalized Jewish texts in German . . .," adding that German-Jewish culture should not be treated "as an object to be "read," but as a critical problem that itself demands new forms of critical writing."[64] She calls us "to imagine German Jewishness as a state of being that exemplifies Benjamin's 'art of being off center.'"[65] In my reading of *Baumgartner's Bombay* as a global novel through multilingual, multilocational, multitemporal narration with a focus on "refugee time," I have tried to answer the query asked by the letter about the travel documents for German Jews in India. The UNHCR archives did not have an immediate answer. But an answer was indeed provided much later, in a fictionalized form by Anita Desai.

Instead of thinking through the "German" lineage of Desai as an author, or the "English" lineage of the novel, I have tried to read it as a novel of refuge. As I have attempted to show, the novel really offers the possibility to trace "touching tales" – now borrowing from Leslie A. Adelson – of Germans, Jews, and Indians.

But the work of literature is not merely to engage or report history or provide easy answers to questions asked in documents buried in the historical archives. Desai's novel acquires its globality not just through the gravity of the subject matter and its multilocational setting. It's an investment in storytelling with claims to future, and for future readers. To express with Adelson again, "readers whom hope will not abandon and who are called upon to make more and better times."[66]

---

[64] Leslie Morris, "How Jewish Is German Studies?," *The German Quarterly* 82.3 (2009): vii.
[65] Morris, "How Jewish Is German Studies?," vii.
[66] Adelson, *Cosmic Miniatures and the Future Sense*, 251.

Works cited

Adelson, Leslie A. *Cosmic Miniatures and the Future Sense: Alexander Kluge's 21st-Century Literary Experiments in German Culture and Narrative Form* (Berlin and Boston: De Gruyter, 2018).

Adelson, Leslie A. *The Turkish Turn in Contemporary German Literature: Toward a New Critical Grammar of Migration* (New York: Palgrave Macmillan, 2005).

Bande, Usha. *The Novels of Anita Desai: A Study in Character and Conflict* (New Delhi: Prestige Books, 1988).

Bhabha, Homi K. *The Location of Culture* (New York: Routledge, 1994).

Da Silva, Tony Simoes. "Whose Bombay Is It Anyway?: Anita Desai's 'Baumgartner's Bombay' Tony," *Ariel* 28.3 (1997): 63–77.

Desai, Anita. *Baumgartner's Bombay* (New York: Vintage, 1988).

Dinnage, Rosemary. "Exiles," *The New York Review of Books*, 1 June 1989, 1–9.

Fachinger, Petra. "India/Sri Lanka, the Holocaust, and the European Gaze in Anita Desai's Baumgartner's Bombay and Jeannette Lander's Jahrhundert der Herren," in *Mapping Channels between Ganges and Rhein: German-Indian Cross-Cultural Relations*. Ed. Jörg Esleben et al. (Newcastle: Newcastle Cambridge Scholars Publ., 2008), 120–136.

Ganguly, Debjani. "The Global Novel: Comparative Perspectives," *New Literary History* 51.2 (2020).

Lotz, Rainer and Rekha Kamath. "Interculturality, a View from Below: Anita Desai's Baumgartner's Bombay," in *Jewish Exile in India, 1933–1945*. Eds. Anil Bhatti and Johannes H Voight, in association with Max Mueller Bhavan (New Delhi: Manohar Publishing, 1999), 163–171.

Mani, B. Venkat. "Multilingual Code-Stitching in Ultraminor World Literatures. Reading Abhimanyu Unnuth's *Lāla Pasīnā* (1977) with Amitav Ghosh's *Sea of Poppies* (2008)," *Journal of World Literature* 3.3 (2018): 373–399.

Mani, B. Venkat. *Recoding World Literature: Libraries, Print Culture, and Germany's Pact with Books* (New York: Fordham University Press, 2017).

Morris, Leslie. "How Jewish Is German Studies?," *The German Quarterly* 82.3 (2009): vii–xii.

Newman, Judie. "History and Letters: Anita Desai's Baumgartner's Bombay," *World Literature Written in English* 30.1 (1990): 37–46.

Ramazani, Jahan. "Code-Switching, Code-Stitching: A Macaronic Poetics?," *ARCADE*, http://arcade.stanford.edu/dibur/code-switching-code-stitching-macaronic-poetics-0. 1 September 2017.

Solanki, Mrinalini. *Anita Desai's Fiction: Patterns of Survival Strategies* (Delhi: Kanishka Publishing House, 1992).

Stähler, Axel. "The Holocaust in the Nursery: Anita Desai's Baumgartner's Bombay," *Journal of Postcolonial Writing* 46.1 (2010): 76–88.

West, Paul. "The Man Who Didn't Belong," *The New York Times*, 9 April 1989, 3.

Multilingualism, Translation, Transfer

Ulrike Vedder and Erik Porath
Gaps and Tatting: Reading, Translating, Collecting (Anna O., Bertha Pappenheim, Uljana Wolf)

> . . . only a keen attention to the important [details] can teach us how to tell the difference.[1]
> Leslie A. Adelson

The many scholarly, gender, textile, collecting, and literary histories associated with the Jewish social pioneer, Bertha Pappenheim, reveal countless gaps of varying provenance. Discontinuities and blanks are inevitable constitutive components in any biography, arising from the epistemological challenges of any attempt to represent and to give meaning to a life story. They are also the practical consequences of any number of decisions made during an individual's lifetime. However, gaps play a special role in Bertha Pappenheim's life and works, in her speaking, writing, and collecting, both restrictive and productive. The following essay will examine them on three levels.

Bertha Pappenheim famously appears in Joseph Breuer's and Sigmund Freud's 1895 *Studies on Hysteria* neither under her full name nor as B. P., but rather as A. O., or more precisely as Fräulein Anna O., thanks to a pseudonymous shift of her initials one letter forward in the alphabet. Of course, the name assigned to her is not the only deferral and omission, for indeed the case history is itself marked by many gaps as it describes the pathological breakdowns of Anna O. during her treatment for hysteria. Bertha Pappenheim's absences and memory lapses are as important for the pre-history of psychoanalytical treatment and its theorization as the filling in of these gaps through free association and the (re-)construction of an unconscious relation. (Part 1 of this essay) Among her symptoms was the temporary inability to speak German – a fragmented English took its place, thereby raising questions of multilinguality, which are especially interesting for the strategic presentation of early psychoanalysis in Vienna, as well as for Uljana Wolf, a contemporary author writing about Anna O. As a patient, author, and translator, Bertha Pappenheim

---

[1] Leslie A. Adelson, "From Erfahrungshunger to Realitätshunger: Futurity, Migrations, and Difference," in *Transatlantic German Studies: Testimonials to the Profession*, eds. Paul Michael Lützeler and Peter Hoeyng (Rochester, NY: Camden House, 2018), 5–22, here 7.

combined several languages and modes of expression – German and Yiddish along with English and other codes, including body language and poetic storytelling, which mixed up the familiar code systems while producing new ones. (Part 2 of this essay.) In addition, Bertha Pappenheim is of interest as an expert in the textile arts. Known for her social-political and journalistic activities, she also gathered together a valuable collection of lace over the years, which she eventually donated to the Vienna Museum for Applied Arts. As femininely connotated handicraft that owes its specific material and spatial structure to the principle of the hole, lace raises the question of what meanings are opened up its "holeyness" and how these take form in, for instance, a thing-story by Bertha Pappenheim or in Uljana Wolf's lyrical text *Tatting*. (Part 3 of this essay.) These aspects around Bertha Pappenheim are brought together through the phenomenon and the mental image of the "gap."

"Private theater:" Biographical and pathological gaps

Bertha Pappenheim's biography is marked by absences and fictions, above all by "Anna O.," the pseudonym for her belated case history. Thirteen years after her treatment ended (1880–1802), Josef Breuer published the case of "Fräulein Anna O." in *Studies on Hysteria*, which generated a series of further psychoanalytical, biographical, and literary texts.

Bertha Pappenheim was born in 1859 into a bourgeois, Jewish orthodox family in Vienna. Two of her sisters died early, a brother survived beyond childhood. He appears in Breuer's case history, whereas the sisters are not mentioned, not even in Breuer's subsequent correspondence with doctors.[2] In the absence of an upper-level school for Jewish daughters, Bertha Pappenheim attended a Catholic girls school, where most of all, she learned new languages.

> Bertha Pappenheim learned English, French, and Italian, though she later complained that she had received little general education. However, her brother Wilhelm, who was far less gifted than she, received a solid education, attended Gymnasium and eventually

---

[2] Even though the death of her sisters during Pappenheim's childhood and youth surely played an important role: "she experienced with intensity the anniversaries of the deaths of her sisters, on which memorial candles were lit in keeping with Jewish tradition," Marianne Brentzel, *Anna O. Bertha Pappenheim: Biographie* (Göttingen: Wallstein, 2002), 19.

studied law. Bertha viewed the difference in treatment between the genders with envy, stating that "daughters were undesired and above all a burden for their families on account of their expensive expectations and costly aspirations.[3]

When she was sixteen, her education ended. There were no plans for her to take up a profession, further education, or university study. "From this time on, the usual course of events would have been to wait for her future role as wife and mother."[4] In *Studies on Hysteria*, Breuer described Anna O. in the following manner:

> She herself had hitherto been consistently healthy and had shown no signs of neurosis during her period of growth. She was markedly intelligent, with an astonishingly quick grasp of things and penetrating intuition. She possessed a powerful intellect which would have been capable of digesting solid mental pabulum and which stood in need of it – though without receiving it after she had left school. She had great poetic and imaginative gifts, which were under the control of a sharp and critical common sense.[5]

According to Bertha Pappenheim's own later memories, her life after she finished school was filled with nothing but needlework. Around the same time, the women's rights activist, Marie Calm, warned against just such feminine activities because it undermined clear thinking: "This dainty needle can still be dangerous for women just as the thorns were to sleeping beauty, for they sink us into an intellectual sleep – a sleep filled with colorful dreams and glittering fantasies, but which allows no serious, clear-headed thought."[6] Even if Bertha Pappenheim gladly and skillfully practiced crafts such as lace-making, embroidering, beadwork, she still referred to the endless hours of women's needlework

---

3 Brentzel, *Anna O. Bertha Pappenheim*, 19. Brentzel cites Bertha Pappenheim writing under the pseudonym P. Berthold in "Zur Erziehung der weiblichen Jugend in den höheren Ständen," *Ethnische Kultur* 6.5 (1898): 61–63, here 62. Brentzel also notes: "Despite contradictory traditions, the Pappenheim family did not frown upon feminine education. Her mother grew up in a lively intellectual atmosphere and had attended a secular school in Frankfurt. Bertha's aunt, Nina Bettelheim, her father's sister, worked in the first Jewish girl school in Preßburg as a teacher," *Anna O. Bertha Pappenheim*, 18.
4 Gudrun Wolfgruber, "The 'Passions' of Bertha Pappenheim (1859–1936) alias Anna O.," in *Spitzen und so weiter . . . Die Sammlungen Bertha Pappenheims im MAK/Laces and so on . . . Bertha Pappenheim's Collections at the MAK*, ed. Peter Noever, trans. Abigail Prohaska (Vienna: Schlegrügge, 2007), 32–37 here 34.
5 Josef Breuer and Sigmund Freud, *Studies on Hysteria*, eds. and trans. James Strachey and Anna Freud (New York: Basic Books, 1955), 21.
6 Marie Calm, "Confirmationsgabe für junge Mädchen [1877]," cited by Christiane Holm, "versponnen – verstrickt – verwoben. Romantische Handarbeit zwischen Spinnstube, Salonmode und Maschinensturm," in *Handarbeit*, ed. Christiane Holm (Berlin: Secession, 2020), 9–17, here 10.

as producing "hundreds of worthless and tasteless nothings, which have become so terribly long-lasting precisely because of their uselessness" – an equally sharp and frustrated critique of the useless nothings that waste away women's productivity.[7] Theodor Fontane also takes up the topos of needlework in his novel *Frau Jenny Treibel* [Mrs. Jenny Treibel, 1892] wherein a young woman tells in skeptically self-ironic terms about her mastery in invisible mending, that is to say she reports on her ability to remove all visible signs of wear and tear as well as of her own needlework.[8] In all these examples, the object is to productively and conclusively remove all indications of the passage of time.

According to Christiane Holm, the Enlightenment foregrounded the utility of feminine needlework, both in the sense of "their household uses" and in their "function as an educational instrument and therapeutic means of binding girls' and women's unfocused thoughts and desires."[9] Romanticism, on the other hand, offered the reverse judgement: needlework became a visible activity displaying salon fashions as well as a poetic expression arising from the "presentation of unrestrained imagination" and the "the secretive inner life of craft-working women and their singular absent presence."[10] By the end of the nineteenth century these had become "useless nothings."

These "nothings" are furthermore symptoms of feminine helplessness. What should one do if the waiting period until marriage, which can be bridged but not filled meaningfully with "doing nothing," drags on endlessly? For Bertha Pappenheim, this was the case, for she "strictly rejected entering into an eligible, arranged marriage after the model of her parents."[11] No wonder that she later was outspoken about the need to professionalize and market women's needlework. "Bertha Pappenheim supported the establishment of handicraft and lacework operations in Galicia and Palestine with the aim of helping married and single Jewish women to become economically independent through occupational training."[12]

---

[7] Bertha Pappenheim, "Zur Erziehung der weiblichen Jugend in den höheren Ständen," partially reprinted in *Blätter des Jüdischen Frauenbundes* (July/August 1936): 4, cited in Brentzel, 22.
[8] Ulrike Vedder, "'in den Ton ausgeprochenster Wirklichkeit verfallend,' Poesie und Prosea in Fontanes *Frau Jenny Treibel*," in *Herausforderungen des Realismus. Theodor Fontanes Gesellschaftsromane*, eds. Peter Hohendahl and Ulrike Vedder (Freiburg/Br: Rombach, 2018), 187–202.
[9] Holm, "versponnen – verstrickt – verwoben," 10.
[10] Holm, "versponnen – verstrickt – verwoben," 11. Holm's beautiful anthology *Handarbeit* could only cover the literature of Romanticism.
[11] Wolfgruber, "The Passions of Bertha Pappenheim," 34.
[12] Wolfgruber, "The Passions of Bertha Pappenheim," 36.

In their reflections about the disposition to hysterical states, Breuer and Freud take needlework into consideration. At the beginning of *Studies in Hysteria*, they state: "We have nothing new to say on the question of the origin of these dispositional hypnoid states. They often, it would seem, grow out of the day-dreams which are so common even in healthy people and to which needlework and similar occupations render women especially prone."[13] And they cite Anna O. using her own expression, "private theater," which she summons up against boredom and "nothings":

> This girl, who was bubbling over with intellectual vitality, led an extremely monotonous existence . . . . She embellished her life in a manner which probably influenced her decisively in the direction of her illness, by indulging in systematic day-dreaming, which she described as her "private theater." While everyone thought she was attending, she was living through fairy tales in her imagination; but she was always on the spot when she was spoken to, so that no one was aware of it. She pursued this activity almost continuously while she was engaged on her household duties, which she discharged impeccably.[14]

Fairy tales, daydreams, and private theater point to a not just literary imaginative capacity, which functioned here fatally, as a displaced parallel world that fostered her "hysterical states" but also provided her with a medium for self-articulation. Narrating stories as "talking away" symptoms played a decisive role in Josef Breuer's treatment of Anna O. – for the patient herself as well as for the practice of psychoanalysis. Breuer describes the stories narrated under hypnosis as "always sad and some of them very charming, in the style of Hans Christian Anderson's *Picture-book without Pictures*, and, indeed, they were probably constructed on that model. As a rule, their starting-point or central situation was of a girl anxiously sitting by a sick bed. But she also built up her stories on quite other topics."[15] With the telling of stories came an easing of the symptoms – paralysis, aphasia, blindness, amnesia. Indeed, Breuer saw "the symptoms disappearing after being 'talked away.'"[16] In any case, his claim that Anna O. was healed in 1882 has been vehemently contradicted: "It is definite that Breuer's suggestion in *Studies on Hysteria* that the patient was almost completely cured does not correspond with the facts."[17]

---

13 Breuer and Freud, *Studies on Hysteria*, 13.
14 Breuer and Freud, *Studies on Hysteria*, 22. The official translation states that she discharged her household duties "unexceptionally," however a better translation for the original "tadellos" would be "impeccably."
15 Breuer and Freud, *Studies on Hysteria*, 29.
16 Breuer and Freud, *Studies on Hysteria*, 43.
17 Albrecht Hirschmüller, *Physiologie und Psychoanalyse in Leben und Werk Josef Breuers* [*Jahrbuch der Psychoanalyse*, Beiheft 4] (Bern: Hans Huber Verlag, 1978), 145. Rather Breuer

Even if the content and conclusions of Breuer's case history are questionable, his description of Anna O. as a "girl, who was bubbling over with intellectual vitality," does correspond with Martin Buber's much later characterizations of Bertha Pappenheim, on the occasion of her death in 1936, as a "person with passionate spirit."[18] By then her "monotonous life" (Breuer) had evolved into a life as an engaged women's rights activist and social reformer, and as an author and translator of literary and scholarly texts, dedicated to Jewish feminine modernity.

> Pappenheim's historic legacy – her attempt to constitute a specifically female ethic through social work based on religious convictions, and the transposition of women's liberation aspirations into the Jewish context – is at the same time a contribution to a specifically Jewish and female project of [modernity].[19]

It is astonishing that Bertha Pappenheim's Jewish identity, which had determined her entire life work (including the founding of the Jewish Women's Alliance in 1904) is never named in *Studies on Hysteria*. Breuer mentions her Jewish identity in his other testimonies about her, and rather, dismisses it there as irrelevant.[20] Here we have one of the many gaps and lacuna in her case history, but also a specific strategic blank spot, intended to foster the general acceptance of psychoanalysis.[21]

> Freud and Breuer removed all references in the case description to the Jewish background of their patient for good reason, given that in Vienna around 1900 hysteria was understood as a codeword for the character of Jewish men. In a double displacement, Freud and Breuer set the racist and confessionally unmarked "feminine hysteria" to substitute for the racist discourse about "Jewish hysteria." They thereby demonstrated their distance from particular religions and grounded psychoanalysis as a universal and meta-confessional project.[22]

---

transferred the patient to the Bellevue Sanitorium in Kreuzlingen from which she was released after several months in an "improved state."

18 Martin Buber, "Worte des Gedankens," in *Schriften zu Literatur, Theater und Kunst: Lyrik, Autobiographie und Drama*, Werkausgabe vol. 7, eds. Emily D. Bilski, Heike Breitenbach, Freddie Rokem, and Bernd Witte (Gütersloh: Gütersloher Verlagshaus, 2016), 444.
19 Wolfgruber, "The 'Passions' of Bertha Pappenheim," 36.
20 See the comment Breuer makes in the medical history he wrote when Anna O. was admitted to the Bellevue Sanatorium in Kreuzlingen: "She [Anna O.] is completely unreligious; the daughter of very orthodox and pious Jews, she is accustomed to obeying her father's strictest rules, so much so that she holds to them still for his sake. Religion played a role in her life only as the object of a quiet battle and resistance." Quoted in Hirschmüller, *Physiologie und Psychoanalyse in Leben und Werk Josef Breuers*, 349.
21 See Mikkel Borch-Jacobsen, *Anna O. zum Gedächtnis. Eine hundertjährige Irreführung* (Munich: Fink, 1997).
22 Louise Hecht, "Übersetzungen jüdischer Tradition. Bertha Pappenheims religiös-feministische Schriften," *Hofmannsthal-Jahrbuch zur europäischen Moderne* 20 (2012): 199–254, here 217.

This displacement from a "Jewish hysteria" to a "feminine hysteria," tantamount to concealing the patients' Jewish origins, found its equivalent in Freud's redefinition of the concept of "conversion" from the religious to the psychic-medical sphere. When Freud speaks of an "hysterical conversion," he takes up a loaded contemporary word that later also preoccupied Bertha Pappenheim in her volume of fictional stories, *Kämpfe* [Struggles]: conversion in the sense of a crossing over from Judaism to Christianity.[23] Freud for his part displaces the concept of conversion into a decidedly non-religious framework.

> If conversion was understood in the Vienna around 1900 as a change in religions, that is to say, the conversion from Judaism to Christianity, then Freud had placed the term in an "unorthodox" context. In his 1894 essay, "The Neuro-Psychoses of Defence," . . . he writes about the conversion of psychic traumas, or socially taboo sexual fantasies, into somatic symptoms in hysteria patients. The "conversion" transforms a strong yet socially unacceptable idea into a weaker acceptable one . . . The strong idea was thus, as it were, inscribed onto the body as a memory trace.[24]

It is also clear here that the hystericized body is to be understood as an historicized one, as the bearer and agent of the subject's memory traces, which are in turn historically conditioned. Leslie A. Adelson's phrase "making bodies, making history" raises an additional question concerning the conditions underlying the relationship between materiality and history: ". . . bodies constitute a nonontological, material ground for action at specific moments in time. Such ground is, moreover, subject to diachronic shifts as well as synchronic instability."[25] The synchronic and diachronic convulsions reverberating on the body – that nonstable material scene-have their equivalent in the specific image of the discontinuous that Freud used to describe hysterical conversion: the "leap" ("Sprung"). As Freud made clear, this leap both provokes *and* articulates gaps in the interpretation and attribution of meaning to hysteria. He first brings up the leap in his 1909 "Notes upon a Case of Obsessional Neurosis," where he states that "the leap from a mental process to a somatic innervation – hysterical conversion – can never be

---

23 "Pappenheim's stories [in *Kämpfe*, 1916] are interventions in a wide-ranging and intense debate about Jewish to Christian conversion: as a threat to Jewish life and identity, or as an opportunity to participate fully in modernity," Peter Davies, "Christian Art, Masculine Crisis, and the Threat of Jewish Conversion in Bertha Pappenheim's Short Stories," *German Life and Letters* 73.4 (2020): 581–602, here 584.
24 Hecht, "Übersetzungen jüdischer Tradition," 202. Hecht cites Freud, *Gesammelte Werke* 1, 59–74, here 217.
25 Leslie A. Adelson, *Making Bodies, Making History: Feminism and German Identity* (Lincoln and London: Nebraska University Press, 1993), 15.

fully comprehensible to us."²⁶ A few years later he speaks of "the puzzling leap from the mental to the physical."²⁷ Despite some progress in psychoanalytical understanding and practice, Freud held onto the enigmatic character of conversions.²⁸

In order to comprehend Anna O.'s hystericized body in terms of its historicity, its external inscriptions, and its willful experiences, it is important to situate this body within its contemporary discursive framework: as a "female Jewish" body in Vienna around 1900, as a symptom of productive and performative bodies, as a readable and writable body within the (pre)history of psychoanalysis. The "hystericized body" is also a "semiotic body," saturated with the effects of power, yet it nevertheless also represents a space for social experiences that allows for different positionings and even resistances. Without mentioning Freud, Leslie A. Adelson points out that "positionality *characterizes* the body of social experience as well as the sign-functions of which it partakes, but we cannot say that positionality *is* the body, since it always implies a complex physical and significatory relationship to structures of power."²⁹

Anna O. is a frequently described and often overwritten figure within such a specific power structure. Her place in the prehistory of psychoanalytical treatment and its theorization, however, repeatedly concerns voids (gaps in consciousness and recollection, absences, and ruptures in attentiveness) and the filling in of these voids or gaps through free association, through the (re)construction of a context that has remained unconscious, and through a language rich in metaphor and imagery. Bertha Pappenheim herself never spoke about her psychoanalytical treatments and its biographical and intellectual consequences – with one exception: a fragment of a report, which she wrote in English during her stay in the Bellevue Sanatorium in Kreuzlingen (July to October 1882) after treatment by Breuer. This brings us to the topic of linguistic and poetic gaps.

---

26 Sigmund Freud, "Notes upon a Case of Obsessional Neurosis," in *Standard Edition of the Complete Psychological Works of Sigmund Freud* (London: Hogarth Press, 1955), 10: 157.
27 Sigmund Freud, "General Theory of the Neuroses," in "Introductory Lectures on Psycho-Analysis," in *Standard Edition of the Complete Psychological Works of Sigmund Freud* (London: Hogarth Press, 1963), 16: 258.
28 Erik Porath, "'Jener rätselhafte Sprung aus dem Seelischen ins Körperliche.' Konzepte und Narrative der Konversion in Freudscher Psychoanalyse, Medizin und Literatur," in *Konversion. Erzählungen der Umkehr und des Wandels*, eds. Ulrike Vedder and Elisabeth Wagner (Berlin: Vorwerk 8, 2017), 153–173.
29 Adelson, *Making Bodies, Making History*, 19.

Aphasia, multilingualism, translation: Linguistic and poetic gaps

Anna O. became anonymously famous not least because of her neologisms. In addition to the already mentioned "private theater," she equally invented the English term, "the talking cure," which she also referred to as "chimney-sweeping," again speaking in English, while she was Josef Breuer's patient from 1880 to 1882. English is one of the foreign languages that Anna O. retained during her aphasiatic phase. For a time, she spoke only English. Breuer describes the situation in the following words:

> On the fifth of April her adored father died. During her illness she had seen him very rarely and for short periods. This was the most severe psychical trauma that she could possibly have experienced. . . . She now spoke only English and could not understand what was said to her in German. Those about her were obliged to talk to her in English . . . She was, however, able to read French and Italian. If she had to read one of these aloud, what she produced, with extraordinary fluency, was an admirable extempore English translation.[30]

The fragment of Bertha Pappenheim's own report which she wrote in English, with minor spelling mistakes, in the middle of September 1882 offers the following:

> I, a native German girl, am now totaly [sic] deprived of the faculty to speak, to understand or to read German [. . .]. The physicians point it out as something very strange and but rarely to be observed; therefore I will try to give, as well, as a person who never has made any medical studies, can do, a short account of my own observations and experiences considering this terrible estate. [. . .] When during this phase two other persons are talking in German, I must take trouble to fix my attention to the conversation, which is quite indifferent me. I feel sorry not to understand; but ame [sic] not interested in it. I have bin [sic] told that after some hours I get my German language through speaking it very badly, [. . .] [end is missing].[31]

In her report, Bertha Pappenheim both describes *and* enacts her linguistic symptoms – her partial speechlessness and her idiosyncratic multilingualism. For example, certain "mistakes" in the fragment quoted above can be recognized as German-language insertions.

This fragment of Pappenheim's report reappears in the literature of contemporary author, Uljana Wolf. In her prose and lyric poetry, Wolf often works with multilinguality and turns Anna O.'s language loss into a language expansion,

---

30 Breuer and Freud, *Studies on Hysteria*, 26.
31 Cited in Hirschmüller, *Physiologie und Psychoanalyse in Leben und Werk Josef Breuers*, 369ff.

thereby ironically challenging the interpretative status of early psychoanalysis. *Method Acting with Anna O.* (2013) is a text saturated with German and English. It consists of three sections: "Annalogue on Oranges," "Annalogue on Flowers," and "Tatting." Uljana Wolf does not offer a new case history, nor she does write an "Anna O." novel.[32] Instead, she takes up themes from the history of her illness, with a particular interest in her aphasia, her word invention, and her translations. The section, "Annalogue on Oranges," brings together a series of symptoms, utterances, and situations from Anna O.'s history, including her neologism, "chimney-sweeping," which in Wolf's text turns into the harsh request "go sweep the chimney, so that the doctor comes again."[33] In another poetic example the symptom that the patient could not drink anything for a while and took to oranges and other fruits as liquid intake is transformed into: "orangenpoetiqqqqq."[34] Uljana Wolf also works with typographical means: the thick prose monologue in the patient's first-person voice (called "annalog") receives its own space on the left-side of the book, while the opposite right page contains a few loosely distributed verses, as if they were fragments left over from an expunged text.

There, on the right-hand page of the book, the first line reads "i. a native irgendwas girl," which references the opening sentence of Bertha Pappenheim's self-analysis ("I, a native German girl").[35] Her origin is subjected to a semantic disorientation, as "German" is turned into "irgendwas" (something-or-other). This move brings the actual proliferation of her origin to the fore. Bertha Pappenheim could be considered German on the basis of her native language, Austrian because she was born in Vienna, Habsburg as a resident of the multi-ethnic state, Jewish in terms of her religion and culture, or English as this is the language she is actually speaking. The first line continues "solide/geistige Nahrung and she digested/ mit affektiver athletik/und orangenpoetiqqqqq."[36] Here, Wolf combined a chopped-up quotation from Breuer's characterization of Anna O.

---

[32] Anna O., or rather Bertha Pappenheim, has often been turned into a literary figure. "The gaps in the documentation of Pappenheim's life that have frustrated some of her biographers have been welcomed by a diverse cadre of creative artists in various media (novel, drama, opera, visual art, film, and performance art) who have embraced ambiguity as an invitation to explore the links between the near-mythical figure of Anna O. and the historical figure Bertha Pappenheim," Elizabeth Loentz, *Let Me Continue to Speak the Truth: Bertha Pappenheim as Author and Activist* (Cincinnati: Hebrew Union College Press, 2007), 239.
[33] Uljana Wolf, "Annalogue on Oranges," in *Sub-sisters: Selected Poems*, trans. Sophie Saita (Brooklyn: belladonna, 2017), 68.
[34] Wolf, "Annalogue," 69.
[35] Wolf, "Annalogue," 69.
[36] Wolf, "Annalogue," 69.

("a strong intellect that could have absorbed sold intellectual sustenance") with a fragment from Gilles Deleuze, who takes up this formulation in his study, *Logic of Sensation*, where he writes about the hysterical body's "affective athletics." Then, she inserts her own neologism "Orangenpoetik," which she immediately estranges, however, by attaching the letters, "qqqqq," which onomatopoetically imitate the gurgling sound produced when drinking.

The multilingual, first-person text on the left side of the book could be characterized as an "orange poetics." This poetics involves both the "drinking" of oranges as a detailed description of this procedure, that not only quenches thirst, but also structures time, challenges language, and brings the body into play to articulate resistance:

> when it is time for oranges, ist keine zeit, no time at all, für nichts. I only eat oranges, at least they exist, even if not much else is, no things at all, not much. Petite little boats and stringy thin skin! I suck on them for hours. keeps me busy. free run for the tongue, looking for thread between teeth, interlace-space, and rooms to own, not much. oranges or existence all round. oranges or residence all round (. . .) while the wardress brings fresh water fresh sheets, all the unemptied glasses, cup., daily a warding off for repair, nicht wahr, that's how they planned it all. later ten rooms on each floor, servants galore, with bow and tie marriage and tea. marriage and in the evening a little riot, then tea. but when it is time for oranges, ist keine zeit, no time at all for thirst, für wasser, for being thus arranged. because oranges are their own maneuvering material. because trains, bridges, and little glimmering glitches keep me going unallayed.[37]

The critique of authority is obvious, as the first-person voice defends itself against "marriage and tea" and "for being thus arranged." She uses the oranges as "maneuvering material" in order to keep herself "unallayed:" o-ranged. But the helplessness of the means available to the first-person voice are clear as well: "because i have no work, no travel only thought-revel . . . hungerstreik. Because oranges are asylum and solid geistig nourishment."[38]

The use of multilinguality and of exclusively using lower case letters as a poetic procedure assure the de-automatization of meaning. Not only do these techniques block an all too hasty identification (e.g., of a young woman as hysteric) but they also draw attention to the materiality and the physicality of language and speech. Her polyphonic speaking also serves as a creative rebuttal to Josef Breuer's description of Anna O.'s speech, which he understands strictly in terms of loss:

---

37 Wolf, "Annalogue," 68.
38 Wolf, "Annalogue," 70.

Later she lost her command of grammar and syntax; she no longer conjugated verbs, and eventually she used only infinitives, for the most part incorrectly formed from weak past participles; and she omitted both the definite and indefinite article. In the process of time she became almost completely deprived of words. She put them together laboriously out of four or five languages and became almost unintelligible. When she tried to write (until her contractures entirely prevented her doing so) she employed the same jargon.[39]

In contrast to Breuer's account, Uljana Wolf's "Annalogue with oranges" focuses on the productive complexity of poetic, multi-lingual and multi-layered speech. In doing so, she not only simply evaluates an otherwise "pathological" speech but also reminds us that multilingualism was an everyday "normality" in Vienna around 1900, as it was for the multi-ethnic state of Austria-Hungary in general. Psychoanalysis's own linguistic environment was no different:

> Freud stands in the tradition of a German that served as the language of cosmopolitanism and beside which, of course, other languages were in circulation. (. . .) In Freud's writings, language change is sometimes noted *en passant* but it does not appear as an isolated problem in need of investigation. Possibly, multilingualism was too much the cultural norm to attract attention to itself or even appear as a source of problems.[40]

Bertha Pappenheim's multilingualism included, in addition to the knowledge of new foreign languages acquired at school, Yiddish, which Breuer refers to as "jargon." Not only did Yiddish allow her to remain articulate during her aphasia, it also comes into play in her later translation work. Among other works, she translated Mary Wollstonecraft's 1792 *A Vindication of the Rights of Woman* from the English as well as the Yiddish memoirs of Glückel von Hameln, a.k.a Glikl bas Judah Leib, ca. 1646–1724, which she published in 1910.[41] Inge Stephan considers these translations to be "self-conscious acts of recollection of two moments in her biography that play no role, or at best a minor one, in the case history Breuer narrates: her Jewish origin and her position as a woman."[42]

In her careful translation of Glückel's memoirs, Bertha Pappenheim made sure to convey the characteristics of Yiddish style into German by preserving

---

39 Breuer and Freud, *Studies on Hysteria*, 25.
40 Esther Kilchmann, "Von short sentences, fancy-dresses und jeux de mots. Die Psychoanalyse und der exilbedingte Sprachwechsel," in *Sprache(n) im Exil. Jahrbuch Exilforschung*, eds. Doerte Bischoff and Christoph Gabriel, 32 (2014): 66–82, here 68ff.
41 In addition, Pappenheim translated into German a collection of old Yiddish stories, known as the Ma'asse or Maysebuch in 1929 and the so-called women's Bible in 1930.
42 Inge Stephan, "Sprache, Sprechen und Übersetzen. Überlegungen zu Bertha Pappenheim und ihrem Erzählungsband "Kämpfe" (1916)," in *Sprache und Identität im Judentum*, ed. Karl E. Grözinger (Wiesbaden: Harrassowitz, 1998), 29–42, here 32.

the sentence construction and rhythm of the Yiddish. Pappenheim also emphasized Glückel's multilingualism in her translation, for Glückel's memoirs were filled with Hebrew and Aramaic quotations. "The literal translation of Hebrew interjections commonly used in Yiddish interrupts the reading flow and calls attention to the description of everyday events."[43] Interestingly, Bertha Pappenheim had herself portrayed as Glückel von Hameln after the publication of her translation. This is where her lace collection comes into play: for the painting (by Leopold Pilichowski) she not only donned a fur coat "borrowed from a friend" but also with old lace from her own collection.[44]

Collecting lace: Women's craftwork and the art of gaps

Bertha Pappenheim's extensive lace collection includes rare historical objects as well as contemporary arts, which she unearthed on her numerous travels, especially in the context of her work with international Jewish women's associations. "Besides classical needle and bobbin lace of the sixteenth to the eighteenth centuries from Italy, France and Belgium, she also collected nineteenth-century lace and, most of all, lace of the twentieth century . . . around 1,850 pieces of lace and textiles."[45] The collection is not only an expression of her private passion but also points to Pappenheim's social-political agenda: the economic independence of Jewish women working in craftwork enterprises. The collection can also be viewed as "a specifically feminine modern project that has the particular

---

43 Hecht, "Übersetzungen jüdischer Tradition," 234. Hecht underscores: "With her innovative reconstruction of Yiddish in the German, Pappenheim situates herself, consciously or not, within the Romantic tradition of translation that can be mapped from Klopstock via Schlegel to Hölderlin in their classical translations from Greek, English and Latin into German," "Übersetzungen jüdischer Tradition," 234.
44 Hecht, "Übersetzungen jüdischer Tradition," 241. Hecht adds, "In 1925 the now lost portrait was shown in Palestine as part of an exhibit of [Leopold] Pilichowski's work," "Übersetzungen jüdischer Tradition," 241.
45 Angela Völker, "Lace and so on . . . The Collections of Bertha Pappenheim – Sigmund and Recha Pappenheim née Goldschmidt Donation – at the MAK," in *Spitzen und so weiter . . . Die Sammlungen Bertha Pappenheims im MAK / Laces and so on . . . Bertha Pappenheim's Collections at the MAK*, ed. Peter Noever, trans. Abigail Prohaska (Vienna: Schlebrügge, 2007), 14–18, here 14.

goal of celebrating the 'preindustrial,' 'feminine,' and 'applied arts.'"[46] Part of the collection includes contemporary lace art by women designers, such as Franziska Hoffmanninger, Mathilde Hrdlička, and Leni Matthaei, so that the craft work could step out from behind its usual feminine anonymity. What distinguishes lace as a textile art is immediately obvious: the filigree delicacy that comes with great expertise and patience. Among its distinguishing features is that lace consists of both threads and gaps that create a productive interplay of ornate patterns and their limits. Lace is neither fabric nor no-fabric. Lace is not made up of plain cloth, yet it can be produced by pulling out threads from a woven cloth. In this technique, lace can be considered holes that have been fabricated elaborately. But they are also not no-cloth, because lace is fabric. This special consistency turns them into elaborate decorative and erotic metaphors, as Bertha Pappenheim explains in one of her travel letters:

> I must admit I'm sometimes homesick – though this is only a kind of yearning for my home, my desk with the paraffin lamp, my amusing silhouettes, my colourful glasses, and first and foremost my lacework, these wonderful varieties and configurations, their element a straight, fine thread of linen. And if I were not an enemy of poetic comparisons, and if all comparisons did not limp, I might say our life should also be made of such fine, firm, genuine material, interlaced and interwoven with identical and straight threads, which, whether simple or complicated, represent ethical as well as aesthetic values. I long to lead such a life as well, and hate the rough fingers that destroy the beautiful pattern, and tear or tangle the threads.[47]

This passage brings out the many attractions of her lace collection. She is writing while separated, far away from the collection for which she yearns. Her affectionate bond for "the wonderful varieties and configurations" can even give

---

[46] Annette Tietenberg, "Strukturprinzipien der Moderne: Die Textilsammlungen von Bertha Pappenheim und Emilie Flöge," in *Textile Moderne*, ed. Burcu Dogramaci (Cologne: Böhlau, 2019), 157–167, here 159.

[47] Wolfgruber "The 'Passions' of Bertha Pappenheim," 34. See the original: "Allerdings habe ich manchmal Heimweh, aber, das ist nur eine Art Sehnsucht nach meinem Heim, nach meinem Schreibtisch mit der Petroleumlampe, nach meinen lustigen Schattenrissen, nach meinen bunten Gläsern und vor allem nach meinen Spitzen, diesen wunderbaren Varietäten und Gebilden, deren Element ein grader feiner Leinenfaden ist. Und wenn ich nicht eine Feindin poetischer Vergleiche wäre, und wenn nicht alle Gleichnisse hinkten, möchte ich sagen, unser Leben müßte auch aus so feinem, festen, echten Material gleich- und gradfadige Verflechtungen und Verwebungen darstellen, die, ob sie einfach oder kompliziert sind, ethische, resp. ästhetische Werte darstellen. Auch danach habe ich Sehnsucht, so ein Leben zu führen, und hasse die groben Finger, die die schönen Plangebilde zerstören und die Fäden zerreißen oder verwirren," Bertha Pappenheim, *Sisyphus-Arbeit. Reisebriefe aus den Jahren 1911 und 1912*, Leipzig 1924, quoted in Wolfgruber, "The 'Passions' of Bertha Pappenheim," 31.

her homesickness. But these feelings are not just the sentimental emotional bonds for her possessions. Her lace represents an ideal life that finds fulfillment by becoming intertwined and interwoven with others who share her ethical and aesthetic values.

Furthermore, her fascination with lace arts is not just a product of its fantastical and delicate visuality, but rather it is also material and haptic, for lace are fashioned by feminine hands to decorate the body and its closest interior spaces. The idea of being "interlaced and interwoven" includes the sense of touching and being touched. As the passage from Pappenheim's letter shows, confirming textile- and thing theory, the haptic quality of things is coupled with modes of memory. Recollections, old stories, genealogical thoughts are woven, spun, stitched, and sewn into the textiles in the form of patterns and motifs as well as in the form of narratives and thoughts arising while doing craftwork.[48] Manual work with textiles is itself connected with the topos of memory: as a bodily recollection of repeated movements and gestures that comprises practiced handicraft and which foster the daydreams of a "private theater." Annette Tietenberg describes such feminine craftwork as an "alternative form of materialization for the unconscious."

While under hypnosis Bertha Pappenheim delivered the raw material that others transmitted it into writing. In the confluence of threads, she discovered an alternative form of materialization for the unconscious, located in the realm of motor skills, at the intersection of technology and handiwork. The slow and consistent repetition of practiced movements produced textiles, that emerged from the operative "synergy of tool and gesture," which could function also as a medium of recollection. Through contemplation and touch, it can narrate the past, but does not require masculine authority nor translation into a written form to be "played" in the present.[49]

Interestingly, Bertha Pappenheim also put the memory medium of lace "into a written form": into a literary form. The "Tale of the Old Lace" is the title of her stories, collected as *In the Junk Shop* and published in 1890 under the pseudonym, "P. Berthold." These are stories about things, such as a coffee

---

[48] Just to mention the famous mythical scene: Philomele is raped by Tereus, who cuts out her tongue. She however weaves the scene for her sisters, so that it can be retold and revenged. Freud famously claimed that the cultural technique of plaiting and weaving was the one feminine contribution to the "discovery and inventions in the history of civilization," Sigmund Freud, "Femininity," *Standard Edition*, 22: 112–135 here 132.

[49] Tietenberg, "Strukturprinzipien der Moderne," 163. When using the phrase "the synergy of tool and gesture," she cites André Leroi-Gourhan, *Hand und Wort. Die Evolution von Technik, Sprache und Kunst* (Frankfurt am Main: Suhrkamp, 1980), 296.

grinder, a bird cage, a thimble, or a music box, that tell their respective "life stories" from their marginal position in the junk shop – how they were passed from hand to hand and linked life paths. The tale of the junk dealer serves as the frame for these stories. He finds a trace of his youthful love through one of these memory objects and eventually adopts their daughter. The interlacing and interweaving of life stories creates the central theme of the collection. One evening, after hours when all the things are alone in the shop, the old lace recounts the story of her importance within changing contexts: as a christening gown, an altar cloth, a museum piece, and then finally in the junk shop. She was predestined for the junk shop not only because of the fine quality of her old Dutch lace but even more so because of her notable burn mark. The lace was scorched by a lightning bolt while the "little countess," whose christening gown it adorned, remained unharmed.[50] In gratitude for this miracle, she was donated for an altar cloth in the village church. The lace refers to this moment as her martyr's stripes.[51] From her place on the altar, the lace observes the childhood encounter between the "little countess" and the teacher's son. Years later, the lace was loaned to a museum for decorative arts: "Only gradually did I learn to adapt to my environment and thereby become aware of my own worth, because everyone who approached the cabinet in which I was hung admired my delicacy and the beauty of my pattern."[52] Eventually, the "little countess," now all grown up, and the boy who had meanwhile become a professor, meet again in front of her cabinet. The two eventually marry in the village church, with the lace back on the altar again. ". . . a little bit of their blissfulness was transferred to me because I knew, I sensed, that I was a part of their union."[53] This traditional thing-narrative is of now great literary value, though it remains interesting because of its format as an object biography and for its focus on interconnectedness.

The object biography has gaps, for the path the old lace travels to the junk shop is missing from the story. It can be assumed that the burn mark, which initially led to the appreciation, later contributed to its devaluation as junk. Object biographies seem always to be concerned with questions of value. Thing narratives, as Walter Benjamin pointedly noted in his essay, "Unpacking my Library," work within an order of things that is deployed against gaps, chaos, and contingency: ". . . any order is nothing more than a hovering over the

---

50 Bertha Pappenheim, *In the Junk Shop and other Stories*, intro. Sander L. Gilman, trans. Renate Latimer (Riverside, CA: Ariadne Press, 2008), 36–43, here 37.
51 Pappenheim, *In the Junk Shop*, 38.
52 Pappenheim, *In the Junk Shop*, 41.
53 Pappenheim, *In the Junk Shop*, 43.

abyss."⁵⁴ A certain narrative is, therefore, important for Benjamin's collector – "the fate of his object."⁵⁵ Thus every collected object is given a "life story:" a history of acquisition and loss, provenance and previous owners, significance and revaluation, and so forth. While in Benjamin's text the metaphor of the object's "life" signifies expressly the perspective of the passionate collector, the term "object biography" is a methodological term commonly used in archeology and ethnography in order to summarize the objects' various uses, revaluations, and meanings.⁵⁶ Object biographies represent an additional literary genre in which most interesting stories involved atypical "life paths" and usages of things. In Joseph Addison's *Adventures of a Shilling* (1710) or James Fenimore Cooper's *Autobiography of a Pocket-Handkerchief* (1853) each respective object acquires "significance only to the extent that it is not subsumed within its general purpose."⁵⁷ Pappenheim's story also employs this productive narrative pattern as the feudal sartorial decoration and quasi sacral object turns into a profane museum piece and finally a bit of junk.

Uljana Wolf is also interested in the form, meaning, and literary productivity of lace: One section of "Method Acting with Anna O." is entitled "Tatting." Wolf again works with typographical means, for the words and verses are arranged on the book pages like lace patterns, while at the same time they tell of making lace, and again there are references to Anna O., for instance, through quotations from her case history or by switching into English. The following provides an example:

for tatted lace   or *occhispitze*   **you wind the thread**
around a shuttle   which then   between fingers   back & forth
then up   &   down so that   ring & arc-shaped   figures also
eye-loops   join   &   one below the other
into larger patterns   lie a crest   in the blink of an eye
(gaze   into the candle)   (direkt in die flamme)⁵⁸

The poem stages instructions for the technique of occhi lace (along with counting instructions "for beginners" in the footnote). At the same time, the poem

---

54 Walter Benjamin, "Unpacking my Library: A Talk about Collecting," trans. Harry Zohn, in *Selected Writings, 1927–1934*, ed. Michael Jennings (Cambridge: Belknap, 1999) 2, 486–493, here 487.
55 Benjamin, "Unpacking," 487.
56 See, Hans Peter Hahn, *Materielle Kultur. Eine Einführung* (Berlin: Reimer, 2005), 40–45.
57 Michael Niehaus, *Das Buch der wandernden Dinge. Vom Ring des Polykrates bis zum entwendeten Brief* (Munich: Hanser, 2009), 268.
58 Uljana Wolf, "tatting" *Subsisters: Selected Poems*, 86.

depicts the procedure itself: both through the patterns on the book page and through the interruptions in work process, as manifested in the blank line and the dreamy distraction of the gaze ("gaze into the candle").

The next page emphasizes women's work. The sexualized connotation of tatting production appears in the name "occhi lace" also called "Frivolité." The appearance of the tatting tool used to make lace, also called "the shuttle," is reminiscent of female genitals. This, in turn, can be connected to the tendency of eroticizing or sexualizing daydreams "to which needlework and similar occupations render women especially prone" as in to "gaze directly into the candle."[59]

The following passage from Uljana Wolf's lyric poetry makes these intersections in the sign of tatting particularly clear:

the tatting shuttle   **or**   *schiffchen der augenspitze*
is thumb-sized   **&resembles**   **a**   **small fold**
mon dieu   une petite occhi-pussy   with which she can   or can't
(not really)   skip   but slip   *how d'you do* knots
as a lady of the upper   in day of candle   light   and if she pulled
first the rascals   then the threads   from this folding   shuttle[60]

The typographical and semantic omissions create a pattern like the textile art of lace, but they also contain breakdowns and gaps, the unsayable and the double meaning. Multilingualism and intertextuality also contribute greatly to the rich associations in Uljana Wolf's lyric poetry. These cannot all be examined here, however one quotation from Breuer and Freud is worth pursuing. Wolf's "tatting" makes reference to Freud in one particular footnote: "(Freud asks, How can such a camel pass through the eye of a needle?)." The main text on the same page reads as follows:

or does *freud* want to   say   (but   doesn't   say   )
if   you   speak   of   the   eye   of   a   needle
language   begins to   totter   lays eyes on you   like the sea
look here an eyelet   is   œillet   is an öhr   for seeing
the eye of a sailor   the seemann ties the knot   & later dreams a lot
(when scrubbing the deck) of the beauty of loops   in every harbour he
gives a lady his lace   for her (neck) rough as rope &   course as cord.[61]

---

59 Breuer and Freud, *Studies on Hysteria*, 13.
60 Wolf, "tatting," 88.
61 Wolf, "tatting," 100.

The associations here range from the tottering rhythm of language to that of the sea, from knots in the production of tatting to seamen's knots, from the little tatting boat to "tatting" to the "dick/coarseness" of the seaman, and so forth. These associations are likewise connected to Sigmund Freud's reflections on the treatment method at the conclusion of *Studies on Hysteria*, where the "eye of the needle" proverb is reintroduced. Thus, the feminine needlework named in the Introduction to the *Studies* recurs at the end and provides the metaphor for the interpretative work of hysteria. Freud writes: "The psychical material in such cases of hysteria presents itself as a structure in several dimensions . . . . The logical chain . . . contains nodal points [*Knotenpunkte* in original] at which two or more threads meet and thereafter proceed as one; as a rule several threads which run independently, or which are connected at various points by side-paths, debouch into the nucleus."[62] He continues:

> after the case had been completely cleared up, to demonstrate the pathogenic material to a third person in what we now know is its complicated and multi-dimensional organization, we should rightly be asked how a camel like this got through the eye of the needle. For there is some justification for speaking of the "defile" of consciousness. . . . The whole spatially-extended mass of psychogenic material is in this way drawn through a narrow cleft and thus arrives I consciousness cut up, as it were, into pieces or strips. It is the psychotherapist's business to put these together once more into the organization which he presumes to have existed. Anyone who has a craving for further similes may think at this point of a Chinese puzzle.[63]

Uljana Wolf takes the eye of the needle metaphor literally and applies it to the textile handiwork in order to critically present the period's tying hysteria to its image of femininity, while also playing out the productivity of holes and empty spaces as figured by lace. Freud blatantly uses the proverb in order to emphasize the vast dimensions of an hysteric's unconscious material and the corresponding amount of interpretive work required in response. The eye of the needle proverb fits in neatly with Freud's metaphorical references to "threads," "knots," and "strips" with which he famously describes his own work. Uljana Wolf also draws attention to how the (anti-authoritarian) tottering, or swaying, of language accounts for holes and gaps: "or does *freud* want to say (but doesn't say) if you speak of the eye of a needle language begins to totter lays eyes on you like the sea."

---

62 Breuer and Freud, *Studies on Hysteria*, 288, 290. Strachey translates "Knotenpunkt" as "nodal point." The knot metaphor is obviously crucial for the argument in this essay.
63 Breuer and Freud, *Studies on Hysteria*, 291.

"Anyone who has a craving for further similes may think at this point of a Chinese puzzle" – one that enters through the ear after having passed through mouths and other bodily openings, even the smallest pores as it betrays the unconscious as language.[64] Jacques Lacan was right to recommend to analysts that they practice solving crossword puzzles in order to learn never to grow impatient with the arduous work of the psychoanalytical process but instead to always take up the task again of finding its rich string of associations. Or one could, in the context of feminine life around 1900, recall the delicate, patient needlework, wherein one had to tie together and entwine threads, while carefully detaching others from the weaving, and then use yet again other threads to create recurring patterns and to create the most beautiful lace around gaps.

"With all my memories:" Touching tales

The transfer of Bertha Pappenheim's valuable collection of laces and iron work to the Austrian Museum for Art and Industry (today the Museum for Applied Art, Vienna) that she undertook in 1935, one year before her death, is also filled with significant gaps. She had already started the process in 1912 and then eventually in 1935 gave her collection, without requiring payment or a pension, first as a loan and then written into her will, from Frankfurt to the museum in Vienna. The relevant documents, including the collection's dedication to the memory of her parents, Sigmund and Recha Pappenheim, and her testament bequeathing the collection to the museum are missing. "It is probable that Bertha Pappenheim's will was destroyed in a bomb attack, along with her entire estate. Her closest friend and confidante Hannah Karminski had passed them on to a friend in Berlin, along with her own memoirs. Hannah Karminski was deported by the National Socialists in 1942 and killed."[65]

The conflict Bertha Pappenheim experienced as she undertook the transfer in 1935 as a Jew under Austro-Fascism becomes apparent in her correspondence with the museum director, Richard Ernst. In her reconstruction of the circumstances, Angela Völker cites two letters from the museum archive that "hint at

---

[64] "He that has eyes to see and ears to hear may convince himself that no mortal can keep a secret. If his lips are silent, he chatters with his finger-tips; betrayal oozes out of him at every pore," Sigmund Freud, "Fragment of a Case of Hysteria," *Standard Edition*, 7: 3–124, here 77–78.
[65] Völker, "Lace and so on . . . The Collections of Bertha Pappenheim," 17. Völker also provides more information on the lengthy history of negotiations between Pappenheim and the museum.

the 'Jewish issue.'" "Certain ideological incongruities that cropped up in our conversations," Pappenheim wrote on July 2, 1935, "are of no importance for me in the context we talked about them. You will understand that I hold the honour of my lineage in high esteem."[66] Even if Pappenheim accommodatingly chose the discreet formulation, "certain ideological incongruities," she also emphasized the "honor" of her Jewish origin and her life's work as a determined Jewish social activist. The museum director Ernst answered first by offering the reassurance that he recognized the "interesting but not inimical contradictions" between them. Then, in the second letter, he referred to the New Testament but in a less Christian formulation that also cited Goethe in order to strike a more tolerant pose: "many dwellings are prepared in the mansion of the Lord – here the words of Goethe ring in my ears."[67]

That the museum held to its obligations to Bertha Pappenheim is certain. It preserved the collection and made it accessible to the public, thereby preserving cultural memory. Gaps and voids still appear in every museum exhibition. Karl-Josef Pazzini has shown that every museum object is constituted through its absences. "Every material thing that can be seen in a museum has been taken from somewhere else. The first significant feature of a museum piece is the absence of any reference to this other location and time."[68] The conflicts of a museum become thus apparent: as a powerful institution the museum preserves objects by leaving absences somewhere else. These gaps can be recognized by a gaze that takes a particular interest in doing so. Gaps played a similarly productive and recollective role in Bertha Pappenheim's life history

---

66 Völker, "Lace and so on . . . The Collections of Bertha Pappenheim," 17.
67 "Richard Ernst answered thus: 'The ideological incongruities touched on in your kind letter shrink in my view into interesting but not inimical contradictions (– many dwellings are prepared in the mansion of the Lord – here the words of Goethe ring in my ears). In the spirit in which you wish your collection to be assessed and see it used, we feel ourselves entirely beholden to you,'" Völker, "Lace and so on . . .," 18. Original text reads as follows: "Darauf antwortete Richard Ernst: 'Die weltanschaulichen Ungleichheiten die Ihr gütiger Brief berührt, schrumpfen meinem Gefühl nach auf interessante aber nicht feindliche Gegensätze zusammen (– in unsres Herrn Hause sind viele Wohnungen bereitet, klingts mir von Goethe her in den Ohren). In dem Geiste, in welchem Sie ihre Sammlung gewertete und benützt sehen wollen, fühlen wir uns Ihnen ganz verbunden,'" Völker, "Spitzen und so weiter . . .," 13. Goethe used Jesus's formulation "In my Father's house there are many rooms" (John 14:2) in a letter to Zelter on July 22, 1816 in which he is not actually discussing tolerance, but rather his accidentally renting three apartments.
68 Karl-Josef Pazzini, "'Das kleine Stück des Realen' – Das Museum als "Schema" (Kant) und als Medium," in *Open Box. Künstlerische und wissenschaftliche Reflexionen des Museumsbegriffs*, ed. Michael Fehr (Cologne: Wienand, 1998), 312–322, here 314.

with the art of lace as perhaps the most visible form and the absences in her psychoanalytical case history as the most powerful example.

In the aforementioned letter from 2 July 1935, Bertha Pappenheim also writes – in material and affective terms – about the last time she touched her lace before giving her collection to the museum: "how happy I was to have them slip through my hands piece by piece with all my memories."[69] Contact, recollection, departure: here we can connect to the concept of "touching tales" that Leslie A. Adelson has developed in the context of contemporary linguistic and cultural alterity but which is thought-provoking also for the constellation we have been discussing here.[70] From an affective perspective (in the sense of stirring), "touching tales" are just as significant as in a bodily (tangible) and transcultural point of view (in the sense of interwoven histories that move and overlap each other). Given their affectivity and bodily articulation, their multilingual and multi-perspectival genres and narrative styles, and their specific materialities, Bertha Pappenheim's many scholarly, gender, textile, collecting and literary histories can be understood as touching tales.

Translation Bettina Brandt

Works cited

Adelson, Leslie A. "From Erfahrungshunger to Realitätshunger: Futurity, Migrations, and Difference," in *Transatlantic German Studies: Testimonials to the Profession*. Eds. Paul Michael Lützeler and Peter Hoeyng (Rochester, NY: Camden House, 2018), 5–22.
Adelson, Leslie A. *Making Bodies, Making History: Feminism and German Identity* (Lincoln and London: Nebraska University Press, 1993).
Adelson, Leslie A. "Touching Tales of Turks, Germans, and Jews: Cultural Alterity, Historical Narrative, and Literary Riddles for the 1990s," *New German Critique* 80 (2000): 93–124.
Benjamin, Walter. "Unpacking my Library: A Talk about Collecting," in *Selected Writings, 1927–1934*. Trans. Harry Zohn, ed. Michael Jennings (Cambridge: Belknap, 1999) 2: 486–493.
Borch-Jacobsen, Mikkel. *Anna O. zum Gedächtnis. Eine hundertjährige Irreführung* (Munich: Fink, 1997).
Brentzel, Marianne. *Anna O. Bertha Pappenheim: Biographie* (Göttingen: Wallstein, 2002).

---

69 Völker, "Lace and so on . . . The Collections of Bertha Pappenheim," 17. The original text reads as follows: "wie froh ich war, sie [die Spitzen] noch einmal Stück für Stück mit allen Erinnerungen durch meine Hände gleiten zu lassen," Völker, "Spitzen und so weiter . . .," 12.
70 Leslie A. Adelson, "Touching Tales of Turks, Germans, and Jews: Cultural Alterity, Historical Narrative, and Literary Riddles for the 1990s," *New German Critique* 80 (2000): 93–124.

Breuer, Josef and Freud, Sigmund. *Studies on Hysteria*. Eds. and trans. James Strachey and Anna Freud (New York: Basic Books, 1955).

Buber, Martin. "Worte des Gedankens," in *Schriften zu Literatur, Theater und Kunst: Lyrik, Autobiographie und Drama*. Werkausgabe vol. 7. Eds. Emily D. Bilski, Heike Breitenbach, Freddie Rokem, and Bernd Witte (Gütersloh: Gütersloher Verlagshaus, 2016), 444–445.

Calm, Marie. "Confirmationsgabe für junge Mädchen [1877]." Cited by Christiane Holm, "versponnen – verstrickt – verwoben. Romantische Handarbeit zwischen Spinnstube, Salonmode und Maschinensturm," in *Handarbeit*. Ed. Christiane Holm (Berlin: Secession, 2020), 9–17.

Davies, Peter. "Christian Art, Masculine Crisis, and the Threat of Jewish Conversion in Bertha Pappenheim's Short Stories," *German Life and Letters* 73.4 (2020): 581–602.

Freud, Sigmund. *Standard Edition of the Complete Psychological Works of Sigmund Freud* (London: Hogarth Press, 1955).

Freud, Sigmund. *Standard Edition of the Complete Psychological Works of Sigmund Freud* (London: Hogarth Press, 1963).

Hahn, Hans Peter. *Materielle Kultur. Eine Einführung* (Berlin: Reimer, 2005).

Hecht, Louise. "Übersetzungen jüdischer Tradition. Bertha Pappenheims religiös-feministische Schriften," *Hofmannsthal-Jahrbuch zur europäischen Moderne* 20 (2012): 199–254.

Hirschmüller, Albrecht. Physiologie und Psychoanalyse in Leben und Werk Josef Breuers [Jahrbuch der Psychoanalyse, Beiheft 4] (Bern: Hans Huber Verlag, 1978).

Kilchmann, Esther. "Von short sentences, fancy-dresses und jeux de mots. Die Psychoanalyse und der exilbedingte Sprachwechsel," in *Sprache(n) im Exil. Jahrbuch Exilforschung*. Eds. Doerte Bischoff and Christoph Gabriel 32 (2014): 66–82.

Leroi-Gourhan, André. *Hand und Wort. Die Evolution von Technik, Sprache und Kunst* (Frankfurt am Main: Suhrkamp, 1980).

Loentz, Elizabeth. *Let Me Continue to Speak the Truth: Bertha Pappenheim as Author and Activist* (Cincinnati: Hebrew Union College Press, 2007).

Niehaus, Michael. *Das Buch der wandernden Dinge. Vom Ring des Polykrates bis zum entwendeten Brief* (Munich: Hanser, 2009).

Pappenheim, Bertha. *In the Junk Shop and other Stories*. Intro. Sander L. Gilman, trans. Renate Latimer (Riverside, CA: Ariadne Press, 2008), 36–43.

Pappenheim, Bertha. "Zur Erziehung der weiblichen Jugend in den höheren Ständen." Partially reprinted in *Blätter des Jüdischen Frauenbundes* (July/August 1936) 12: 3–5.

Pazzini, Karl-Josef. "'Das kleine Stück des Realen' – Das Museum als "Schema" (Kant) und als Medium," in *Open Box. Künstlerische und wissenschaftliche Reflexionen des Museumsbegriffs*. Ed. Michael Fehr (Cologne: Wienand, 1998), 312–322.

Porath, Erik. "'Jener rätselhafte Sprung aus dem Seelischen ins Körperliche.' Konzepte und Narrative der Konversion in Freudscher Psychoanalyse, Medezin und Literatur," in *Konversion. Erzählungen der Umkehr und des Wandels*. Eds. Ulrike Vedder and Elisabeth Wagner (Berlin: Vorwerk 8, 2017), 153–173.

Stephan, Inge. "Sprache, Sprechen und Übersetzen. Überlegungen zu Bertha Pappenheim und ihrem Erzählungsband "Kämpfe" (1916)," in *Sprache und Identität im Judentum*. Ed. Karl E. Grözinger (Wiesbaden: Harrassowitz, 1998), 29–42.

Tietenberg, Annette. "Strukturprinzipien der Moderne: Die Textilsammlungen von Bertha Pappenheim und Emilie Flöge," in *Textile Moderne*. Ed. Burcu Dogramaci (Cologne: Böhlau, 2019), 157–167.

Vedder, Ulrike. "'in den Ton ausgeprochenster Wirklichkeit verfallend.' Poesie und Prosa in Fontanes *Frau Jenny Treibel*," in *Herausforderungen des Realismus. Theodor Fontanes Gesellschaftsromane*. Eds. Peter Hohendahl and Ulrike Vedder (Freiburg/Br: Rombach, 2018), 187–202.

Völker, Angela. "Lace and so on . . . The Collections of Bertha Pappenheim – Sigmund and Recha Pappenheim née Goldschmidt Donation – at the MAK," in *Spitzen und so weiter . . . Die Sammlungen Bertha Pappenheims im MAK / Laces and so on . . . Bertha Pappenheim's Collections at the MAK*. Ed. Peter Noever, trans. Abigail Prohaska (Vienna: Schlebrügge, 2007), 14–18.

Wolf, Uljana. "Annalogue on Oranges," in *Sub-sisters: Selected Poems*. Trans. Sophie Saita (Brooklyn: belladonna, 2017).

Wolfgruber, Gudrun. "The 'Passions' of Bertha Pappenheim (1859–1936) alias Anna O," in *Spitzen und so weiter . . . Die Sammlungen Bertha Pappenheims im MAK/Laces and so on . . . Bertha Pappenheim's Collections at the MAK*. Ed. Peter Noever, trans. Abigail Prohaska (Vienna: Schlegrügge, 2007), 32–37.

John Namjun Kim
A Betweenness that Beckons: Rhythm and Rhyme in Tawada's Poetic Time

Betweenness

Of the many tropes used to describe cultural productions by ethnicized subjects, few are as innocuous yet often cited as the seemingly humble word "between." Such subjects are envisaged as suspended "between" one thing and another, "between" a point of departure and a forever deferred point of arrival, "between" their imagined "homelands" and their no less imagined "hosts." This preposition that acts more like a verb enforcing separation and distance introduces a protocol of reading in which the sociological status of such subjects determines the reading of their cultural productions in advance of their actually being read by anyone. But, it does so only by presupposing the empirical givenness of the objects *between* which the ethnic status of such subjects is also made to appear all the more given. "Between" is not a mere preposition, it is a trope that *ethnicizes*.

This trope is the most incisively critiqued by Leslie A. Adelson in her highly influential article, "Against Between: A Manifesto," on how literary works by migrants and their descendants in Germany have been read or, more precisely, *not* read.[1] "'Between Two Worlds,'" Adelson argues, "is the place customarily reserved for those authors and their texts on the cultural map of our time, but the trope of 'betweenness' often functions literally like a reservation designed to contain, restrain, and impede new knowledge, not enable it."[2] Her critique of betweenness rests on two critical observations.

First, the trope of betweenness "contain[s], restrain[s] and impede[s] new knowledge," on Adelson's account, by virtue of the apparently empirical givenness of a place called "Germany" and the places from which these writers are thought to hail, as though the cultures of these places were as bounded and stable as the territorial borders of these places. Even if imagined as a celebratory "bridge" of mutual understanding, Adelson argues, the figure of "'between two worlds' is designed to keep discrete worlds apart as much as it pretends to bring them together. Migrants are at best imagined as suspended on this bridge in perpetuity."[3] She

---

[1] Leslie A. Adelson, "Against Between: A Manifesto," *New Perspectives on Turkey* 28–29 (2003): 19–39, here 18.
[2] Adelson, "Against Between," 21.
[3] Adelson, "Against Between," 22.

thus concludes, "we do not need more understanding of different cultures if understanding only fixes them *as* utterly different cultures. Instead of reifying different cultures as fundamentally foreign, we need to understand culture itself differently."[4] Implicit in Adelson's critique is that the trope of "betweenness" rests on the catachresis of metonymy confounding territorial place with cultural practice; it occludes the latter by means of the former.

Second, this catachresis of metonymy permits readers of literary productions by such ethnicized subjects *not to read* what these subjects have written but only the ethnicity they are thought to be. They are "read" sociologically. As Adelson remarks, "This positivist approach presumes that literature reflects empirical truths about migrants' lives and that authors' biographies explain their texts so well that reading the texts themselves becomes virtually superfluous."[5]

Through these observations, Adelson raises one of the fundamental questions of literary studies, the curiously conjunctive status of literary figuration and social referentiality. In other words, because the writers in question are imagined to hail from "elsewhere," their literary works are "read" strictly through the grid of intelligibility of this sociological frame, as though the social text coincided with the literary text in an interchangeable manner. Frameworks of "betweenness" thereby introduce a tautological protocol of reading in which wherever ethnics appear writing, their writing appears ethnic. As Adelson sharply quips, "This saves readers and critics a good deal of time. Meanwhile, the literary elephant in the room goes unremarked."[6]

Adelson's two-fold critique touching upon one of the most fundamental questions of literary studies prompts the further query: do *all* figurations of betweenness serve to "contain, restrain, and impede new knowledge"? For Adelson, the answer is *no*. Turning to literary texts by such ethnically marked authors, she highlights one figuration of "betweenness" in particular for its alternative citation of this preposition, Yōko Tawada's "The Translator's Gate or Celan Reads Japanese" ["Tor des Übersetzers oder Celan liest Japanisch"].[7] In this text, Tawada ponders the "translatability" of Celan's poetry in Japanese through its Japanese translation, which throughout includes the Sino-Japanese

---

4 Adelson, "Against Between," 23.
5 Adelson, "Against Between," 21.
6 Adelson, "Against Between," 21.
7 Adelson cites from the German original, published in Yoko Tawada, "Das Tor des Übersetzers oder Celan liest Japanisch," in *Talisman* (Tübingen: 1996), 121–134. Susan Bernofsky's English translation of Tawada's essay is available in "The Translator's Gate, or Celan Reads Japanese," *Mantis: A Journal of Poetry, Criticism & Translation* 8 (2009): 223–232.

character (*kanji*) *mon*, 門, or "gate," in combination with other *kanji*, such as *aida* or *kan*, 間, or "between." As Tawada writes and Adelson cites, "'I began to regard Celan's poems as gates and not, say, as houses in which meaning is stored like possessions.'"[8] For Adelson reading Tawada reading Celan, "the word is a site of opening, a threshold that beckons."[9] Betweenness need not foreclose the reading of literature but opens it in the form of a threshold.

Adelson's critique generates yet another question that is fundamental to not only the reading of literature but also literary studies as an institution: Why is literary criticism so quick to read writings by ethnicized writers according to a protocol of referential reading in which the texts are assumed to be sociological reproductions of the ethnicity that such writers are thought to be? Might not some texts lure acts of criticism into the aesthetic phantasmagoria of "ethnicity" only to undo its referential illusions through the tropological dimension of language?

With these two questions in mind, I now turn to two poetic texts by Tawada, her German-language poem, "A Poem for a Book" ["Ein Gedicht für ein Buch"; hereafter "A Poem"] and her Japanese-language poem "Yokohama" [よこはま] to consider the opposed senses of betweenness cited by Adelson, one that opens reading and the other that forecloses it, and to pose two questions in elaboration and extension of her critical observations: What is the status of language in the figure of a "threshold that beckons"? And, what is precisely imagined in the foreclosing trope "between two worlds"? That is, what underlies this imagination of "between two worlds"?

In posing these questions, the aim of this essay is to understand how Tawada's poetic text might invoke figurations of ethnicity only to revoke them in language. It may do so, I suggest here, not necessarily through language's tropological dimension or even its referential function but rather through its sonic materiality, namely, through rhythm in "Yokohama" and rhyme in "A Poem."

Ein Gedicht für ein Buch
   ein wort
1 ein mord
   wenn ich spreche
   bin ich nicht da
   ein wort
5 in seinem käfig
   fesselnd gefesselt
   spuckt einen bericht

---

8 Tawada, "Das Tor," 130, cited in Adelson, "Against Between," 24.
9 Adelson, "Against Between," 24.

über meine taten
über meine karten
10   kein wort
nur sein schatten
in dem ich ruhe
mein schatten verschwindet darin
nichts wird bewertet
15   wenn ich schweige
bin ich aus demselben stoff gemacht
wie du
stoffliche zeit
zwischen einem wort
20   und einem schluck wasser
dort
wo die stimme im fleisch aufwacht
hört man ohne ohren
ein wort
25   befreit von seinem dienst
ein wort
direkt auf das trommelfell geschrieben
die trommel fällt
lautlos
30   stimmhaft
ein wort
ein ort[10]

A Poem for a Book
a word
1   a murder
when i speak
i am not there
a word
5   in its cage
arresting arrested
spits a report
about my crimes
about my cards
10   no word
only its shadow
in which i rest
my shadow disappears in it
nothing is judged

---

10 Yōko Tawada and Stephan Köhler, *Ein Gedicht für ein Buch* (Hamburg: Edition Lange, 1996). This poem is reprinted in Yoko Tawada, *Aber die Mandarinen müssen heute abend noch geraubt werden* (Tübingen: Konkursbuch, 2003), 93–94.

15 when i am silent
    i am made of the same material
    as you
    material time
    between one word
20 and a sip of water
    there
    where the voice awakes in the flesh
    one hears without ears
    a word
25 liberated from its duty
    a word
    written directly on the eardrum
    the drum falls
    soundless
30 voiced
    a word
    a place[11]

Rhyme: "A Poem for a Book"

A betweenness that beckons pervades Yoko Tawada's "A Poem," not only in its words but also in the material form in which it was first published. First published in 1996 in an artist's book created in collaboration with the photographer and papermaker Stephan Köhler and the bookmaker and designer Clemens-Tobias Lange, this poem appeared in the material context of a book bound in ray-leather printed on loose-leaf folios made of hand-made Japanese paper (*washi*) by Köhler within photographs, also by Köhler, of everyday scenes in Japan: a man bathing, people riding on trains while reading, and temple installations.[12] The effect of this collaborative endeavor with its ray-skin binding and hand-made paper is that of a highly corporealized and singular mode of delivering a poem for reading, lending each of its copies, in a highly limited print-run of just forty-five copies, as Jeremy Redlich argues, "a very material, corporeal

---

[11] Translation by Bettina Brandt in "Scattered Leaves: Artist Books and Migration, A Conversation with Yoko Tawada," *Comparative Literature Studies* 45.1 (2008): 12–22, here 18. Line 24 has been amended to accord with this essay's reading of the German.

[12] These philological details are based on Bettina Brandt's illuminating interview with Tawada in "Scattered Leaves: Artist Books and Migration, a Conversation with Yoko Tawada," *Comparative Literature Studies* 45.1 (2008): 12–22, 13 and 16.

experience pre-figuring the linguistic text."[13] In other words, the poem is presented in a context requiring not just "reading" the text, but also *feeling* the texture and weight of the binding and hand-made paper as well as *seeing* the photographic images in conjunction with the poem.

In view of the synaesthetic experience of interpreting the sensorial interplay of the book's presentation, readers such as Redlich have shown that the material "background" of this book must be accounted for in co-constitutive terms with the "foreground" of the poem appearing within this multi-sensorial book. Yet, as Bettina Brandt notes, Tawada's poem "simultaneously centers and de-centers this book"[14] as the relation between the poem and the other material aspects of the book are largely ambiguous; its lines, printed one per folio, "center" the book in terms of creating a thematic continuity between the pages but "de-centers" it insofar as its lines bear no clear relation to the images, the book's paper and its ray-leather binding "unifying" it as "a book." What then is the relation between this poem and the book in which it appears and of which it is a constitutive member?

Reading this poem in relation to the synaesthetic experience of reading, feeling, and seeing this text, Redlich argues that Tawada's citation of the word *wort* (word) as the poem's "self-reflexive and central theme" suggests "that language has both a symbolic (in the discursive sense) and material (in the corporeal sense) effect on the body."[15] In Redlich's reading, the lines "wenn ich spreche / bin ich nicht da",[16] "wenn ich schweige / bin ich aus demselben stoff gemacht wie du"[17] and "ein wort / befreit von seinem dienst"[18] suggest "a kind of displacement of the 'word' from its conventional function as a communicative sign, pointing towards a kind of liberating potential for the 'word.'"[19]

However compelling Redlich's reading may be with respect to the material conditions of the poem – the book's binding, its hand-made paper, its photographic images – the self-reflexive word in question in Tawada's poem need not be restricted to the word "word" (wort) alone. Rather a rereading suggests that the word in question need not be *wort* itself, but the most literally *self-*

---

[13] Jeremy Redlich, "Bringing the Background into Focus: Reading the Linguistic and Bibliographic Codes in Yoko Tawada's Das Bad," in *Scholarly Editing and German Literature: Revision, Revaluation, Edition*, eds. Lydia Jones, Bodo Plachta, Gaby Pailer, and Catherine Karen Roy (Leiden and Boston: Brill Rodopi, 2016), 78.
[14] Brandt, "Scattered Leaves," 17.
[15] Redlich, "Bringing the Background," 79.
[16] Tawada, "A Poem," l. 3–4: "when i speak / i am not there."
[17] Tawada, "A Poem," l. 16–19: "when i am silent / i am made of the same material / as you."
[18] Tawada, "A Poem," l. 25–26: "a word liberated from its duty."
[19] Redlich, "Bringing the Background," 79.

reflexive word available in language *ich* (I). This is suggested by the rhyme of the first two lines and meter of next two lines in blank verse, "ein wort / ein mord / wenn ich spreche / bin ich nicht da."[20] The rhyme of the first two lines equates "a word" with "a murder"; the iambic dimeter of the next two lines[21] literally redoubles the one iambic meter of the first two lines suggesting that "wenn ich spreche / bin ich nicht da" is in apposition to "ein wort / ein mord," such that the "I" in third line elaborates the "word" (wort) in the first line and that the "I" that is "not there" (nicht da) in fourth line describes the results of a "murder" (mord) in the second line. This poem harkens to Saint Paul's second letter to the Corinthians, "the letter killeth, but the spirit giveth life,"[22] except that in Tawada's poetic practice there is no "spirit," no *subject*. Rather, if there is a subject, it is immediately "not there" (nicht da) when it "speaks." If there is a beckoning in Tawada's poem, it is not from a speaking subject but from the materiality language itself in the form of the *word* "I."

Rather than a profoundly enigmatic Heideggerian observation, the claim that it is language that beckons both in this poem in particular and in linguistic life in general is grounded in one of the most basic observations of structuralist linguistics with respect to the exceptional status of the "I" in discourse. Unlike terms with "objective reference" – such as "chair," "stone" or even terms of fantasy such a "unicorn" – the enunciation of the word "I" initiates a temporality entirely internal to language and refers, not to its speaker, but to the instance of discourse in which it is uttered. If this were not the case, a contradiction would immediately ensue within a dialogue in which the two parties predicate their "I's" differently.[23] Moreover, statements such as the Cretin's paradox "I am lying," which tracks closely to Tawada's lines "when I speak / I am not there," would be unintelligible were a distinction not made between the subject of the enunciated and the subject of the enunciation, that is, between the subject posited in an utterance as the agent of the verb and the subject retroactively posited as the "source" of the utterance but who appears nowhere in the utterance itself. This critical distinction that makes linguistic expression possible can be made even more vivid in analogy to self-portraiture in photography, such as Cindy Sherman's *Untitled Film Stills* series in which her "self"-portraits (the subject of the enunciated) are never to be confused with the photographer herself (the subject of enunciation), especially as her photographs show how the

---

20 Tawada, "A Poem," l. 1–4 "a word / a murder / when i speak / i am not there."
21 Tawada, "A Poem," l. 3–4.
22 The Bible, 2 Corinthians 3:6.
23 Émile Benveniste, "Subjectivity in Language," in *Problems in General Linguistics* (Coral Gables, FL: University of Miami Press, 1971), 223–230.

subject of the enunciated retroactively produces the imagination of a living subject of enunciation. The temporality of the enunciated and that of the enunciation never intersect, even in the presence of a speaker to his or her own speech. Were it not so, it would be impossible to say "I" in a theatrical performance to refer, not to its speaker, but to the character one plays.

As a consequence of this temporal rupture between the subject of the enunciated and the subject of enunciation, the subject of enunciation – as a theoretical "object" known only through the enunciated – is permanently foreclosed to representation, linguistic, photographic, or otherwise. For, if it were represented, it would immediately be of the enunciated, not of enunciation itself. As such, Tawada's lines "when I speak / I am not there" are not just a poetic conceit but a poetic performance of the most basic function of language to represent beyond the determinations or intentions of the representer. As such, the "I" can simultaneously "speak" and "not be there" in the sense that the subject of enunciation can *never* be marked within the enunciated. However, within the enunciated itself, the "I" can assume any guise regardless of the identity of the subject of enunciation, who cannot assume any guise whatsoever in language without rendering itself the subject of the enunciated. It is thus *literally* language or representation that beckons, not the speaking subject, for beckoning always takes place at the level of *some sign*, be it linguistic, photographic, or even gestural such as a waving hand.

In Émile Benveniste's analysis, upon which the distinction between the subject of the enunciated and of enunciation are based, the term "I" is not only a "shifter" that shifts in temporal reference, it is also the opening of an address. The moment "I" is uttered, it inaugurates a social relation between an addresser (I) and an addressee (you). The "I" and the "you" mutually necessitate each other, as Benveniste argues, "neither of the terms can be conceived without the other; they are complementary, although according to an 'interior/exterior' opposition, and, at the same time they are reversible."[24] Nevertheless, he also argues, "This polarity does not mean either equality or symmetry: 'ego' always has a position of transcendence with regard to *you*."[25] In other words, for Benveniste, all statements are ultimately reducible to first-personal utterances, even if they are explicitly in the second or third person. However, he does not justify this claim, presumably because he gives primacy to the subject of enunciation as the

---

[24] Benveniste, "Subjectivity in Language," 225.
[25] Benveniste, "Subjectivity in Language," 225.

center of language, even as the consequences of his analysis have shown *the opposite*.²⁶

Inasmuch as Tawada's poem performs the linguist problem of marking subjectivity in language, it also offers a poetic critique of the reducibility of language to the subject of enunciation. But it does so through a performative paradox in the lines, "when i am silent / i am made of the same material / as you / material time."²⁷ The paradox of these lines is that it gestures toward this relation in the absence of language (silence) *through* the semantics of language. It is simultaneously an address made by an "I" (ich) to a "you" (du) inaugurating a relation of betweennesss *and* a poetic appeal to that which is the precondition of language, "material time" ("stoffliche zeit"). In other words, though language inaugurates a relation of betweenness between addresser and addressee, Tawada's poem points to a greater kind of relation of betweenness that beckons: the oscillation *between* soundlessness and voicedness ("lautlos / stimmhaft"²⁸), *between* no sign and sign.

The poem gestures toward this radical perspective external to language but once again *through* language in its pronominal citations, moving first from the first person "I" (ich), then to the second person "you" (du), and culminating with the perspective of the impersonal third person "one" (man) framed by the rhyme *dort* and *wort*: "dort / wo die stimme im fleisch aufwacht / hört *man* ohne ohren / ein wort"²⁹). In so doing, it suggests that language takes place beyond the determinations of an addresser or addressee, beyond any determinate consciousness, on the impersonal order of the third person, which Benveniste excludes from linguistic "personhood" as the third person is exterior to the field of address. In this radically other perspective, the word *wort* is tied again by the materiality of rhyme to yet another figure, the word *ort* (place³⁰). In terms of Adelson's reading of Tawada reading Celan, the betweenness that beckons here is the oscillation between *wort* (word) and its rhyming pair *ort* (place), that is, the *interval* between the two, between language and its material

---

26 For an incisive analysis of first-personal deixis in Tawada's works, see Brett de Bary's "Deixis, Dislocation, and Suspense in Translation," in *The Politics of Culture: Around the Work of Naoki Sakai*, eds. Richarch F. Calichman and John Namjun Kim (New York: Routledge, 2010), 40–51.
27 Tawada, "A Poem," l. 16–19: "wenn ich schweige / bin ich aus demselben stoff gemacht wie du / stoffliche zeit."
28 Tawada, "A Poem," l. 30–31.
29 Tawada, "A Poem," l. 22–25, emphasis added; "there / where the voice awakes in the flesh / one hears without ears / a word."
30 Tawada, "A Poem," l. 33.

formation. This oscillation *between* the silence of the materiality of language and its semantics *is* the *beckoning* of this poem. Its rhymes create its time.

    よこはま

1 むな
    むなむな
    むなむなぐるしい
5 むなむなぐるしいむらの
    むなむなぐるしいむらのなかに
    むなむなぐるしいむらのなかにむれる
    むなむなぐらしいむらのなかにむれるむれが
    むなむなぐらしいむらのなかにむれるむれがむれて

10 くろ
    くろふね
    くろふねがくる
15 くろふねがくるくる
    くろふねがくるくるくるって
    くろふねがくるくるくるってまわって
    くろふねがくるくるくるってまわってもどって
    くろふねがくるくるくるってまわってもどってくるって
    くろふねがくるくるくるってまわってもどってくるっててんのうせいもどって

20 なみ
    なみなみ
    なみなみだぶつ
    なみなみだぶつおだぶつ

25 ひろ
    ひろびろ
    ひろ
    ひろびろ
30 のんびり
    びり
    びりでもいい
    ひろ
    ひろおおおおい[31]

---

[31] Tawada Yōko (多和田葉子), "Yokohama" (よこはま). *Gendaishi Techō* (現代詩手帖) 53.12 (2010): 255.

Yokohama

1   muna
     muna muna
     muna muna gurushii
     muna muna gurushii mura no
5   muna muna gurushii mura no naka ni
     muna muna gurushii mura no naka ni mureru
     muna muna gurushii mura no naka ni mureru mure ga
     muna muna gurushii mura no naka ni mureru mure ga murete

     kuro
10 kurofune
     kurofune ga kuru
     kurofune ga kuru kuru
     kurofune ga kuru kuru kurutte
     kurofune ga kuru kuru kurutte mawatte
15 kurofune ga kuru kuru kurutte mawatte modotte
     kurofune ga kuru kuru kurutte mawatte modotte kurutte
     kurofune ga kuru kuru kurutte mawatte modotte kurutte tennōsei modotte

     nami
     nami nami
20 nami namida butsu
     nami namida butsu odabutsu

     hiro
     hirobiro
     hiro
25 hirobiro
     nonbiri
     biri
     biridemoii
     hiro
30 hiroooooi[32]

Yokohama

1   chest
     chests

---

32 This transliteration of the Japanese is provided here to facilitate readers who do not read Japanese and to show the alliteration of this poem. However, the parsing of the text into individual words here is not definitive. Because Japanese does not require spacing between words and because Tawada's original is written without *kanji*, which would otherwise determine which word is "meant," this parsing of the text could be otherwise, as discussed in the essay.

    chests in distress
    the chest-distressing town
5   in the chest-distressing town
    in the chest-distressing town it is crowded
    in the chest-distressing town the crowded crowd is
    in the chest-distressing town the crowded crowd is crowded and

10 black
    blackships
    blackships come
    blackships come come
15 blackships come come crazing
    blackships come come crazing turning
    blackships come come crazing turning returning
    blackships come come crazing turning returning crazing
    blackships come come crazing turning returning crazing the emperor-system returns and

20 wave
    waves
    wave, tear strikes
    death strikes a wave, tear

    deep
25 awide
    deep
    awide
    carefree
    last
30 last is fine
    deep
    wiiiiide[33]

Rhythm: "Yokohama"

In a similar vein as Adelson's critique, Nahum Dimitri Chandler also critiques the trope of betweenness with reference to racialized ethnicity in his study *X – The Problem of the Negro as a Problem for Thought*. However, whereas Adelson directs her critique at the institution of literary criticism for reading literary texts sociologically, Chandler directs his critique at the institution of sociology

---

[33] This translation is my own. It is based on the parsing provided in the transliteration. As discussed in the essay, an alternative parsing is possible changing the meaning of text.

for not reading closely one of its most foundational texts for its *literary* strategies. Rereading W.E.B. Du Bois's 1902 *The Souls of Black Folk* more closely than is usually demanded of literary criticism – and is almost never demanded of sociology – Chandler offers an extended meditation upon Du Bois's opening first lines, "Between me and the other world there is ever an unasked question: [. . .] How does it feel to be a problem?"[34]

As with Adelson, the stakes of this one word are high for Chandler, for Du Bois's opening word *between* is the primary term that enables one of the foundational concepts of African American critical race studies, *double consciousness*, which in Du Bois's words, designates a:

> second sight in this American world, – a world which yields him no true self-consciousness, but only lets him see himself through the revelation of the other world. It is a peculiar sensation, this double-consciousness, this sense of always looking at one's self through the eyes of others, of measuring one's soul by the tape of the world that looks on in amused contempt and pity.[35]

Yet, for Chandler, something is remiss in the way in which this one word has been read. Betweenness, for Chandler, "appears as that quite solid structure which gives the referent for this prepositional phrase, 'me *and* the other,' its specific and determining sense."[36] Betweenness confers upon "me" and "the other [world]" the sense of a *given* opposition, that is, the same sense in which Adelson critiques the trope of "between two worlds" as "contain[ing], restrain [ing], and imped[ing] new knowledge, not enab[ling] it."[37]

Yet, just as Adelson pauses to reread its possible alternatives through Tawada's citation of a form of betweenness that beckons, Chandler too rereads the aberrant syntax of Du Bois's opening line, "*between* me and the other world there is ever [. . .]," as suggesting that more is at work in Du Bois's invocation of betweenness than it would first appear. The prepositional phrase introduced by the word *between* need not be read as just a third-personal propositional truth claim about "two determinate or stable objects."[38] Rather, Du Bois's "syntactical style" suggests that it can also be read as a first-personal "enunciation" or, in Benveniste's sense to which Chandler hews closely, "the enactment of

---

34 Nahum Dimitri Chandler, *X – The Problem of the Negro as a Problem for Thought* (New York: Fordham University Press, 2014), 2; the citation of Du Bois is from W. E. B. Du Bois, *The Souls of Black Folk* (Oxford: Oxford University Press, 2007), 2.
35 Du Bois, *The Souls*, 3.
36 Chandler, *X – The Problem*, 4.
37 Chandler, *X – The Problem*, 21.
38 Chandler, *X – The Problem*, 4.

language through an individual act of use."³⁹ In enunciation, language is not just third-personal "objective" statement but an *enactment*. In this sense, the word *between* in Du Bois's opening line "may be understood to name the *opening* of the sense of space, of spatiality, rather than confirm it."⁴⁰ It does not merely describe a space but enacts its *opening* in *time*.

Moreover, Chandler adds, nothing in the history of the term *between* precludes it from governing just two objects; it can govern more. As a consequence, Chandler concludes of Du Bois's concept of double-consciousness, "the double is never only double, proliferating its marks without end" and extends to what Chandler calls "the unnamable" to other terms not expressly mentioned in a prepositional phrase introduced by the word *between*.⁴¹ Or, to appropriate and rephrase Jonathan Culler's quip on Jacques Derrida's critique of "context": Betweenness binds, but betweenness itself is boundless.⁴²

Chandler's critical intervention shows how even the referential language of sociology has a temporally enunciative dimension standing in tension with its spatially referential dimension. In so doing, he shows how referential language may exceed the limits of the sociological referent it seeks to render in language. Language overtakes the referent to make it do and say more than it might have been thought to do or say of itself. What then of the reverse? What then of poetic language that explicitly refers to a major historical event that fundamentally transformed a social body? How might it render this event in language yet also disrupt its own referential gesture in a mode of poetic critique?

Such are the questions posed by a reading of Tawada's Japanese-language poem "Yokohama" as the poem gestures toward the single most socially, politically and culturally significant event in modern Japanese history, the forced "opening" of Japan in 1854 after over 200 years of its "isolated country" (鎖国) policy. Like Tawada's "A Poem" in the context of the artist book in which it was first published, "Yokohama" is a multi-medial text that is not only to be "read," but also *seen* and *heard*, if not also "felt," in its materiality. A shape poem outlining the visual profile of a nineteenth-century ship of three masts, with its first stanza forming the bow and the final stanza its stern, its shape gestures visually toward its second stanza in which the coming of a blackship is

---

39 Émile Benveniste, "The Formal Apparatus of Enunciation," in *The Discourse Studies Reader*, eds. Johannes Angermuller, Dominique Maingueneau, and Ruth Wodak (Amsterdam: John Benjamins Publishing Company, 2014), 12–18, here, 12.
40 Chandler, *X – The Problem*, 7, emphasis added.
41 Chandler, *X – The Problem*, 7.
42 Jonathan Culler writes, "[. . .] meaning is context-bound [. . .] but [. . .] context itself is boundless," in Jonathan D.Culler, *The Literary in Theory*, 181.

announced. Moreover, it is a poem that Tawada frequently reads – that is, performs – in her public readings. Oddly, it has remained unmentioned in the scholarship on Tawada's works.

Yet, before a close reading of this poem can take place with reference to the sense of "betweenness," a contrastive account of the differences and similarities between "Yokohama" and "A Poem" is called for as their intersection is not immediately "clear." Though both poems make their address at the level of the materiality of language, they do so through sharply differing registers. Formally, the extreme hypotaxis of "Yokohama," in which each line of each stanza repeats and further completes the preceding line in a rigid order, contrasts sharply with the equally extreme parataxis of "A Poem" in which words cited in one line are associated with words in even distant lines by virtue of rhyme. Semantically, the hypotaxis of "Yokohama" and the parataxis of "A Poem" also stand in sharp contrast with respect to the words that compose them. Whereas the hypotaxis of "Yokohama" rigidly coordinates the relation between each line of each stanza, the words within the lines themselves are semantically ambiguous as the poem is written entirely in the phonetic script of *hiragana* without *kanji* to disambiguate which word is "meant." Compounding the challenges of parsing the text, as written Japanese does not use spaces to distinguish one word from the next, it is impossible to determine if one mora belongs to one word or to the adjacent word; in this poem, it could belong to both simultaneously. As Gizem Arslan argues, such moments are not mere hermeneutic challenges of interpretations, but constitutive moments of Tawada's poetic practice, "Illegibility, intermediality and misreadings are pivotal for Tawada's writerly and readerly practice. Her texts often feature accidental illegibilities, that is, diegetic moments of textual erasure and excision, lost or blurred texts, as well as a plethora of misreadings and mistranscriptions."[43]

By contrast, whereas the parataxis of "A Poem" allows for unconnected lines to be read together, the words of "A Poem" themselves are not semantically unambiguous but vividly "clear" with only their semiotic relation to one another in question due to the poem's parataxis. One could argue that, at first blush, these poems *appear* to have nothing to do with one another, except for their common provenance in Tawada's poetic hand.

Nevertheless, just as "A Poem" points to language itself as that which beckons a closer reading through its use of rhyme – "wort" (word), "mord" (murder), "dort" (over there) and "ort" (place) – so too does "Yokohama" with its rhythm

---

[43] Gizem Arslan, "Making Senses: Translation and the Materiality of Written Signs in Yoko Tawada," *Translation Studies* 12.3 (2019): 338–356, here 340.

of its alliterations point to language itself: "kuro" (black), "kuru" (to come), "mawatte" (turning around), "modotte" (returning) and so forth. Moreover, both are thematically concerned with the formation and dissolution of subjectivity in language: in the case of "A Poem," the formation and dissolution of individual subjectivity; in that of "Yokohama," the formation and dissolution of collective, or "national," subjectivity. Both poems evoke figurations of betweenness by virtue of their concern with subjectivity in language; they both beckon but beckon differently.

To the extent that "Yokohama" submits to a semantic reading even in the absence of *kanji* to disambiguate its words, the poem evokes the history of Japan's formation into a modern nation-state, from a feudal military-police state (the Tokugawa shogunate) to an imperial state among Euro-American imperial states. Thus unlike "A Poem," "Yokohama" relies on an extra-textual imagination of history to confer "meaning" upon its words, doing so through its rhythm of alliteration to disrupt this imagination. The first stanza evokes the image of confined and crowded space prior to Japan's opening to the Euro-American world, possibly referencing Edo (now Tokyo, just north of Yokohama) as the most populated city in the world, already in the nineteenth century, "in the town that crushes chests the crowding crowd is crowded."[44] However, the historical specificity of this image comes in the second stanza, referencing "blackships" and the "return of the emperor system": "the blackships are coming coming going crazy turning around and returning and going crazy and the emperor system is returning."[45] In 1853, the American Commodore Matthew Perry first sailed his flotilla of "blackships" to Japan just south of Yokohama to demand trade relations with the Tokugawa shogunate under the threat of force, promising to return a year later to negotiate what would become the first in a series of unequal treaties conferring extra-territorial rights upon Western powers, or the Treaty of Kanagawa 1854. These unequal treaties then triggered a series of political crises in Japan concluding in a coup d'état against the Tokugawa shogunate and the instauration of the emperor system in which the emperor, who was previously a nominal figurehead, became a political entity with sovereign, governmental authority. Read historically, the final two stanzas appear to be poetic commentaries on the previous two stanzas, with the third stanza referring to the second and the fourth and final stanza with its images of "carefree" (nonbiri) openness referring back, in contrast, to the first stanza with its images of confinement and crowdedness. If

---

[44] Tawada, "Yokohama," l. 8: "muna munagurashii mura no naka ni mureru mure ga murete."
[45] Tawada, "Yokohama," l. 17: "kurofune ga kuru kuru kurutte mawatte modotte kurutte tennousei modotte."

read "historically" alone, this poem would appear to be a celebration of Japan's opening after some two hundred or so years of strictly regulated isolation from the outside world. It would appear to be a celebration of an "opening" *between* two stable and predefined positions, a "Japan" and "the other world."

However, at the level of the letter, this poem disrupts this imagination of stable positions, showing the institution of history to be that of repetition: the institution of history repeats history in order to institute itself in the service of the nation-state. Though the thematic turning point of the poem may be the second stanza with its images of an external threat resulting in an internal reorganization of state sovereignty, the poetic turning point is in the third stanza. In the third stanza, the extreme hypotaxis of the poem – its rigidly syntactical coordination of each line relative to the others – breaks down at the level of the rhythmic letter rendering a univocal translation all but impossible: "nami / nami nami / nami namida butsu / nami namida butsu odabutsu."[46] This stanza could be translated as "wave / wave wave / wave tear strike / death strikes wave, tear," this translation would only be possible by ignoring that the verbs that normatively accompany "nami" (wave) and "namida" (tear) are not "butsu" (to strike) but "utsu" (to strike) for "nami" and "nagasu" (to flow) for "namida." In other words, something is going on in this stanza, for its language is beginning to break from the referential function of language, renouncing meaning for sound.

If read not for its "words" but its sounds, the line "nami namida butsu" sonically harkens to the Pure Land Buddhist chant "Namu Amida Butsu" (南無阿弥陀仏), which is ritually repeated at Japanese funerals, meaning "Hail Amitabha Buddha," which in turn also evokes the image of the Great Buddha statue at Kotoku Temple in Kamakura, just south of Yokohama. This reading of the third line of this stanza is further suggested by its extension in the fourth line of this stanza, which completes the phrase "nami namida butsu" with "odabutsu," a trope literally citing the Buddha and figuratively used to mean "death."

This multiplication of the signified for each signifier prompts a rereading of the poem's other lines to track the possibility of other readings. While there are several salient lines in this regard, one in particular calls for attention, the second to the last line of the second stanza (l. 16) already read above: "kurofune ga kuru kuru kurutte mawatte modotte kurutte."[47] Though this passage can be parsed as such and translated as "blackships come come crazing turning returning crazing," the Japanese can also be parsed as "kurofune ga kurukuru

---

46 Tawada, "Yokohama," l. 18–21.
47 Tawada, "Yokohama," l. 18.

kuru *tte* mawatte modotte kuru *tte*," or "the blackships are coming (kuru) whirling around (kurukuru), I hear (tte), coming turning and returning, I hear (tte)." In other words, this passage can be read *both* as a third personal statement about a state of affairs *and* as a first personal statement inaugurating a relation between an addresser and addressee. Nothing in the purely phonetic script of this lines precludes "kurutte" (crazing) from also being parsed as "kuru tte" (I hear, [the blackships] are coming), in which the quotative particle *tte* indicates reported speech heard by a first person. As no distinction is possible, only *both* can be taken as referentially "meant." The third person is simultaneously a first person reporting on a third personal event for the sake of a second person, a *you*, the reader.

My double reading destabilizes the solemn image of sovereignty – the emperor system – cited in the second stanza's final line. The state sovereignty cited in the second stanza is in one reading asserted as a given fact, while in another reading presented as the consequence of mere *hearsay*. Moreover, when read together with the double reading of the third stanza whose waves and tears "strike" with an unconventional verb "butsu," it can also be read as a sonic evocation of the figure of death, thereby suggesting less the celebratory exuberance cited in the final stanza of "new" Japan than the instauration of modern sovereignty generating *death*.

Though this text is written entirely in one language, Tawada's "mother tongue" of Japanese, it can be read as standing under what Yasemin Yildiz has called the "bilingual gaze" in reference to Tawada's other works that disrupt the assumed contiguity of the "mother tongue" with its associated nation-state.[48] Yet, in this case, the "other" language is not German, but the silence of death itself. It is here that a return to Adelson's and Chandler's critiques of the reified sense of betweenness is necessary in reference to this poem's citation of state sovereignty. The image of state sovereignty not only establishes the two poles of the binary suspending ethnicized subjects "between two worlds" in Adelson's critique; at the same time it occludes them as the "unnamable" in Chandler's critique. The image of state sovereignty always rests on that which is *excluded* from the ken of sovereignty in a zone of indeterminacy suspended in social death.

---

[48] Yasemin Yildiz, *Beyond the Mother Tongue: The Postmonolingual Condition* (New York: Fordham University Press, 2012), 126.

Works cited

Adelson, Leslie A. "Against Between: A Manifesto," *New Perspectives on Turkey* 28–29 (2003): 19–39.
Arslan, Gizem. "Making Senses: Translation and the Materiality of Written Signs in Yoko Tawada," *Translation Studies* 12.3 (2019): 338–356.
Benveniste, Émile. "The Formal Apparatus of Enunciation," in *The Discourse Studies Reader*. Eds. Johannes Angermuller, Dominique Maingueneau, and Ruth Wodak (Amsterdam: John Benjamins Publishing Company, 2014), 12–18.
Benveniste, Émile. "Subjectivity in Language," in *Problems in General Linguistics* (Coral Gables, FL.: University of Miami Press, 1971), 223–230.
Brandt, Bettina. "Scattered Leaves: Artist Books and Migration, A Conversation with Yoko Tawada," *Comparative Literature Studies* 45.1 (2008): 12–22.
Chandler, Nahum Dimitri. *X – The Problem of the Negro as a Problem for Thought* (New York: Fordham University Press, 2014).
Culler, Jonathan D. *The Literary in Theory* (Stanford: Stanford University Press, 2007).
de Bary, Brett. "Deixis, Dislocation, and Suspense in Translation," in *The Politics of Culture: Around the Work of Naoki Sakai*. Eds. Richard F. Calichman and John Namjun Kim (New York: Routledge, 2010), 40–51.
Du Bois, W. E. B. *The Souls of Black Folk* (Oxford: Oxford University Press, 2007).
Redlich, Jeremy. "Bringing the Background into Focus: Reading the Linguistic and Bibliographic Codes in Yoko Tawada's *Das Bad*," in *Scholarly Editing and German Literature: Revision Revaluation, Edition*. Eds. Lydia Jones, Bodo Plachta, Gaby Pailer, and Catherine Karen Roy (Leiden and Boston: Brill Rodopi, 2016), 71–96.
Tawada, Yōko and Stephan Köhler. *Ein Gedicht für ein Buch* (Hamburg: Edition Lange, 1996a).
Tawada, Yoko. *Aber die Mandarinen müssen heute abend noch geraubt werden* (Tübingen: Konkursbuch, 2003).
Tawada, Yoko. "Das Tor des Übersetzers oder Celan liest Japanisch," in *Talisman* (Tübingen: Konkursbuch, 1996b), 121–134.
Tawada, Yoko. "The Translator's Gate, or Celan Reads Japanese," *Mantis: A Journal of Poetry, Criticism & Translation* 8 (2009): 223–232.
Tawada, Yoko. (多和田葉子). "Yokohama" (よこはま). *Gendaishi Techō* (現代詩手帖) 53.12 (2010).
Yildiz, Yasemin. *Beyond the Mother Tongue: The Postmonolingual Condition* (New York: Fordham University Press, 2012).

Deniz Göktürk
Beyond Fidelity and Treason: On the Ironic Poetics of Translation

> depth of commitment to correct cultural politics, felt in the details of personal life, is sometimes not enough. The history of the language, the history of the author's moment, the history of the language-in-and-as-translation, must figure in the weaving as well.
>
> Gayatri Chakravorty Spivak

Preamble

Those who have translated literature know that the labor of translation is rarely concerned with rendering a clear-cut meaning, but rather with creating approximations, activating slumbering resonances, and unfolding possible readings within new contexts. Translators are continuously engaged in a dual movement of deep immersion and distancing; they have to keep stepping inside the world of the text and back outside to converse with readers who see the world through different words. Precision and purpose are driving forces for good translators: precision to tease out poetic nuances and purpose to unlock these for readers in another language, thereby complicating given categories of identification and classification.

Leslie A. Adelson has been such a translator and mediator with a keen sense of purpose throughout her career, opening up spaces for transnational voices in the realm of German literature. In "Coordinates of Orientation," the introduction to her collection and translation of Zafer Şenocak's essays, *Atlas of a Tropical Germany*, she framed his texts as interventions into the politics of memory and collective identity in a recently reunified Germany and post-Cold War Europe of the 1990s, tracing a "shared history," "a history of 'touch' among

---

Note: This essay is based on a talk given at the conference "WORT.BRÜCHE: Fragmente einer Sprache des Vertrauens" at the Warburg-Haus in Hamburg in July 2016 in the context of Zafer Şenocak's Visiting Professorship for Intercultural Poetics. The German version will be published in the forthcoming volume: Ortrud Gutjahr, ed. *Wortbrüche. Fragmente einer Sprache des Vertrauens*. The English version has been significantly expanded. Landon Reitz helped with translating some parts from the German.

https://doi.org/10.1515/9783110778922-008

Germans, Turks, and Jews."[1] Alongside the political relevance of these writings, she highlighted "a call to poetic language, a mode of articulation that creates more labyrinthine ways of knowing time and space, that rescues them from the poverty of dualistic coordinates but makes no pretense at redemption."[2] With reference to Şenocak's essay on Paul Celan, Adelson acknowledges the European Jewish poet and translator from Czernowitz as "an imaginary guide on the byways of this atlas." Her analysis channels an appeal "to a negative hermeneutic, 'which critically interrogates what is presumed to be understood'"[3] and points "the way, not to understanding cultural difference, but to understanding culture differently."[4]

Attempts to "understand" culture frequently run into challenges of translatability in Şenocak's writings. The protagonists in his novels and autobiographically inspired essays are often translator-mediator figures who receive cases of old documents, letters and diaries, often written in scripts that remain illegible to them. Disinterested in any homogenizing categories of cultural identification, their encounters with unreadable archives and scattered fragments from the past do not easily converge into coherent storylines; instead, they open up uncertainties and spark the imagination. Archival resistance to grand socio-political narratives of culture-clash, which deploy rigid compartmentalizations such as West vs. East, Christian or Jewish vs. Muslim, German vs. Turkish, native vs. migrant has been a distinguishing feature of Şenocak's writing as well as Adelson's scholarship.[5] In a recent book, Şenocak promotes a scaled-down focus on personal experiences and memories put into conversation with findings from the archives. Fissures and negotiations in families, neighborhoods, and various kinds of border zones reveal entanglements: rather than coming as an invasion from outside, "the foreign dwells in everyone," and "differences keep our society together."[6] I will argue in the following that the multiple alliances of translators who dwell both inside and outside, and keep moving back and forth between particular places, time-zones, and languages, often find expression in tactics of irony such as masking, defamiliarization, and ventriloquism. Survival amid

---

1 Zafer Şenocak, "Coordinates of Orientation: An Introduction," in *Atlas of a Tropical Germany: Essays on Politics and Culture, 1990–1998*, trans. and ed. Leslie A. Adelson (Lincoln and London: University of Nebraska Press, 2000): xi–xxxvii, here xxx.
2 Şenocak, "Coordinates of Orientation . . .," xxxi.
3 Şenocak, "Coordinates of Orientation . . .," xxxi.
4 Şenocak, "Coordinates of Orientation . . .," xxxv.
5 See also Leslie A. Adelson, *The Turkish Turn in Contemporary German Literature. Toward a New Critical Grammar of Migration* (New York: Palgrave Macmillan, 2005).
6 Zafer Şenocak, *Das Fremde, das in jedem wohnt. Wie Unterschiede unsere Gesellschaft zusammenhalten* [The Foreign Dwells in Everyone: How Differences Keep Our Society Together] (Hamburg: Edition Körber, 2018).

the minefields of categorical language in our times of societal polarization depends on irony-savvy translators and readers who can navigate the murky waters of trust and suspicion without reverting to judgements on fidelity and treason, original and copy, authentic and fake.

Reader – translator – writer

In his oft-cited essay, "The Task of the Translator," Walter Benjamin wrote:

> Translatability is an essential quality of certain works, which is not to say that it is essential for the works themselves that they be translated; it means, rather, that a specific significance inherent in the original manifests itself in its translatability.[7]

Over and above the "afterlife"[8] or "continued life"[9] of the original in its translation, Benjamin stresses its "unfolding"[10] and "maturing process."[11] Zafer Şenocak emerged as a translator early on, particularly with his translation of poems by Yunus Emre (c. 1238–1320), a wandering dervish mystic revered as the father of Turkish vernacular literature. *Das Kummerrad / Dertli Dolap* [Wheel of Sorrow] was published in a dual language edition by Dağyeli Verlag in 1986. The grace of these thirteenth-century poems is astonishing to this day, and raises questions about the temporal and geographic positioning of the modern worldview. In this broader horizon, it seems shortsighted to uphold "modernity" as

---

6 Zafer Şenocak, *Das Fremde, das in jedem wohnt. Wie Unterschiede unsere Gesellschaft zusammenhalten* [The Foreign Dwells in Everyone: How Differences Keep Our Society Together] (Hamburg: Edition Körber, 2018).
7 Walter Benjamin, "The Task of the Translator," trans. Harry Zohn in *Walter Benjamin: Selected Writings*, eds. Marcus Bullock and Michael W. Jennings vol. 1 (Cambridge: Belknap Press, 1996), 253–263, here 254. German orig.: "Übersetzbarkeit eignet gewissen Werken wesentlich – das heißt nicht, ihre Übersetzung ist wesentlich für sie selbst, sondern will besagen, daß eine bestimmte Bedeutung, die den Originalen innewohnt, sich in ihrer Übersetzbarkeit äußere." "Die Aufgabe des Übersetzers," in Walter Benjamin, *Gesammelte Schriften* vol. IV/1 (Frankfurt am Main: Suhrkamp, 1972), 9–21.
8 Benjamin, "The Task of the Translator," 254. Cf. "Überleben" in "Die Aufgabe des Übersetzers," 10.
9 Benjamin, "The Task of the Translator," 254. Cf. "Fortleben" in "Die Aufgabe des Übersetzers," 11.
10 Benjamin, "The Task of the Translator," 255. Cf. "Entfaltung," in "Die Aufgabe des Übersetzers," 11.
11 Benjamin, "The Task of the Translator," 256. Cf. "Nachreife," in "Die Aufgabe des Übersetzers," 12.

the monolithic achievement of western Enlightenment. In his afterword, Şenocak hails Yunus Emre, the *Wunderkind* of the Islamic Enlightenment, as our contemporary [*Zeitgenossen*].[12] Retrospectively commenting on his own translation practice in his book *Das Fremde, das in jedem wohnt* [*The Foreign Dwells in Everyone*], Şenocak notes:

> In a translation, it is important that the language no longer appears as a foreign language. Yunus Emre migrated into the German language, because I, his translator, was at home in German.[13]

Şenocak's stated goal to carry the writer towards the reader echoes a discussion famously started by Friedrich Schleiermacher – a translator of Plato's works who himself favored "foreignizing" translations that would expand the German language and world-view – in "Über die verschiedenen Methoden des Übersetzens" ["On the Different Methods of Translating"], a series of lectures first presented at the Prussian Academy of Sciences in 1813.[14] Şenocak's active formulation with regard to an author from the past ("migrated into the German language") implies that the Benjaminian potential for movement, "translatability" and "maturing process" are inherent in the original poems. As Gayatri Spivak tells us, translation is "the most intimate act of reading."[15] And indeed, Şenocak's intensive engagement with Emre's lyrical poetry and other Turkish literary texts was a source of inspiration for his own poetic language, which often disrupts supposedly self-contained unities and dichotomies. Beginning with his early published collections of poems including *Rituale der Jugend* [Rituals of the Youth, 1987], *Das senkrechte Meer* [The Perpendicular Sea, 1991], and *Fernwehanstalten* [Wanderlust Institutions, 1994] and continuing throughout his entire work in poetry and prose, he has been interweaving influences from modernist poetry in German by Paul Celan, Ingeborg Bachmann and others with the rich tradition of poetry in Turkish.

---

12 Yunus Emre, *Das Kummerrad / Dertli Dolap*, trans. Zafer Şenocak (Frankfurt am Main: Dağyeli 1986), 89f.
13 "Wichtig bei einer Übersetzung ist, dass ihre Sprache nicht mehr als Fremdsprache erscheint. Yunus Emre wanderte in die deutsche Sprache ein, weil ich, sein Übersetzer, im Deutschen zu Hause war." Zafer Şenocak, "Die dritte Sprache des Übersetzers," in Şenocak, *Das Fremde, das in jedem wohnt. Wie Unterschiede unsere Gesellschaft zusammenhalten*, trans. Landon Reitz. (Hamburg: Edition Körber, 2018), 65–74, here 65.
14 Friedrich Schleiermacher, "On the Different Methods of Translating" (1813), trans. Susan Bernofsky, ed. Lawrence Venuti, in *The Translation Studies Reader*, 2nd ed. (New York: Routledge, 2012), 43–63.
15 Gayatri Chakravorty Spivak, "The Politics of Translation," in *The Translation Studies Reader*, ed. Lawrence Venuti, 2nd ed. (New York: Routledge, 2012 [¹1993]), 312–330, here 315.

This work across languages often took shape against common assumptions about the incommensurability of western and eastern cultures. When Şenocak and I co-edited an anthology of contemporary Turkish literature in conjunction with a series of readings at the Literarisches Colloquium Berlin in 1991, we were on a mission to correct misconceptions about Turkish culture. Pairing visiting writers with German counterparts, we wanted to bring the modern urban literature of Turkey – at this time all but unknown in Germany – to a German-reading public to arouse interest and curiosity, and forge points of contact and convergence. In our preface, we ironically polemicized against the imbalance of translation traffic and the popular perception of Turkish literature as social-realist stories in rural settings, far removed from large metropolitan centers.[16] On several occasions, the work on the series and the collection made us aware of the market forces of compartmentalizing preconceptions, which determine the circulation or non-circulation of world literature. Thinking about translation became key to our analyses of cultural representation in terms of obstacles and access to networks of publication, recognition, and value.

Şenocak continued to explore shifting perspectives, expanding horizons, and the uneven circulation of cultural capital in his journalistic work and in other books, including *Atlas des tropischen Deutschland* [1993, *Atlas of a Tropical Germany*, 2000], *War Hitler Araber?* [Was Hitler an Arab?, 1994], and *Der gebrochene Blick nach Westen* [The Broken Gaze toward the West, 1994] as well as *Deutschsein* [Being German, 2011] and *Das Fremde, das in jedem wohnt* (2018). In his essay "Die bastardisierte Sprache" ["The Bastardized Language"], he reflects on inequities and blind spots in German-Turkish cultural exchange:

> Is only one white language allowed? Is there a world language? Is such a world language audible or legible, or is it too much for ears to bear? When the black whites not only sing and dance but write, what happens then? Do they become white? The Turk of German tongue knows the German, but is there a German of Turkish tongue who knows the Turk? Is there 'the German,' 'the Turk'? Can languages embrace cultures, can cultures embrace peoples, can peoples embrace a person? The Turkish writer knows Goethe, Schiller, Hölderlin, Benn, Trakl, Eich, Celan, Bachmann, Kafka, Camus. And the German writer? Does he know Cansever, Uyar, Süreya? Has he ever heard the name Ibnül Emin? Does he know who Ahmet Rasim was, or Fuzuli or Nedim? The German has an idea but knows nothing; the Turk knows but has no idea. Which of the two is the ignoramus, which is the one in the dark? The German's dark ideas frighten him. But then he thinks of Prince Eugene, "Terror to the Turks," and leans back, calm again.[17]

---

16 Deniz Göktürk and Zafer Şenocak, "Vorwort," in *Jedem Wort gehört ein Himmel: Türkei literarisch*, eds. Göktürk and Şenocak (Berlin: Babel, 1991), 7–15.

17 Zafer Şenocak, "The Bastardized Language," trans. Tom Cheesman, in *Germany in Transit: Nation and Migration, 1955–2005*, eds. Deniz Göktürk, David Gramling, and Anton Kaes (Berkeley:

The turn from a radical questioning of cultural identities ("Is there *the* German, *the* Turk?") to a generalizing assertion ("*The* German has an idea but knows nothing; *the* Turk knows but has no idea.") could appear at first contradictory; however, the passage takes an ironic turn with the use of the epithet "Türkenschreck" [Terror to the Turks] for Prince Eugen, the commander who fought back the Ottoman army at Vienna in 1716/17 thereby becoming known as the savior of the West. In my reading, this passage does not reinstate cultural identities as given, but aims to recognize them as relational constructs that arise out of the complex and contentious interplay between assigned and assumed identifications. The longer history of cultural contact through translation is deeply intertwined with ideas of modernization and civilization.[18] In the twentieth century, German into Turkish translation activity by far exceeded translation from Turkish into German. In recent years, the reception of Turkish literature and culture in Germany has seen a slight updraft. The reputation of Turkish authors has increased since Orhan Pamuk received the 2006 Nobel Prize, and the 2008 Frankfurt Book Fair highlighted Turkey as that year's focus. Between 2005 and 2010 Unionsverlag published 20 translated volumes as *Die türkische Bibliothek* [*The Turkish Library*]. Literature from Turkey has aroused greater interest, and more translations have been published; however, blind spots and clichés still abound in the perception of Turkey and other cultures of the Near and Far East.

The passage quoted above shows clear resonances with postcolonial critiques, which insist on taking the language of the Other seriously on an equal footing rather than exoticizing and relegating it to the sphere of traditionalist

---

University of California Press, 2007), 402–405, here 403. German orig.: "Darf es nur eine weiße Sprache geben? Gibt es eine Weltsprache? Ist eine solche Weltsprache hörbar oder lesbar, oder ist sie unerträglich für Ohren? Wenn die schwarzen Weißen nicht nur singen und tanzen, sondern schreiben, was passiert dann? Werden sie dann weiß? Der Türke deutscher Zunge kennt den Deutschen, aber gibt es einen Deutschen türkischer Zunge, der den Türken kennt? Gibt es den Deutschen, den Türken? Kann Sprache Kulturen umfassen, können Kulturen Völker umfassen, und Völker einen Menschen? Der türkische Schriftsteller kennt Goethe, Schiller, Hölderlin, Benn, Trakl, Eich, Celan, Bachmann, Kafka, Camus. Und der deutsche Schriftsteller? Kennt er Cansever, Uyar, Süreya? Hat er je den Namen Ibnül Emin gehört? Weiß er, wer Ahmet Rasim war, wer Fuzuli oder Nedim? Der Deutsche ahnt, ohne zu wissen, der Türke weiß, ohne zu ahnen. Wer von beiden ist der Ignorant, wer der Ahnungslose? Dem Deutschen machen seine Ahnungen Angst. Doch dann denkt er an Prinz Eugen den 'Türkenschreck' und lehnt sich beruhigt zurück."
Zafer Şenocak, "Die bastardisierte Sprache," in *War Hitler Araber? IrreFührungen an den Rand Europas* (Berlin: Babel Verlag Hund & van Uffelen, 1994), 29–33, here 30f.
18 Kristin Dickinson, *DisOrientations: German-Turkish Cultural Contact in Translation, 1811–1946* (University Park: Penn State University Press, 2021).

folklore.¹⁹ The aspiration to a "world language" that is not only "white" reflects more recent debates on "postcolonial literature as world literature."²⁰ Şenocak's ironic formulation of "black whites" alludes to, again following Spivak, "the post-colonial as the outside/insider [who] translates white theory as she reads, so that she can discriminate on the terrain of the original."²¹ Innovation, irony, and "the staging of language as the production of agency"²² in such writing deserve even greater attention than with texts written in major European languages where linguistic registers might be more readily understood. In our increasingly polarized world, the nuanced work of multilingual translators, writers, and readers acquires new significance, sharpening our senses for ambiguities that can confront calcified binary stereotypes.

Unreadable archives

The translation of texts from one language into another is but one factor in processes of cultural exchange; central to the circulation of cultural forms is also the legibility of sources. In his book, *In deinen Worten. Mutmaßungen über den Glauben meines Vaters* [*In Your Words. Speculations on the Belief of My Father*, 2016], Şenocak refers to the documents and books that became illegible to subsequent generations after Turkey's transition from the Arabic to the Latin alphabet in 1928:

> Every revolution has a melancholic aftermath. So, too, the Turkish. In the shadow of Kemal Atatürk, who took on the alphabet, discarding the Arabic and imposing the Latin, to orient his cultural revolution unmistakably towards the West, the abandoned letters became burial shrouds for the old words. The old libraries could no longer be distinguished from cemeteries.²³

---

19 The question of exclusionary recognition for non-native writers was addressed by Salman Rushdie in his essay "'Commonwealth Literature' Does Not Exist" [1983], *Imaginary Homelands* (London: Granta, 1991), 61–70. In the German context, *Ausländerliteratur* [the literature by foreigners] served as a similarly exclusionary category. Aras Ören, the first recipient of the Adelbert von Chamisso Prize for non-native writers of German literature, in his acceptance speech in 1986, staked his claims to be read as writer abreast of fundamental transformations of his time (Göktürk et al., *Germany in Transit*, 391–394).
20 Pheng Cheah, *What is a World? On Postcolonial Literature as World Literature* (Durham: Duke University Press, 2016).
21 Spivak, "The Politics of Translation," 327.
22 Spivak, "The Politics of Translation," 320.
23 Zafer Şenocak, *In deinen Worten. Mutmaßungen über den Glauben meines Vaters*, trans. Landon Reitz (Munich: Babel, 2016), 43: "Jede Revolution hat ein melancholisches Nachspiel.

Yet, these indecipherable documents arouse the writer's fantasy:

> There were no Arabic characters on my father's typewriter. The Arabic script belonged to the hand. The Latin alphabet is public, the Arabic private. I imagined that the letters with the Arabic characters – the handwritten, private letters – were meant just for my father. While the typewritten letters that piled up on the table were accessible to everyone.[24]

Precisely the mysterious secrecy of unreadable documents becomes a source of poetic imagination and inspiration.

In *Gefährliche Verwandtschaft* [1998, *Perilous Kinship*, 2009], Sasha Muhteshem, the somewhat sluggish offspring of Turkish-Jewish-German ancestry, self-declared "grandchild of victims and perpetrators," whose grandiose last name (muhteşem: magnificent) is ironic in itself, inherits a box with his grandfather's notebooks, written mostly in Arabic script, but also containing passages in Cyrillic.[25] Despite efforts to enlist help with deciphering the old handwriting, the notebooks remain illegible to the protagonist. The grandfather's complicity in the deportation of Armenians in the eastern border town of Kars, intertwined with hints at a forgotten love story, remains speculation. The novel stages various archival practices, contrasting, for example, Sasha's half-hearted attempts at uncovering his family history with his partner Marie's research toward a realistic documentary film about Talat Pasha in Berlin. For Sasha, fiction uncovers a truth different from that achieved by the historians' quest to reconstruct facts from archival documents.

> I regularly visited the city archives. My reading concentrated on the thirties. I read the newspapers of the period, trying to form a comprehensive picture of opinions and moods. History always has a used-up side and an un-used-up side. On the used-up side the historians labour. They attempt to reconstruct. I wanted to work on the un-used-up side. I knotted together the threads in my mind to form the idea of a novel with my grandfather as its central figure. My task was to construct what could not be reconstructed. Grandfather might have been a character invented just for this purpose. Much in his life had

---

So auch die türkische. Im Schatten Kemal Atatürks, der sich nicht zuletzt an die Schriftzeichen machte, die arabischen abschaffte und die lateinischen einführte, um seiner Kulturrevolution unmissverständlich die Richtung nach Westen vorzugeben, wurden die abgelegten Schriftzeichen zu Leichentüchern der alten Wörter. Die alten Bibliotheken unterschied nichts mehr von Friedhöfen."

24 Şenocak, *In deinen Worten*, 124: "Vater hatte keine arabische Schrift auf seiner Schreibmaschine. Die arabische Schrift gehörte der Hand. Die lateinischen Buchstaben sind öffentlich, die arabischen privat. Ich stellte mir vor, dass die Briefe mit den arabischen Schriftzeichen, die handgeschriebenen, privaten Briefe sind, nur für den Vater bestimmt. Während die Schreibmaschinenbriefe, die sich auf seinem Tisch stapeln, jedermann immer zugänglich sind."

25 Zafer Şenocak, *Gefährliche Verwandtschaft* (Munich: Babel, 1998), 13f and passim.

remained concealed. His death was mysterious, ultimately unsolved. I had his diaries which I could not read. What did I need the archives for?[26]

While the writer Şenocak clearly does draw on various personal and public archives, he shares his protagonist's belief in the power of imagination. His poetic work often plucks moments out of the past and stages them in the imagined present, configuring historical elements in new constellations.

Critics have read *Gefährliche Verwandtschaft* in the context of Şenocak's essayistic works as an intervention in the cultural memory of the German nation.[27] His question whether it is possible for someone to migrate into a country's past has resonated strongly with discussions of German memory culture.[28] His project is, however, even more radical. His interventions cannot be subsumed under one national project of collective memory. His texts transcend the space of national unity and adjourn to places of entanglement. Tracing back the history of Turkish German contact, he deterritorializes it beyond the scope of "the language of the land" ("[j]enseits der Landessprache"[29]). He writes not only in German but also in Turkish, as in his novel discussed below, *Alman Terbiyesi* [*Deutsche Schule*,

---

26 Şenocak, *Gefährliche Verwandtschaft*, 51: "Ich besuchte regelmäßig die Archive der Stadt. Ich konzentrierte mich bei meiner Lektüre auf die dreißiger Jahre. Ich las in Zeitungen aus dieser Zeit, wollte mir ein umfassendes Bild von den Meinungen und Stimmungen machen. Geschichte hat immer eine verbrauchte und eine unverbrauchte Seite. An der verbrauchten Seite sind die Historiker am Werk. Sie versuchen zu rekonstruieren. An der unverbrauchten Seite wollte ich tätig sein. Ich verknüpfte die Fäden in meinem Kopf zu einem Roman, dessen zentrale Figur mein Großvater sein sollte. Meine Aufgabe war es zu konstruieren, was nicht zu rekonstruieren war. Großvaters Figur war wie geschaffen für dieses Vorhaben. Vieles in seinem Leben war verdeckt geblieben. Sein Tod war mysteriös, letztlich unaufgeklärt. Ich hatte seine Tagebücher, die ich nicht lesen konnte. Wozu brauchte ich Archive?" Şenocak, *Gefährliche Verwandtschaft*, trans. Tom Cheesman, *Perilous Kinship* (Swansea: Hafan Books, 2001), 42.
27 On the question of migration with regards to collective memory, see Leslie A. Adelson, "Touching Tales of Turks, Germans, and Jews: Cultural Alterity, Historical Narrative, and Literary Riddles for the 1990s," *New German Critique* Special Issue on the Holocaust 80 (2000): 93–124; Andreas Huyssen. "Diaspora and Nation: Migration into Other Pasts," *New German Critique* Contemporary German Literature 88 (2003): 147–164; Margaret Littler, "Guilt, Victimhood, and Identity in Zafer Şenocak's *Gefährliche Verwandtschaft*," *The German Quarterly* 78.3 (2005): 357–373; Elke Segelcke. "National History and Politics of Memory in Turkish-German Literature," *Colloquia Germanica* Special Issue: Transnational Hi/Stories 44.4 (2011): 396–407.
28 Zafer Şenocak posed the question about migrating into a country's past in an interview with Karin Yeşilada: "Kann man Türken und Juden vergleichen, Herr Şenocak?," *Der Tagesspiegel*, 13–14 April 1995. "May One Compare Turks and Jews, Mr. Şenocak?," trans. Leslie A. Adelson, in *Atlas of Tropical Germany*, 53–57.
29 Zafer Şenocak, "Jenseits der Landessprache," in *Zungenentfernung. Bericht aus der Quarantänestation* (Munich: Babel, 2001), 87–90.

German Education]. Readings that focus on claiming his place in German literature therefore fall short of grasping the broader horizon of his participation in Turkish-language literature.

It bears repeating that unreadable archives as a source of poetic inspiration are a recurring trope in Şenocak's texts. Blind spots in the legibility of his fictional figures intimate the impossibility of encapsulating a story totally and presenting it as a linear narrative. Such gaps that resist full knowability and translatability are key elements of an ironic citational poetics. In tune with the dual movement of the translator who speaks from both inside and outside the boundaries of culture, Şenocak stages figures who collect, cite and comment, framing fragments of public language from distancing vantage points. This tactic of distanced exposure makes it difficult to determine the ideological or political stance of the writer and his characters in terms of resistance or conformism. The irony in these stagings deserves a closer look.

Ironic ventriloquism

The rhetorical figure irony (*eirōneía*) is the art of disguise. Ironic speech acts are marked by performative pretense and calculated deception that enact the limitations of supposed certainties, defamiliarize conventions, and parade modes of speech in order to expose their ignorance and fallibility. Romantic irony, according to Friedrich Schlegel, is characterized by parody, self-deprecation, and metafictional reflection staged in the creation and framing of a text. This irony manifests itself in fragmentary narration punctuated by interruptions containing reflections on the possibility or, as the case may be, impossibility of narrating stories.[30] Precisely at the point where certainty and interpretation dissipate, where hermeneutics chafes against its limitations, imagination comes into play. Fragments interact in resonance and dissonance, while silences and gaps ("Leerstellen"[31]) remain unresolved, instigating readers to activate their associative intuition. A focus on such blind spots and silences highlights an awareness of the fundamental role that indeterminacy and ambiguity play in human communication and knowledge formation. However, in his pursuit of a hermeneutics of

---

30 Friedrich Schlegel, "Über die Unverständlichkeit," *Kritische Friedrich-Schlegel-Ausgabe*, 1st ed.: Critical new edition, Vol. 2 (Munich, Paderborn, Vienna, Zurich, 1967), 363–373, First Print in: Athenäum (Berlin), Vol. 3, 2. Stück, 1800. Permalink: http://www.zeno.org/nid/2000561905X.
31 For the reader-response term "Leerstelle" see Wolfgang Iser, "Die Appellstruktur der Texte," in *Rezeptionsästhetik*, ed. Rainer Warning (Munich: Wilhelm Fink, 1975), 228–252.

trust and good will (in contrast to Paul Ricoeur's hermeneutics of suspicion), Hans-Georg Gadamer insists that while the intentional deception (*Verstellung*) of irony challenges interpretation, it nonetheless calls for a sophisticated form of understanding, which requires pre-textual, verbal communication about its signals and premises of social solidarity.[32] In this sense, irony comes to fruition only in acts of reading and translation that unpack the signals of defamiliarization. Citational poetics do indeed invite negotiations about common grounds of understanding, trust, and social bonding. Forms of echoing allusion are characteristic for a post-modern intertextual-ironic position.[33] The author operates as a collector and ventriloquist, who performs set pieces drawn from the archives and plays them off of each other, leaving it to the reader to make sense of the assemblage.

This latter from of irony – the staging of voices and the montage of real and putative quotations – is pronounced in Şenocak's works, present already in *Gefährliche Verwandtschaft* (1998), but especially apparent in his novel *Alman Terbiyesi* (2007), written in Turkish and translated as *Deutsche Schule* (2012) by Helga Dağyeli-Bohne. This text that moves along the German-Turkish axis, written first in Turkish, translated into German, and feeding on layers of historical context in both languages, poses particular challenges when it comes to unpacking its framework of references.

The novel transports us to Turkey during the Second World War, when the country was still officially neutral. Turkey did not sever its diplomatic and commercial relations with Germany until August 1944 and held off on declaring war against Nazi Germany until 23 February 1945. In June 1941, German ambassador to Turkey Franz von Papen and Turkish Minister of Foreign Affairs Şükrü Saracoğlu signed the German-Turkish Treaty of Friendship in Ankara as a mutual non-aggression pact. *Alman Terbiyesi* depicts Istanbul in late summer of the same year, a city caught in a peculiar twilight that blurs fidelity and treason, a city populated by figures with dubious alliances: admirers of Prussian discipline – some of them avid Hitler-supporters – Turkish nationalists, duped wives, and disappeared lovers. In this atmosphere of diffuse suspicion, no one trusts anyone as the city teems with informers and double agents – their own special kind of translators.

---

[32] Hans-Georg Gadamer, *Wahrheit und Methode*, Vol. II (Tübingen: Mohr, 1993 [¹1986]), 347f. See also Robert J. Dostal, "Gadamerian Hermeneutics and Irony: Between Strauss and Derrida," *Research in Phenomenology* 38.2 (2008): 247–269.

[33] Cf. Uwe Wirth, "Ironie," in *Komik. Ein interdisziplinäres Handbuch*, ed. Wirth (Stuttgart: J.B. Metzler, 2017), 16–21, here 20. Wirth borrows the concept of "echotischen Erwähnens" from Dan Sperber and Deirdre Wilson, "Irony and the Use-Mention Distinction" [1981], in *Pragmatics. A Reader*, ed. Steven Davies (New York: Oxford University Press, 1991), 550–564.

The prehistory of the book's protagonist, Lieutenant Colonel Salih Bey, is rendered in fragments. He had served as an officer in Berlin under the Kaiser, fought as a German intelligence officer on the eastern front in the First World War, received German citizenship, converted to Christianity, married an officer's daughter named Annette, and lived through the Weimar Republic and the rise of the Nazis in a villa in Berlin-Zehlendorf. In 1939, he left Germany at the request of his wife and moved into an apartment in the Cihangir neighborhood of Istanbul with a view of the still green hills along the Bosporus. The narration begins after Annette's death and alternates between the memoirs of Salih Bey set in italic font (which, in the German translation becomes a Courier typeface) and a narrative voice in the third person that sets the scene of a shrouded city and a figure sitting at a Biedermeier desk by candlelight, or exercising in the early morning to the sounds of a gramophone playing Beethoven. A suitcase contains his personal archive on the move:

> Salih Bey had arrived from Berlin with a suitcase full of papers. Photographs, diplomas, certificates, commendations, maps, and a stack of notes in his neat handwriting, mostly written in German, a few put on paper in old Turkish.[34]

In his pocket, he carries an article by Yunus Nadi on the "Turkish-German Friendship," cut from the 26 June 1941 edition of *Cumhuriyet*, a newspaper sympathetic to Germany. Salih Bey compares the dictatorial tendencies of Mustafa Kemal Paşa, who died in 1938, to those of Hitler. He regards both with reservation; his loyalty is primarily to the Prussian officer class: "The one important thing is that the Prussian army still stands. His trust in his fellow soldiers was unflappable. Surely, they would put Hitler in his place one day."[35]

---

34 This and the following quotations from this book trans. into Engl. by Deniz Göktürk and Landon Reitz. Turkish orig.: "Berlin'den bir bavul dolusu evrakla gelmişti Salih Bey. Fotoğraflar, diplomalar, takdirnameler, haritalar, şehir planları ve muntazam el yazısıyla tutulmuş bir tomar not. Bu notlar çoğunlukla Almancaydı, pek azı eski Türkçe kaleme alınmıştı."
Zafer Şenocak, *Alman Terbiyesi* (Istanbul: Alef Yayınları, 2007), 30. In German: "Salih Bey war mit einem Koffer voller Papiere aus Berlin gekommen. Fotografien, Diplomen, Belobigungen, Landkarten, Stadtplänen und einem Stapel Notizen in seiner gestochenen Handschrift. Sie waren zumeist auf Deutsch verfasst, einige wenige in altem Türkisch zu Papier gebracht," Zafer Şenocak, *Deutsche Schule*, trans. Helga Dağyeli-Bohne (Berlin: J&D Dağyeli, 2012), 27.
35 Şenocak, *Alman Terbiyesi*, 11: "Önemli olan Prusya ordusunun yerinde durup durmadığıydı. Silah arkadaşlarına itimadı sonsuzdu. Hitler'in taşkınlıklarına elbette bir gün dur diyeceklerdi." "Das einzig wichtige ist doch, dass das preußische Heer steht. Sein Vertrauen in die Kriegskameraden war unerschütterlich. Sie würden irgendwann Hitler in die Schranken weisen," (Şenocak, *Deutsche Schule*, 11).

With his faith in Prussian militarism, this Germanized Turkish officer in Istanbul appears as an anachronistic figure, staged in retrospect from an ironic distance. His admiration of German discipline and order implies a brotherhood of both peoples, hailed already during the pre-World War I rapprochement between both empires, especially in 1899, when Sultan Abdülhamid granted the construction of the Baghdad Railway to Kaiser Wilhem II.[36] In contrast to his deceased wife, Salih's worldview of national-socialist Germany in *Alman Terbiyesi* is not entirely negative:

> When Adolf Hitler came to power, he, like many others, underestimated the ragtag private and regarded him as brash and arrogant. However, the great achievements he accomplished for Germany in such a short time could not be denied. Even more importantly: the people loved him. They virtually deified him. He became Germany's prophet. What Atatürk was for the Turks, Hitler was for the Germans. What a privilege it was to be both a Turk and a German. To belong simultaneously to two free peoples that had, in the same century, the makings to harness their immanent wills and determine history . . .[37]

While he perceives Hitler condescendingly as a ragged upstart with a formation unequal to that of the Prussian ranks, Salih nonetheless gives the dictator credit for his unifying popularity and achievements for the German people. The comparison with Mustafa Kemal Atatürk, the founder of the Turkish nation-state, might be a thought-provoking irritation, at least for a post-World War II Turkish readership educated in the spirit of modernization. But Salih does not dwell on nuanced comparisons regarding governmental style, social transformation, and destructive militarism. As a twice displaced and detached dual citizen, he holds on to his belief in the greatness and power of both nations, as the

---

36 Şenocak, *Alman Terbiyesi*, 28; Şenocak, *Deutsche Schule*, 25f.
37 "Adolf Hitler iktidara geldiğinde birçok kişi gibi o da bu serseri onbaşıyı küçümsemiş, onun küstah ve haddini bilmez tavırlarından iğrenmişti. Ama Almanya'da kısa zamanda elde ettiği başarı reddedilemezdi. En önemlisi millet onu seviyordu. Adeta tapıyorlardı ona. Almanların peygamberi olmuştu. Atatürk Türkler için ne ise, Almanlar için de Hitler oydu. Hem Türk hem Alman olmak ne kadar kıvanç vericiydi. Aynı asırda başıbuyruk, tarihe hükmedebilen iki hür millete birden mensup olmak . . ." (Şenocak, *Alman Terbiyesi*, 20f);
"Als Adolf Hitler an die Macht gelangte, hatte er wie viele andere auch diesen abgerissenen Gefreiten unterschätzt und ihn als dreist und überheblich empfunden. Dennoch war nicht zu leugnen, welch großes Werk dieser in kurzer Zeit für Deutschland geschaffen hatte. Noch wichtiger als das: das Volk liebte ihn. Es vergötterte ihn geradezu. Er war zu Deutschlands Propheten geworden. Was Atatürk für die Türken, das war Hitler für die Deutschen. Was für ein Privileg, sowohl Türke als auch Deutscher zu sein. Zwei freien Völkern zugleich anzugehören, die im selben Jahrhundert das Zeug dazu hatten, aus ihrem ureigenen Willen die Geschichte [zu] lenken . . ." (Şenocak, *Deutsche Schule*, 19).

bifold alliance becomes increasingly contentious over the course of a world war that would ultimately claim 75 million lives.

The author's opinions are not to be confused with those of the character. Şenocak renders Salih Bey's musings, ideologically confused and often contradictory, in a kind of ventriloquy. Comparable to Sasha Muhteshem in *Gefährliche Verwandtschaft*, *Alman Terbiyesi* stages Salih Bey and other figures as puppets or vessels through which fragments of ideologized language are rehearsed and played against each other. Ventriloquy serves as a poetic tactic of ironic distancing through which the narrative voice performs and mediates the rhetoric of the narrated figure. Rather than delivering accounts of authentic experiences and figures of identification, Şenocak's emphasis is on exposing layers of mediation through language. His figures relay a language that feeds on resonances with the *Zeitgeist* in Istanbul and Berlin both in 1940s and the 2000s. Tracing these resonances remains a job left to the reader.

Double agent translators

Salih Bey arrives at the weekly conspiratorial meeting in the legendary Café Markiz with the *Völkischer Beobachter* and the *Deutsche Allgemeine* newspapers as identifying signs. However, the new go-between, a Gestapo officer, questions Salih's loyalty to the party. The brawny fellow, with no sensibility for art or culture asks outright, and a bit skeptically, why Salih has not joined the party before steering the discussion to the developments in the war in Russia. He then speaks about the necessity for a "comprehensive purge" and "the fight against a people bastardized by Jews."[38]

In terms of racial and religious identity, Salih Bey's alliances are diffuse. He is a man of the old cosmopolitan Istanbul, where Christians, Jews, and Muslims lived side-by-side as neighbors. 62% of Istanbul's population in 1914 were non-Muslims who lived mainly in the neighborhoods in the European part of the city, especially in Pera, later renamed Beyoğlu. After the massive population exchange of 1922, the founding of the nation state with its new capital in Ankara brought a Turkification of the citizenry. On his way to meet a cultivated prostitute, Elena, who speaks Turkish with an accent, Salih Bey reminisces:

---

38 Şenocak, *Alman Terbiyesi*, 46; Şenocak, *Deutsche Schule*, 41.

He simply could not get used to the fact that Tatavla is now called Kurtuluş. Tatavla is simply Tatavla, just like Pera is Pera. The non-muslims live here. As they have for centuries. If that were to change, these places would disappear. No one, not even the pashas, had the power make that happen.[39]

The coexistence of ethnicities, confessions, and languages that was a matter of course in the Istanbul of the Ottomans was increasingly diminished in the new nationalistic formation of the city. Nationalistic thought that defamed minorities as scapegoats was brewing in the years after WWI on both the German and Turkish sides, while Berlin with its many refugees was deemed "the stepmother of all Russian cities, [. . .] the main train station of the sleepless, the impotent, the vindictive, and the hateful."[40] This invocation of 1920s Berlin as a migrant-metropolis resonated not only in 1940's Istanbul but also in reunified post-Cold War Berlin after 1989, where traces of this history were still evident.

The key figures responsible for the Armenian genocide, the Young Turks Talât and Enver Pasha, were also in Berlin in the years following World War I. In a retaliatory act, the assassin Soghomon Tehlirian shot Talât Pasha in the Hardenbergstraße on March 15, 1921. Şenocak has his protagonist Salih Bey ride through the Tiergarten Park with Enver Pasha – presumably in 1919 or 1920 – as they discuss Pan-Turkish ideas, the alliance among "brothers in middle Asia" and their liberation "from the non-Muslims."[41] The debt owed by immigrants to their host society also figures in this conversation. They discussed those gentlemen who shuttle back and forth between Istanbul and Berlin, where they keep to themselves in Turkish clubs while the Germans do not even know of their existence: "What did we [Turks] have to offer except for nuts and dried fruit? [. . .] Humans exist through identity. [. . .] Who was our Goethe and Schiller?"[42] With subtle irony, Şenocak lets recurring questions about the (self-)ghettoization of migrants in millennial Berlin shine through the indirect speech of that fictional conversation between Enver Pascha and Salih Bey in the past. Attributed identity and self-awareness stand in a strained reciprocal relationship both in the past and the present.

---

39 Şenocak, *Alman Terbiyesi*, 14: "Tatavla'ya Kurtuluş denilmesine bir türlü alışamamıştı. Tatavla Tatavla'dır, Pera da Pera. Gayri Müslimler oturur buralarda. Asırlardır böyledir bu. Bunun değişmesi buraların yok olması anlamına gelir. Kimsenin gücü buna yetmez. Paşaların bile." "Er konnte sich einfach nicht daran gewöhnen, dass Tatavla jetzt Kurtuluş hieß. Tatavla ist nun einmal Tatavla, so wie Pera eben Pera ist. Hier wohnen die Nicht-Muslime. Und zwar schon seit Jahrhunderten. Unvorstellbar, dass das sich jemals ändern würde," (Şenocak, *Deutsche Schule*, 13).
40 Şenocak, *Alman Terbiyesi*, 32f; Şenocak, *Deutsche Schule*, 30.
41 Şenocak, *Alman Terbiyesi*, 34; Şenocak, *Deutsche Schule*, 31.
42 Şenocak, *Alman Terbiyesi*, 35; Şenocak, *Deutsche Schule*, 32.

In Istanbul, where Salih Bey considers himself to be a liaison for Imperial Germany, by 1941 long defunct, he is tailed by the Germans as well as the Turks. A new neighbor turns out to be an informant. A history teacher at the Istanbul German School, Şerafettin Bey, encounters Salih Bey with suspicion. Şerafettin is an undercover agent for the Turkish secret police driven by his respect for the achievements of the Nazi regime; he is a faithful nationalist who longs for the German disciplining of the Turkish people. After an event at the German club Teutonia, where he wore a leather belt with a swastika, he stands at his window to catch a cool breeze from the sea. Irritated by the smell of garbage, he bemoans his neighbors who throw their trash into the courtyard and reflects on the Istanbulites' lack of a national spirit. He dreams of enforcing order and discipline through German-style *Blockwarts* whom he watched with envy when he was studying in Dresden for a few months in the 1930s. The use of the German word "Blockwart" in the original Turkish text is a strong signal. The neighborhood guard ("bekçi") mutates here into an unscrupulous, violent figure armed with a baton ("eli sopalı acımasız") and part of a surveillance apparatus ("gözaltı mekanizması"). The desire for a block warden, an emblematic figure of the Nazi regime that stood for neighborhood watch and discipline, reads as a simulation of duplicitous ventriloquy with satirical nods both to the memory of National Socialism and contemporary digital surveillance. Şerafettin Bey continuous his soliloquy:

> The Germans had the necessary qualities to prove their status as a people. They were not some kind of thrown-together raw mass like the Turks, who descended from a mixture of seventy-two-and-a-half peoples that would never coalesce. This Turkish Republic had not even produced one respectable architect. If he had not become a history teacher, he would have become an architect. The important thing was to bring order to, to structure people's lives and to keep their memories awake. But what had the politicians in Ankara decided?
>
> Instead of educating architects for the construction and development of Ankara as the capital, architects who would go to work with the nation in mind, they frivolously employed the services of any architect that the *Führer* had banished from his country. The result is obvious: cold, inhospitable buildings that are foreign to the Turkish people and do not consider their feelings or way of life in the least. They've made Ankara into a stomping ground for uprooted master builders.[43]

---

43 Şenocak, *Alman Terbiyesi*, 65: "Almanlar da millet olmanın bütün vasıflarını haizdi, öyle Türkler gibi yetmiş iki buçuk milletin karışımından oluşan, bir türlü mütecanis bir kitleye dönüşemeyen ham bir güruh değildi. Doğru dürüst bir mimar bile yetişmiyordu şu Türkiye Cumhuriyeti'nde. Tarih öğretmeni olmasa mimar olmak isterdi. İnsanların barındıkları mekanları düzenlemek, onların hayatlarını tanzim etmek, hafızalarını canlı tutmak kadar mühim bir işti. Başkent Ankara'nın inşası ve inkişafı için milli bir zihniyetle çalışacak mimarlar yetiştirmek

Şenocak's ironic staging of the history teacher's disdain for the architecture of exiles from Nazi Germany – such as Clemens Holzmeister and Bruno Taut who gave Ankara, the capital of the Turkish Republic founded in 1923, its modern imprint – highlights a nationalistic mentality full of internal contradictions: skepticism regarding top-down bureaucratically prescribed modernization, i.e., westernization does not preclude a desire for German discipline and order.

The restructuring of Ankara as the new capital was, in fact, a central element of the modernization efforts. Esra Akcan based her study of the role of German-speaking architects in the Turkish adaptation of modern architecture on a theory of translatability and historical non-simultaneity.[44] In the transference and reinterpretation of modern structural designs, from Hermann Jansen's masterplan for Ankara during the Weimar Republic to Bruno Taut's cosmopolitan late work, various approaches for the planning of the city were negotiated. These included weighing functionality versus tradition, and the modernist housing projects versus the more reactionary model of garden estates. The biography of a German architect from those years, Robert Vorhoelzer, reads like a story from the novel *Alman Terbiyesi*. The Nazis relieved Vorhoelzer, whom they called a "Baubolschewist" (a Bolshevik architect), of his Munich professorship in architecture. In 1939, succeeding the late Brunto Taut, he would take over the directorship of the department of architecture at the Academy of Fine Arts in Istanbul, only to be accused, due to his interest in aerial photography, of spying for Germany in 1941. Upon returning to Germany, he was drafted into

---

yerine, Führer'in memleketinden kovulmuş ne idüğü belirsiz mimarlardan medet umuluyordu şimdilerde. Sonuç ortadaydı: Türk milletinin hissiyatı ve hayat tarzıyla hiçbir ilgisi olamayan, ona yabancı, soğuk ve sağlıksız bir yapılanma. Ankara'nın manzarası acayip bir tecrübe tahtasını andırıyordu."

"Die Deutschen hatten eben alle Eigenschaften, um sich als Volk zu bewähren. Sie waren kein so zusammengewürfelter Haufen wie die Türken, die einer Mischung von zweiundsiebzigeinhalb Völkern entstammten und wohl kaum zusammenwachsen würden. Noch nicht einmal einen anständigen Architekten hat diese Türkische Republik hervorgebracht. Wenn er nicht Geschichtslehrer geworden wäre, hätte er Architekt werden wollen. Das Wesentliche war doch, in das Leben der Menschen Ordnung zu bringen, es zu strukturieren und ihr Gedächtnis wach zu halten. Was aber hatte man in Ankara entschieden? Statt für den Bau und die Entwicklung der Hauptstadt Ankara Architekten heranzubilden, die national gesinnt ans Werk gehen, bediente man sich heute leichtfertig irgendwelcher Architekten, die der Führer aus dem Land geworfen hatte. Das Ergebnis ist offensichtlich: kalte, lebensfeindliche Bauwerke, die dem türkischen Volk fremd sind und keinerlei Rücksicht auf seine Gefühle und seine Lebensweise nehmen. Aus Ankara ist ein Tummelplatz entwurzelter Baumeister geworden," (Şenocak, *Deutsche Schule*, 56).

44 Cf. Esra Akcan, *Architecture in Translation: Germany, Turkey, and the Modern House* (Durham, NC: Duke University Press, 2012).

the *Wehrmacht* at the age of 58.[45] Border crossers and translators in the broadest sense all too easily have found themselves suspected of treason.

The emigration from Nazi Germany to Turkey received attention rather late.[46] From 1933 to 1945 about a thousand expatriates from the German-speaking region found refuge in Turkey and were employed in the civil service and universities, where they were to help establish a western education system. Among the emigrated literary scholars, Erich Auerbach is perhaps the most famous, having taught at the University of Istanbul as a professor of Romance Philology from 1936–1947, During those years he wrote his widely known book *Mimesis: The Representation of Reality in Western Literature* (1946), which Emily Apter has praised as the origin of Comparative Literature, unfolding a transnational humanism of "global *translation*."[47] Kader Konuk contextualizes this genesis story more precisely and shows how the "rescue" of certain emigrants, carefully selected on the basis of their qualifications, served not so much humanistic ideals as national interests in the framework of a state-driven modernization project.[48] A lecture given by Auerbach at the University of Istanbul in 1941 makes clear that he was well aware of the militaristic-nationalistic dimensions of this educational project:

> A nation that is self-aware and understands that the national defense is the concern of the entire populace also has to understand the intellectual needs of this task that comes with modernization; in order to protect itself, it has to have knowledge at its disposal. Compulsory military service and obligatory schooling go hand-in-hand. They complement each other. School prepares one for the barracks. And the barracks often found and foster the education of the nation not only in a militaristic but also in a professional and general sense.[49]

---

45 Cf. Jan Lubitz, "Robert Vorhoelzer 1884–1954," www.architekten-por-trait.de/robert_vo rhoelzer/index.html. On the role of German-speaking architects in the construction of the new capital in Ankara see Oya Atalay Franck, "Deutschsprachige Architekten in der frühen Republik," www.goethe.de/ins/tr/ank/prj/urs/arc/deindex.htm.
46 Cf. the exhibition catalogue for the Akademie der Künste, Sabine Hillebrecht ed., *Haymatloz – Exil in der Türkei 1933–1945* [Katalog zur Ausstellung des Vereins Aktives Museum und des Goethe-Institutes mit der Akademie der Künste, 8. Januar bis 20. Februar 2000, Akademie der Künste, Berlin], (Berlin: Verein Aktives Museum, 2000).
47 Emily Apter, "Global *Translation*: The 'Invention' of Comparative Literature, Istanbul, 1933," *Critical Inquiry* 2.29 (2003): 253–281. Also see Apter, *The Translation Zone: A New Comparative Literature* (Princeton: Princeton University Press, 2006).
48 Cf. Kader Konuk, *East/West Mimesis: Auerbach in Turkey* (Stanford: Stanford University Press, 2010), 75.
49 Erich Auerbach, "Literatur und Krieg," in Auerbach, *Kultur als Politik. Aufsätze aus dem Exil zur Geschichte und Zukunft Europas (1938–1947)*, ed. Christian Rivoletti, from the Turkish trans. Christoph Neumann (Paderborn: Konstanz University Press, 2014), 33–49, here 41: "Eine Nation, die zum Bewusstsein von sich selbst findet und versteht, dass die nationale Verteidigung Angelegenheit des ganzen Volkes ist, muss auch die intellektuellen Erfordernisse dieser Aufgabe

Although Auerbach refers paradigmatically to the national armament of Napoleon's France in this passage, resonances with the modern Turkish education project, in which he took part, cannot be ignored. The novel *Deutsche Schule* also illuminates the modern education project as the militarization of society. Contrary to the history of emigration and exile as rescue, Şenocak turns the attention of his novel toward conspiracy, collaboration, and entangled alliances.

Intertextual resonances

Although not itself a translation, the novel *Alman Terbiyesi* serves as a stage for acts of translation as well as the "continued life" and "maturation process" of works in the literary imagination as conceived by Benjamin. The boundaries between the fictional perpetualization and revitalization of a past language and conceptual world and the translation in the interlingual sense appear fluid. With this novel Şenocak writes himself back into the Turkish language and literature of that time, a Turkish that is no longer spoken today, that is to be found in the early works of Sait Faik, Istanbul's melancholic storyteller. Faik captures the atmosphere of the city by means of everyday objects – a samovar or a young boy's handmade model ship – which play decisive roles in the lives of inconsequential people.[50] During the above mentioned operative meeting between Salih Bey and the Gestapo officer, Sait Faik has an anonymous cameo in Café Markiz. Salih greets the unnamed man and explains:

> "Everyone knows him. He writes stories, mostly about Istanbul."
>
> "I don't have much respect for writers. It's good that thanks to the *Führer* we have freed ourselves from most of them. But we can't trust even those who remain."[51]

---

begreifen, die die Moderne mit sich bringt; um sich selbst schützen zu können, muss es über Wissen verfügen. Wehrpflicht und Schulpflicht hängen eng miteinander zusammen. Und sie ergänzen einander. Die Schule ist die Vorbereitung auf die Kaserne. Und die Kaserne fundiert und fördert oftmals die Erziehung der Nation nicht nur in militärischer, sondern auch in professioneller und allgemeiner Hinsicht."

50 Cf. Sait Faik Abasıyanık. *Semaver* [1936] (Istanbul: Yapı Kredi Yayınları, 2004). On life in the former Pera district see Sait Faik Abasıyanık, *Tüneldeki Çocuk* (İstanbul: Varlık Yayınları, 1955).

51 "Onu herkes tanır. O da nerdeyse herkesi. Hikayeler yazıyor, çoğu İstanbul üzerine." Halinden zaten belli, dercesine başını salladı adam.
"Yazarlardan hoşlanmam. Führer sayesinden çoğundan kurtulduk neyse ki. Ama kalanlara da güvenilmez" (Şenocak, *Alman Terbiyesi*, 48).

Meanwhile Salih recalls the famous Romanisches Café in Berlin in 1924 and the circle of poets gathered around Else [Lasker-Schüler], the Piscator performance in the theater on Nollendorfplatz, and the Turkish café in the Haus Vaterland entertainment center on Potsdamer Platz run by the UFA.

Şenocak's narrative along the Turkish-German axis corresponds intertextually with Sabahattin Ali's novel *Kürk Mantolu Madonna* [1943, *Die Madonna im Pelzmantel*, 2008 / *Madonna in a Fur Coat*, 2016], the love story of Raif Efendi and Maria Puder in Berlin during the Weimar Republic, told in retrospect through Raif's notes, a fictional character who works as a corporate translator of German and dies in Ankara.[52] Particularly Karla, Salih Bey's Jewish lover in *Deutsche Schule*, who arrives in Istanbul on her journey to Palestine, is a figure from the sphere of 1920's Berlin with a clear resemblance to Maria Puder. It is in this context that the Struma is mentioned in Deutsche Schule: the ship was sunk by a Soviet torpedo attack in the Black Sea on 24 Feb 1942, while carrying almost 800 Jewish refugees to whom Turkish authorities had refused entry.[53] In the confusing surveillance conditions of the war years, breaches of trust had fatal consequences for agents: death lurked around every corner – on the front, or in flight from the gears of the killing machine.

Sabahattin Ali was recently rediscovered as a pioneer of Turkish-German literature.[54] *Madonna in a Fur Coat*, Ali's last novel, bears an autobiographical stamp. Ali was born in 1907 in Eğridere, which, at the time, belonged to the Ottoman Empire, but today is the city of Ardino in Bulgaria. He lived through the First World War, the Turkish War of Independence, and the founding of the Republic of Turkey in 1923. In 1928, he travelled to Berlin on a government-funded scholarship to study language, literature, and philosophy, but discontinued his studies after a year and a half. Following his return in 1940, he worked as an editor and translator for the ministry of culture's translation office, which had been founded that same year by Education Minister Hasan Ali Yücel, and was directed by Nurullah Ataç. There, Ali became a part of the *Dünya Edebiyatından Tercümeler* [Translations From World Literature] project,

---

"Jeder kennt ihn. Er schreibt Geschichten, meist über Istanbul."
"Ich halte nicht viel von Schriftstellern. Gut, dass wir dank des Führers uns von den meisten befreit haben. Aber auch denen, die geblieben sind, kann man nicht über den Weg trauen" (Şenocak, *Deutsche Schule*, 42).
52 Sabahattin Ali, *Die Madonna im Pelzmantel*, trans. Ute Birgi (Zurich: Dörlemann, 2008).
53 Cf. Şenocak, *Alman Terbiyesi*, 140; Şenocak, *Deutsche Schule*, 123.
54 Cf. Şeyda Ozil et al., ed. *The Transcultural Critic: Sabahattin Ali and Beyond*, *Türkisch-deutsche Studien Jahrbuch 2016* (Göttingen: Universitätsverlag, 2017). https://doi.org/10.17875/gup2017-1012.

which, guided by European humanistic educational ideals, translated world literary classics into Turkish and published them in affordable editions. Despite his role as a public servant, Ali, a passionate translator of German literature, was skeptical of a westernization project conceived of as a transfer of civilization. For him translation was not a simple transfer of meaning, and 'the West' was not an ideal entity that should be emulated blindly. In 1944, Ali was placed under government surveillance for alleged destructive political activities. In 1948, he was murdered near the Bulgarian border under mysterious circumstances.[55]

Madonna in a Fur Coat was initially published in the newspaper *Hakikat* from 1940 to 1941 as a serial novel. During the same period, Ali published his translation of Heinrich von Kleist's novella "Die Verlobung in St. Domingo" [1811, "The Betrothal in St. Domingo"], a text that deals with the crisis of colonial German and European identity during the slave-led Haitian revolution. Kristin Dickinson analyzes the implicit sexual act in *Madonna in a Fur Coat* as a central intertextual reference to "Die Verlobung in St. Domingo" and underscores the resonances between the two texts with regards to the mingling of the races: the mestiza Toni and the half-Jewish Maria Puder are both hybrid figures who question a "pure" German or European identity in tragic ways.[56] On a walk through Berlin, the novel's protagonist Raif stands on the shore of the Wannsee at the place where Kleist shot his friend Henriette Vogel and then committed suicide. Ali's engagement with Kleist is an important source of inspiration for his examination of the ambiguities of modernity.

The frame narrative in *Madonna in a Fur Coat* begins as a white-collar novel (*Angestelltenroman*). In Ankara, the new capital of the bureaucrats, the narrator, a destitute and jobless young man with writerly ambitions, finds employment with a company through a friend, where he shares an office with Raif Efendi, an old translator of German. Raif is a quiet, inconspicuous man, a gentle, humble outsider ("Außenseiter"[57]), dismissed by colleagues and his family, immersed in his own world, and removed from the materialistic society that surrounds him. In time, the narrator discovers deeper dimensions in the ailing man and begins to admire his resistance of the superficial urbanity of his surroundings: "with those people whose entire appearances seem to scream 'We

---

55 Another text that returns to the Second World War and continues the story of Sabahattin Ali is Doğan Akhanlı's *Madonna'nın Son Hayali* [*The Madonna's Final Fantasy*] (Ankara: Olasılık, 2015). This novel begins with the murder of the writer Sabahattin Ali in 1948 near the Bulgarian border and imagines Maria Puder on board the *Struma*.
56 Cf. Kristin Dickinson, "Intervening in the Humanist Legacy: Sabahattin Alis Kleist Translations," in *The Transcultural Critic*, ed. Ş. Ozil et al., (2017), 45–62.
57 Ali, *Die Madonna im Pelzmantel*, 33.

understand foreignness,' he didn't share the slightest resemblance" ("mit jenen Menschen, deren ganzes Wesen 'Wir verstehen ausländisch!' zu schreien schien, hatte er nicht die geringste Ähnlichkeit"[58]). The enigma that is Raif is only understood after his death when the narrator reads Raif's notebook, which he finds in one of Raif's desk drawers and, contrary to Raif's wishes, does not burn. The notebook was written in 1933 shortly after he learned of Maria Puder's death, and it gives a retrospective account of his 1923 meeting with her. The betrayal of his lover's confidence is the tragic secret of the solitary translator. By selecting a translator as the protagonist of his novel, Ali takes on the invisibility of the translator and opposes the model of a functional transference of meaning as a strategy of goal-oriented modernization with a nuanced multilingual, transcultural, and melancholic-ironic subjectivity. David Gramling and Martina Schwalm read the novel as a documentation of translators' interventions into political power structures and the order of modern monolingual nationalistic consolidation and the development of the translator's aesthetic-ethic imperative: "an ethics of translation practice and a complex *ars poetica* for translators in the era of modern, nationalized monolingualism."[59]

With *Alman Terbiyesi*, Şenocak wrote himself into this tradition of a literature in Turkish that thrives on translation, corresponds with world literature across borders, and maintains a critical distance to nationalist framings of collective identity. In addition to reading Şenocak's text as an intervention in the cultural politics of remembrance in Germany, it is therefore equally important to appreciate his contribution to Turkish literature and cultural memory in the vein of Sabahattin Ali, Sait Faik and others. In fact, Şenocak's textual production both in German and Turkish points to the inadequacy of the national as a category for containing cultures on the move.

Ironic poetics beyond national culture

Let us now return to the question of trust and treason, fidelity and liberty with regard to translation. Walter Benjamin wrote:

> The traditional concepts in any discussion of translation are fidelity and license – the freedom to give a faithful reproduction of the sense and, in its service, fidelity to the

---

[58] Ali, *Die Madonna im Pelzmantel*, 19.
[59] David Gramling and Martina Schwalm, "World Literature (Already) Wrote Back: Sabahattin Ali after Germany," in *The Transcultural Critic*, ed. Ş. Ozil et al. (2017), 25–44, here 42.

word. These ideas seem to be no longer serviceable to a theory that strives to find, in a translation, something other than reproduction of meaning.[60]

Beyond the semantic approach of representation theory and literal equivalency, the atmospheric qualities of language are paramount and resonances with intertexts ring out in the translation process. Şenocak often stages these voices in a satirical light. It is precisely in this way that one must understand the basic principle of translation in an ironic poetics beyond fidelity and treason. As readers we must usurp this "language of languages,"[61] we must continually expand our frames of reference and archives in order to keep the borders of national literatures permeable. For Emily Apter, translation is, in the broadest sense, a way to obtain a cosmopolitan consciousness, "a way of denaturalizing citizens, taking them out of the comfort zone of national space, daily ritual, and pre-given domestic arrangements."[62] This breaking away from familiar group rituals and the awareness of possible alternatives make it possible to win, in processes of reading and writing, a critical distance from the language of society. Cultural practices of translation, publication, exhibition, and criticism entail implicit value judgments. Meanwhile, undervalued silences, which are not transferred, recognized, or appreciated in the market merit attention.

The negotiation of national character and "western" modernity portrayed in *Deutsche Schule* demonstrates that cultural heritage and a sense of community cannot be contained within static national categories; they are, instead, constantly in motion and produced collaboratively. Models of straightforward translatability are not adequate. The work of "outside/insider" translators generates, rather, ambiguities and nuances through processes of adaptation and incorporation. The fidelity to a national language and history remains a central category in educational and cultural politics; I would propose that it is even more virulent today than ever, as witnessed by the mobilization of nationalism around the globe. Ironic tactics of masking, defamiliarization, and ventriloquism in texts like *Gefährliche Verwandtschaft*, *Alman Terbiyesi* and its precursor, *Kürk Mantolu Madonna*, serve as correctives to essentializing notions of self-contained, pure identities. The focus on multiple affiliations of translators

---

60 Benjamin, "The Task of the Translator," 259. German Orig.: "Treue und Freiheit – Freiheit der sinngemäßen Wiedergabe und in ihrem Dienst Treue gegen das Wort – sind die althergebrachten Begriffe in jeder Diskussion von Übersetzungen. Einer Theorie, die anderes in der Übersetzung sucht als Sinnwiedergabe, scheinen sie nicht mehr dienen zu können," (Benjamin, "Die Aufgabe des Übersetzers," 17).
61 Akşit Göktürk, *Çeviri: Dillerin Dili* [1986] (Istanbul: Yapı Kredi Yayınları, 2010).
62 Apter, *The Translation Zone*, 6.

sharpens our awareness for continuous processes of translation, actualization, and negotiation that make up the core of any culture.

Works cited

Abasıyanık, Sait Faik. *Semaver* [1936] (Istanbul: Yapı Kredi Yayınları, 2004).
Abasıyanık, Sait Faik. *Tüneldeki Çocuk* (Istanbul: Varlık Yayınları, 1955).
Adelson, Leslie A. "Touching Tales of Turks, Germans, and Jews: Cultural Alterity, Historical Narrative, and Literary Riddles for the 1990s," *New German Critique*, Special Issue on the Holocaust 80 (2000): 93–124.
Adelson, Leslie A. *The Turkish Turn in Contemporary German Literature. Toward a New Critical Grammar of Migration* (New York: Palgrave Macmillan, 2005).
Akcan, Esra. *Architecture in Translation: Germany, Turkey, and the Modern House* (Durham: Duke University Press, 2012).
Akhanlı, Doğan. *Madonna'nın Son Hayali* (Ankara: Olasılık, 2015).
Ali, Sabahattin. *Die Madonna im Pelzmantel*. Trans. Ute Birgi (Zurich: Dörlemann, 2008).
Apter, Emily. "Global *Translation*: The 'Invention' of Comparative Literature, Istanbul, 1933," *Critical Inquiry* 2.29 (2003): 253–281.
Apter, Emily. *The Translation Zone: A New Comparative Literature* (Princeton: Princeton University Press, 2006).
Atalay Franck, Oya. "Deutschsprachige Architekten in der frühen Republik," www.goethe.de/ins/tr/ank/prj/urs/arc/deindex.htm
Auerbach, Erich. "Literatur und Krieg," in Auerbach, *Kultur als Politik. Aufsätze aus dem Exil zur Geschichte und Zukunft Europas (1938–1947)*. Ed. Christian Rivoletti, trans. from Turkish Christoph Neumann (Paderborn: Konstanz University Press, 2014), 33–49.
Benjamin, Walter. "Die Aufgabe des Übersetzers," in *Gesammelte Schriften* vol. IV/1 (Frankfurt am Main: Suhrkamp, 1972), 9–21.
Benjamin, Walter. "The Task of the Translator." Trans. Harry Zohn in *Walter Benjamin: Selected Writings*, ed. Marcus Bullock and Michael W. Jennings vol. 1 (Cambridge: Belknap Press, 1996), 253–263.
Cheah, Pheng. *What is a World? On Postcolonial Literature as World Literature* (Durham: Duke University Press, 2016).
Dickinson, Kristin. *DisOrientations: German-Turkish Cultural Contact in Translation, 1811–1946* (University Park: Penn State University Press, 2021).
Dickinson, Kristin. "Intervening in the Humanist Legacy: Sabahattin Alis Kleist Translations," in *The Transcultural Critic: Sabahattin Ali and Beyond*. Eds. Şeyda Ozil et al. (Göttingen: Universitätsverlag, 2017), 45–62.
Dostal, Robert J. "Gadamerian Hermeneutics and Irony: Between Strauss and Derrida," *Research in Phenomenology* 38.2 (2008): 247–269.
Emre, Yunus. *Das Kummerrad / Dertli Dolap*. Trans. Zafer Şenocak (Frankfurt am Main: Dağyeli, 1986).
Gadamer, Hans-Georg. *Wahrheit und Methode*. Vol. II (Tübingen: Mohr, 1993 [^{1}1986]).

Gramling, David and Martina Schwalm. "World Literature (Already) Wrote Back: Sabahattin Ali after Germany," in *The Transcultural Critic: Sabahattin Ali and Beyond*. Eds. Şeyda Ozil et al. (Göttingen: Universitätsverlag, 2017), 25–44.
Göktürk, Akşit. *Çeviri: Dillerin Dili* [Translation: The Language of Languages] (Istanbul: Yapı Kredi Yayınları, 2010 [1986]).
Göktürk, Deniz and Zafer Şenocak, eds. *Jedem Wort gehört ein Himmel: Türkei literarisch* (Berlin: Babel 1991).
Göktürk, Deniz, David Gramling, and Anton Kaes, eds. *Germany in Transit: Nation and Migration, 1955–2005* (Berkeley: University of California Press, 2007).
Hillebrecht, Sabine, ed. *Haymatloz – Exil in der Türkei 1933–1945* [Katalog zur Ausstellung des Vereins Aktives Museum und des Goethe-Institutes mit der Akademie der Künste, 8. Januar bis 20. Februar 2000, Akademie der Künste, Berlin] (Berlin: Verein Aktives Museum, 2000).
Huyssen, Andreas. "Diaspora and Nation: Migration into Other Pasts," *New German Critique* Contemporary German Literature 88 (2003): 147–164.
Iser, Wolfgang. "Die Appellstruktur der Texte," in *Rezeptionsästhetik*. Ed. Rainer Warning (Munich: Wilhelm Fink, 1975), 228–252.
Konuk, Kader. *East/West Mimesis: Auerbach in Turkey* (Stanford: Stanford University Press, 2010).
Littler, Margaret. "Guilt, Victimhood, and Identity in Zafer Şenocak's Gefährliche Verwandtschaft," *The German Quarterly* 3.78 (2005): 357–373.
Lubitz, Jan. "Robert Vorhoelzer 1884–1954," www.architekten-portrait.de/robert_vorhoelzer/index.html.
Ozil, Şeyda et al., eds. *The Transcultural Critic: Sabahattin Ali and Beyond* (Göttingen: Universitätsverlag, 2017), doi.org/10.17875/gup2017-1012.
Rushdie, Salman. "'Commonwealth Literature' Does Not Exist" [1983], in *Imaginary Homelands* (London: Granta, 1991), 61–70.
Schlegel, Friedrich. "Über die Unverständlichkeit." Kritische Friedrich-Schlegel-Ausgabe, 1st ed.: Critical New Reissue, Vol. 2 (Munich, Paderborn, Vienna, Zurich, 1967), 363–373, First Print in: Athenäum (Berlin), Vol. 3, 2. Stück, 1800. Permalink: http://www.zeno.org/nid/2000561905X.
Segelcke, Elke. "National History and Politics of Memory in Turkish-German Literature," *Colloquia Germanica* Special Issue: Transnational Hi/Stories 4.44 (2011): 396–407.
Şenocak, Zafer. *Alman Terbiyesi* (Istanbul: Alef Yayınevi, 2007).
Şenocak, Zafer. *Deutsche Schule*. Trans. Helga Dağyeli-Bohne (Berlin: J&D Dağyeli, 2012).
Şenocak, Zafer. "Die bastardisierte Sprache," in *War Hitler Araber? Irreführungen an den Rand Europas* (Berlin: Babel, 1994), 29–33, 30f.
Şenocak, Zafer. "The Bastardized Language." Trans. Tom Cheesman. In *Germany in Transit: Nation and Migration, 1955–2005*. Eds. Deniz Göktürk, David Gramling, and Anton Kaes (Berkeley: University of California Press, 2007), 402–405.
Şenocak, Zafer. "Coordinates of Orientation: An Introduction," in *Atlas of a Tropical Germany: Essays on Politics and Culture, 1990–1998*. Trans. and ed. Leslie A. Adelson (Lincoln and London: University of Nebraska Press, 2000), xi–xxxvii.
Şenocak, Zafer. "Die dritte Sprache des Übersetzers," in *Das Fremde, das in jedem wohnt. Wie Unterschiede unsere Gesellschaft zusammenhalten* (Hamburg: Edition Körber, 2018), 65–74.

Şenocak, Zafer. *Das Fremde, das in jedem wohnt. Wie Unterschiede unsere Gesellschaft zusammenhalten* (Hamburg: Edition Körber, 2018).
Şenocak, Zafer. *Gefährliche Verwandtschaft* (Munich: Babel, 1998).
Şenocak, Zafer. *In deinen Worten. Mutmaßungen über den Glauben meines Vaters* (Munich: Babel, 2016).
Şenocak, Zafer. "Jenseits der Landessprache," in *Zungenentfernung. Bericht aus der Quarantänestation* (Munich: Babel, 2001), 87–90.
Şenocak, Zafer. "Kann man Türken und Juden vergleichen, Herr Şenocak?," *Der Tagesspiegel* 13–14 April 1995.
Şenocak, Zafer. *Perilous Kinship*. Trans. Tom Cheesman (Swansea: Hafan Books, 2001).
Schleiermacher, Friedrich. "On the Different Methods of Translating" [1813]. Trans. Susan Bernofsky, ed. Lawrence Venuti. In *The Translation Studies Reader*, 2nd ed. (New York: Routledge, 2012), 43–63.
Sperber, Dan and Deidre Wilson. "Irony and the Use-Mention Distinction [1981]," in *Pragmatics. A Reader*. Ed. Steven Davies (New York: Oxford University Press, 1991), 550–564.
Spivak, Gayatri Chakravorty. "The Politics of Translation," in *The Translation Studies Reader*. Ed. Lawrence Venuti. 2nd ed. (New York: Routledge, 2012 [^{1}1993]): 312–330.
Wirth, Uwe. "Ironie," in *Komik. Ein interdisziplinäres Handbuch*. Ed. Uwe Wirth (Stuttgart: J.B. Metzler, 2017), 16–21.

Yuliya Komska
Jews, Animals, Migration: H. A. Rey's Commercial and Non-Commercial Nature Drawings in Brazil

Introduction: Drawing on lined paper

Although the creatures did not look particularly unusual, Hans August Reyersbach fumbled for the adjectives with which to describe them. He finally opted for a gaggle of non-committal attributes in -ish. "White-yellowish quills, dark brown on top, hairy nose, reddish muzzle," one annotation read.[1] "Face, head, back: whitish olive gray, body olive gray, the back darker. Paws, shoulders, thighs olive brown. Muzzle a brownish flesh color. Flesh pink soles. Bluish green claws," went another. Reyersbach, now known as children's author H. A. Rey, was sketching quickly, his soft graphite pencil flying across loose sheets of paper to trace little but the animals' roughest contours. A smattering of eyes, limbs, stripes, spots, or quills materialized.[2] All of those sheets were lined and obviously not intended for drawing. Did he stumble across the animals in the wild? Did they catch him off guard, without his draughtsman's materials?

Because Hans would have hardly entered a zoo thus unprepared. Not only was he a compulsive zoo-goer, wherever his serial migrant life carried him from his native Hamburg – first to Rio de Janeiro in 1925, then back to Hamburg in 1936, then to Paris in 1937, and finally to New York by way of Rio in 1940 – but those zoo visits also shaped his artist practice from the earliest years. Already as a child, Hans, pen and paper in hand, would make his way to a zoo. The zoo's proximity to the Jewish Reyersbachs' residences in the bourgeois district Harvestehude (the family moved several times, always within the same few blocks) comes up repeatedly in the sources, although the zoo is never identified by name. Both of these circumstances suggest a reference to Hamburg's Zoological Garden. It was the city's original zoo, founded in 1860 by the merchant elites on the acres leased from the Hamburg Senate (the current site of the park

---

[1] "Rodents & sundry," de Grummond Children's Literature Collection, University of Southern Mississippi, H.A. & Margret Rey Papers, DG0812, 137/18. Henceforth abbreviated as DGRP. The subsequent references are to the same file, unless otherwise indicated.
[2] For consistency, I use "Hans August Reyersbach" to refer to H. A. Rey before his immigration to the United States in October 1940. While he did adopt "Rey" as an alias in Brazil, using it to sign his work, its appearance remained sporadic and unofficial.

https://doi.org/10.1515/9783110778922-009

Planten un Blomen) and opened to the public in 1863.³ The locations of Tierpark Hagenbeck, the Zoological Garden's competitor and nemesis, to this day famous for its pioneering cage-free design and the landscaping of habitats and infamous for its namesake animal tycoon owner's vast colonial networks and ethnographic displays of live human subjects, lay further away. Born in 1898, the boy would quickly become "more familiar with elephants and kangaroos than with cows or sheep" and excel at imitating the lion's roar.⁴

Harvestehude's Wilhelm Gymnasium, the elite all-boys school that Hans attended between 1907 and 1916, made the most of the same topographical proximity.⁵ Observational drawing en plein air, on playgrounds and especially at the zoo, was a go-to instrument in the reform-pedagogical toolkit of the school's art teacher Fritz Müller, nicknamed Fietje, or little Fritz.⁶ In contrast to other teachers, serious men with doctoral degrees, Fietje was untethered to the podium. With some regularity, he would ask his students to pack up their art supplies and go on a field trip. There is little doubt that observing and sketching wild animals in the expressly unnatural setting of the colonial zoo was a bedrock of Hans's artistic training. Both activities would remain integral to his subsequent work process to an underappreciated extent. The same does not appear to apply to his future wife and collaborator Margret (born Margarete Elisabeth Waldstein in 1906), although she was a formally trained artist, and he was not.

---

3 A rare brief sketch of the zoo appears in Herman Reichenbach, "A Tale of Two Zoos: The Hamburg Zoological Garden and Carl Hagenbeck's Tierpark," in *New Worlds, New Animals: From Menagerie to Zoological Park in the Nineteenth Century*, eds. Robert J. Hoage and William A. Deiss (Baltimore: Johns Hopkins University Press, 1996), 51–62. On Tierpark Hagenbeck, see Nigel Rothfels's *Savages and Beasts: The Birth of the Modern Zoo* (Baltimore: Johns Hopkins University Press, 2002) and Eric Ames, *Carl Hagenbeck's Empire of Entertainments* (Seattle: University of Washington Press, 2009).

4 "The Life of H. A. Rey, told by himself in Chronological Order" (c. 1945), DG0812, 1/3. "In Hamburg, Germany, where both of us were born, H. A. lived close to the famous Hagenbeck Zoo," Margret Rey explained years later, "and, as a child, spent much of his free time there. That's where he learned to imitate animal voices. He is proudest of his lion roar, and once he roared for 3,000 children in the Atlanta Civic Auditorium, thus making the headlines in the *Atlanta Constitution* for the first and last time." "Rey, Margret (Elizabeth)," *Something about the Author: Facts and Pictures about Authors and Illustrators of Books for Young People*, vol. 26 (Detroit: Gale Research Company, 1982), 167.

5 Gerstenberg, Oberschulbehörde-Statistik, Hamburg State Archive (further abbreviated as HSta), Oberschulbehörde 2_Wilhelm-Gymn_DStatistik, 361–2II-A2, 6.1.

6 Ernst Albers-Schönberg, "Die Schule," DGRP, D0812, 175/15, 33. H. A. Rey mentioned sketching in the zoo in almost all author questionnaires for American publishers, especially his main publisher, Houghton Mifflin. See untitled autobiographical sketches, undated, DGRP, D0812, 1/2.

Only later would she join her husband on such outings, a camera in tow: "One of the things we do when we come to a new town is visit the Zoo," she would report.⁷ In zoos, she photographed, while he drew.

The animal drawings on lined paper are thus undoubtedly Hans's, from the handwriting to the style. Yet they are undated and lack explicit references to place, although the annotations – messy, unsystematic, and scattered all over each sheet – offer clues about the setting. First, there are the languages: Hans's native German, occasionally Latin, and sometimes also Portuguese. *Coendou prehensilis, coandú, Greifstachler*: the arboreal Brazilian porcupine. *Dasyprocta, cutia*: Brazilian agouti. *Paca*: spotted paca. *Proechimys guyannensis, Cayenne Ratte*: Cayenne spiny rat. *Choloepus didactylus*: the two-toed sloth. Ever the linguistic chameleon, Reyersbach enjoyed showing off his privileged schooling; he also tended to adopt the language of his surroundings quickly and rarely suffered from his other compatriots' "terrible sense of useless tongue," to borrow writer Bernard Malamud's turn of phrase.⁸ This occasion was no different. And while German and Latin added scientific flair, Portuguese and the range of species divulged the location – Brazil.

The second clue is the amount of text and the layout. Hans's extant zoo sketches from Hamburg, Paris, or New York contain few words and generally do not record the animals' appearance or behavior in a format mimicking a naturalist's rather than an artist's. The inscriptions, where they are available, usually supply intimate details, such as the animal's pet name.⁹ Besides, like many artists before and after him, Reyersbach tends to capture zoo animals from several angles at once (*en face*, three quarters, in profile, from the back, or from above). He also frequently does closeups, as if to confirm that visibility is an obvious effect of confinement – "each cage is a frame," in John Berger's words.¹⁰ A confined animal, scant annotations on his zoo drawings underscore, can be revisited; the missing minutiae of its appearance and habits can be recollected. The extensive scribblings and the jotted silhouettes on the lined sheets of paper, by contrast, suggest fleeting, difficult-to-replicate encounters outside a zoo. Why

---

7 "Rey, Margret (Elizabeth)," *Something about the Author: Facts and Pictures about Authors and Illustrators of Books for Young People*, vol. 26 (Detroit: Gale Research Company, 1982), 167.
8 Bernard Malamud, "The Refugee," *The Saturday Evening Post*, 14 September 1963, 39. I have written about the couple's multilingualism in "Why Curious George Could Not Speak: The Conspicuous Multilingualism of Margret and H. A. Rey," *The German Studies Review* 43.3 (2018): 505–528.
9 A vivid example are H. A. Rey's sketches of chimpanzees from 1948. Sketchbook and loose pages with pencil drawings of scenes in Washington Square Park, Greenwich Village, New York City, June 1948, DGRP, DG0812, 136/20.
10 John Berger, "Why Look at Animals?," in *About Looking* (London: Vintage, 1980), 23.

was Reyersbach drawing these animals, why did he give his sketches the naturalist veneer, and how do they fit into the hitherto unexplored continuum of his artistic practice in and outside Brazil? The question goes to the heart of this case study that probes the relationship between Jewish migration, animals, and creativity.

For this purpose, I situate Reyersbach's live sketches in three contexts: first, within Jewish animal studies; second, in relation to the material archive of the couple's creativity; and third, vis-à-vis the sum and the significance of Reyersbach's surviving Brazilian oeuvre. This last, as I explain, sits at the intersection between modernism and commercial graphic arts (advertising), commissioned both by local and by multinational companies engaged in settler-colonial projects. Reyersbach's migration to Brazil, during which he began to develop his style and to live off his animal stories, deserves to be reconsidered as more than an escape from the economic privation and political misfortunes in Germany. To be a commercial artist of European extraction in Brazil of that era verged on being coopted by the same forces of colonialism-fueled industrial modernity that had once emancipated Hans's forebears.[11] And at times, I argue, it meant stopping short of being coopted, as may have been the case with Hans's rough animal sketches on lined paper.

The animals of Jewish animal studies and settler colonialism

Reyersbach may have been a Jew sketching animals in Brazil, yet his pencil sketches do not speak the idiom of Jewish animal studies, which has been notable for its strong humanist slant. Analyses of the philosophical and religious negotiations of human animality, the term with two dominant meanings, tend to take center stage within the subfield.[12] The first meaning reflects the place of

---

[11] On how the gains of modernity entangled the Jewish subjects in colonialism, see Ethan B. Katz, Lisa Moses Leff, and Maud S. Mandel, "Introduction: Engaging Colonial History and Jewish History," in *Colonialism and the Jews*, eds. Ethan B. Katz, Lisa Moses Leff, and Maud S. Mandel (Bloomington, IN: Indiana University Press, 2017), 7 and other articles in this volume.

[12] The landmark contributions referenced in this paragraph include Andrew Benjamin, *Of Jews and Animals* (Edinburgh: Edinburgh University Press, 2010); Maya Barzilai, *Golem: Modern Wars and Their Monsters* (New York: New York University Press, 2016); Jay Geller, *Bestiarium Judaicum: Unnatural Histories of the Jews* (New York: Fordham University Press, 2017); David I. Shyovitz, *A Remembrance of His Wonders: Nature and the Supernatural in Medieval Ashkenaz* (Philadelphia: University of Pennsylvania Press, 2017); Mira Beth Wasserman, *Jews,*

all human animals, including Jews as human animals, in the great chain of being and highlights the ethical ramifications of such positioning. The second meaning refers more narrowly to the non-Jewish persons' antisemitic rhetorical constitution of Jews as the Other in animal form (alternatively known as dehumanization or animalization) and encompasses a range of Jewish responses. In both, the status of the animals that are not human – as such or qua representations – remains marginal by comparison.[13] A vivid example is Franz Kafka's short story "A Report to an Academy," most commonly read as an allegory of the limits of human passing or race-mixing, and almost never as the "animal story" (*Tiergeschichte*) that the author insisted it be.[14] Only recently have such scholars as Naama Harel broken new ground by advocating a posthumanist perspective.[15]

One could chalk up the longevity of this trend to the dubious cliché of "Jewish zoophobia," the existence of which scholar Steven G. Kellman hypothesized decades ago.[16] Limiting himself to the context of the United States, Kellman puzzled over the confluence of several distinct socio-cultural circumstances, from the low numbers of Jewish veterinarians to the "*judenrein*" (his word) condition at animation studios such as Disney, to the overwhelmingly pet-free existence of fictional characters scripted by Jewish authors. "*Shtetl* and immigrant urban life," he reasoned, "kept Jews remote from the intimacy with the natural world."

In contradiction to this assumption, recent scholarship on Jewish migration, to which this essay contributes, suggests that mobility increased, rather than constrained the amplitude of relationalities between Jews and animals. Jews, wherever and whenever they moved, did not enter urban environments in today's western understanding of them. Sometimes, this was because such environments did not yet exist, in which case the history of Jewish migration is also a history of settler colonialism and its workaday practices, such as trapping, cattle ranching, agriculture, or fearing the wild. All of these presuppose a broad range of decidedly unmetaphorical human-animal encounters, some life-,

---

Gentiles, and Other Animals: The Talmud after the Humanities (Philadelphia: University of Pennsylvania Press, 2017).
13 See also Samuel J. Spinner, "Plausible Primitives: Kafka and Jewish Primitivism," *The German Quarterly* 89.1 (2016): 28–29. Many thanks to Kerry Wallach for sharing this reference.
14 Geller, *Bestiarium Judaicum*, 123. For a very different, zoo-historical reading on Kafka's Red Peter, see Nigel Rothfels, *Savages and Beasts*, 145–147 and 189–194.
15 Naama Harel, *Kafka's Zoopoetics: Beyond the Human-Animal Barrier* (Ann Arbor, MI: University of Michigan Press, 2020).
16 Steven G. Kellman, "Jews, Beasts, and Americans," *Studies in American Jewish Literature* 5 (1986): 62–63.

habitat-, and body-image-changing and others less so.[17] On other occasions, this was because "urban" may have meant "unnatural" but not "nature-less." For a long time, cities teemed with domesticated species, including cattle, horses, and stray pets, all of whom lived active "social lives" in but also outside enclosures.[18] The same streets also accommodated "exotic" creatures, which (depending on the location) could be local or runaways from zoos, animal trade shops, or private homes. In short, avoiding animals was impossible.

The utilitarian, exploitative, and extractive outcomes of the resulting interspecies contact or bioprospecting – food, clothing, labor, or profit from the local and global circulation of animals-as-commodities – are familiar enough. The Reyersbachs' extended family, especially on Margret's side, was no stranger to such blunt transactionalism. Margret's ancestors owned the Hamburg firm S. Samuel & Rosenfeld, which at an early point may have traded in furs and "exotic" skins (fur trade being a widespread Jewish occupation); her uncle Carl Johann Cohn was a partner in Arndt & Cohn, another Hamburg company that very likely imported pelts, among other colonial goods, from South Africa; and her brother-in-law Günther Eichenberg was briefly employed by the Hide and Skins Corporation upon emigrating to New York in 1937.[19]

However, not all interactions between Jewish immigrants and animals evidenced utility. Reyersbach's annotated lined-paper sketches may belong in this category. As I trace them to Brazil prior to Hans and Margret's return to Europe in 1936 (in 1940, their second Brazilian stay lasted less than two months, and the work and life schedules did not leave much room for sketching in the wild), I suggest that the duo did not attempt to monetize this work in any of their ventures, from advertising to private artist sales. As far as we know, Hans would never again draw a porcupine, a sloth, an agouti, or a Cayenne spiny rat. The

---

17 Histories of U.S. immigration are especially rich with examples, although most do not appear focally. See Judith Levin Cantor, *Jews in Michigan* (East Lansing, MI: Michigan State University Press, 2001), 3–22; Natalie Ornish and Sara Alpern, *Pioneer Jewish Texans* (Austin, TX: Texas A&M University Press, 2011), 71–85; Sarah Imhoff, *Masculinity and the Making of American Judaism* (Bloomington, IN: Indiana University Press, 2017), 163–175; David S. Koffman, *The Jews' Indian: Colonialism, Pluralism, and Belonging in America* (New Brunswick, NJ: Rutgers University Press, 2019), 20–81.

18 As Sarah Amato observes, urbanization "did not bring a separation from the animals that were constituent parts of agricultural life." Sarah Amato, *Beastly Possessions: Animals in Victorian Consumer Culture* (Toronto: University of Toronto Press, 2015), 5–6.

19 David Felix Waldstein to Senator Nöldeke, 1 March 1923, HSta, Justizverwaltung, Personalakten, Hans Waldstein, Dr. d. R., 241_2_A1410. Guenther Eichenberg, draft card, Ancestry.com. *U.S., World War II Draft Cards Young Men, 1940–1947* [database on-line]. Lehi, UT, USA: Ancestry.com Operations, Inc., 2011.

sketches, as a result, had no public material afterlives. Instead, they remained private documents. But documents of what? Precisely because Hans and Margret would become famous for their animal characters – the American press and the city of Cambridge, their last place of residence, would naturalize the authors as "parents" of their fictional simian, Curious George – this question is inescapable.[20]

The Reyersbachs' usable archive

The facile "parent" moniker aside, where do fictional animals come from? This is a fraught question in the studies of classic children's books, which, some allege, have peddled a warped image of nature by anthropomorphizing animals.[21] However, there is mounting evidence against such blanket judgments. Recent research has highlighted the naturalist streak of some children's authors and uncovered their manifest interest in "life sciences, natural history, and Darwinian ideas," as a scholar puts it.[22] The Reyersbachs boiled no pet carcasses and performed no dissections, as some other authors had done. But their stylized animal portrayals did take root in animal observation and in regular consumption of popular zoological knowledge, despite the H. A. Rey's contradictory claim that Curious George "sprang from [his] head the way Athena did from Zeus," prototype-free.[23]

This claim is contradictory not only because it ostensibly excludes Margret from Curious George's progeniture, but also because Hans's popular-naturalist approach is well-documented. Reyersbach organized all his animal sketches, the Brazilian sketches included, into voluminous "files" – a backbone of his creative practice.[24] It is difficult to tell when exactly he began to collect and

---

20 Resolution by City of Cambridge, Massachusetts, for Margret Rey's 80th birthday with clipping, May 1986, DGRP, DG0812, 225/1.
21 Paul Bisceglio, "Are Picture Books Warping How Kids Understand Animals?" *Pacific Standard Magazine*, 27 March 2014, https://psmag.com/social-justice/picture-books-warping-kids-understand-animals-77550; Marla V. Anderson and Antonia J. Z. Henderson, "Pernicious Portrayals: The Impact of Children's Attachment to Animals of Fiction on Animals of Fact," *Society and Animals* 13.4 (2005): 297–314.
22 See Rose Lovell-Smith, "The Animals of Wonderland: Tenniel as Carroll's Reader," *Criticism* 45.4 (2005): 385 and Linda Lear, *Beatrix Potter: A Life in Nature* (New York: St. Martin's Griffin, 2016).
23 Carolyn F. Hummel, "Authors Tell of Writing 'Curious George' Series," *The Christian Science Monitor*, n. d., 10B, Autobiographical sketches of H. A. Rey, DGRP, DG0812, 1/2.
24 Sketchbooks and assorted drawings, DGRP, DG0812, 136/13–137/19.

systematize the materials (or to what extent Margret, as the main writer of the books and the engine behind their promotions as well as her husband's advisor and confidante, was involved), since many of the couple's papers did not survive the migrations. Some clippings and drawings date back to the mid-1930s. By the 1960s, Hans counted about a hundred slim folders that ranged "from Aircraft all through the alphabet to Zoology and containing several thousand sketches, photographs and [press] clippings about a great variety of subjects."[25]

Devising the six books in the Curious George series (1941–1966) as well as the prequel, *Cecily G. and the Nine Monkeys* (1939), the authors relied on this collection intermittently. Their forays into the files' depths exemplified how the material became useful, especially in the sense of being monetized, although they also suggest that one-to-one correspondences did not always exist. "Back in 1953," H. A. Rey explained on one occasion in 1959, "I clipped a news item about two mice who had been sent up in a rocket for a story of the effects of acceleration and weightlessness. Four years later I used this in a book 'Curious George gets a Medal': I had George go up in an experimental space ship." The plot thus preempted the historical launch of primates into space and had little to do with any primatological news.

On other occasions, the files provided immediate fodder for illustration and writing, especially when it came to shaping the animal characters' appearances. Here again, Curious George is a prominent example. His figure is stylized, no doubt, and the descriptor "monkey" follows him, like a shadow. Still, he possesses a chimpanzee's physique and other attributes of a young ape: the absence of a tail, bipedal locomotion, brachiation (swinging from branch to branch). There are also cognitive benchmarks – the ability to paint, for example, to recognize the letters of the alphabet, or to eat with a spoon at the table, like many real-life chimps had done under the watchful eyes of zoo and circus trainers.[26] These features, the couple steadfastly believed, qualified him as an animal and nothing but an animal. To anthropomorphize and allegorize, they assured their interviewers, was beneath them.[27]

---

[25] "Where do I go to get ideas," Articles on creative writing techniques by H. A. Rey, undated (circa 1959), DGRP, DG0812, 1/4. Subsequent citations are from the same source, unless otherwise indicated.

[26] I have greatly benefited from the generous advice of my colleagues in anthropology and primatology, especially Jeremy DaSilva and Nathaniel J. Dominy.

[27] These assertions ranged from the couple saying that they don't anthropomorphize their animals to defending Curious George as decidedly unmetaphorical. Jane Holtz Kay, "Curious George Lives Here," *Christian Science Monitor*, 9 May 1979, 15 and Elizabeth Mehren, "Monkey Business," *The Los Angeles Times*, 30 May 1996, https://www.latimes.com/archives/la-xpm-1996-05-30-ls-9779-story.html.

The assertions were not groundless. The misnomer "monkey" appears to have been a publicity-related convenience: the distinction between monkeys and apes would not have been widely familiar to readers in the United States at the time. However, the authors were also unmistakably aware of the differences, semantically absent though these were in either their native German or in French, the language of their first children's books. The accuracy of George's portrayals was thus no coincidence. The files allotted several folders to primate-related topics. Hans's zoo studies included a variety of clearly identifiable (albeit unlabeled) primates species – usually in motion – as well as a selection of extreme closeups, as was the case with the chimpanzees Mary, Congo, and Bobo, whom he drew in New York in 1948.[28] The collection of press clippings, interspersed with the sketches and Margret's photographs, swelled with news reports about behavioral primatology, private zoos, apes as war casualties, and animal acquisitions, to name a few examples.

In the news stories, "displaced animals" was an especially resonant theme. There is the Brookfield Zoo's baboon Mr. Moto, incongruously named for Hollywood's Japanese detective played by the German-Jewish exile Peter Lorre; visitors pelt him after the Pearl Harbor attack. There is Francis, the "German-speaking" orangutan from Tierpark Hagenbeck, who learns English faster than his caretakers can pick up German. Another striking example is the "displaced" phalanger, gifted to a "U.S. sailor by a New Guinea native for not having been shot."[29] Menace, in this case, is twofold and extends to the marsupial as much as the animal's Indigenous captor. One might, of course, read in these examples a not-too-subtle innuendo to the authors' first-hand experience of serial dislocation. But most obviously, they are evidence of zoos as quintessentially colonial institutions, predicated on the animals' cyclical uprooting that predates the artists' own migrations, both chosen and forced.

In addition, the key anatomical monkey-ape distinction, the tail, is quite prominently featured in the authors' work outside the *Curious George* series. A case in point is the manuscript of illustrated alphabet verse, *Pictionary* or *Nonsense ABCs* (c. 1941). The book was welcomed by the couple's friend and influential literary editor Ursula Nordstrom at Harper & Brothers but remained unpublished for

---

[28] Sketchbook and loose pages with pencil drawings of scenes in Washington Square Park, Greenwich Village, New York City, June 1948, DGRP, DG0812, 136/20.

[29] "Mr. Moto Lands behind the '8' Ball," source unknown, 13 January 1942; "Orangutan Has Learned English," source unknown, undated (circa 1945), 'Monkeys' file of clippings and pencil drawings and 'Gorillas, orangs, gibbons' file of clipping, DGRP, DG0812, 137/13–15. "Displaced Animals (Continued)," source unknown, undated (circa 1947), Rodents and sundry, DGRP, DG0812, 137/18.

unclear reasons. Possibly, H. A. Rey felt guilty about penning frivolities as the war raged on. Be that as it may, the mock-up aligned witty rhymes and drawings of undeniably anthropomorphic animals with the letters of the alphabet. On the page for the letter T, for example, a relaxed monkey is drawing a self-portrait with the tail on a thick sketchpad. Underneath, a slightly accented rhyme: "The monkey's Tail is prehensil [sic]: / He can use it to hold a pencil. / What an utterly useful utensil!"[30] The drawing documents both Rey's familiarity with simian anatomy and his terminological savvy in English. The misspelling of "prehensile," by contrast, betrays the recency of his arrival in the United States. In preparation for *Pictionary*, he maintained several German-English word lists with possible rhymes, idiomatic translations, and new animal names.[31]

The unused archive and advertising in Brazil

The Brazilian sketches, albeit stored in the same files, appear to have played no role in Reyersbach's further work, in Brazil or thereafter. This is not to say that during his eleven years in the country, he did not draw animals for commercial purposes. On the contrary, this is where animals became a linchpin of his artistic identity and a source of income to be sustained over decades to come. As early as 1933, a year before Margret's arrival, four samples of Hans's advertising designs appeared in the third issue of *base*, a new Brazilian review of the arts, technology, and ideas. Only one of these reproductions, a flyer for a bridge-tournament arts fundraiser, included no animal figures – unless one counts Reyersbach's signature, a heron atop a wave flowing over a capital letter "R," a pun on his name and the German word for "heron", as well as a reference to his physique and his receding hairline with a stray waft of hairs.[32] Among the three other designs, a promotion for a bridge tea party on 9 August 1933 pictured a set of card jacks decked out as knights on horseback, spears ready for a joust. A poster for Moinho Fluminense, a vast grain mill in Rio, featured cheerful donkeys rushing to deliver heavy flour sacks on their backs. And on a New Year's greeting card for 1933 – the annus horribilis for the future of Jews in Germany – two modernist armadillos, looking like line-graphed cylinders on four feet, gingerly

---

30 "Nonsense ABC / Nonsense Rhymes / Rhyming Pictionary," DGRP, DG0812, 81/3.
31 Handwritten word lists, DGRP, DG0812, 81/2.
32 "Obra de Hans Reyersbach," *base: revista de arte, técnica e pensamento* 1.3 (1933): 60–61, DGRP, DG0812, 124/9.

approached a pineapple. This dawning year, Reyersbach's choice of the animal seemed to foretell, would require more than just a thick skin.

Modernist sensibilities dictated not only the armadillos' amusing shapes. They saturated all four of Reyersbach's designs and manifested themselves in the black-and-white sparseness, in the dense yet uncluttered geometries of the layout, and in the fonts – variants of the popular Futura styles recently devised by the German graphic designer Paul Renner. These European markers, remote from the artistic rediscoveries of "Brazilianness" in the 1920s, characterized the more conservative, west-facing modernism of the 1930s.[33] Reyersbach's typographic decisions aligned closely with the editors', who opened the issue with a programmatic loyalty oath to all-lower-case Futura. Performatively, in the aforesaid typeface, they explained that their choice was no head-in-the-clouds futurist manifesto but an issue of material and labor economy. Modern times ostensibly called for modern measures to make not only aesthetic or political but also practical sense.

First arriving in Rio de Janeiro in January 1925, Hans did not immediately become swept up by the Brazilian Southeast's brisk modernist ascendancy, underway since the late 1910s.[34] Much less bohemian prospects awaited him initially. He was about to join a relative's export-import company as an assistant: merchant James Magnus, married to Hans's sister Luisa since 1920, had been doing business in Brazil since about 1903.[35] Quite simply, Hans needed money. Germany after World War I, he reflected in a later biographical sketch, "contrasted sharply with happy times of [his] youth": "inflation, no money, and no chance of going to art school."[36] Having graduated from the Wilhelm Gymnasium in 1916, Hans had ostensibly intended to study medicine in Munich. But by November 1916 the war draft had disrupted those plans. Returning from the war to find his "family fortunes in bad shape" left him adrift. Psychology, philosophy, languages: at the University of Hamburg he sampled wildly from a smorgasbord of disciplines, without completing a full course of study in any of them. Between 1921 and 1923, he "eked out" a living, designing a few circus posters for Central Europe's foremost lithographer, Adolph Friedländer (these were Hans's earliest extant depictions of animals in print), and illustrating Christian Morgenstern's *A Daylight Lamp and Other Poems* [*Zwölf Lithographien*

---

33 Icleia Maria Borsa Cattani, "Places of Modernism in Brazil," in *Brazil: Body and Soul*, ed. Edward J. Sullivan (New York: Guggenheim Museum Publications, 2001), 385.
34 NARA, Passenger and Crew List Vessels Arriving at New York, NY, 1897–1957, Microfilm T715, 1897–1957, Roll 3600, group 4, p. 123.
35 HSta, Hamburger Passagierlisten, Volume: 373–7 I, VIII A 1 Band 146, p. 2228, Microfilm No.: K_1781.
36 "The Life of H. A. Rey, Told by Himself in Chronological Order."

zu Chr. Morgensterns Grotesken] for publisher and school friend Kurt Enoch (1923), although it is unclear how lucrative either endeavor was.[37] Brazil was meant to remedy the dire financial situation, provide a direction, and, by way of a distance, mitigate the deleterious psychological aftereffects of World War I. There was no way of knowing that the New York stock market crash of 1929 would send economic and political shockwaves across this country, too.

That Hans was a university dropout without much business experience must not have perturbed his new brother-in-law, a fellow-Hamburger twenty-two years his senior. Traditionally, the city-state's merchant class, to which the middling Reyersbachs belonged, preferred having their offspring learn by doing, ideally overseas, to a formal university education. Brazil, on their mental maps, was far from far-flung. Hamburg elites had yearned for that country's raw materials and its labor since the days of Portuguese colonialism. For some, Brazil's proclamation of independence from Portugal in 1822 merely portended new Nordic dependences, so much so that a representative of Hamburg's Chamber of Commerce pompously welcomed the news by announcing, "Hamburg has now received colonies."[38]

The crude neocolonial spoils of which Magnus and through him, other family members, were partaking, did not entice the neophyte Hans. In his later autobiographical sketches, he would complain about having to compose commercial letters that he was not "allowed to adorn with illustrations" and to sell "bathtubs up and down the Amazon river," which, given the aggressive push of foreign and domestic industrial manufacturing and trade companies into Brazil's interior, may well have been more than a fabulist's fanciful flourish. "Obviously it was not the right road," he would later confess, "but it took me twelve years to find out."[39] However, there were more subtle ways in which a newcomer like Reyersbach could become a cogwheel in the neocolonial machine. The aforesaid 1933 special issue of *base*, dedicated to the arts of persuasion, his new profession, revealed that early on.

The magazine exploited the elastic semantics of the Portuguese word *propaganda*, which could also refer to advertising. Yet the political examples, including four Soviet posters and one fascist specimen from Italy, appeared mostly for

---

[37] Hans Reyersbach, *Zwölf Lithographien zu Chr. Morgensterns Grotesken* (Hamburg: Kurt Enoch, 1923), published in the United States as *The Daylight Lamp and Other Poems* (Boston: Houghton Mifflin, 1973). Roland Jäger speculates that the original printing of 400 copies sold well, resulting in a second, abridged printing in 1925. "Der Schöpfer von 'Curious George': Kinderbuch-Illustrator H. A. Rey," *Aus dem Antiquariat* 10 (1997): A 544.
[38] W. Manshard, "Effects and Consequences of the 'Age of Discovery' for Central Europe," *GeoJournal* 26.4 (1992): 493.
[39] "The Life of H. A. Rey, Told by Himself in Chronological Order."

contrast and were squeezed onto a single page. Otherwise, the focus was unabashedly commercial. The goal was to highlight the graphic artists working in Brazil, rather than the foreign imports, although these, by and large, were first- and second-generation Jewish immigrants.[40] This was significant, since Europeans and Americans were poised to dominate Brazil's entire advertising industry at the time. Reyersbach and his peers featured in *base*, Americo Rosenberg (better known as Erico), Gerhard Orthof, Franz Kohout, were no different.

The work of all four was sandwiched between two objects. One was a series of photographs of New York billboards; perhaps a flashback to Gilberto Freyre's ode to New York's "dress" of "illuminated advertisements," perhaps a testament to the Madison Avenue's tightening grip in and beyond Rio.[41] The other was a review of the Soviet film about youth reeducation, *Road to Life* [Путёвка в жизнь; dir. Nikolai Ekk, 1931]. Persuasion, a preface to the issue expounded, "educates man to a better standard of existence." Underneath, a black-and-white illustration by Hans depicted a two-legged rectangular, flat, and faceless creature, presumably a personified advertising poster with the word *propaganda* written across it.[42] This angular but agile being was deftly wrapping a bowler-hat-wearing banker type into a roll of paper. The token capitalist, eyes shut, screamed powerlessly into his chin and waved two dollar-filled sacks above his head, as though they could ransom him from the trap. According to the caption, this was how advertising wrapped its customers. But was this fact to be criticized as manipulative or to be praised as ingenious? Reyersbach's own stance remained opaque.

The drawing was the issue's only special commission, in addition to the two-page spread with Reyersbach's reproduced designs. Notably, his work was alone in picturing animals of any sort. All other artists focused on buildings and abstract human figures to peddle imported goods, from Odol toothpaste to Cinzano vermouth to Bayer's flu medication Grippe-Instantina, or Brazilian products such as Normandia orangeade or Orygam de Gally cosmetics, or services in transportation, hospitality, and gastronomy. Representing animals, by all appearances, was fast becoming Reyersbach's calling card, and his footprint

---

40 Art historians observe similar patterns in other art currents, such as constructivism. See Agnaldo Farias, "Apollo in the Tropics: Constructivist Art in Brazil," in *Brazil: Body and Soul*, 398.

41 Cited in James P. Woodard, *Brazil's Revolution in Commerce: Creating Consumer Capitalism in the American Century* (Durham: The University of North Carolina Press, 2020), 1. On the influence of the United States, see 6–7 and passim.

42 A. Xavier da Silva, "a arte e propaganda," *base: revista de arte, técnica e pensamento* 1.3 (1933): 49, DGRP, DG0812, 124/9.

in the issue was a benchmark of recognition. Within eight years of arrival – rather than twelve, as he suggested – he had carved a name for himself as a graphic artist, hitting upon a new line of income that married modernism with commercialism and garnished the whole with a sprinkling of *animalia brasiliana*.

In Brazil, as Flora Süssekind has argued with an eye to the literati, artistic dalliances with writing copy had produced a distinct "brand of intellectual" already by the 1920s.[43] Notorious cough syrup bards, these professionals embraced ornate commercialism, then imported the flourishes back into the belles lettres.[44] An example was Emílio de Meneses, who took the fusion as far as to anoint himself "Gabriel d'Anúncio," a pun on the name of Gabriele D'Annunzio and the word for "advertisement," *anúncio*.[45] The tendency was in step with the brisk advances of consumer capitalism. "Posters, sandwich men, throwaways, signboards, movie theater curtains" and especially advertising-covered electric trams were everywhere in Rio and São Paulo.[46] A stealth cultural elitist with ambitions that went beyond his interrupted education, Reyersbach and, upon her arrival in 1934, Margret, felt in their element.[47]

The almost-married Reyersbachs quickly established a joint reputation in the Southeast's network of advertisers and publishers, a remarkable feat for a couple in a near exclusively male profession. In August 1935, their work appeared in the São Paulo issue of "the modern life review," *Espelho*. He glorified the Paulist splendors with a detailed map of the province's riches. She, known primarily as a photographer, praised her Leica in a short feature. In September of that year, a double cameo – her photographs, his drawings – ran under the title "Under the Sun of Copacabana" ["Au sol de Copacabana"].[48] The playful photo-essay was all about the pleasures of the beach, the sun, the toned bodies, and, in a charming non-sequitur, the "beautiful soup" steaming on the table at the end of the day. "Beautiful parasols – it's true! But they hide so much . . . I would rather see the beauty that they hide," proclaimed a caption attributed to Margret. The mood was one of "tropical idyllism," to borrow from James Woodard, with a spotlight on the ostensibly harmonious and energizing mixing of

---

[43] Flora Süssekind, *Cinematograph of Words: Literature, Technique, and Modernization in Brazil*, trans. Paulo Henriques Britto (Palo Alto: Stanford University Press, 1997), 46.
[44] Süssekind, *Cinematograph of Words*, 38 and 41.
[45] Süssekind, *Cinematograph of Words*, 43.
[46] Süssekind, *Cinematograph of Words*, 45 and Maria Claudia Bonadio, "Consumerism and Advertising in 20th-Century Brazil," *Oxford Research Encyclopedia of Latin American History*, https://doi.org/10.1093/acrefore/9780199366439.013.831.
[47] Reyersbach became a Brazilian citizen on 23 April 1934 and married Margret on 21 December 1935.
[48] "Au sol de Copacabana," *Espelho*, September 1935, 35–37, DGRP, DG0812, 124/11.

races and body types that made Brazil famous.⁴⁹ Thinking of their relatives' missives from Germany ("the Nazis are growing wilder daily," Margret's brother Hans Waldstein wrote in August 1935), the couple seemed to embrace the stereotype unquestioningly.⁵⁰ Brazilian editors reciprocated. In brief introductions, they admired Hans's "brilliant irony" and his "gracious wit" as much as they trumpeted Margret's Bauhaus credentials and her expertise in advertising.⁵¹ Collectively, these commissions earned them about one thousand and fifty mil-réis, enough to cover two monthly apartment rent payments.

The couple's account ledger that Margret kept since September 1935 suggests that they were serious about the business.⁵² A desk, a typewriter, card stock, and immeasurable quantities of art supplies had to be procured in its service. The investments paid off: within months, the couple's income outweighed their expenses. Hans's drawing style, humorous and light, drew admirers almost instantly. Alas, the same relegated Margret to the less visible roles of a creative advisor and a business manager. Expertly, she handled commissions that were beginning to come in not only from Brazilian businesses but also from some of the biggest multinational corporation of the era: Nestlé and the pharmaceutical giant Hoffmann-La Roche, Inc.⁵³ These companies, as cultural historian Maria Claudia Bonadio has written, were in the process of breaking down the remaining Native and local chains of consumption, nutrition, and healing (promotions of medicines being especially abundant).⁵⁴ The advertising industry was these enterprises' right hand. And the financially precarious Reyersbachs, who in September 1935 earned only three mil-réis more than they spent – doing laundry or buying paper required triple as much – an instrument in it.

Foreseeably, Hans's advertisements for Hoffmann-La Roche's panaceas and cosmetics privileged human figures. Pets and "pests" – cats, dogs, mice –

---

49 Woodard, *Brazil's Revolution in Commerce*, 3.
50 Hans Waldstein to Margret Waldstein [Reyersbach], postcard, 5 August 1935, Correspondence and photograph for Hans Waldstein, DGRP, DG0812, 173/8.
51 "Os autores deante do *Espelho*," *Espelho*, August 1935, 5–6, DGRP, DG0812, 124/10.
52 Margret Rey, "Account book for advertising business, September 1935–September 1936," DGRP, DG0812, 124/8. The dates and sums of the commissions stem from this document, unless otherwise indicated.
53 This was not the couple's first experience working on a commission for a multinational company. In the early 1930s, Margret helped write copy for Unilever while working at Crawford's Reklame Agentur, a Berlin subsidiary of the British advertising firm W. S. Crawford. Ann Mulloy Ashmore, "Margret before Rey: The Early Life and Career of Margarete Elisabeth Waldstein, 1925–1935," *Journal of Historical Biography* 14 (Autumn 2013): 86–87.
54 Bonadio, "Consumerism and Advertising in 20ᵗʰ-Century Brazil."

were more at home in the artist's work for Nestlé. It is conspicuous how familiar these animals are, how free from any stamp of the place in and for which they were created, how transplantable from one culture or home into another – a good fit for a multinational corporation. A few of these creatures scamper across the pages of the free dessert recipe booklet that H. A. Rey finished by January 1936 for the payment of one thousand five hundred mil-réis, the last and most substantial of his four Nestlé commissions in 1935.[55] They are lured by the saccharine concoctions made with the company's iconic tinned milk and chocolate products on which every recipe inevitably hinges. The same bait, by extension, would entrap the booklet's target audience, "the Brazilian ladies." Reyersbach conjures this consumption-fueled interspecies tandem to create an illusion of the sugary delights' universal appeal and benefit. Over time, the illusion would abet the country's obesity epidemic.[56] The tandem's workings were simple. At the forefront were Hans's human figures, the elegant housewives and the starched-looking chefs proudly carrying the puddings, the cakes, the cookies, and the jellies to the table; occasionally they tripped for a humorous effect. The animals, ever ready to clean up the mishaps, lurked on the sidelines.

Brazilian companies, however, were interested in something quite different than the multinationals. Or else Reyersbach sought to anticipate their wishes with the designs that Nestlé and its ilk would have found unpalatable. The genesis of these advertisements is difficult to reconstruct with certainty due to the gaps in documentation, but the designs tend to be quite eloquent. While working on the serial projects for *Elspelho* and Nestlé in 1935, Reyersbach was also busy with several other sets of narrative single-page or multi-page advertisements. Three were for the insecticide manufacturer Dr. Blem & Cia., Ltd., and one, for the Perfumery Myrta S/A. The products may appear dissimilar, but Hans's storytelling – the advertisements are his unsung animal-story debuts – approximates them through the uses of animal imagery. In none do the creatures play second fiddle to humans, as they did in the booklet for Nestlé. And in all, they are Brazilian species with rich significance in Native folklore: the anteater and the armadillo.

---

[55] *Livros de receitas Nestlé*, undated, publisher unknown, DGRP, DG0812, 124/6. Other Nestlé commissions from this year do not appear to have survived in the authors' archive. Reyersbach retained his connections with Nestlé Brazil in the years to come and met with the company's influential representative and future CEO Oswaldo Ballarin on 29 August 1940, upon returning to Rio. "H. A. Rey's annual journals," 1940, DGRP, DG0812, 166/5.

[56] Andrew Jacobs and Matt Richtel, "How Big Business Got Brazil Hooked on Junk Food," *The New York Times*, 16 September 2017, https://www.nytimes.com/interactive/2017/09/16/health/brazil-obesity-nestle.html.

This said, the genres differ. The booklet for Myrta is a classic piece of rhymed and illustrated didacticism with therianthropy (shapeshifting) as the looming punishment for disobedience.[57] The title, *The Story of a Boy who Became an Anteater* [*História do menino que verou tamanduá*] gives away the gist readily. Against his mother's admonitions, an otherwise nice little boy neglects to brush his teeth with Eucalol toothpaste.[58] Days pass, and on a stroll through the forest he runs into a group of anteaters, notably toothless animals. They intimate that they, too, had once neglected to take care of their teeth, with obvious outcomes. Within seconds, the terrified boy turns into a "cold, dizzy, and dumb" anteater, condemned to preying on "ticks, flies, ants, termites" while a tasty dinner at home goes uneaten and parents panic. A search and rescue mission brings no result. Only the anteater-boy's sincere contrition can restore him to human form, by summoning an anthropomorphized tube of toothbrush-wielding Eucalol. But not only the child is born again. On the pamphlet's last page, an actual anteater, too, embraces Eucalol in every consistency – be it talcum, soap, or powder.

In the promotions for Dr. Blem, a pest control manufacturer, martial tones prevail. Two out of three are thinly veiled war stories for adults. They mark no radical rupture with the work for Myrta, however. Well into the late 1930s, Reyersbach toggles with ease between the child and adult audiences, aiming to satisfy both. The militant subtext speaks to the entrenched scientific and metaphorical interdependencies between combat and pest control – since World War I, propagandists and scientists habitually imagined war as pest control, and nature, as a battlefield.[59] Yet the designs may also reflect, and possibly displace, Hans's own unexpressed combat memories. No creature better embodies war than the armadillo, a known ant- and termite-scavenger suited in proverbial armor. Still, the choice is not Reyersbach's creative license. The animal – *tatú*, in Portuguese – is the company's mascot, imprinted on every tin.[60]

Reyersbach takes this abstract emblem, first individualizes it, then turns it into a multitude. The series for the ant poison "Comet Tatú" ["Cometa Tatú"] starts with a single armadillo, Dr. Blem's companion. It ends with dozens marching in a tin-drumming, spade-wielding battalion. On behalf of the porcelain-skinned,

---

[57] "História do menino que verou tamandua." Booklet for Eucalol toothpaste, DGRP, DG0812, 124/7.
[58] I have outlined the book's hygienic dimension in the settler-colonial context in "Toothless in Brazil," *The Hypocrite Reader* 98 (July 2021), https://hypocritereader.com/98/toothless-in-brazil.
[59] Edmund P. Russell, "'Speaking of Annihilation': Mobilizing for War Against Human and Insect Enemies, 1914–1945," *The Journal of American History* 82.4 (1996): 1510.
[60] Sequence of 3 promotional flyers for Cometa Tatú, an ant poison, DGRP, DG0812, 122/3.

ruddy-cheeked, bespectacled, boater-hat-wearing, impeccably turned out, and decidedly civilian Dr. Blem (indistinguishable from those days' token capitalist caricature), this army readies to wage war on the insolent insect aggressors. The cause is the ants' attack on the tree kingdom and their rejection of a peace treaty. Earlier, the tree kingdom's delegates, disheveled, distressed, and with visibly downturned mouth corners, storm into Tatú and Dr. Blem's quarters, evoking real-life refugees.

In an even bolder plot concocted for the same product, Dr. Blem and Tatú meet as military volunteers packing bags to fight yet another ant attack.[61] Following the armadillo's expert reading of a warzone map, accomplished in front of a proper campaign chair and to the sound of the company's martial *propaganda* blaring from a gramophone, their combat plan unfolds into a sequence of a World War I–inspired maneuvers, transported to Brazilian soil. The duo drives tanks and flies a bomber plane over the terrified ant populations, dropping cans of poison in an uncanny echo of the war that Reyersbach had witnessed seventeen years earlier. Throughout, Tatú walks on hind legs and gesticulates with a passion, much like Hans's anteaters do, while Dr. Blem responds enthusiastically.

The tension between the armadillo as a Brazilian Indigene and an agent of nature-managerial neocolonialism reaches its apogee in "A History of Créo-Tatú" ["A história de Créo-Tatú"], meant to advertise Dr. Blem's eponymous antibacterial farm animal treatment.[62] Here, the undercurrent is clinical rather than martial, although the goal remains the same: the subjugation of nature in the interest of settler agriculture. In the opening, Tatú walks in on an anguished bovine friend, who is drowning his insect-caused sorrow in liquor, and decides to help. It takes going to the Amazon and falling into the river as he watches the Native people fish with the toxic timbo plant. The accident is salubrious. Tatú comes out of the water parasite-free, thanks to the workings of timbo, and sets his sights developing a water-soluble animal pest cure.[63] His eureka moment prompts a journey to a British laboratory, where a similar formula has already been tried. Having learned from the Empire, Tatú returns to Brazil, heals the

---

61 Sequence of 6 promotional flyers for Cometa Tatú, an ant poison, DGRP, DG0812, 122/2.
62 "A história de Créo-Tatú." A sequence of 9 promotional flyers for ant poison, DGRP, DG0812, 122/1.
63 At the same time, Native uses of timbo and similar plants became of interest to the United States officials. See R. C. Roark, *Lonchocarpus (Barbasco, Cube, and Timbo): A Review of Recent Literature* (Washington, DC: United States Department of Agriculture/Bureau of Entomology and Plant Quarantine, 1938), https://ufdc.ufl.edu/AA00022944/00001/3j.

farm animals, and founds an "Armadillo Academy," streamlining the expertise and the production alike.

The story encapsulates the gist of how Reyersbach used both the anteater and the armadillo: by relying on a few essential facts about each species without granting full animality or full indigeneity to either. It is unsurprising that no live sketches of either animal survive. From the start, the creatures materialize as figments of Hans's imagination. Their roles in local cultures, Native or not – for the Mundurucu in the Amazon basin, the armadillo is the creator god's constant companion, while some cattle breeders in São Roque de Minas hold that the anteater can bring bad luck, asphyxiate the adversary, and never be male – remain extrinsic to the advertisements.[64]

Coda

Compared to the rest of Reyersbach's Brazilian oeuvre, the live sketches on lined paper are outliers. By all appearances, Hans probably did not sketch the animal protagonists of his advertisements, opting for a cartoonish style instead. And conversely, the animals whom he did sketch live do not re-appear in his commercial (or any other) work. If anything, his pencil drawings of Brazilian animals most closely resemble his pencil drawings of Brazilian vegetation. These were executed around October 1930 and also left manifestly unused: mangosteen, kapok, yucca, and palm trees, among them.[65] He drew the plants on plain (rather than lined) paper, with bursts of colorful pencilwork occasionally illuminating the stern black-and-white scheme. On these occasions, presumably, he had his drawing materials ready. Besides, the greenery was unlikely to scamper away and disappear in a blink of an eye, affording access to such visual details as color, pattern, or texture. This distinction aside, both sets share the vestiges of Linnean nomenclature and the extensive if haphazard annotations: "Slim long leaves, part dark green with a smooth yellow mid-rib, part black-brown with carmine," one botanical caption reads, "Stem gray, birch-like with whitish and blackish spots." A deracinated transplant uncertain about his status,

---

64 Angus K. Gillespie, "The Armadillo," in *American Wildlife in Symbol and Story*, eds. Angus K. Gillespie and Jay Mechling (Knoxville, TN: University of Tennessee Press, 1987), 110 and Alessandra Bertassoni, "Perception and Popular Reports about Giant Anteaters (*Myrmecophaga tridactyla* Linneus, 1785) by two Brazilian Traditional Communities," *Edentata* 13 (2012): 10–17.
65 Pencil and color pencil drawings of vegetation with clipping, DGRP, DG0812, 137/22.

Hans may have deployed the Latin names as well as analogies to the familiar species (e.g., the birch) to conjure a modicum of control.

As a chronotope, the early sketches also stand apart from the more canonical immigrant Jewish artists' depictions of animals. Painter Marc Chagall, for example, transformed farm animals into a nostalgic shorthand for rootedness "in a land far off."[66] Chaim Soutine's pig portraits, painted while he was in hiding from the Nazis, mystify with polysemous "iconic metaphors" and innuendos that range from religious taboos to sexual aversion.[67] Reyersbach's Brazilian paca, agouti, and others, however, appear to be neither *lieux de mémoire* nor enigmatic ciphers. They are a trace of how the artist experienced his present, in part by directing his attention to a rather unspectacular array of Brazil's mammals. Most of them are humble rodents, except the sloth. The drawings seem devoid of any introjections of reflection, self-identification, reminiscence, or desire. They are also free from the cumbersome references to nature's opposite – "civilization" – and from abstractions like *Getier* (the collective singular noun for "animals"), with which another Germanophone Jewish exile, Stefan Zweig, peppered his *Brazil: A Land of the Future* (1941).

They are ambiguous artifacts. On the one hand, they attest to Reyersbach's refusal to sequester himself on Rio's immigrant island, with its European-style cafés, cinemas, shops, and refurbished boulevards, with its studiously cosmopolitan comforts. Instead, he seems to recognize nature as a fundamental constituent of this new place – a place with more than just a social reality – and uses his pencil to express curiosity about it. On the other hand, curiosity in colonial settings is hardly an innocent notion. Writing about the art of Maria Sybilla Merian, historian of science Tomomi Kunikawa distinguishes between a personal inquisitiveness and an investigative disposition. When curiosity coincides with the inquisitive disposition, Kunikawa argues, it can fuel an entire "ideological apparatus that Europeans constructed to promote and justify European colonization of knowledge and resources depletion." Within it, nature art is both a coveted commodity and an epistemic vehicle.[68] In Brazil, this tradition is deep-seated, reaching as far back as the mid-seventeenth century. At the time,

---

[66] Allyn Weisstein, "Iconography of Chagall," *Kenyon Review* 16.4 (1954): 45–46. Hazel Frankel, "Home and the Holocaust in Selected Paintings of Marc Chagall and Yiddish Poems of David Fram," *Soundings: An Interdisciplinary Journal*, 101.4 (2018): 345–346.

[67] Avigdor G. W. Posèq, "Soutine's Two Paintings of Pigs," *Notes in the History of Art* 14.2 (1995): 38–46.

[68] Tomomi Kunikawa, "Science and Whiteness as Property in the Dutch Atlantic World: Maria Sybilla Merian's *Metamorphosis Insectorum Surinamensium* (1705)," *Journal of Women's History* 24. 3 (2012): 102 and 106.

Albert Eckhout and Frans Post painted carefully constructed and highly realistic paintings of people, landscapes, plants, and animals, offering "a view of a beautiful, fertile, well-ordered, and conquered Brazil" that both pleased the Dutch colony's governor-general and simulated the extent of his access to the country's deepest depths.[69] It is also, however, obvious that Reyersbach's drawings were rather the opposite of this kind of curiosity. In contrast to his advertisements, they remained private documents well outside his commercial entanglements. They lacked the polish of either the naturalist or the artist. Perhaps, the curiosity that the sketches document prefigures the model of curiosity that Hans and Margret would later develop in the Curious George's series, where they would envision and over the years contend with the aesthetics and ethics of animal capture and captivity. This model would be predicated on frequently irrational and deeply personal impulses and outbursts that, from story to story, generate no orderly system of knowledges, championing, instead, cycles of learning and unlearning.

Works cited

Amato, Sarah. *Beastly Possessions: Animals in Victorian Consumer Culture* (Toronto: University of Toronto Press, 2015).

Ames, Eric. *Carl Hagenbeck's Empire of Entertainments* (Seattle: University of Washington Press, 2009).

Anderson, Marla V. and Antonia J. Z. Henderson. "Pernicious Portrayals: The Impact of Children's Attachment to Animals of Fiction on Animals of Fact," *Society and Animals* 13.4 (2005): 297–314.

Ashmore, Ann Mulloy. "Margret before Rey: The Early Life and Career of Margarete Elisabeth Waldstein, 1925–1935," *Journal of Historical Biography* 14 (Autumn 2013): 73–101.

Barzilai, Maya. *Golem: Modern Wars and Their Monsters* (New York: New York University Press, 2016).

Benjamin, Andrew. *Of Jews and Animals* (Edinburgh: Edinburgh University Press, 2010).

Bertassoni, Alessandra. "Perception and Popular Reports about Giant Anteaters (*Myrmecophaga tridactyla* Linneus, 1785) by two Brazilian Traditional Communities," *Edentata* 13 (2012): 10–17.

Bisceglio, Paul. "Are Picture Books Warping How Kids Understand Animals?," *Pacific Standard Magazine*, 27 March, 2014. https://psmag.com/social-justice/picture-books-warping-kids-understand-animals-77550.

Bonadio, Maria Claudia. "Consumerism and Advertising in 20th-Century Brazil," in *Oxford Research Encyclopedia of Latin American History*, doi.org/10.1093/acrefore/9780199366439.013.831.

---

[69] Rebecca Parker Brienen, "Albert Eckhout and Frans Post: Two Dutch Artists in Colonial Brazil," in *Brazil: Body and Soul*, 63.

Cantor, Judith Levin. *Jews in Michigan* (East Lansing, MI: Michigan State University Press, 2001).

Farias, Agnaldo. "Apollo in the Tropics: Constructivist Art in Brazil," in *Brazil: Body and Soul*. Ed. Edward J. Sullivan (New York: Guggenheim Museum Publications, 2001), 398–405.

Frankel, Hazel. "Home and the Holocaust in Selected Paintings of Marc Chagall and Yiddish Poems of David Fram," *Soundings: An Interdisciplinary Journal*, 101.4 (2018): 341–359.

Geller, Jay. *Bestiarium Judaicum: Unnatural Histories of the Jews* (New York: Fordham University Press, 2017).

Gillespie, Angus K. "The Armadillo," in *American Wildlife in Symbol and Story*. Eds. Angus K. Gillespie and Jay Mechling (Knoxville, TN: University of Tennessee Press, 1987), 99–132.

Cattani, Icleia Maria Borsa. "Places of Modernism in Brazil," in *Brazil: Body and Soul*. Ed. Edward J. Sullivan (New York: Guggenheim Museum Publications, 2001), 380–387.

Imhoff, Sarah. *Masculinity and the Making of American Judaism* (Bloomington, IN: Indiana University Press, 2017).

Jacobs, Andrew and Matt Richtel. "How Big Business Got Brazil Hooked on Junk Food," *The New York Times*, 16 September 2017. https://www.nytimes.com/interactive/2017/09/16/health/brazil-obesity-nestle.html.

Jäger, Roland. "Der Schöpfer von 'Curious George': Kinderbuch-Illustrator H. A. Rey," *Aus dem Antiquariat* 10 (1997): A 543–A 451.

Katz, Ethan B., Lisa Moses Leff, and Maud S. Mandel. "Introduction: Engaging Colonial History and Jewish History," in *Colonialism and the Jews*. Eds. Ethan B. Katz, Lisa Moses Leff, and Maud S. Mandel (Bloomington, IN: Indiana University Press, 2017), 1–25.

Kellman, Steven G. "Jews, Beasts, and Americans," *Studies in American Jewish Literature* 5 (1986): 61–68.

Koffman, David S. *The Jews' Indian: Colonialism, Pluralism, and Belonging in America* (New Brunswick, NJ: Rutgers University Press, 2019).

Komska, Yuliya. "Why Curious George Could Not Speak: The Conspicuous Multilingualism of Margret and H. A. Rey," *The German Studies Review* 43.3 (2018): 505–528.

Kunikawa, Tomomi. "Science and Whiteness as Property in the Dutch Atlantic World: Maria Sybilla Merian's *Metamorphosis Insectorum Surinamensium* (1705)," *Journal of Women's History* 24.3 (2012): 91–116.

Lear, Linda. *Beatrix Potter: A Life in Nature* (New York: St. Martin's Griffin, 2016).

Lovell-Smith, Rose. "The Animals of Wonderland: Tenniel as Carroll's Reader," *Criticism* 45.4 (2005): 383–415.

Malamud, Bernard. "The Refugee," *The Saturday Evening Post*, 14 September 1963. 38–43.

Manshard, W. "Effects and Consequences of the 'Age of Discovery' for Central Europe," *GeoJournal* 26.4 (1992): 489–495.

Ornish, Natalie and Sara Alpern. *Pioneer Jewish Texans* (Austin, TX: Texas A&M University Press, 2011).

Parker Brienen, Rebecca. "Albert Eckhout and Frans Post: Two Dutch Artists in Colonial Brazil," in *Brazil: Body and Soul*. Ed. Edward J. Sullivan (New York: Guggenheim Museum Publications, 2001), 62–75.

Posèq, Avigdor G. W. "Soutine's Two Paintings of Pigs," *Notes in the History of Art* 14.2 (1995): 38–46.

Reichenbach, Herman. "A Tale of Two Zoos: The Hamburg Zoological Garden and Carl Hagenbeck's Tierpark," in *New Worlds, New Animals: From Menagerie to Zoological Park in the Nineteenth Century*. Eds. Robert J. Hoage and William A. Deiss (Baltimore: Johns Hopkins University Press, 1996), 51–62.

Rothfels, Nigel. *Savages and Beasts: The Birth of the Modern Zoo* (Baltimore: Johns Hopkins University Press, 2002).

Russell, Edmund P. "'Speaking of Annihilation': Mobilizing for War Against Human and Insect Enemies, 1914–1945," *The Journal of American History* 82.4 (1996): 1505–1529.

Shyovitz, David I. *A Remembrance of His Wonders: Nature and the Supernatural in Medieval Ashkenaz* (Philadelphia: University of Pennsylvania Press, 2017).

Spinner, Samuel J. "Plausible Primitives: Kafka and Jewish Primitivism," *The German Quartlerly* 89.1 (2016): 17–35.

Süssekind, Flora. *Cinematograph of Words: Literature, Technique, and Modernization in Brazil*. Trans. Paulo Henriques Britto (Palo Alto: Stanford University Press, 1997).

Wasserman, Mira Beth. *Jews, Gentiles, and Other Animals: The Talmud after the Humanities* (Philadelphia: University of Pennsylvania Press, 2017).

Weisstein, Allyn. "Iconography of Chagall," *Kenyon Review* 16.4 (1954): 38–48.

Woodard, James P. *Brazil's Revolution in Commerce: Creating Consumer Capitalism in the American Century* (Durham: The University of North Carolina Press, 2020).

Narratological Itineraries

Claudia Breger
Belonging in the Folds of Fact and Fabulation: Fictionality, Narration, and *Heimat* in Saša Stanišić's *Herkunft*

Introduction

"*Heimat*," Saša Stanišić spells out in an interview at the occasion of his 2019 *Herkunft* [Where You Come From], for which he was awarded the annual German Book Award, "is a structurally regressive, usually repressive and antiemancipatory concept, since it is defined by way of delineating an external You from an internal We."[1] The notion doesn't translate easily: it roughly means home and homeland, with an emphasis on the local or regional and the emphatic affects of communal belonging more than abstract citizenship, as well as a history of association with nationalist and fascist mythologies.[2] In the past few years, *Heimat* has seen a controversial revival in German politics. Widely deployed by rightwing movements including Pegida (Patriotic Europeans against the Islamization of the Occident) and AfD (Alternative for Germany), the concept was catapulted into the political spotlight in 2018, when newly appointed federal minister Horst Seehofer decided to rename his domain as that of "the Interior, Building and Community [*Heimat*]."[3] Critical responses to these relegitimizations of a term historically charged "with myths of national unity, traditional gender roles and 'natural' hierarchies" have included the call to "De-Heimatize Belonging" along with attempts to reclaim *Heimat* for more inclusive projects.[4] In early

---

1 "Heimat ist ein strukturell regressiver, meist repressiver und antiemanzipatorischer Begriff, da er sich über die Abgrenzung eines äußeren Ihr von einem inneren Wir definiert" ("Saša Stanišić im Interview: 'Heimat ist ein Fantasiekonstrukt.'" Interview by Ulrich Thiele. *Szene Hamburg* [no date], https://szene-hamburg.com/sasa-stanisic-im-interview-heimat-ist-ein-fantasiekonstrukt/). All translations from the German are my own, unless otherwise noted.
2 See, e.g., Gisela Ecker ed., *Kein Land in Sicht: Heimat – weiblich?* (Munich: Wilhelm Fink, 1997).
3 See Daniel Schreiber, "Deutschland soll werden, wie es nie war," *Zeit online*, 2 October 2018 (https://www.zeit.de/kultur/2018-02/heimatministerium-heimat-rechtspopulismus-begriff-kulturgeschichte/komplettansicht).
4 The "De-Heimatize Belonging" conference was put on by the Maxim Gorki Theater in fall 2019 (I quote the critical summary of the terms' meanings from their website: https://www.gorki.de/en/de-heimatize-belonging-konferenz). On the resignification attempts, see Annika Orich, "Archival Resistance: Reading the New Right," *German Politics and Society* 38.2 (2020): 1–34, here 12–13, 16–17.

https://doi.org/10.1515/9783110778922-010

2020, for example, Federal President Frank-Walter Steinmeier suggested that the ("very German") term might be spelled in different ways today, including *Haymat* per its adoption by Turkish German artists and journalists.[5]

Stanišić's *Herkunft* (the title notion translates as "origin," "source," "family background," "ancestry," and more) makes a more layered contribution to this debate than perhaps indicated by the author's swift critical analysis of the *Heimat* concept. One of the most renowned voices in the field of contemporary German literatures of migration, Stanišić has imaginatively explored questions of collective identity and affective belonging across contexts. His 2006 debut novel *Wie der Soldat das Grammofon repariert* [*How the Soldier Repairs the Gramophone*] tells of emigration in the wake of the Bosnian War, while the 2014 *Vor dem Fest* [*Before the Feast*] is set in the East German provinces and has been discussed as part of a new genre of contemporary German "Heimat" literature.[6] Against the backdrop of these earlier texts, *Herkunft* has been marketed and read, including by the author himself, as a shift onto more – respectively more solidly – autobiographical and documentary terrain. Missing the earlier texts' categorization as "a novel," *Herkunft*'s authorial "I" makes a different "pact" with the reader than the thematically resonant 2006 debut, which – in the author's retrospective analysis – had erected "protective shields" between himself and the semi-autobiographical first person narrator Aleksandar.[7] *Herkunft* in part also draws on Stanišić's 2017 Zurich poetology lectures and might be categorized as a memoir with reflexive, essayistic elements, or as an extensive essay probing approaches to autobiographical writing.[8]

---

5 Orich, "Archival Resistance," 17.
6 See, e.g., Philipp Böttcher, "Fürstenfelde erzählt: Dörflichkeit und narrative Verfahren in Saša Stanišić's 'Vor dem Fest,'" *Zeitschrift für Germanistik* 30 (2020): 306–325. See also Katrina Nousek's contribution to this volume on *Vor dem Fest*. Interestingly, Stanišić reports that he first conceived the idea for *Vor dem Fest* in relation to the village that now features prominently in *Herkunft*. See "Was erzählte uns ein Fuchs über uns, über die Stadt und das Dorf?" "Saša Stanišić im Gespräch mit Alexander Gumz und Katrin Schumacher," in *Über Land: Aktuelle literatur- und kulturwissenschaftliche Perspektiven auf Dorf und Ländlichkeit*, eds. Magdalena Marszalek, Werner Nell, and Marc Weiland (Transcript: Bielefeld, 2018), 27–35, here 27.
7 Saša Stanišić, "'Manche Dinge würde ich lieber vergessen,' Interview by Karin Janker," *Süddeutsche Zeitung* [no date given]; https://www.goethe.de/ins/in/de/kultur/lw/soc/sst/21635544.html. The notion of the "autobiographical pact" is Philippe Lejeune's: "Le pacte autobiographique (bis)," in *Moi aussi. Collection Poétique* (Paris: Seuil, 1986), 13–36.
8 On the poetology lectures, see Karin Janker, "Zürcher Poetikvorlesung: Wie Saša Stanišić seine Heimat erfindet," *Süddeutsche* (13 November 2017). Marjorie Worthington defines the "memoir" in contrast to "autofiction" as "referential or mostly so," while acknowledging that the "distinction" is "difficult to maintain" in a historical moment in which "conceptions of life writing have evolved to also include more creative and, often, fictional elements" ("Fiction in

What interests me most about this shift in genre, however, is how *Herkunft* does not leave fictionality behind, but continues to deftly probe the means of invention, myth making and fantasy.[9] To be sure, the presence of fictionality also in non-fictional genres is arguably structural and certainly "ubiquitous in our culture."[10] Ilja Trojanow's thematically resonant *Nach der Flucht* [After the Flight, 2017], for example, carries the explicit subtitle "an autobiographical essay," but features various elements of fictive discourse.[11] In part facilitated by intertextual references to works of art and literature, these elements range from small dramatic dialogues to the ways in which the figure of the "refugee" (*Geflüchteter*) or also "stranger/foreigner" (*Fremder*) becomes a quasi-character evoked in more or less typical situations.[12] Comparing Trojanow's essay to *Herkunft*, however, also showcases the particular significance of fictionality for Stanišić's project.[13] Despite its familial "kernel," the author himself reports, *Herkunft* "in the end transforms" memories into stories, family members into (full-fledged) "characters."[14] *Herkunft*'s uses of fictionality are both local and larger-scale. They take on thematic prominence in the author's poetological reflections and,

---

the 'Post-Truth' Era: The Ironic Effects of Autofiction," *Critique: Studies in Contemporary Fiction* 58.5 (2017): 471–83, here 472; with reference to Gerard Genette's definition of autofiction). The distinction then is one of degree, and to me ultimately less interesting than a closer investigation of fictionality's workings in specific texts and contexts.

9 Alternatively, we could then characterize the text as autofiction after all, perhaps less by Genette's definition, but Serge Doubrovsky's ("fiction, of strictly real events and facts"), who has inspired uses of the category to emphasize fictional, imaginary and/or fantastic elements in autobiographical writing. See Yvonne Delhey, Rolf Parr, and Kerstin Wilhelms, "Autofiktion als Utopie: Zur Einleitung," in *Autofiktion als Utopie/Autofiction as Utopia*, eds. Yvonne Delhey, Rolf Parr, and Kerstin Wilhelms (Paderborn: Fink, 2019), 1–8, here 2.
10 Henrik Skov Nielsen, James Phelan and Richard Walsh, "Ten Theses about Fictionality," *Narrative* 23.1 (2015): 61–73, here 62.
11 Ilja Trojanow, *Nach der Flucht* (Frankfurt am Main: Fischer, 2017).
12 Trojanow's book features an advance note acknowledging inspiration by Jacob Lawrence's "The Migration Series" and an appendix specifying references ranging from Mahmud Darwisch to Ralph Ellison (Frankfurt am Main: Fischer, 2017), 7. The small dramatic dialogues ("Dramolett[e]," first 20) are in part adapted from a range of sources.
13 A more general comparison between Stanišić and Trojanow was made as early as 2008 as one between "Weltensammler" (Trojanow) and "Welterfinder" (Stanišić). See Špela Virant, "Der Weltensammler und der Welterfinder: Zu *Der Weltensammler* von Ilja Trojanow und *Wie der Soldat das Grammofon repariert* von Saša Stanišić," *Pismo – Časopis za jezik i književnost* 6 (2008): 286–296 (https://www.ceeol.com/search/article-detail?id=185188).
14 "Saša Stanišić spricht über sein Buch 'Herkunft'" (video interview), *Youtube*, https://www.youtube.com/watch?v=dwocYKZhDqY.

as I propose in this chapter, specifically include practices of *fabulation*.[15] On the most straightforward level of autobiographical narration, *Herkunft*'s authorial protagonist deploys such fabulation as a "pragmatic filler" for the memory gaps of his maternal grandmother, who is struggling with dementia.[16] Beyond this specific context, however, I show how Stanišić explores fabulation to generate "a steadfast home within crisis": fabulation functions as "one of the most important pillars" of his origin/background.[17]

In a nutshell, my chapter then proposes that *Herkunft* explores the affordances, and potentiality, of critically imaginative fabulation for a reparative project of creating belonging against the explicit backdrop of Stanišić's critical awareness of the exclusionary, often deadly workings of hegemonic fictions of collective identity.[18] Importantly, this fabulatory project does not operate in the mode of blatant disregard for reality that characterizes today's right-wing deployments of post-factuality. When Stanišić's German Book Award was announced in the immediate aftermath of Peter Handke's controversial Nobel Prize, critics underlined that Stanišić's literature commits to creating worlds that, "transferred to reality," do not become "clownish lies" (*plump[e] Lüge*).[19] As I detail in the following, Stanišić's commitment to a notion of truth and the creation of worlds "full of reality" (*realitätsgesättigt*) does, however, not require that his work – as they also worded rather defensively – remains "barely fictionalized."[20] Imaginatively defying this zero-sum premise, *Herkunft*'s fabulatory project makes creative – while ethical – use of fiction's hypothetical or conditional (*as if*) mode, even as it complicates delineations between different modes of speech in a complex field of memory and fantasy shaped by asymmetrical power structures and legacies of historical violence. In this way, *Herkunft*

---

15 As detailed below, my use of this concept adapts Saidiya Hartman's and Tavia Nyong'o's work on "critical fabulation" and "Afro-fabulation" respectively. See Saidiya Hartman, "Venus in Two Acts," in *Small Axe* 26 (2008): 1–14; Tavia Nyong'o, *Afro-Fabulations: The Queer Drama of Black Life* (New York: New York University Press, 2019).
16 "Saša Stanišić im Interview: 'Heimat ist . . .'"
17 Stanišić uses the (per my conceptualization below, more general) notion of "fiction" here: fiction creates an "unerschütterliches Zuhause in der Krise" and forms "eine der wichtigsten Säulen meiner Herkunft" ("Saša Stanišić im Interview: Heimat ist . . .").
18 On the reparative, see Eve Kosofsky Sedgwick, *Touching Feeling: Affect, Pedagogy, Performativity* (Durham: Duke University Press, 2003), and below for detail.
19 Mely Kiyak, as quoted in Steffen Hendel's summary of the debate, "'Das soll Literatur eigentlich nicht.' Die Debatte um Wesen und Wert der Literatur anlässlich der Preisvergaben an Peter Handke, Saša Stanišić und Olga Tokarczuk 2019," in *undercurrents: Forum für linke Literaturwissenschaft* (Frühjahr 2020): 1–21.
20 Hendel, "Das soll Literatur," 7–8 (quoting Andreas Platthaus and Marie Schmidt).

answers Leslie A. Adelson's forceful call for the future of literary studies: against the backdrop of violence and loss, Stanišić's text explores the potential of the "literary imagination" towards cultivating "new forms of social practice."[21]

Invention in the folds of the real: Fiction and fabulation

My thesis clearly needs unpacking. In this section, I begin by engaging recent narratological discussions around fictionality towards delineating a fuller understanding of how fictionality operates within larger surrounding lifeworlds and delineate the contours of fabulation (as a particular practice of fictionality) starting from Stanišić's own mapping of the relations between fiction and truth. In "Ten Theses about Fictionality," Henrik (Skov, now Zetterberg-)Nielsen, James Phelan, and Richard Walsh analyze "fictionality" – or the mode of "fictive discourse" – as "a specific communicative strategy" across genres, which operates within an "actual world" context.[22] Specifically, fictive discourse "invites the reader or listener to imagine something."[23] It attains its rhetorical contours in contrast to acts of "lying," which "deceive" audiences in that they "are designed to be taken as referring to actual states of affairs," whereas fictive discourse asks "What if?" in a hypothetical, counterfactual, or speculative way.[24] For Nielsen, Phelan, and Walsh, reading discourse as fictive therefore entails assuming "that it is not making referential claims, and that its relevance is indirect rather than direct."[25] This delineation prompted theoretical pushback: in positioning fictionality as a "rhetorical resource" rather than an "ontological category," Paul Dawson charged, Nielsen, Phelan and Walsh seek "to bypass" questions of referentiality and truth altogether.[26] As I have argued previously

---

[21] Leslie A. Adelson, "Literary Imagination and the Future of Literary Studies," *DVjs* 89.4 (2015): 675–82; with reference to Appadurai's work on imagination as a creative force more generally.
[22] Nielsen, Phelan, and Walsh, "Ten Theses," 62. More precisely, they define fictional*ity* as a "quality," 62.
[23] Nielsen, Phelan, and Walsh, "Ten Theses," 64.
[24] Nielsen, Phelan, and Walsh, "Ten Theses," 63–64.
[25] Nielsen, Phelan, and Walsh, "Ten Theses," 68.
[26] Paul Dawson, "Ten Theses Against Fictionality," *Narrative* 23.1 (2015): 74–100, here 82. Dawson cites Walsh's earlier *The Rhetoric of Fictionality* here but Nielsen, Phelan, and Walsh confirm this distinction in their response ("Fictionality as Rhetoric: A Response to Paul Dawson," *Narrative* 23.1 (2015): 101–111, here 103).

myself, this accusation does not do justice to the spirit of Nielsen, Phelan, and Walsh's insistence on fictionality's non-lying engagement with the real world, but it does entail a challenge to describe referentiality's contributions to fictive discourse in more positive terms, towards more fully grounding it within and against the backdrop of the real.[27]

Different from factual discourse by degree rather than ontological status, I hold, fictive discourse does not operate "non-referentially" but through a *more piecemeal* process of *productive* reference.[28] The backdrop to this argument includes the understanding that the "real" of scientific or documentary discourse is, as Jacques Rancière reminds us, "always . . . a matter of construction, too."[29] The notion of productive reference is Bruno Latour's, who develops it in contrast to the legacy of referentiality's restrictive definitions as (mere) "*reproduction*" or "*mimetic* resemblance."[30] Etymologically, Latour underlines, "to refer" means "to *report*, to *bring back*"; and reference can be defined as an effect of continuity achieved through a "discontinuous series of markers," or the "mediation" of a "network."[31] Principally shared across genres, the process follows different rules in "factual" vs. "fictional" speech: while both are "made of the same material, the same figures," we "authorize beings of fiction to . . . 'carry us away', as we say, into another world," while "chaining down" those of fact with disciplinary protocols of "procedure."[32] In loosening these chains, I propose, fictional discourse deploys reference in piecemeal ways, with piecemeal understood in the sense of both *fragmentary* and *unsystematic*, short of

---

[27] Claudia Breger, "Affects in Configuration," *Narrative* 25.2 (May 2017): 227–251.

[28] Nielsen, Phelan, and Walsh concur that upholding a distinction between fictive and non-fictive discourse does not require declaring fiction a separate ontological category. I emphasize that this does not mean that fictive discourse has no ontological weight: emphasizing fictionality and construction across genres does not amount to postmodern deconstructivism (in dialogue with Ryan, "Postmodernism," 165).

[29] Jacques Rancière, *Dissensus: On Politics and Aesthetics*, ed. and trans. Steven Corcoran (London: Continuum, 2010), 148.

[30] Bruno Latour, *An Inquiry into Modes of Existence* (Cambridge, MA: Harvard University Press, 2013), 73, 76 (Latour's emphases). As I would argue, this legacy of restrictive definitions is largely responsible for the "foreclosure" of reference in structuralist and poststructuralist criticism (as diagnosed by Marie-Laure Ryan, "Postmodernism and the Doctrine of Panfictionality," *Narrative* 5.2 (1997): 165–187, here 175). Paul Ricoeur also struggles with the notion of reference and wants to replace it with "refiguration," but intriguingly describes refiguration as "something like a productive reference" in the sense of Kant's "productive imagination" (*Time and Narrative III*, trans. Kathleen McLaughlin and David Pellauer (Chicago: University of Chicago Press, 1988), 100, 158).

[31] Latour, *An Inquiry*, 79; Latour's emphasis (77–78; see 92).

[32] Latour, *An Inquiry*, 251–252.

entirely dissolving the material-semiotic continuity at stake.[33] I understand the "real world pieces" thus circulating through fictional along with non-fictional discourse in an encompassing sense: they include affective charges, embodied memories and fantasies along with (or attached to) discourse fragments and intertextual associations. In that sense, the operations of reference in fictional discourse underscore the fundamental openness even of full-fledged fictional worlds (such as those created by Stanišić's earlier novels): they are always multiply interwoven with their surrounding life worlds.[34] In Rancière's words again, "[t]here is no 'real world' that functions as the outside of art. Instead, there is a multiplicity of folds in the sensory fabric of the common."[35]

The authorial protagonist of Stanišić's *Herkunft* articulates a resonant theory of his writing in response to his grandmother's question as to whether his first novel was "about us."[36] On the one hand, he underlines the affordances of letting oneself get carried away into different worlds or realms not governed by mimetic constraints. In more precise narratological terms, the first person narrator (writing in 2018) reports on the earlier conversation in the gently distanciating syntax of past tense and subjunctive mood: "Fiction, as I saw it, I said, was building its own world rather than reproducing ours."[37] On the other hand, this world of its "own" is neither disconnected from nor discrete vis-a-vis the lifeworlds surrounding it (as the narrator reports slightly more assertively): "Fiction, as I conceive of it, I said, is an open system of invention, perception, and memory that rubs against that which really happened."[38] "Rubs?" the grandmother asks, highlighting the verb with its layered implications of contact along with conflict, before she concludes, with an apparent mixture of disbelief

---

33 Nielsen, Phelan and Walsh capture part of this idea with their distinction between "local" and "global" operations of (non-)fictionality ("Ten Theses," 67); however, multiple reconfigured real-world-fragments can add up to quite encompassing referential operations without obeying any protocol for documentary standards.
34 This is in dialogue with more conventional fiction-nonfiction distinctions. Ryan suggests that non-fictional texts invite readers to orient themselves by performing comparisons with "other texts" and "source[s] of knowledge," while "fictional texts do not share their reference world with other texts" ("Postmodernism and the Doctrine of Panfictionality," *Narrative* 5.2 (1997): 166; 166–168).
35 Rancière, *Dissensus*, 148.
36 Saša Stanišić, *Herkunft* (Munich: Luchterhand, 2019), 20.
37 Stanišić, *Herkunft,* 20, "Fiktion, wie ich sie sähe, sagte ich, bilde eine eigene Welt, statt unsere abzubilden."
38 Stanišić, *Herkunft,* 20, "Fiktion, wie ich sie mir denke, sagte ich, ist ein offenes System aus Erfindung, Wahrnehmung, und Erinnerung, das sich am wirklich Geschehenen reibt." Dementia then perhaps dramatizes, he will suggest later, how (transient) memory tilts into fiction, or operates as a practice of fictionality unaware of its figurality (Stanišić, *Herkunft,* 46, 169).

and satisfaction, that her grandson is making a living by "inventing and exaggerating."[39] As the narrator fills in, she had characterized Saša's propensity for storytelling in these same terms already when he was a child, with the emphasis that "I would never deceive or lie, but only always invent and exaggerate."[40] Per his grandmother Kristina, our authorial protagonist thus deploys fictionality properly in Nielsen, Phelan, and Walsh's sense. The narrator himself, however, is less sure about her distinction: "I probably didn't know that difference back then (and I don't always want to know it today), but I liked that she seemed to trust me."[41] The narrator's comment simultaneously questions and affirms the difference between deceiving/lying and exaggerating/inventing. As it seems, we shouldn't rely on him respecting the boundary at every single moment. Nonetheless, he does indirectly position the distinction between fiction and deception as the accomplishment of a grown-up mindset – and even as a boy, he cherished the trust that rewards an ethical deployment of storytelling. How might we resolve, or productively conceptualize, the apparent tensions in this speech act?

In the following, I probe the suitability of a concept of critically reparative fabulation that I adapt via recent African American cultural theory and aesthetics, specifically Saidiya Hartman's and Tavia Nyong'o's work on histories of slavery and queer Black performance respectively. Let me note at the outset that the context of Stanišić's writing is, of course, a very different one, and that theoretical conceptualization is never context-free, even as I believe in the productivity of transfers, as long as they are undertaken with deliberate care and respect for the limits of comparison. In the case at hand, the shared ground might be described as the problem of ethical storytelling against the backdrop of, and from within, asymmetrical power dynamics and histories of violence. Of course, Hartman and Nyong'o in turn build on heterogeneous conceptual genealogies. Thus, Hartman reminds us that in classical narratology, "'[f]abula' denotes the basic elements of story, the building blocks of the narrative," "a series of logically and chronologically related events that are caused and experienced by actors."[42] She then proposes her "method" of "critical fabulation" as an answer specifically to the "founding violence" of "the archive of slavery": since its records do not yield the experiences of the human beings whom they list as "commodities and corpses," "fiction" is needed to counter "the fictions

---

[39] Stanišić, *Herkunft*, 20, "[E]rfinden und übertreiben."
[40] Stanišić, *Herkunft*, 19, "ich würde niemals täuschen und lügen, sondern immer nur übertreiben und erfinden."
[41] Stanišić, *Herkunft*, 19, "Den Unterschied kannte ich damals wohl nicht (will ihn auch heute nicht immer kennen), ich mochte aber, dass sie mir zu vertrauen schien."
[42] Hartman, "Venus in Two Acts," 11; with reference to Mieke Bal.

of history" by "narrating stories which are impossible to tell."⁴³ As a practice of fictionality, critical fabulation exploits "the capacities of the subjunctive (a grammatical mood that expresses doubts, wishes, and possibilities)," and thereby, as Hartman underlines with Lisa Lowe, "symbolizes aptly the space of a different kind of thinking, a space of productive attention to the scene of loss."⁴⁴

For his context of queer Black performance, Nyong'o speaks of *Afro-fabulations*. With reference also to Donna Haraway's method of "speculative fabulation," he circumscribes the method as a way of doing "things" with "archives."⁴⁵ From my angle, this links to the role of productive referentiality within fictional discourse. As Nyong'o spells out further, "Afro-fabulation" is less "a matter of inventing tall tales from whole cloth" than the (I might stress, *piecemeal*) "tactical fictionalizing of a world that is, from the point of view of black social life, already false."⁴⁶ In Stanišić's yet different context, the falseness of the world at hand, and the archival gaps and distortions at stake, include the dissolution of the (socialist Yugoslav) nation he was born into, the legacies of war, displacement, and the racism and anti-refugee hostility he experienced in the new German home country. Further complicating matters, however, Stanišić's authorial protagonist and narrator is also struggling to make sense of a familial heritage spanning both victim and perpetrator sides in the Bosnian genocide: in some respects, *Herkunft*'s project foregrounds precisely the challenge of working through (what Michael Rothberg calls) implication in a legacy of historical violence.⁴⁷ In this layered context, I suggest, Stanišić's practice of "fabulative archiving" towards reflexive imaginations of belonging does intriguingly resonate with Hartman's and Nyong'o's conceptualizations, including in how it navigates the folds of fiction and truth vis-à-vis dissemblance and documentation.⁴⁸

As Nyong'o emphasizes, the fabulist "is nothing like a liar."⁴⁹ Like Stanišić's narrator, they may admit to perhaps being "confused on a point or two," but that doesn't mean they are an "'untrustworthy' narrator."⁵⁰ The similarly judgmental narratological category of unreliable narration, I will echo, does not get us very far; it is much more helpful to situate the tactics of fabulation in

---

43 Hartman, "Venus in Two Acts," 10.
44 Hartman, "Venus in Two Acts," 11.
45 Nyong'o, *Afro-Fabulations*, 13.
46 Nyong'o, *Afro-Fabulations*, 6.
47 Michael Rothberg, *The Implicated Subject: Beyond Victims and Perpetrators* (Palo Alto: Stanford University Press, 2019).
48 Nyong'o, *Afro-Fabulations*, 3.
49 Nyong'o, *Afro-Fabulations*, 5.
50 Nyong'o, *Afro-Fabulations*, 6.

a framework of (generally) *nonsovereign* narration.⁵¹ Even where *"anexact"* in the mode of "intensifications" and "manipulations," the "factual fictions" of Nyong'o's fabulist are no "malicious mistruths," and – again – they inspire "trust."⁵² Rather than "sign[s] of dissemblance," the points of "incoherence" in the narrative may be sites of *"incompossibility"*: faced with the realities created by hegemonic social forces, they investigate "possibilities outside our present terms of order."⁵³ In challenging these terms, the tactics of fabulation perform acts of reflexively nonsovereign narration: the fabulist lacks the privilege (or megalomania) needed to pretend that a world, even a fictional one, could ever be fully under their control or wholly of their own making.⁵⁴ This does not

---

51 See Breger, "Affects in Configuration," 239, for a critique of the unreliability trope in a framework of nonsovereign narration, that is, most generally, the idea that narration is always shaped by a sociosymbolic network of (variously non/conscious) affects and meanings, in which no agent ever has pseudo-divine control over their words or worlds. Per Krogh Hansen's amendment of rhetorical narratology's concept of unreliability for the generic borderland terrain of autofiction presents a step in the right direction: it replaces the notion that unrelialibility depends on an intentional act by the implied author (as distinct from the narrator) with the criterion of "accordance with the norms, values or facts of the storyworld," as determined by a *"sensus communis"* ("Autofiction and Authorial Unreliable Narration," *Emerging Vectors of Narratology*, eds. Per Krogh Hansen, John Pier, Philippe Roussin, Wolf Schmid (Berlin and Boston: De Gruyter 2017), 57). However, Krogh Hansen's continued reliance on a norm of sovereign authorship is indicated when he specifies that unreliability in autofiction takes the form of either "intentional auto-mocking" or "seemingly unintentional self-deception" (57). I am more interested in a nonsovereign author's search for ethical orientation in a field of affect and power, in which any *sensus communis* needs to be assembled from a plurality of voices. For example, Stanišić's narrator stages the dissolution of Yugoslavia's "multiethnic idea" in the onslaught of "new voices" after the loss of Tito's hegemonic "narrative voice" (*Herkunft*, 95). His own response to this chorus, "Hadn't we hailed the goals of Red Star all together? Apparently not" questions his earlier insistence that the heightened affects of soccer were just about soccer back then (Herkunft, 97, 14). But rather than categorical unreliability, the tension between the two passages indicates an ongoing process of sensemaking. For a part resonant critique of narratological un/reliability models as implicated in colonial ideologies, see also Greta Olson, "Questioning the Ideology of Reliability in Mohsin Hamid's *The Reluctant Fundamentalist*: Towards a Critical, Culturalist Narratology," in *Narratology and Ideology: Negotiating Context, Form, and Theory in Postcolonial Narratives*, eds. Divya Dwivedi, Henrik Skov Nielsen, and Richard Walsh (Columbus: Ohio State University Press, 2018), 156–172.
52 Nyong'o, *Afro-Fabulations*, 15 (his emphasis), 6. Nyong'o relates this back to "the classic paradox of fiction": "a story we know to be untrue can nonetheless inspire belief, emotion, and attachment" (New York: New York University Press, 2019), 7.
53 Nyong'o, *Afro-Fabulations*, 6.
54 This is in dialogue with the formalist position that in fiction, the author, or narrator as endowed by the author, is epistemologically equipped with imaginative sovereignty over the

mean that they (or we) refuse all responsibility for (evaluating) the fabulist's creative agency in reassembling affects, memory and fantasy scraps, culturally dominant topoi, genre conventions and other intertextual inspirations.[55] That the fabulist takes liberties vis-à-vis socially accepted "fact-check[ing]" standards does not equal a license to ruthlessly "untether both history and memory from the grounds of veridiction" altogether: the "powers of the false," Nyong'o emphasizes, need "to be critically interrogated" in terms of their (however unsystematic) relation to historical contexts and surrounding social fantasies.[56] In other words, fabulation is a practice of fictionalization under real life conditions that put some stress on neat theoretical and moral delineations of truth-telling, invention, and deception, but it remains ethically accountable for the contours of its imagination. With Bruno Latour, we might say that it is bound not by (seemingly simple) "matters of fact" but to (complicated and controversial but nonetheless "real") "matters of concern."[57]

Stanišić's authorial character narrator, who relishes his grandmother's trust even while admitting to residual confusions about the difference between invention and deception, opens *Herkunft* with a brief introductory vignette introducing the grandmother's dementia, immediately followed by a chapter addressed "TO THE IMMIGRATION AUTHORITIES."[58] After thus establishing a framework of tactical response to a "false world," he sets out in a mode of flamboyant fabulation, momentarily reminiscent of the earlier *Wie der Soldat*'s toying with the picaresque novel and its modernist reception by Günter Grass and others.[59] Namely, *Herkunft*'s autobiographical narrator evokes the scenario of his birth during a fierce March storm: "my Drina," the river in his birth town

---

created world. See Dawson, *The Return of the Omniscient Narrator: Authorship and Authority in Twenty-First Century Fiction* (Columbus: The Ohio State University Press, 2013), 32, with reference to Sternberg.

55 In the context at hand, the insistence on a positive notion of (creatively forceful) nonsovereign agency facilitates an answer to Hendel, who develops the comparison between Stanišić's reality-saturated prose and Handke's fictions into an (ostensibly leftwing) apology of Handke's presumed artistic sovereignty ("'Das soll Literatur eigentlich nicht'"). Artistic "ability" (*Können*, 10), I will underline strongly, does not require a fantasy of god-like potency.
56 Nyong'o, *Afro-Fabulations*, 15 (with Mark Siegel), 7.
57 Bruno Latour, *Reassembling the Social: An Introduction to Actor-Network-Theory* (Oxford: Oxford University Press, 2005), 114.
58 Stanišić, *Herkunft*, 6.
59 On the picaresque in *Wie der Soldat*, see Christian Rink: "Vom transkuturellen Erschreiben der Gegenwart. Saša Staniić's Roman 'Wie der Soldat das Grammofon repariert,'" in *Erzählen von Zeitgenossenschaft: Zur Darstellung von Zeitgeschichte in deutschsprachiger Gegenwartsliteratur*, eds. Linda Karlsson Hammarfelt, Edgar Platen, Petra Platen (Munich: Iudicium, 2018), 106–115, here 106. See Günter Grass, *Die Blechtrommel* (Hamburg: Luchterhand, 1974).

Višegrad, was "nervous," and a lightning strike made everyone believe that "the devil" had come into the world.[60] Playfully asserting instant consciousness, the narrator claims to have been somewhat pleased with that perception: "It's not a bad thing after all for people to be a little afraid of you before it even starts."[61] Perhaps especially so if "[t]hirty years later," the immigration authority's demand for a handwritten narrative resume will cause "a giant amount of stress" (*Riesenstress*) in your life.[62] In response to that demand, the narrator reports, he was initially unable to write anything at all, feeling "as if my biography had been flushed away by the Drina."[63] For readers with contextual historical knowledge, the personified river's erasure agency – which in this latter sentence is syntactically marked as fictional – may be particularly haunting given its role in the Bosnian genocide, when bodies were regularly dumped into the Drina.[64] In any case, the river's imagined power provides a hypothetical explanation for the experience of losing one's sense of biographical trajectory under duress. Saša then attempted to fill the gap by making a table of factual life data. Even knowing they were "correct," however, he felt "as if this had nothing to do with me": "I didn't trust such a life."[65] A list of data does not connect (in)to an identity or a reliable sense of one's biography.

This is where the fabulative birth scenario comes into play. Starting from it, *Herkunft*'s protagonist begins crafting a narrative that establishes an affective connection with the world and, through this connection, a sense of trust, agency and belonging (in time and space, among people, at least virtually both in – former – Yugoslavia and Germany). As indicated here, the turn to fabulation has a strongly *reparative* layer in Stanišić's work – more fully than in Nyong'o's and certainly more than in Hartman's conceptualizations.[66] As introduced by Eve Kosofsky Sedgwick (with reference to Melanie Klein's psychoanalysis), the reparative process is oriented at a goal of assembly or "'repair'" in a spirit variously of "love," the "*seeking of pleasure*," self-care, empathy or ethical

---

60 Stanišić, *Herkunft*, 6.
61 Stanišić, *Herkunft*, 6, "Ist doch ganz gut, wenn die Leute ein bisschen Angst haben vor dir, bevor es überhaupt losgeht."
62 Stanišić, *Herkunft*, 6.
63 Stanišić, *Herkunft*, 7.
64 https://en.wikipedia.org/wiki/Vi%C5%A1egrad_massacres.
65 Stanišić, *Herkunft*, 7.
66 Stanišić, *Herkunft*, 214, "Telling stories" (*Erzählen*), the narrator offers later, "made what was shit more absurd and somehow more bearable." Nyong'o marks the partial departure of his (neither pessimist nor optimist) work from Hartman's critical emphasis on "irredeemable loss" (*Afro-Fabulations*, 20).

recognition of the other as "once good."⁶⁷ In contrast to paranoia, reparative practice mitigates "hatred, envy, and anxiety," although it is grounded in "the depressive position," or, as I would word it less clinically, in a full acknowledgment of negative – broken, hurting, and haunting – world realities. In *Herkunft*'s opening writing scenario, reparative fabulation actually brings only a moment of relief: Saša's narrative imagining quickly leads him onto dangerous terrain, at least from the angle of the implied audience of the immigration authority. His name, he writes, was chosen by his paternal "grandmother Kristina," who was affiliated with the "Mafia," an occupation that afforded her the time to bring up the child while his parents worked and studied.⁶⁸ Her husband, "grandfather Pero, was a communist with both heart and party membership book" (*Herz und Parteibuch*); the time spent around him and his comrades allowed the child to hold his own in political conversations at age four.⁶⁹ Unsurprisingly, Saša quickly resorts to the eraser. Probing more or less tactical perspectives and narrative building blocks, he arrives at another reasonably straightforward fact: "religion: none," only to supplement it with a questionable interpretation: "And that I had all but grown up among heathens."⁷⁰ Bracketed by the "all but" modifier once more indicating fictionality, or figural rather than literal referentiality, the dated topos flamboyantly dramatizes the fact's likely interpretation through the lens of majority German Christian *Leitkultur*.⁷¹ A fierce atheist, Saša continues, his grandfather came from a mountain village that worshipped St. George, or, "as it seemed to me even back then, more so the dragon side."⁷²

---

67 Sedgwick, *Touching Feeling*, 128, 137 (Sedgwick's emphasis).
68 Stanišić, *Herkunft*, 7.
69 Stanišić, *Herkunft*, 7.
70 Stanišić, *Herkunft*, 7, "quasi unter Heiden aufgewachsen sei."
71 Expressing expectations of asymmetrical "integration"/assimilation, the concept of *Leitkultur* (leading/guiding culture) has featured prominently in hegemonic German immigration discourse since its turn-of-the-twenty-first-century introduction by Günther Beckstein and Friedrich Merz. See Deniz Götürk, David Gramling, and Anton Kaes, "An Immigration Country? The Limits of Culture," in *Germany in Transit: Nation and Migration 1955–2005*, eds. Götürk, Gramling, and Kaes (Berkeley: University of California Press, 2007), 287–288.
72 Stanišić, *Herkunft*, 8.

Dragons, narrative forks, and historical virtuality

Mafia connections, worldly communism, and dragon (slaughter) worship: just about a page of tentative stabs at tactical autobiography writing has produced a repertoire of topoi that, as we will see, ambiguously index key issues to be tackled *and* fictional tools for solving the *Herkunft* puzzle. Of course, the suspicious reader may also wonder how strictly documentary the scene of resume writing itself is in relation to the biography of the book's flesh-and-blood-author. But whatever its exact configuration from perception, memory, and invention, the scene forcefully lays out the book's literal and symbolic, bureaucratic and experiential starting point. The status of having become a refugee, or, as the narrator words later, a "human" no longer allowed to or wanting to live at the particular place they happened to have been born in, produces a reckoning with *Herkunft* – or "identity stress" (*Identitätsstress*).[73] The latter, casually depreciating wording indexes the pressure exerted by the narrator's simultaneous critical sense that it seemed "backward, downright destructive, to speak about my or our origin in a time in which descent and birthplace served as markers of distinction again, and borders were newly mounted . . . In a time when exclusion became programmatic and regained legitimacy in electoral politics."[74] After his mother was threatened as a "Muslim" in Višegrad because of her ethnic background in 1992, the adolescent Saša had found himself in Germany where soon after his arrival, Neo-Nazis were throwing Molotov cocktails on a home for Vietnamese workers in Rostock.[75] And as he is writing in 2018, thousands are demonstrating against an open society: once more, "affiliations" function as "kindling."[76] The original German word used here, "*Zugehörigkeiten*," translates as both membership and belonging, indicating the challenge of articulating the latter – affectively affirmative – idea.

The authorial protagonist was confronted with this challenge head-on when in 2009, he felt interpellated into another line of his familial heritage, which implicates him into the very histories of genocide he had fled. Just before her memory started to fail, grandmother Kristina took him to Oskoruša, the village where his (communist Serbian) grandfather Pero was born, a village where almost all the gravestones featured the name Stanišić, and where he felt pressured to profess a belonging/affiliation he would rather deconstruct: "Genes, ancestors, dialect? However you spin it, descent remains a construct after

---

[73] Stanišić, *Herkunft*, 63.
[74] Stanišić, *Herkunft*, 62, "Ausgrenzung programmatisch und wieder wählbar wurde."
[75] Stanišić, *Herkunft*, 118, 136.
[76] Stanišić, *Herkunft*, 97.

all!"⁷⁷ When his grandmother and Gavrilo, one of the few old people still living in the village, urged him to drink from a well, he worried about bacteria, but gave in so as to not disappoint them, and to his surprise felt that it was "the best water I had ever drunk."⁷⁸ Even as the critical commentary continues in his mind ("affiliation kitsch!"⁷⁹), Saša is not unaffected by the taste of belonging he is offered. In the narrator's retrospective summary, already his high school essays, the seed of his literary practice, had characterized him as a "kitschy nostalgic suffering from homesickness."⁸⁰

In navigating the dilemma, fabulation again comes to his rescue. In the narrator's account of the Oskoruša expedition, a story was "whizzing and hissing" up on the mountains when he asked Gavrilo about the origin of his huge scar.⁸¹ The story, which is thus acting as if it was a dragon, alternatively begins with a farmer called Gavrilo, with a stormy night in Višegrad, grandmother's dementia, or "the lighting [*Befeuern*] of the world by way of adding stories."⁸² In explicitly poetological terms, the narrator explains that he will begin repeatedly, and find several endings; as he suggests, "deviation" or "meandering" (*Abschweifung*) is the very "mode of my writing. *My own adventure.*"⁸³ English in the German original, the latter phrase refers to the "*Choose your own adventure*" genre that Saša had discovered as an adolescent, as the narrator spelled out earlier.⁸⁴ Beyond young adult reading habits, interactive multifork narratives were widely hailed in the 1990s as a promising (nonlinear, egalitarian . . .) route towards literary futures in the age of new media.⁸⁵ Years later, our authorial narrator returns to the idea. Aware of both pleasures and limits of deconstructive techniques of "ironic multiplication," he explores the reparative potential of fabulatory world building from "minuscule" (again, piecemeal) impulses: "a memory here, a legend there, a single remembered word over there."⁸⁶

---

77 Stanišić, *Herkunft*, 32.
78 Stanišić, *Herkunft*, 33.
79 Stanišić, *Herkunft*, 33.
80 Stanišić, *Herkunft*, 160.
81 Stanišić, *Herkunft*, 36, "zischte und fauchte." Gavrilo's scar, which looked "like/as if [*wie*] ripped by a giant muzzle," connects him to Saša's father, who returns from the war with a similar scar – about the origin of which Saša has not asked him. Stanišić, *Herkunft*, 66, see 224.
82 Stanišić, *Herkunft*, 36.
83 Stanišić, *Herkunft*, 36.
84 Stanišić, *Herkunft*, 12.
85 See, e.g., Janet H. Murray, *Hamlet on the Holodeck: The Future of Narrative in Cyberspace* (Cambridge, MA: MIT Press, 1997).
86 Stanišić, *Herkunft*, 30, 37.

As if it were an adventure novel in its own right, *Herkunft* ends with an experiment in multifork poetics put into biographical writing practice. Following an "EPILOGUE," the choose-your-own-adventure story "THE DRAGON SHELTER" (*Drachenhort*) puts the reader in the shoes of the narrative "I," grandson of a "Mafia godparent" and a grandfather whose identity the narrator at this point can no longer determine at all ("yes – what actually?"[87]). In a mode of role taking, the concluding adventure offers the reader to explore their own relation to such (be)longing and fantasy, choosing our own path and, perhaps, finding closure among ten possible endings.

The overarching theme of the multi-fork adventure plot is the response to loss; its most explicit personal – while politically entangled – layer is the authorial protagonist's struggle with his grandmother's dementia and, eventually, death. Saša's fantasies of keeping her alive offer a variation on, and at moments converge, with a *leitmotif* of *Wie der Soldat*, which opens with the death of "grandpa Slavko," the novel's Pero equivalent.[88] The collective, political resonances of this loss are indicated when the adolescent protagonist of *Wie der Soldat* hopes to reawaken him with the magic wand that the grandfather had just carved for him, promising a revolutionary force circumscribed by adherence to Tito's socialist ideas but powered by "invention" and "imagination."[89] In *Herkunft*, it is grandmother Kristina who has been looking for her Pero throughout. In the last regular chapter preceding the adventure, Saša visits her in the home where the family reluctantly brought her in fear for her safety, and spontaneously fabulates a resurrection when the grandmother keeps insisting on going to a funeral scheduled only in her mind. Aware of the deception involved, the narrator comments for the reader that he is "a hundred percent certain" that what he is doing is "not right"; the grandmother, however, "smiles" (*lächelt*).[90] The ethics of fabulation are not exhausted by conventional delineations of truth telling-vs-lying.

In the following epilogue, Saša leaves for the airport but at the last minute decides to turn around and arrives back at the home an hour before midnight, where the narrative transitions into a more global fabulatory mode via German romantic topoi. (Joseph von Eichendorff is featured in the acknowledgments

---

[87] Stanišić, *Herkunft*, 291.
[88] Saša Stanišić, *Wie der Soldat das Grammofon repariert: Roman* (Munich: btb, 2008), 11.
[89] Stanišić, *Wie der Soldat*, 11, "Erfindung," "Fantasie."
[90] Stanišić, *Herkunft*, 283. Reasoning further, he considers that insisting on the truth with grandmother would also lead to grandfather's "daily dying anew." Stanišić, *Herkunft*, 305.

and plays a role throughout *Herkunft*.)⁹¹ The transition to fiction is marked syntactically as well: In the light of a storm lamp, it looks "as if there were" branches growing from the back of the gardener cutting a rose hedge, "as if he were" part of the hedge ("als wüchsen . . . [a]ls sei,"⁹²). Once the reader "you" has slipped into the protagonist's skin (or at least accepted the charge of operating in the role) and enters the home in the initial segment of the multi-fork plot, the grandmother asks whether "you" are Pero.⁹³ The adventure ends quickly for both the reader who outright *"lies"* (claiming to be the grandfather) and the reader who insists on *"the truth,"* proceeding to explain that grandfather has long been dead.⁹⁴ This quick end isn't necessarily bad: as you tuck the grandmother into bed, she articulates content and takes your hand.⁹⁵ However, if you identify yourself as the grandson but proceed to mention dragons in a more ambiguous follow-up to grandmother's questions about Pero's whereabouts,⁹⁶ things get much more interesting.

To back up, the dragon theme had made repeated re-appearances throughout the main part of *Herkunft*. In the narrator's further report on the 2009 visit to Oskoruša, he commented on the equestrian-aiming-at-dragon motif on the paneled walls of Gavrilo's house, along with the framed photographs of "the war criminals Radovan Karadžić und, in uniform, Ratko Mladić" on a shelf.⁹⁷ Both Karadžić, the president of Republika Srpska during the Bosnian War, and Mladić, the leader of the republic's army, were later convicted of genocide, crimes against humanity, and war crimes by the International Criminal Tribunal for the former Yugoslavia (ICTY).⁹⁸ Under the influence of the liquor being served, Saša was inclined to see more on the walls "than meets the eye ostensibly" (*vordergründig*): he concludes that the "holy equestrian," whose eye color is the same as that of everyone around including Saša, "is the beast" himself.⁹⁹

---

91 Stanišić, *Herkunft*, 353. Reading Eichendorff, Saša emphasizes that he likes his "friendly" attitude directed emphatically "towards" the world ("freundlich," "der Welt . . . zugewandt"), Stanišić, *Herkunft*, 228.
92 Stanišić, *Herkunft*, 287.
93 Stanišić, *Herkunft*, 293.
94 Stanišić, *Herkunft*, 293, see 295. The italics mark the instructions for the reader about the choices offered here.
95 Stanišić, *Herkunft*, 342.
96 Stanišić, *Herkunft*, 295.
97 Stanišić, *Herkunft*, 47–48.
98 See "Cases," *United Nations: International Criminal Tribunal for the Former Yugoslavia*, https://www.icty.org/en/cases, 31 January 2022.
99 Stanišić, *Herkunft*, 49. Adelson quotes Michael Young on "on seeing '>more than meets the eye,< taking or treating or construing what is sensibly present as something other, or something

The reversibility, or mutual contamination, of the roles of murderous saint and slaughtered-while-dangerous dragon is further underscored when Gavrilo shows Saša a pretend-old notebook to document the family's beginnings in three Montenegrin brothers' uprising against the Ottoman governor. In his story, the third brother rises into the air as a dragon.[100] As Saša faces these origin tales, the ethical concern is not primarily with fabulation's failure to uphold the contract of fiction: upon Saša's request for further detail on the dragon, Gavrilo himself admonishes him not to take "everything literally."[101] Literal or figurative, the confrontation with the Serbian mythmaking practices at the ancestral place to which his beloved grandmother had taken him ensures that the "primal scene" (*Urszenerie*) for Saša's "self-portrait with ancestors" simultaneously becomes "a portrait for my being overwhelmed with the self portrait."[102] When he returns to Oskoruša with his parents in 2018, they continue to encounter dragon tattoos and Saint George portraits as the signs of Serbian nationalism; intuitively, Saša's mother introduces herself with a Serbian name.[103] In return, Sretoje, Gavrilo's brother, orders her to complete household tasks before indirectly justifying the Muslim genocide. In anger, Saša's mother eventually requests to break off the expedition. Saša, no longer sure what he was even looking for, instantly complies and reiterates his inability to understand religion, nationalism, and the determining force attributed to "Herkunft."[104]

The multi-fork narrative at the end of *Herkunft* aims to engage these experiences reparatively by rewriting the dragon myth in a non-heroic way that presents an alternative to the bloody legacy of ethnic fiction.[105] The reader willing to explore the possibilities of fabulation may find out soon that dragons, in the existence of which "you, of course, don't believe," have been inhabiting the world "for five thousand years."[106] Their "origin" (*Herkunft*), to be sure, is in the "legendary realms" of the Caucasus Mountains and Mesopotamia; in the

---

more, than what immediately appears,'" and asks what such 'more than meets the eye' might be "in the literary imagination of our own times." Adelson, "Literary Imagination," 17.
100 Stanišić, *Herkunft*, 50–51.
101 Stanišić, *Herkunft*, 51. In fiction's "as if" mode, the virtual dragons (or something unseen by the eye in the imagination space created by syntax) also come to the rescue of Saša's father when he almost falls into a snake hole: "As if something had grabbed me by the neck and carried me across the hole!" Stanišić, *Herkunft*, 219.
102 Stanišić, *Herkunft*, 49.
103 Stanišić, *Herkunft*, 263, 265, 272.
104 Stanišić, *Herkunft*, 275.
105 "Origin, origination, no heroism," the narrator probes his alliteration skills ("Herkunft, Hervorbringung, keine Heldengeschichten"). Stanišić, *Herkunft*, 229.
106 Stanišić, *Herkunft*, 296, see 298.

area around Oskoruša they can be found only because of the "migration movements" of the last several millennia.[107] National myths, *Herkunft*'s fabulatory practice thus establishes matter-of-factly, are preceded by and contingent on transnational movement and cultural translation. As you return to Gavrilo's house during the adventure, the "photographs of the war criminals have disappeared" while St. George and the dragon are still on the wall: a piecemeal glimpse at different possibilities?[108] The further unfolding of the adventure is secured by several layers of comic relief and metanarrative reflexivity. Thus, making it into the mountain is contingent on evading the call of the sirens, who – be warned – don't have a Netflix subscription.[109] Once inside, you can choose the path of *"never ending storytelling,"* which further descends into the mountain.[110] Even on the level of dialogue, to be sure, grandmother now protests: "You are exaggerating! *Herkunft* as a picture puzzle [*Wimmelbild*] with dragons?"[111] When you finally encounter the multi-headed (and multi-voiced), bickering dragons, including one who identifies as an irregular immigrant from a Russian legend, the drinks on offer include "blood, water," and "all foreign languages;" the narrative "I" chooses "Spanish."[112] Grandmother and I/you now imaginatively perform the trick that *Wie der Soldat's* adolescent magician had failed at: we retrieve grandfather Pero from the dragons' guard, if with the order to return "the comrade after 48 hours at the latest."[113] One of the dragon heads comments on the irony that "for millennia," it hadn't occurred to anyone that "backwards might be doable as well."[114]

By "rearranging" the "basic elements" of the story and "re-presenting the sequence of events" from divergent viewpoints, Hartman submits, critical fabulation underlines the contested character of event and history while "imagin[ing] what might have happened."[115] More ambitiously, Nyong'o conceptualizes Afro-fabulation as, not least, "a theory and practice of black time and temporality."[116] He syncretically outlines the idea at the intersection of Henri Bergson and Gilles Deleuze's conceptualization of the "virtual" with Brechtian theater's

---

107 Stanišić, *Herkunft*, 298.
108 Stanišić, *Herkunft*, 301.
109 Stanišić, *Herkunft*, 343.
110 Stanišić, *Herkunft*, 331, "Niemals aufhören, Geschichten zu erzählen."
111 Stanišić, *Herkunft*, 345.
112 Saša Stanišić, *Herkunft*, 346–347.
113 Stanišić, *Herkunft*, 348.
114 Stanišić, *Herkunft*, 347, "dass Zurück auch machbar wäre."
115 Stanišić, *Herkunft*, 11.
116 Nyong'o, *Afro-fabulations*, 5.

epic pressure on history's naturalized story.[117] Sometimes just a gesture of "belated . . . protest . . . shut down" by "narrative logic," fabulation "tethers together worlds that can and cannot be" in "mingling what was with what could have been."[118] Even before getting into full-fledged fabulation mode, *Herkunft*'s autobiographical narrator admitted that he is "a little like" those "Yugoslavs, who don't exist anymore" but then do again momentarily as they annually celebrate the anniversary of the Socialist Federal Republic.[119] Of course, he is also perfectly capable of making fun of their simplistic cosmopolitan idealism and drunken stumblings.[120] Retrieving the grandfather "comrade" for a dragon-administered forty-eight hour-window certainly does not provide a magical solution to the question of whether, or how, socialism's decomposition into genocidal nationalism could have been prevented. The answer that family memory attributes to Pero is analytically unsatisfactory: "'Racists are fundamentally impolite people,' he is supposed to have said once."[121] Even on the level of the fabulated adventure plot, Pero fails to deliver "the political message" that "I expect" from him, as they drive by the "Serbian aggression graffiti" (*Aggro-Graffiti*) that have not magically disappeared, either.[122] Again, fabulation does not offer comprehensive new worlds from "whole cloth."[123]

But perhaps, the "disjunctive synthesis" performed by fabulation's "'anarrang[ing]'" of the "linear timeline of history" does not need to deliver ready-made solutions to maintain its "family resemblance" with "hope."[124] Further calling on Ernst Bloch (via José Esteban Muñoz) and his stern dialectic counterpart Theodor W. Adorno, Nyong'o suggests that "the powers of the false point to a potential correction of our dystopic present, but not necessarily by providing a picture of the true."[125] Figuratively bringing back – for a moment, virtually, and piecemeal – the socialist "melting pot" that had provided Saša with a childhood free from "the coercion of difference in origin and religion" does not solve the *Herkunft* puzzle; it just fuels the ongoing reparative process of narration at the intersection of memory and imagination.[126] Perhaps, Pero's

---

117 Nyong'o, *Afro-fabulations*, 14.
118 Nyong'o, *Afro-fabulations*, 5–7.
119 Nyong'o, *Afro-fabulations*, 87.
120 Stanišić, *Herkunft*, 90.
121 Stanišić, *Herkunft*, 98.
122 Stanišić, *Herkunft*, 348.
123 Nyong'o, *Afro-fabulations*, 6, as quoted above.
124 Nyong'o, *Afro-fabulations*, 18, 26.
125 Nyong'o, *Afro-fabulations*, 18.
126 Stanišić, *Herkunft*, 13, "den Zwängen unterschiedlicher Herkunft und Religion." Alternatives to the backward route in the company of dragons include a scenario that Saša imagines earlier for

legacy is to be found primarily in Saša's pleasure in storytelling: "Allegedly, grandfather rarely answered my many childhood questions directly but wrapped the answer in a little story."[127] The narrator certainly has even more trouble committing to narrative endings than to beginnings. The proliferation of adventure plot endings – per se inviting us to start over – includes recursive pathways to the scene of writing ("I open the file *Herkunft.doc*") as well as back to *Herkunft*'s opening scene with the grandmother seeing herself as a child.[128] Critically, the point of these loops is not the kind of deconstructive undoing that questions or cancels the power of narration.[129] Rather, the point is to keep intertwining the "virtually endless . . . possibilities" of telling a story with a process of productive reflexivity, ever more firmly entangling the genres, or modes, of fabulation and essay writing.[130]

As assembled by such generically syncretic narration, "Herkunft," then, indexes "the sweet-bitter accidents" that carried us here or there; "Herkunft" is "belonging to which one didn't contribute anything;" it also is "war" and the "flinching" of Saša's mother when someone calls her name in her birth town.[131] Perhaps, the transience of memory indicates that it ultimately matters little where one is "at home."[132] However, *Heimat* (or *Haymat*, or *Hajmat*: choose your own spelling) also points to "grandmothers" and, in the context of a German

---

reviving the mountain village: "A painter from Leipzig could have come by Oskoruša . . .," initiating a series of events (then told in the present indicative) involving lesbian Commerzbank culture managers with the cash to buy art, yoga workshops in the mountains and an emerging commune teaching Gavrilo how to meditate. Stanišić, *Herkunft*, 81.
127 Stanišić, *Herkunft*, 85.
128 Stanišić, *Herkunft*, 323; Stanišić, *Herkunft*, 324.
129 Existing scholarship on *Wie der Soldat* and even *Herkunft* slants in this deconstructive direction. See, e.g., Joscha Klueppel, "Emotionale Landschaften der Migration: Von unsichtbaren Grenzen, Nicht-Ankommen und dem Tod in Stanišićs *Herkunft* und Varatharajahs *Vor der Zunahme der Zeichen*," *Transit* 12.2 (2020); https://escholarship.org/uc/item/3vr5v24v. Klueppel reads the text as a "commitment" [*Bekenntnis*] against conceptualizing 'Herkunft,' 'Heimat' and similar notions and concludes with an emphasis on "fragmentation" ("Emotionale Landschaften der Migration," 14, 19). On *Wie der Soldat*, see Brigid Haines, "Sport, Identity and War in Saša Stanišić's *Wie der Soldat das Grammofon repariert*," in *Aesthetics and Politics in Modern German Culture: Festschrift in Honour of Rhys W. Williams*, eds. Brigid Haines, Stephen Parker, and Colin Riordan (Oxford: Peter Lang, 2010), 153–164. Frauke Matthes and David Williams quote Haines affirmatively to the effect that Stanišić's "novel is about the limits of storytelling – some events will never be told, some wounds never do heal" ("Displacement, Self-(Re)Construction, and Writing the Bosnian War: Aleksandar Hemon and Saša Stanišić," *Comparative Critical Studies* 10.1 (2013): 27–45, here 41; see Haines, "Sport," 164).
130 Stanišić, *Herkunft*, 229.
131 Stanišić, *Herkunft*, 66, 117.
132 Stanišić, *Herkunft*, 327.

adolescence, to the dentist "Dr. Heimat."[133] He not only took care of the cavities in the mouth of an young refugee without health insurance, but also modeled a form of cosmopolitan conviviality by taking Saša and his grandfather fishing, providing permits, sandwiches, and a few hours free of "fear."[134] In short, "Herkunft" is "a tree-like structure" (*Geäst*) made up of "multiple paths, forks in the road, possibilities and improbabilities."[135] The ongoing narrative process of choosing and linking paths involves nonsovereign agency: "I decide," the narrator reminds himself a bit anxiously as he once more redescribes the taste of the Oskoruša well water.[136] In this sense, the "taste of well water is made of language," although we should arguably never rely on words being "only words," as indicated by Saša's memory of Serbian guests starting to toss around genocide talk in 1987.[137] Since worlds, and affiliations, have material layers and very real effects, the agency we have in making them is so fragile – and simultaneously crucial.

To conclude, the ongoing narrative process of reflexive fabulation, or fabulation-enriched reflexivity, navigates the folds of world and word, fact and fiction in a dynamic and productive way: neither fetishizing nor disregarding the boundaries, it invites us to join an ethical journey of imaginatively exploring reparative possibilities against the backdrop of potentially overwhelming realities of violence and loss. In our cultural moment of freewheeling paranoia and all-encompassing conspiracy theory, reflexive fabulation's disjunctive syntheses of piecemeal memories and fantasies perhaps demonstrate that – and indicate how – caring about historical truth does not require abandoning the powers of literary imagination.[138] Instead of just relying on genre boundaries for safeguarding the fact/invention divide, Stanišić's *Herkunft* project creatively exploits the affordances of the "as if" even as it commits to an ongoing process of evaluating the representation of actual matters of concern. In conjoining the powers of the real with those of the false, the fabulist can offer more, precisely because they remain aware of their own embedding into the folds of unredeemed histories.

---

133 Stanišić, *Herkunft*, 63.
134 Stanišić, *Herkunft*, 10, 173. On conviviality, see Paul Gilroy, *Postcolonial Melancholia* (New York: Columbia University Press, 2005), first 8.
135 Sandra Kegel, "A World Where Rivers Have A Voice," *Frankfurter Allgemeine Zeitung* (16 March 2019) (German and English at: https://www.goethe.de/ins/in/en/culture/lak/soc/sst/21635615.html).
136 Stanišić, *Herkunft*, 34.
137 Stanišić, *Herkunft*, 286, 187.
138 See, again, Adelson, as quoted above. My wording is also in dialogue with Worthington who emphasizes that autofiction readers maintain "a line of demarcation between fact and fiction" by way of appreciating irony, indicative of increasing cultural investments in (non-capitalized versions of) truth (Worthington, "Fiction in the Post-Truth Era," 471, see 475–476).

Works cited

Adelson, Leslie A. "Literary Imagination and the Future of Literary Studies," *DVjs* 89.4 (2015), 675–682.
Böttcher, Philipp. "Fürstenfelde erzählt: Dörflichkeit und narrative Verfahren in Saša Stanišić's 'Vor dem Fest,'" *Zeitschrift für Germanistik* 30 (2020): 306–325.
Breger, Claudia. "Affects in Configuration," *Narrative* 25.2 (May 2017): 227–251.
"Cases." *United Nations: International Criminal Tribunal for the Former Yugoslavia.* https://www.icty.org/en/cases, 31 January 2022.
Dawson, Paul. *The Return of the Omnisicent Narrator: Authorship and Authority in Twenty-First Century Fiction* (Columbus: The Ohio State University Press, 2013).
Dawson, Paul. "Ten Theses Against Fictionality," *Narrative* 23.1 (2015): 74–100.
Delhey, Yvonne, Rolf Parr, and Kerstin Wilhelms. "Autofiktion als Utopie: Zur Einleitung," in *Autofiktion als Utopie/Autofiction as Utopia*. Eds. Yvonne Delhey, Rolf Parr, and Kerstin Wilhelms (Paderborn: Fink, 2019), 1–8.
Ecker, Gisela, ed. *Kein Land in Sicht: Heimat – weiblich?* (Munich: Wilhelm Fink, 1997).
Gilroy, Paul. *Postcolonial Melancholia* (New York: Columbia University Press, 2005)
Göktürk, Deniz, David Gramling, and Anton Kaes. "An Immigration Country? The Limits of Culture," in *Germany in Transit: Nation and Migration 1955–2005*. Eds. Deniz Göktürk, David Gramling, and Anton Kaes (Berkeley: University of California Press, 2007), 1–17.
Grass, Günter. *Die Blechtrommel* (Hamburg: Luchterhand, 1974).
Haines, Brigid. "Sport, Identity and War in Saša Stanišić's *Wie der Soldat das Grammofon repariert*," in *Aesthetics and Politics in Modern German Culture: Festschrift in Honour of Rhys W. Williams*. Eds. Brigid Haines, Stephen Parker, and Colin Riordan (Oxford: Peter Lang, 2010), 153–164.
Hartman, Saidiya. "Venus in Two Acts," *Small Axe* 26 (2008): 1–14.
Hendel, Steffen. "'Das soll Literatur eigentlich nicht.' Die Debatte um Wesen und Wert der Literatur anlässlich der Preisvergaben an Peter Handke, Saša Stanišić und Olga Tokarczuck 2019," *undercurrents: Forum für linke Literaturwissenschaft* (Frühjahr 2020): 1–21.
Janker, Karin. "Zürcher Poetikvorlesung: Wie Saša Stanišić seine Heimat erfindet," *Süddeutsche Zeitung* (13 November 2017).
Kegel, Sandra. "A World Where Rivers Have A Voice," *Frankfurter Allgemeine Zeitung*. 16 March 2019 (available in both German and English translation at: https://www.goethe.de/ins/in/en/culture/lak/soc/sst/21635615.html).
Klueppel, Joscha. "Emotionale Landschaften der Migration: Von unsichtbaren Grenzen, Nicht-Ankommen und dem Tod in Stanišićs *Herkunft* und Varatharajahs *Vor der Zunahme der Zeichen*," *Transit* 12.2 (2020). https://escholarship.org/uc/item/3vr5v24v.
Krogh Hansen, Per. "Autofiction and Authorial Unreliable Narration," in *Emerging Vectors of Narratology*. Eds. Per Krogh Hansen, John Pier, Philippe Roussin, and Wolf Schmid (Berlin and Boston: De Gruyter, 2017), 47–60.
Latour, Bruno. *Reassembling the Social: An Introduction to Actor-Network-Theory* (Oxford: Oxford University Press, 2005).
Latour, Bruno. *An Inquiry into Modes of Existence* (Cambridge, MA: Harvard University Press, 2013).

Lejeune, Philippe. "Le pacte autobiographique (bis)," in *Moi aussi. Collection Poétique* (Paris: Seuil, 1986), 13–36.
Matthes, Frauke and David Williams. "Displacement, Self-(Re)Construction, and Writing the Bosnian War: Aleksandar Hemon and Saša Stanišić," *Comparative Critical Studies* 10.1 (2013): 27–45.
Murray, Janet H. *Hamlet on the Holodeck: The Future of Narrative in Cyberspace* (Cambridge, MA: MIT Press, 1997).
Nielsen, Henrik Skov, James Phelan, and Richard Walsh. "Ten Theses about Fictionality,"*Narrative* 23.1 (2015a): 61–73.
Nielsen, Henrik Skov, James Phelan, and Richard Walsh. "Fictionality as Rhetoric: A Response to Paul Dawson," *Narrative* 23.1 (2015b): 101–111.
Nyong'o, Tavia. *Afro-Fabulations. The Queer Drama of Black Life* (New York: New York University Press, 2019).
Olson, Greta. "Questioning the Ideology of Reliability in Mohsin Hamid's *The Reluctant Fundamentalist*: Towards a Critical, Culturalist Narratology," in *Narratology and Ideology: Negotiating Context, Form, and Theory in Postcolonial Narratives*. Eds. Divya Dwivedi, Henrik Skov Nielsen, and Richard Walsh (Columbus: Ohio State University Press, 2018), 156–172.
Orich, Annika. "Archival Resistance: Reading the New Right," *German Politics and Society* 38.2 (2020): 1–34.
Rancière, Jacques. *Dissensus: On Politics and Aesthetics*. Ed. and trans. Steven Corcoran (London: Continuum, 2010).
Ricoeur, Paul. *Time and Narrative III*. Trans. Kathleen McLaughlin and David Pellauer (Chicago: University of Chicago Press, 1988).
Rink, Christian. "Vom transkuturellen Erschreiben der Gegenwart. Saša Stanišić's Roman 'Wie der Soldat das Grammofon repariert,'" in *Erzählen von Zeitgenossenschaft: Zur Darstellung von Zeitgeschichte in deutschsprachiger Gegenwartsliteratur*. Eds. Linda Karlsson Hammarfelt, Edgar Platen, and Petra Platen (Munich: Iudicium, 2018), 106–115.
Rothberg, Michael. *The Implicated Subject: Beyond Victims and Perpetrators* (Stanford: Stanford University Press, 2019).
Ryan, Marie-Laure. "Postmodernism and the Doctrine of Panfictionality," *Narrative* 5.2 (1997): 165–187.
Schreiber, Daniel. "Deutschland soll werden, wie es nie war," *Zeit online*, 10 February 2018 https://www.zeit.de/kultur/2018-02/heimatministerium-heimat-rechtspopulismus-begriff-kulturgeschichte/komplettansicht.
Sedgwick, Eve Kosofsky. *Touching Feeling: Affect, Pedagogy, Performativity* (Durham: Duke University Press, 2003).
"Saša Stanišić im Gespräch mit Alexander Gumz und Katrin Schumacher," in *Über Land: Aktuelle literatur- und kulturwissenschaftliche Perspektiven auf Dorf und Ländlichkeit*. Eds. Magdalena Marszalek, Werner Nell, and Marc Weiland (Transcript: Bielefeld, 2018), 27–35.
Stanišić, Saša. *Herkunft* (Munich: Luchterhand, 2019).
Stanišić, Saša. "'Manche Dinge würde ich lieber vergessen.' Interview by Karin Janker," *Süddeutsche Zeitung* [no date given]; Goethe.de/ins/kr/de/kul/sup/sct/sst/21635544.html, 31 January 2022.
Stanišić, Saša. *Wie der Soldat das Grammofon repariert: Roman* (Munich: btb, 2008).

"Saša Stanišić spricht über sein Buch 'Herkunft'" (video interview). *Youtube* https://www.youtube.com/watch?v=dwocYKZhDqY, 31 January 2022.

Trojanow, Ilja. *Nach der Flucht* (Frankfurt am Main: Fischer, 2017).

Virant, Špela. "Der Weltensammler und der Welterfinder: *Zu Der Weltensammler von Ilija Trojanow und Wie der Soldat das Grammofon repariert von Saša Stanišić*." Pismo – Časopis za jezik i književnost 6 (2008): 286–296 (https://www.ceeol.com/search/article-detail?id=185188).

Worthington, Marjorie. "Fiction in the 'Post-Truth' Era: The Ironic Effects of Autofiction," *Critique: Studies in Contemporary Fiction* 58.5 (2017): 471–483.

Paul Michael Lützeler
Intertextuality in Peter Schneider's Narrative Fiction from *Lenz* to *Couplings*: An Essay

I

Peter Schneider's critical comments on university reform stood out during the anti-authoritarian student protest movement of the 1960s. Although little immediate structural change took place within the German ivory tower, a few academics had addressed topics that, thanks to the student protests, now were no longer considered taboo. Particularly important in this respect were the critical engagement with National Socialism, the Holocaust, and World War II. A radicalized fraction of the student body established political cadre groups in the spirit of Lenin or Mao Zedong at the universities, i.e., were preparing for a revolution that would lead to the overthrow of liberal democracy. Their goals, however, stood in sharp opposition to what the anti-authoritarian-inspired students of the mid-1960s envisioned as a university in democracy.[1] In the early 1970s Peter Schneider, then a student of German literature, felt growing discomfort with the increasingly extreme and out-of-touch student political cults.

Schneider did not respond to the crisis of the student movement with pamphlets and polemics, or with speeches or manifestos. He reacted as a literary author, offering doubt instead of slogans; compromise instead of unambiguity; questions instead of dogmas; narratives instead of structures; life stories instead of abstracts; subtlety instead of radicalism; imagination instead of analysis. Schneider knows his German literary history very well, and like others of his Berlin circle who had been taken by the student movement – Friedrich Christian Delius or Hans Christoph Buch come to mind – Schneider was an up-and-coming young writer who not only wanted to passively read poetry, but

---

[1] As I have shown in my article "The Role of Literature in the German Studies Association," *German Studies Review* 30.3 (2016): 505–516 the early student movement reforms within literary scholarship were oriented towards interdisciplinarity and socio-historical contextualization. These are goals that Leslie A. Adelson has dealt with in a sophisticated manner and from a contemporary point of view in her article: "DAAD Faculty Summer Seminar 2012: 'The Futures of Interdisciplinary German Studies,'" *German Studies Review* 35.3 (2012): 511–520.

https://doi.org/10.1515/9783110778922-011

also produce it. Peter Schneider identified comparable crisis constellations in the lives and works of Jakob Michael Reinhold Lenz and Johann Wolfgang Goethe, two authors from the Sturm und Drang period. In his first prose text *Lenz* (1973) as well as in his next text . . . *schon bist du ein Verfassungsfeind* [. . . Already You Are An Enemy of the Constitution, 1975] Schneider creates intertextual references to Georg Büchner's story "Lenz" and Goethe's novel *Die Leiden des jungen Werthers* [*The Sufferings of Young Werther*]. The literary movement of the Sturm und Drang also had been a youth protest phase, and its rebels (including Lenz, Goethe, Schiller, Bürger, Schubart, Heinse) not only opposed traditional ideas of order and norms but also questioned the morals and social conditions of their time in the name of freedom and imagination. Already the young Georg Büchner, whose work is closely intertwined with the 1830 revolution, had been taken in by authors such as Lenz. The field of German Studies, inspired by the student movement, rediscovered Büchner's socialist pamphlet *Der Hessische Landbote* [*The Hessian Courier*] and his drama on revolution *Dantons Tod* [*Danton's Death*] during the 1960s and 1970s. During the crisis years of the student revolt, Büchner's "Lenz" enjoyed a quasi-cultlike status. An unillusioned analyst of revolutionary dialectics, Büchner had closely studied the account of the ailing Lenz as it had been written down by the social reformer Johann Friedrich Oberlin. But in Büchner's work, this simple medical document became literature. In Büchner's novella "Lenz," the inner world of Jakob Michael Reinhold Lenz, the Sturm und Drang author (1751–1792), unfolded in its subjectivity, its artistic aspirations (realism instead of idealism), and its theological reflections (nature as a revelation of God.) Most of all, Büchner's Lenz was eager to get out of the social confinement that surrounded him. He wanted to escape a claustrophobic environment that instilled fear, loneliness, and feelings of persecution in him. His despair stemmed from the realization that he couldn't change the social conditions. His suicide was prompted by the knowledge that he lived in a "world" that had suffered an "immense rift." When his suicide attempt failed, he sank into apathy. The novella ends with the famous sentence: "Sein Dasein war ihm eine notwendige Last – So lebte er hin."("He saw his existence as a necessary burden – And so he lived on.")

Peter Schneider transposes Büchner's Lenz to the West Germany of the early 1970s. His narrative makes clear that it was written just as strongly with Büchner's text in mind as in response to it. This is especially obvious in the altered ending of Schneider's narrative. Both Büchner's and Schneider's Lenz experience being marginalized by their societies. But Schneider's Lenz reacts with a defiantly active "Stay here" – a far cry from the apathy and hollowness that characterizes Büchner's Lenz.² Büchner's Lenz is "finished" in both senses: his opinions are set, his health is poor, he is exhausted and tired of life. Schneider's hero, by contrast, is still developing; he turns his back on ideological dead-ends, still learns new things, and the end of the story implies a fresh start for the protagonist. For Schneider's 1970s Lenz everything is in flux and crisis moments are presented as opportunities. Whether he is engaged in social analysis, an erotic relationship, a literary discussion, or political activities, the hero is constantly extracting himself from constricting constellations associated with the rigidities and self-deceptions of the student protest movement. Schneider's Lenz is keen to gain distance from his university town and the people in it.

When German poets and intellectuals, artists, and scholars feel that life in Germany is too constricting they tend to travel to Italy, often an effective remedy. Since *Italian Journey*, Goethe has been such travelers' unrivaled role model. Schneider's Lenz is but one of many Germans to undertake a pilgrimage to Rome: at the *Piazza del Popolo* he unwinds, determined to renew his mind and body on the banks of the Tiber. In Büchner's "Lenz," there is no transalpine digression, much to the detriment of the protagonist who travels only as far as the Upper Rhine and Alsace. A divinely imposed suffering from the German condition blocks his path to rebirth in Italy. Before Schneider's Lenz buys a ticket to Rome in search of subjective fantasy and dreams, he must pass through a vale of ideological frustration in Berlin, which has its roots in the dogmatic constraints of a utopia, far removed from the world, and grounded in intellectual asceticism. The story's first few sentences describe a dream that illustrates, in a nutshell, the twofold absence that torments the hero. In this dream, he is riding for kilometers "in a mine cage through a building without doors and windows." Next, he is falling down a "dark shaft" but then is caught by a conveyer belt, and ultimately, welcomed by a troupe of Fellini characters ("women with gigantic breasts, sorcerers, clowns, somersaulting children").³ Lenz is unhappy in his local university town, he feels as if he is about to fall into a void. His dream ends with the Italian promise of change, play, creativity, and erotic adventure.

In the first part of the narrative, the worn-out activities of the politicized students take center stage. A Marx poster adorns the wall of his student room but suddenly Lenz can't "endure the sage face of Marx over his bed any longer."⁴

---

2 Peter Schneider, *Lenz*, trans. A. Leslie Willson, in *Three Contemporary German Novellas*, ed. A. Leslie Willson (New York: Continuum, 2001), 78.
3 Schneider, *Lenz*, trans. A. Leslie Willson, 3.
4 Schneider, *Lenz*, 3.

"What were your dreams, old know-it-all, at night, I mean?" "Were you really happy?"[5] He remains distrustful of the spiritual exercises of the political theory groups. It just couldn't be true that "all these comrades with their secret wishes, their difficult and exciting life stories (. . .) wanted to know nothing more of one another than these clean sentences from Mao Zedong."[6] Lenz no longer had any desire to be dragged along by his comrades to demonstrations.[7] During his "political work" he suffers from a lack of consideration for his "personal difficulties."[8] The latter includes, above all, his "Loss of L." the female love interest who had abandoned him.[9] Lenz is unable to get away from her. He always looks for her, thinks about her all the time, writes her many unsent letters, is furiously jealous when he learns about a new relationship in L.'s life, and even dreams of scenes in which L. has sex with others. It is not far-fetched to interpret "L." as a reference to Lotte in Goethe's *Werther*.

Just as Lotte is "the key to the world," for Werther, "L." is for Schneider's Lenz the prerequisite for "conquering the world with the senses."[10] Like Werther, Lenz attempts to cure his lovesickness by taking leave from the woman, who no longer loves him, and, in both cases, traveling does not help. On the contrary, afterward – as both Lenz and Werther experience – the "invisible band" between them and their beloved becomes all the "tauter."[11] Even conversations with an older fellow writer (Günther Grass comes to mind) and a literary critic who goes by the telling name of "Neidt" (sounds like "Neid" in German and "envy" in English), are not conducive to keeping Lenz in Germany. The colleague tells him "to come to his senses" regarding the end of the student movement and insists on "practical political activity," such as leveling the "European mountain of butter."[12] Neidt, by contrast, presents himself as extremely proletarian-revolutionary and only wants to read authors such as Willi Bredel.[13]

In Schneider's *Lenz*, Italy is not simply the counter-world to Germany. In some respects, his disillusioned learning process continues. In Rome, the actress Pierra becomes Lenz's confidante, advisor, and, finally, sisterly friend. She tells him bluntly that he was looking for a woman "who did not exist, who

---

5 Schneider, *Lenz*, 3.
6 Schneider, *Lenz*, 23.
7 Schneider, *Lenz*, 5.
8 Schneider, *Lenz*, 7.
9 Schneider, *Lenz*, 16.
10 Schneider, *Lenz*, 38.
11 Schneider, *Lenz*, 49.
12 Schneider, *Lenz*, 22.
13 Schneider, *Lenz*, 32.

only haunted his mind."[14] Through Pierra, Lenz can enter and get a sense of Rome's social life. She takes him along to glitterati parties. There, he meets a young, wealthy Italian who is writing "a dissertation on the early writings of Marx." He, likewise, meets a Swiss millionaire, a member of the Communist Party of Italy, for whom this party is gradually becoming too "reformist."[15] One of Pierra's colleagues, a young film actor, walks around in the "work clothes of a gas station attendant" at the party. Dressed up in dungarees, he is preparing for the leading role in a film about "Che Guevara."[16] The halls of the villa in which the friends are gathering are decorated with pictures that portray "the suffering and struggles of the working masses," pictures that "were affordable only to people" who "shared responsibility for the sufferings depicted there."[17] Here, everything leftist is *en vogue*, as part of a rapidly changing fashion that has little to do with an understanding for workers and their problems, and a political will for change. Lenz vents his resentment by dropping flowerpots from the balcony on the rooftops of fancy cars yet, in doing so, puts himself on the level of pseudo-revolution. When he realizes that in Rome, with Pierra and her circle of friends, he finds himself in a "similarly closed world" as earlier in Germany when he hung out with "political groups," that he had "not been able to endure any longer," he departs from the Italian capital and travels to northern Italy.[18]

In Trento Lenz finally finds like-minded students and workers whose aspirations and actions, subjective desires, and objective conditions, intentions and goals, dreams and realities, at least at first, do not seem to be irreconcilable. He is impressed by the "impartiality" of his new friends and their helpfulness, spontaneity, and realism. Ultimately, however, the contrast between ideological utopia and concrete improvement of social conditions, i.e., trade unions, reaches a crisis point here as well. Roberto, one of the workers, indicates that he trusts his "union official" more than Lenz, the intellectual since he feels that politically active academics were always "hiding something." "What do you want for yourselves" is Roberto's central question to intellectuals like Lenz. Roberto has good reason to presume that the ideologues want to seize power, and fears that the workers can expect nothing good from the socialist dictatorship in which this will result. However, such thoughts are only hinted at, never discussed in detail. Before the argument gets more heated, the Italian police

---

14 Schneider, *Lenz*, 56.
15 Schneider, *Lenz*, 57.
16 Schneider, *Lenz*, 59.
17 Schneider, *Lenz*, 58.
18 Schneider, *Lenz*, 61.

arrest Lenz on the grounds of being a foreign agitator and send him home to Germany. Back in his university town, Lenz realizes that time has not stood still there either. He notes that the mood has changed from a hardcore cadre mood to a hangover mood: the old friends and comrades are now preparing for exams and a bourgeois career, they have moved out of their communes, and now profess wanting "to have their own place" or simply to "go away, far away." Asked what Lenz wants to do now he responds with the laconic "stay here."[19]

Schneider's first narrative was a bestseller. For many, the text was a breath of fresh air. It openly voiced many of the frustrations, contradictions, and dead-end experiences that the students of Schneider's generation, both male and female, personally had lived through in the protest movement. Schneider's text did not raise a warning finger, did not declare a theoretical pseudo-solidarity with all the underprivileged in the word, but responded to subjective desires and did not devalue dream and phantasy, but rather confirmed these in their own right. At the same time, it wasn't a book that simply reverted to the old and outdated either. *Lenz* is not an exercise in nostalgia but acknowledges the need for political change and, in this sense, is also similar to the earlier texts of the writers from the Sturm and Drang period. One insight that the book conveys, is that it is futile to advocate for structural social reforms if they do not also lead to individual-subjective expansions of freedom. Schneider's *Lenz* (1973) marked the beginning of a new phase in literary history, the so-called "New Subjectivity" which lasted until 1980. In contrast to many other texts written during that time, Schneider's *Lenz* does not only reveal a personal point of view or reports a purely private experience, but rather conveys and unites subjective and social goals.

To "stay here," seems to have implied: to work toward a symbiosis of subjective and objective freedoms in everyday life of the Federal Republic. That is, at any rate, how one can interpret Peter Schneider's next literary work. During the discussions about the Federal Republic's emergency laws that took place in West Germany during the second half of the 1960s, it had become obvious that authoritarian behavior and surveillance state thinking were, by no means, a thing of the past. Ideological policing was (still or again) rampant, even the railroad workers were suddenly required to swear allegiance to the constitution. Freedom of expression is a fundamental component of the Basic Law and to restrict this freedom through the use of state power is contrary to its essence. Schneider's second literary text " . . . Already You Are An Enemy of the Constitution. The Unexpected Expanding of the Personal File of Teacher Kleff" deals with such contradictions.

---

19 Schneider, *Lenz*, 78.

The intertext in Schneider's second narrative is Goethe's *The Sufferings of Young Werther*. Both texts are epistolary novels and in both the opening letter is dated 4 May. Some other letter dates overlap in both epistolary novels as well, but there are also letters in Schneider's text, with dates that do not correspond to any of the letters found in *Werther*. These partly identical, partly non-identical correspondence dates already make clear that despite various similarities there are also serious differences between the two novels and their protagonists. Schneider's text, in contrast to the Goethean model, does not have a part two. Kleff's last letter is dated 2 October and the last letter of the first part of *Werther* is dated 10 September. Schneider deliberately omitted references to Werther's suicide. Neither Lenz nor Kleff is a tragic hero in Schneider's texts. Kleff's crisis-ridden relationship with his girlfriend Renate is oddly normal. Between it and Werther's relationship with Lotte two hundred years of de-romanticization of love had taken place. Kleff does not share Werther's experience of unhappy love, but the two do share experiences of social bondage, of feeling isolated, confined, and locked in, lacking development opportunities. Like Schneider's first literary text his second is written not only with but also against the earlier intertext that serves as a model. In Goethe's epistolary novel the addressee of the letters is Werther's sensitive friend, Wilhelm, in whom he confides the secret emotions of his soul. The relationship of Kleff, the letter writer, to Dr. Schäuble, the recipient of the letters, is different. The trust and intimacy of Goethe's letters have been replaced by business-like neutrality, caution, distrust, and even aversion. The high school board has informed teacher Kleff that "doubts had arisen" as to whether he stood by the "Constitution of the Federal Republic of Germany."[20] According to a "Decree of the Prime Minister," "public servants" were "obligated to positively acknowledge their support for the free democratic Basic Order in the sense of the Basic Law."[21] As his client, Kleff tries to make the lawyer understand that his "problem" is that he does not know "what exactly" the case against him was and that he has also no idea what kind of materials "the German intelligence service agency" has gathered about him.[22] Consequently, he keeps speculating, suspecting that a short-term membership in the "socialist working group at the Otto Suhr Institute at the Free University" had perhaps put the constitutional guards on alert. Or, perhaps it was because years ago he had once "insulted the Shah of Persia as a murderer."[23] To a certain extent, Kleff even agrees with his lawyer,

---

20 Peter Schneider, . . .*und schon bist du ein Verfassungsfeind. Das unerwartete Anschwellen der Personalakte des Lehrers Kleff* (Berlin: Rotbuch Verlag, 1975), 5.
21 Schneider, . . .*und schon bist du*, 14.
22 Schneider, . . .*und schon bist du*, 5 and 8.
23 Schneider, . . .und schon bist du, 21.

who states that he is showing symptoms of "paranoia."[24] He feels that his "phone is being tapped," but also is "not sure."[25] Kleff's situation is reminiscent of the problems K. faces in Kafka's *The Trial*. If one abbreviates Kleff's last name to only the letter K., the reference to Kafka's novel becomes most obvious. Kleff, too, is under a general suspicion that is not substantiated in detail, here, too, slander seems to be involved, here, too, the protagonist tortures himself with conjectures about the reasons for the trial that is being brought against him, here, too, one is in the dark about which authority is involved, here, too, the accused is surrounded by self-appointed guards who simply presume the right to supervise him, here, too, the legal officials are accused of corruption, here, too, it is quasi impossible for the persecuted to pursue his day job. In Schneider's case, however, the protagonist does not accept quasi-metaphysical guilt. There is likewise no equivalent in Schneider's narrative to the execution, at which Kafka's K. ends "like a dog."

The official doubts about Kleff's loyalty to the constitution, however, have harsh professional consequences, which the incompetent lawyer cannot prevent: Kleff is dismissed from his position as a teacher and becomes unemployed. His offense, the high school board finally informs him, consists in his opinion "that there are undemocratic laws in the Federal Republic of Germany which should be resisted."[26] Unlike in Kafka's novel, there is a clearly defined offense in Schneider's text, albeit one that is not an offense at all in the defendant's sense, but rather one that shows civic virtue. Like Kleist's Kohlhaas – another infamous "K" in German literature –, Kleff insists on his right to resist, and like Kohlhaas, he tries to compensate for his powerlessness by usurping power. Like in the case of Kohlhaas, resistance becomes concrete when, like the representative of sovereign power, he declares war on noble rulers. Kleff, on the other hand, sublimates his opposition to megalomaniacal dreams. In these, he sees himself as a "much sought-after advisor" to "chancellors and ministers" and, in general, to the "World's greats" – from the "Minister of Culture" to the "German Chancellor" to "Mao Zedong."[27] Towards the end of the book, one gets the impression that the authorities had fabricated the thesis of the teacher's alleged will to resist. Kleff now believes that the "disclosure of the interrogation transcript and letter of dismissal" to his union friends is the reason he was suspended by the school board because that action violated a "duty of

---

24 Schneider, . . .*und schon bist du*, 25.
25 Schneider, . . .*und schon bist du*, 25 and 53.
26 Schneider, . . .*und schon bist du*, 55.
27 Schneider, . . .*und schon bist du*, 87.

loyalty."[28] Schneider's novel has an open ending. Kleff did not show up for the last hearing date on his case. The reader is told that he had "disappeared."[29] Where did he go? Has he resigned? Did he, like Jutta, one of his former girlfriends, disappear into the anarchist-terrorist underground?[30] This is unlikely given that he had distanced himself from that scene.[31] Has he changed professions and finds the trial about himself now only ridiculous? Or, does he want to appeal anyway "to the highest court," as he once claimed, in which case he will not care how the initial court's decision, to which – as the last lines of the novel state – "the court retires for deliberation," ultimately turns out?[32] As is often the case in the postmodern novel, the conclusion is left open. The readers can continue to spin the narrative thread in their imagination.

II

Several of Peter Schneider's stories published under the title *Die Wette* [*The Bet*,1978] also has an open ending.[33] In these stories, human relationships dominated by hatred are depicted in which a struggle rages – sometimes even to the death – between men and men, women and men, and women and women. The precision and the laconic way in which the narrator's evil eye captures the criminal energy, the envy, and the coldness of heart of the characters is admirable. They reveal a side of Schneider's narrative prose that is little known. Some of the stories – particularly the title story "The Bet" – ought to be part of all relevant collections of German master novellas. It is the most profound of these texts. The first-person narrator is on a boat trip with a friend and acquaintances and has bet that he will kill a two-kilo fish with a harpoon. While hunting, the images of a giant fish – reminiscent of Herman Melville's *Moby Dick* – and the hated rival blend into one, and it remains unclear whom or what he has caught with his harpoon. In order not to drown, he must resurface without the harpoon. The underwater battle becomes a Darwinian parable: "All of the creatures that were darting back and forth below me never knew a second in which they were not prepared for a deadly threat. Every life could be perpetuated only

---

28 Schneider, *. . .und schon bist du*, 106.
29 Schneider, *. . .und schon bist du*, 106.
30 Schneider, *. . .und schon bist du*, 19.
31 Schneider, *. . .und schon bist du*, 97.
32 Schneider, *. . .und schon bist du*, 105.
33 Peter Schneider, *Die Wette. Erzählungen* (Berlin: Rotbuch, 1978).

through the annihilation of another, and I had become part of this system through my harpoon." The story "Big Brother and Little Brother" deals with the hostile Tarquini brothers, who belong to different schools of magic, with the older of the two, the first-person narrator Antonio, emphasizing his superiority over the younger, Carlo. "The real magician is me," Antonio points out.[34] The structure and the style of the story are reminiscent of Kafka's "Report for an Academy." The younger brother is portrayed as an imitator who soon reached the limits of his abilities, after which he no longer could control his envy and jealousy. Carlo wants to expose his older brother's deceit, an action during which Antonio is seriously wounded. (Here one is reminded of parallels to the author's own life: the brothers Peter Schneider – the older – and Michael Schneider – the younger – were both magicians and writers in their early years and fell out for many reasons.)

There is no mention of society, politics, or contemporary history in the novellas contained in *Die Wette*. At first glance, the novellas of *Der Mauerspringer* [*The Wall Jumper*], published four years later, therefore seem to have little in common with the earlier volume.[35] The actual "hero" in the 1982 *Wall Jumper* is the Berlin Wall, the very naming of which evokes political-historical associations with the Yalta division of the world, Europe, Germany, and the city of Berlin. Similarities can be found on the level of the formal literary aspects which here are strikingly postmodern. The wall stories are narrated by different characters, and already the first story makes clear that it is deliberately – as it were – constructed before the reader's eyes. Unlike in *Die Wette*, however, there is a narrative frame in which a first-person narrator introduces himself. The setting is reminiscent of E. T. A. Hoffmann's cycle *The Serapion Brethren*. Here, too, writer friends tell each other stories. Unlike in Hoffmann, in *The Wall Jumper* the narrators do not meet as a group, instead, a dialogical situation arises between the first-person narrator and one of the other two authors. Also, in the *Serapions Brethren* quite heterogeneous novellas are brought together, whereas the stories in Schneider's collection all address a specific theme: They are all about "wall jumpers," i.e., about characters who ignore the Berlin Wall or the fortified German-German border. Yet, most of the people at the center of these narratives are not at all interested in Politics, with a capital P. There is resistance in these stories: their protagonists do not want to see their desires curtailed by the existence of the senseless border fortifications. Here, we are on

---

34 Schneider, *Die Wette*, 97.
35 Peter Schneider, *Der Mauerspringer. Erzählung* (Darmstadt und Neuwied: Luchterhand, 1982), *The Wall Jumper. A Berlin Story*, trans. Leigh Hafrey (Chicago: University of Chicago Press, 1998).

familiar Schneiderian fictional terrain, for already his first work *Lenz* lived from the tension between subjective dream and unwieldy social reality.

The intertextual allusions to E.T.A. Hoffmann are even more direct in Schneider's next text, the novel *Paarungen [Couplings]*, which, while published after German reunification, is set in pre-unification Berlin.[36] Here, the topographical realities of the divided city play only a subordinate role. Allusions to Berlin are plentiful, however, through the many references to the city's literary and musical history. The narrative's focus is on the love-and-hate relationships of three couples who get together and separate after a while. References to political events of the early 1980s do occur but do not take over the plot. The novel contains multiple allusions to the narrative work of E.T. A. Hoffmann, Goethe's *Elective Affinities*, and Mozart/da Ponte's *Don Giovanni*.

Three friends (Eduard, Theo und André) meet in "The Tent," their local Berlin stomping ground, and talk about their relationships with their girlfriends, Klara, Esther, and Pauline, whom they want to marry soon. The name of their café, "The Tent," already contains a reference to E.T.A. Hoffmann.[37] During his time in Berlin, the romantic writer liked to spend time in the northern part of the Berlin Tiergarten, which then was called "in the tents." (The small terrace that now bears this name in the same area is not identical with the historic location. The original was much larger and located just south of what is now the John Foster Dulles Allee). Since the middle of the eighteenth century, there had been tented inns there, but these already had been replaced by wooden and stone buildings in E.T.A. Hoffmann's time. The poet was often seen in Weber's tent, and he mentioned "In The Tents" in his novella of the "Knight Gluck" (from the collection *Fantasy Pieces in Callot's Manner*). The character in Peter Schneider's novel about whom one learns the most is called Eduard Hoffmann. The protagonist's last name, "Hoffmann," is an allusion to the Romantic author with the same name, and Eduard is, of course, the name of the protagonist in Goethe's *Elective Affinities*. While there are few direct references to Goethe's classic no contemporary author in Germany writes a novel about married couples who are friends without having this masterpiece in mind. As in Peter Schneider's earlier texts, the differences in the intertexts are emphasized more than the similarities. In Goethe's text the law of attraction and repulsion of chemical elements, which Goethe transferred to human conditions to present the problem of freedom and necessity, forms the backdrop of the novel. In

---

36 Peter Schneider, *Paarungen. Roman* (Berlin: Rowohlt, 1992), Peter Schneider, *Couplings*, trans. Philip Boehm (New York: Farrar, Straus and Giroux, 1996).
37 Schneider, *Couplings*, 7.

Schneider, by contrast, the unresolved dispute between sociological and biogenetic theories about the role of heredity and milieu in the behavior of individuals is addressed. Eduard Hoffmann, the molecular biologist, is a strong proponent of the heredity thesis, while his brother Lothar, a sociologist, is a staunch advocate of the environment thesis. While these theories stand in opposition to each other in the novel, they have no discernible influence on the development of the characters. Schneider does not want to stretch the behavior of his novel's characters on the Procrustean bed of these theories, both of which leave too little room for human freedom of choice. As in his earlier literary works, Schneider does not present any heroic developments in the life trajectories of the literary characters in *Couplings*. *The Elective Affinities* ends tragically with death and renunciation, with images of saints and angels; *Couplings*, on the other hand, has a life and pleasure-affirming comic ending that illustrates an aesthetic experience. Here, too, Schneider alludes ironically to Goethe's *The Sorrows of Young Werther*. "Lotte" is the name of the creature that has full control over Eduard because his career, his future as a scientist, depends on her. After she vanishes, he is plagued by sleepless nights. He searches desperately for her, sees her again briefly, but then she leaves him forever. Lotte is Eduard's lab mouse on which he is conducting experiments to find a cure for multiple sclerosis. A militant group of animal rights activists, who refer to Eduard's lab as a "mouse concentration camp,"[38] have set all the laboratory mice free. "The star of his future earth-shaking paper and his spectacular publication in *Nature*, the worthy occasion for the next Leibniz prize, possibly even for a trip to Stockholm" had run away.[39] Unlike Werther, Eduard feels "a strange relief" after Lotte's "departure."[40] Instead of committing suicide, he goes on vacation.

Right at the beginning of the novel, Eduard notices a young woman in "The Tent" who is reading E.T.A Hoffmann's *The Serapion Brethren*.[41] In contrast to *The Wall Jumper*, however, *Couplings* shows no formal similarities to the *Serapion Brethren*. Friends do gather here as well but the novel has a conventional structure with an omniscient narrator, and it is only from this one perspective that readers learn about the plot. The "Serapiontic principle," that already determined the problem of Schneider's first story *Lenz*, is in effect here as well. This principle could be stated as: one should strive to balance the inner and outer world, fantasy and reality, as well as mind and body. But what is fascinating about Hoffmann's *Serapion Brethren* (as well as his other story cycles) is

---

38 Schneider, *Couplings*, 211.
39 Schneider, *Couplings*, 214.
40 Schneider, *Couplings*, 215.
41 Schneider, *Couplings*, 6.

that the literary characters in these narratives completely lack harmony and balance. His texts are full of eccentrics, demonic figures, madmen, and automatons. This is no different in Peter Schneider's writings although in his texts everything appears in a less sinister light, if only because Hoffmann's characters are quoted ironically. The irrationality of love relationships unfolds in Schneider's *Couplings* against a merely imagined foil of reason, thwarting all notions of rule, reliability, and duration. At the beginning of the novel, the three friends start with some good intentions. Eduard is aware that, statistically speaking, any given relationship has "a maximum average life expectancy"[42] of three and a half years. Theo railed against the fragility and "base instability of all relationships"[43] in general and the "dissolution" of the "institutions of love"[44] in particular. After discussing various aspects of Eros–including "disloyalty as a rule" and "transience" as a "normal attribute of love" – all three decide to declare war on the "dragon of separation" after a night of heavy drinking at The Tent.[45] They even make a bet: "Whoever failed to show up in The Tent one year later today, still coupled with his current partner, would have to finance an entire ski vacation for six people in the ski resort of Sils Maria."[46] One year later – when love has come and gone – all the couples have broken up, and so no one remembers the bet.

Eduard's girlfriend is called Klara: her name is reminiscent of Clara in E.T.A. Hoffmann's story "Der Sandmann" ["The Sandman"]. In both texts, the love relationship is wrecked by another woman. In Hoffmann's story, it is the automaton Olympia who is the disruptive factor. She materializes in Schneider's text as well, where she does not disrupt the relationship between Eduard and Klara but rather the one between Theo and Pauline. In "The Sandman," Nathanael projects his erotic desires onto Olympia. In *Couplings,* Olympia is Theo's "phantom image of a fantasy woman,"[47] a fictional character introduced into the story by Pauline to help cure Theo of his illusional "male fantasies." But things do not work as planned. The phantom woman eventually develops a life of her own in which the East German Secret police then become interested. Theo doesn't find the Olympian games that Pauline plays with him funny at all, and eventually, they contribute to the dissolution of their relationship. Pauline, for her part, flees from Theo because she is convinced that he will not commit himself to any

---

[42] Schneider, *Couplings*, 9.
[43] Schneider, *Couplings*, 47.
[44] Schneider, *Couplings*, 48.
[45] Schneider, *Couplings*, 49.
[46] Schneider, *Couplings*, 49–50.
[47] Schneider, *Couplings*, 124.

concrete woman and that their "love could only survive at a distance."[48] In general, Theo is a person who does not like to commit himself. He possesses a so-called "double passport,"[49] a privilege that allows him to live in both parts of the divided Germany and Berlin. So, he commutes between these different worlds, finds an alternative to the West in the East and a corrective to the East in the West.

E.T.A. Hoffmann's cast of characters includes–not only, but especially in *The Elixirs of the Devil* – the Doppelgänger. This figure has an ominous presence in *Couplings* as well. The student leader of the militant animal lovers group who is giving Eduard a hard time in the lab strikes him as "a youthful copy"[50] of himself. For this very reason, he frightens him: "Lord have mercy," Eduard reflects, "if such children come to power. They pass judgment on you, finish you off, wipe you out with the best conscience, presumably all for your own good."[51] Many roads lead from Ernst Theodor Amadeus Hoffmann to Wolfgang Amadeus Mozart. Schneider undermines the tragic potential of *The Elective Affinities* and the descent into madness of Hoffman's characters by giving the three friends in *Couplings* the traits of Don Juan. The Don Giovanni material, in turn, is made lighter by leaving out the opera's end in death and damnation. Eduard fails to remain faithful to Klara. He begins affairs with Laura and Jenny. Unlike Petrarch's beloved in *The Canzonieri*, Schneider's Laura is no ideal and lacks all mysteriousness. On the contrary, her unabashed sexual desire and strong physical presence in her sexual relationship with Eduard are very concrete and can almost not be outdone. Whenever and wherever they are together, they can be overcome by desire. Eduard embodies a special variant of the Don Juan type. His Anna, Elvira, and Zerlina are called Klara, Laura, and Jenny. But instead of abandoning one woman to conquer the next (like the heroes in the works from Tirso de Molina to Mozart tend to act) Eduard loves three women at the same time and does not want to give up any of them. "He did love," we read in Schneider's *Couplings* "the only problem was that there were three women! He didn't suffer from an inability to love, he merely lacked the talent for exclusivity."[52] The women he loves, however, insist on exclusivity, and both Klara and Laura pull out. Laura is even pregnant with him but chooses to have an abortion. That leaves Jenny. Her name was likely also introduced as an ironic allusion. Just like Schneider's Laura plays the extreme opposite of Petrarch's love cipher, Eduard's Jenny has nothing in common with the disloyal

---

[48] Schneider, *Couplings*, 238.
[49] Schneider, *Couplings*, 40.
[50] Schneider, *Couplings*, 181.
[51] Schneider, *Couplings*, 183.
[52] Schneider, *Couplings*, 255.

spelunker Jenny in Brecht's *Threepenny Opera*. Jenny is also expecting a child, and she manages temporarily to wean Eduard off his polygamous passions. The two lovers move in together, marry, and have offspring.

Theo and André, on the other hand, cannot be dissuaded to give up their Don Giovanni-like behavior. As soon as they fall for one woman another one beckons. Soon after marrying Esther André divorces her. Tellingly, Theo, the writer and librettist, and André, the composer, are working on a new opera about Don Juan, and, needless to say, they are constantly talking about their great model, Mozart. The score itself is not mentioned in the novel, but there are clear indications that the work is developing in the tradition of the *opera buffa* and the *dramma giocoso*. In Mozart's work the "Buffa" and the "Seria," the comic and the seriously tragic, come together to form a synthesis, but in Theo's and André's new adaptation of the old material there never is any mention of the "Seria." Before the composition work is completed André becomes deathly ill with cancer and is treated in a Parisian clinic. But the prospect that his Don Giovanni opera will have its premiere in Warsaw the next spring and the fact that he falls in love with the Parisian nurse treating him – they will marry soon – lifts his spirits and helps him to get his health back.

The end of the contemporary opera seemed to have caused a few headaches, having to do with the intertwining of art and life. "The concept was in a state of permanent revision," we are told since "the authors' constantly changing love lives kept influencing their view of the protagonist."[53] The ideas for their title kept fluctuating, depending on their situation, between "The Unchastened Libertine"[54] and the "The Rake Reformed."[55] Theo considers it unnecessary to address the guilt issue. André also dislikes the avenging commander and the ride to hell but still thinks that their hero should not get off scot-free. He wants to "condemn the libertine" and confine him to a library where he would spend his days as "a struggling writer laboring over his life confessions."[56] This ending recalls the fate of Giacomo Casanova, in other words, the biography of a Don Giovanni disciple. *Couplings* is Peter Schneider's funniest and most ironic, lightest and most exhilarating text, even if here and there – as in all good comedies – abysses briefly open. Finally, we hear a bit of reverberation from the Champagne Aria "Fin ch'han dal vino/As long as the wine" in Mozart's *Don Giovanni* and the Aria

---

53 Schneider, *Couplings*, 67–68.
54 Schneider, *Couplings*, 67.
55 Schneider, *Couplings*, 151.
56 Schneider, *Couplings*, 282–283.

"Die Liebe fürs Leben ist nur ein Wahn/lifelong love is just a delusion" from Jacques Offenbach's *The Tales of Hoffmann*.

Translation Bettina Brandt

Works cited

Adelson, Leslie A. "DAAD Faculty Summer Seminar 2012: 'The Futures of Interdisciplinary German Studies,'" *German Studies Review* 35.3 (2012): 511–520.
Büchner, Georg. *Lenz*. Trans. Richard Sieburth (Brooklyn, NY: Archipelo Books, 2004).
Burgess, Gordon J.A. "Büchner, Schneider and 'Lenz.' *Two Authors in Search of a Character,*" in *Georg Büchner. Tradition and Innovation*. Ed. Ken Mills (Bristol: University of Bristol Press, 1990), 207–226.
Clare, Jennifer. *'Auf dem Kopf gehen.' Peter Schneiders Lektüre von Büchners Lenz vor dem Horizont der Literatur der deutschen Studentenbewegung* (Leiden: Brill, Rodopi, 2017).
Lützeler, Paul Michael. "The Role of Literature in the German Studies Association," *German Studies Review* 30.3 (2016): 505–516.
Menke, Timm Reiner. "Peter Schneider: Lenz," in *Lenz-Erzählungen in der deutschen Literatur* (Hildesheim, Zurich, New York: Olms, 1984), 105–117.
Schneider, Peter. *Lenz. Eine Erzählung* (Berlin: Rotbuch Verlag, 1973).
Schneider, Peter. "Lenz." Trans. A. Leslie Willson. In *Three Contemporary German Novellas*. Ed. A. Leslie Willson (New York: Continuum, 2001), 1–78.
Schneider, Peter. . . . *Schon bist du ein Verfassungsfeind. Das unerwartete Anschwellen der Personalakte des Lehrers Kleff* (Berlin: Rotbuch Verlag, 1975).
Schneider, Peter. *Die Wette. Erzählungen* (Berlin: Rotbuch, 1978).
Schneider, Peter. *Der Mauerspringer. Erzählung* (Darmstadt and Neuwied: Luchterhand, 1982).
Schneider, Peter. *The Wall Jumper. A Berlin Story*. Trans. Leigh Hafrey (Chicago: University of Chicago Press, 1998).
Schneider, Peter. *Paarungen* (Berlin: Rowohlt, 1992).
Schneider, Peter. *Couplings*. Trans. Philip Boehm (New York: Farrar, Strauss & Giroux, 1996).
Scholz, Anna-Lena. "Rebellion und Wahn? 'Lenz' 1839/1973/2008," in *Enttäuschung und Engagement. Zur ästhetischen Radikalität Georg Büchners*. Eds. Hans Richard Brittnacher and Irmela von der Lühe (Bielefeld: Aisthesis, 2014), 259–275.
Sharman, Gundula M. "Integration: Georg Büchner's and Peter Schneider's *Lenz*," in *Twentieth-Century Reworkings of German Literature*. Ed. Gundula M. Sharman (Rochester, NY: Camden House, 2002), 96–122.
Williams, Rhys W. "'Er klammerte sich an alle Gegenstände.' Büchner, Peter Schneider and the Uses of Germanistik," in *Experiencing Tradition. Essays of Discovery*. Eds. Hinrich Siefken and Anthony Bushell (York: Sessions, 2003), 228–234.
Willson, A. Leslie, ed. *Three Contemporary German Novellas* (New York: Continuum, 2001).

Katrina L. Nousek
(Re)constructing *Heimat*: Intermedial Archives in Saša Stanišić's *Vor dem Fest* and Alexandra Saemmer's "Böhmische Dörfer"

"He learned all that from role-playing, who says it's just a waste of time?"[1] quips Johann in Saša Stanišić's novel, *Vor dem Fest* [*Before the Feast*, 2014]. An active fantasy roleplay gamer just finishing high school, Johann finds an unlikely moment to practice his healing skills during an apprenticeship with the town bell ringer. When he finds his mentor bleeding in front of the church, Johann carefully bandages his wounds with a knowledge gained from the video games he plays in his free time. His joking and proud defense of the skills he gains in virtual worlds is a playful gesture to be sure, yet it also brings up important questions about the medial affordances of narrative. The immersive learning garnered from gaming returns to serve a real purpose for Johann while incorporating medial figures of video game technology into a narrative that spans from sixteenth-century chronicles to a postsocialist present. What do readers learn from Johann learning from gaming?

The reciprocal interactions binding virtual and actual worlds in this moment may be read as a cipher for Stanišić's project more generally, which turns to print as well as digital media to create a portrait of a small town in the eastern German Uckermark. Complete with a "Homeland House" archive where episodes from almost 500 years of town history are collected, edited, and at times substantially revised, the novel as well as the website that temporarily accompanied it offer important insights into the construction of place and community through medial means.[2] In a present moment marked by purportedly global connectivity, readers have much to learn from the social worlds forged and fabricated through intermedial texts.

To investigate the affordances of intermedial engagements with notions of *Heimat*, the following analysis juxtaposes digital and print forms of Saša Stanišić's literary *Heimat* with Alexandra Saemmer's digital-born memory project, "Böhmische Dörfer. Sudeten Germans: Germanophone inhabitants of Bohemia

---
1 Saša Stanišić, *Before the Feast*, trans. Anthea Bell (Portland: Tin House Books, 2016), 45.
2 After reimagining cultural archives in eastern Germany in *Vor dem Fest*, Stanišić's next novel, *Herkunft* (2019), returns closer to the author's home to explore related questions of imagination and authenticity. On these, see Claudia Breger's analysis in this volume of genre and collectivity in *Herkunft*.

https://doi.org/10.1515/9783110778922-012

and Moravia," housed in Volume 3 of *Electronic Literature Online*. Because the town on which Stanišić's novel focuses is shrinking as inhabitants pass away or move out, the work suggests a creative interest in capturing and developing for readers an often-overlooked *Heimat* in all its violent histories and loveable idiosyncrasies. Heimat, which loosely translates to homeland, is a notion of home understood as a place of origin closely tied to nature and territory. A literary account of Heimat opens imaginative points of access to this sociolinguistic particularity through a co-constructed literary world, which Stanišić develops in print and digital forms. At stake for Saemmer, however, is a home that was forcibly removed from the speaker's family, which was part of an ethnic German minority expelled from Czechoslovakia at the end of World War II. When the family returns to their former house many years later, the site provokes an act of remembrance despite the impossibility of the speaker remembering directly given her young age at the time of expulsion. Saemmer's lyrical demonstration of the recuperation and failures of memory regarding this moment suggests a need for continued attention to finding new forms for negotiating contested histories despite the inevitable failure of reconstructing the memory itself. Both works test the horizons of tales that touch where virtual and actual meet, thus bringing literary, historical, and medial questions to bear on the imaginative configurations of *Heimat* that result.[3]

Archiving Heimat: *Vor dem Fest* and fürstenfelde.de

Saša Stanišić's novel, *Vor dem Fest* (2014), chronicles the fictionalized village of Fürstenfelde in the Uckermark region of Brandenburg, Germany. Written in five parts composed of short vignettes, the narration is marked by a collective first-person plural "We" of the village itself and focalized through various human and non-human figures. The resulting heteroglossia and wide-reaching temporal breadth establish intricate relationships among literary, archival, and interview material the author collected over four years living in Fürstenwerder, an

---

3 The conceptual underpinnings of this article are indebted to Leslie A. Adelson's notion of "touching tales," which recognizes the affective and creative dimensions of narratives that bring together historical references not traditionally considered in relation in order to "stress a broad range of common ground, which can be thicker or thinner at some junctures." See Leslie A. Adelson, *The Turkish Turn in Contemporary Literature: Toward a New Critical Grammar of Migration* (New York: Palgrave, 2005), here 20.

actual town in northeast Germany. The scope of Stanišić's narrative technique has prompted critics to underscore its literariness, dubbing the prize-winning novel a testament to "everything of which literature is capable."[4] Although the novel levels distinctions among discourses, combining advertising slogans with an antique chorus and church bells with hip-hop, it employs formal and aesthetic strategies through stylized narrative voices that never leave readers wondering if they picked up an Uckermark visitor's guide in place of a novel.

As the title suggests, the story largely takes place during the day and night before the town celebrates its annual Anna festival, though forays into history and fantasy far exceed this single moment. Poignant portraits present readers with the motley cast of characters composing the town while lending gradual insight into the personal feuds and historical traumas that mark the village over several centuries. The social contours of Fürstenfelde are shaped around a few key social and geographic landmarks. In addition to the lakes, city wall, and promenade distinguishing the town, villagers gather informally for beer and gossip in Ulli's garage, their stories are collected in a village archive run by Frau Schwermuth, and their traces are picked up by a fox through whom the narrative is occasionally focalized as well. Other notable figures include the former secret police officer, Dietmar Dietz (called, like many of the figures by a nickname, Ditzsche), who is known for his questionable service as a postal worker during the GDR period, and subsequently for his devotion to raising prize-winning chickens after unification. Readers catch additional anecdotal glimpses into German history through the suicidal, chain-smoking Wilfried Schramm, a former NVA [National People's Army] officer who oversaw air defense missiles stationed for the GDR in the woods beyond the town. Although the village distinguishes between those born within it and those coming from outside, a few figures successfully establish themselves as transgressors of these boundaries. The town painter Ana Kranz, for example, had fled the Banat region bordering present-day Serbia, Romania and Hungary near the end of World War II, and chronicles the town in art ever since having witnessed Red Army members rape six women while she was in hiding upon her arrival.[5] Another Anna represents a younger generation of the village moving in the opposite direction–literally. Poised to leave Fürstenfelde for studies in Rostock soon

---

[4] Gerrit Bartels, "Die wertvollste Gabe ist die Erfindung," *Tagesspiegel* 14 March 2014, https://www.tagesspiegel.de/kultur/sasa-stanisics-roman-vor-dem-fest-die-wertvollste-gabe-ist-die-erfindung/9617570.html, 7 September 2019.

[5] For an insightful reading of this obliquely narrated moment, see Dora Osborne's analysis through the lens of trauma theory in "'Irgendwie wird es gehen': Trauma, Survival, and Creativity in Saša Stanišić's *Vor dem Fest*," *German Life and Letters* 72.4 (2019): 476–477.

after the festival, this Anna is known for her running, which is in keeping with her last name "Geher," and associated with the town festival as its namesake.

Anna represents a larger trend in the decrease of Fürstenfelde's population after German unification, yet the plural voice of the village refuses to interpret the present moment as a sign of erasure. Instead, the seemingly eternal "we"-narration inserts this present moment of decline into a longue durée marked by continuity and transformation. This occurs thematically and formally through analepses and prolepses of centuries, as well as through figures that straddle traditional and contemporary medial forms. In so doing, the narrative establishes a constitutive tension between continuity and loss that begins with the epigraphic assurance that "For billions of years since the outset of time / Every single one of your ancestors has survived / . . . passed onto you life."[6] When readers confront the markers of loss that open the novel, mourning the death of the village ferryman and the shutting down of the only gas station in town, they have already been conditioned to read this passing moment in a longer narrative of transient life. The epigraphic excerpt, which comes from a song by the English rap project, *The Streets*, also returns in homodiegetic narration focalized through Johann, the aforementioned teenage apprentice of the town's bell ringer, as he paraphrases the music while listening and pondering his own existence.[7] Johann, in contrast to Anna, signifies the continuation of Fürstenfelde through the transformation and maintenance of traditional forms in a younger generation.

The self-reflexive narration that Johann focalizes and the medial mixing of pop culture and *Leitkultur* that he figures are distinguishing features of the narration more widely, which mixes linguistic and cultural forms across centuries. Although readers enter Fürstenfelde in the twenty-first century, contemporary figures and town landmarks are interspersed with entries from the village chronicles that recall sixteenth-century episodes inspired by the historical *Prenzlau Chronicle*.[8] These violent and wonderful events, such as the children left in an oven on a previous Anna festival and a pig born with a human head in 1587, punctuate the narration to incorporate the present moment into a longer trajectory of history as storytelling. Wonderful figures also transgress boundaries between Fürstenfelde's chronicles and the town's manifestation in the present, which has particularly porous boundaries between present and past in the night before the festival. In one case, two mythical figures appear as rappers

---

6 Saša Stanišić, *Vor dem Fest* (Munich: Luchterhand, 2014), 7.
7 Stanišić, *Vor dem Fest*, 48.
8 See Philipp Böttcher's comparison of passages from the Prenzlau Chronicle with Stanišić's adaptation and linguistic imitation in "Fürstenfelde erzählt. Dörflichkeit und narrative Verfahren in Saša Stanišićs 'Vor dem Fest,'" *Zeitschrift für Germanistik* 30.2 (2020): 320–321.

speaking in rhyme and have escaped the archive to help Anna Geher redeem the living and bury the dead properly.[9] In another case, the present literally becomes possessed by the past when Frau Schwermuth wields a (water) gun and threatens to shoot Anna while acting out tales from the archive. This blending of diegetic levels is implicitly related to Frau Schwermuth's visible alterations of the archive, which are thematized typographically for readers as "handwritten" revisions of the village folklore that substantially change it.[10] The archive can rewrite Frau Schwermuth as much as she rewrites it. These imbrications of author and text reveal that neither present nor past is inert or subordinate to the other, but rather mutually influence one another in a living, dynamic relationship.

Stanišić's narrative construction of Fürstenfelde has been located by scholars variously in traditions of *Dorfliteratur*, *Provinzerzählen*, *Heimatroman*, and *Weltliteratur* [village literature, provincial narration, homeland novel, and world literature].[11] All of these designations attest to Stanišić's renewal of genres focused on rural communities. Through the author's allusions to transnational currents of postwar migration to the village and flows of globalization sending resources and labor forces elsewhere, the otherwise traditional setting of a village is tailored specifically to its eastern German context in the twenty-first century. According to Anna Sandberg's reading of the novel through the lens of ecocriticism, for example, Stanišić maintains and critiques key characteristics of *Heimatliteratur*, a genre burdened with conservative ideologies based on exclusionary notions of territorialized national identity. The genre is recognizable in the novel's typical plot, which involves a community that is threatened and then

---

9 Stanišić, *Vor dem Fest*, 119–120 and 281–283 respectively. In the first case, the figures, Q and Henry, bring Anna to Herr Schramm as he is on the cusp of suicide in his car. In the other, they bury skulls in two anonymous graves that surface under a tree used for hangings at the edge of town.
10 Stanišić, *Vor dem Fest*, 187–190.
11 These genres are attributed by the following authors respectively. See Olivia Albiero's comparative analysis of *Dorfliteratur* in "Fürstenfelde and Unterleuten: Two Literary German Villages and Their Digital Representation," *Pacific Coast Philology* 54.2 (2019): 135–160. Philipp Böttcher delivers a convincing and thorough narratological analysis of *Provinzerzählen* in "Fürstenfelde erzählt." Anna Sandberg frames her ecocritical reading by demonstrating Stanisic's intervention in *Heimatliteratur* in "Etische Ökokritik der Gegenwartsliteratur: Saša Stanišić *Vor dem Fest* (2014)," in *Ökologischer Wandel in der deutschsprachigen Literatur des 20. und 21. Jahrhunderts*, eds. Gabriele Dürbeck, et al. (Berlin: Peter Lang, 2018), 91–105. Frauke Matthes explores the productive tension between regionalism and transnationalism in "'Weltliteratur aus der Uckermark': Regionalism and Transnationalism in Saša Stanišić's *Vor dem Fest*" in *German in the World*, eds. James Hodkinson and Benedict Schofield (Rochester: Camden, 2020), 91–108.

restored to peace.¹² However, as part of a diverging trend in *Heimatliteratur*, Stanišić's work reimagines the idea of *Heimat* as a social relation to space that can produce deterritorialized forms of belonging as well. Stanišić's deliberate choice of a genre deeply embedded in German cultural history, according to Sandberg, may also be read as an explicit distancing from reception of his work that, due to his biography, locates him as an author primarily concerned with the migration experience. Although his work includes transnational figures who have moved to Fürstenfelde in addition to those born there, the novel takes as given a landscape inflected with movement and migration and focuses instead on the social construction of *Heimat* as a "fragile construction and even in part a forgery."¹³

This construction does not end at the novel, but rather extends into the digital forms of its public epitext¹⁴ as well. In addition to the published novel, Stanišić made related material available in a so-called "Haus der Heimat" village archive, which was housed on the website fürstenfelde.de. Here readers could access otherwise unpublished draft excerpts, interviews, and photos, and comment sections allowed them to append their own impressions, reactions, and questions for the author, who responded periodically in the years after the novel's publication. Intended as a home for fragments cut from the finalized manuscript and as a promotional site where the fictional village continued to engage readers, the author's posts included links to press and radio reviews of the book. Stanišić maintained the website and responded to comments through 2019, at which point his attention turned to a much more streamlined promotional site for his next novel, *Herkunft* (2019), while his social media presence remained active.¹⁵ The website remained online until 2021 when the URL was removed. Fürstenfelde.de therefore offered a temporary archive and promotional platform that was more widely accessible to interested readers in reach of the Internet, but also more subject to the pressures of time and continued upkeep than the printed book.

---

12 Sandberg, "Etische Ökokritik," 93.
13 Sandberg, "Etische Ökokritik," 95. Translation my own.
14 "Epitext" is Gérard Genette's term for paratextual features that are not physically connected to the text. Key features of these types of textual appendages include being addressed not only to readers of the text, but also to the public more generally, and having a functional difference from the text itself, such as promotion. See Gérard Genette, *Paratexts: Thresholds of Interpretation*, trans. Jane E. Lewin (Cambridge: Cambridge University Press, 1997), 334–370.
15 Interested readers may access the *Herkunft* website at http://kuenstlicht.de/. Also hosted by WordPress, this site consists of a single page promoting the novel with links to the publishing house (Luchterhand). Stanišić is perhaps most frequently active on Instagram, where he posts runs from his reading tours, promotes other authors, and advertises his works.

The website was both an extension of the completed novel and a digital avatar of the novel's town, which is mostly based on the actual town of Fürstenwerder, Germany. When users navigated through the website header to the "Haus der Heimat" page, they came to a set of fifteen icons derived from photographs Stanišić likely collected during his extended stay and post-publication reading tours. The page's title alludes to the *Heimatstube* (Homeland Museum) in Fürstenwerder, where Stanišić conducted research for his novel. Many of the icons were black-and-white circular images that resonated with the figures and landscapes of the novel and linked to various texts collected in the site. The images were interspersed with four icons presenting magnified portions of the text to which they linked, thus continuing the author's play with typography that is also present in the novel. When users hovered over the icons, they turned from black-and-white to color, losing their grayscale patina and coming alive as portals into the draft fragments and interviews.

The website's presentation of information continued the novel's practice of interweaving fact and fiction, archived and imagined, yet blurred boundaries even closer to readers. At the interface of life and works, the site visually and tactilely leveled distinctions among texts from the author's research, writing process, and reader reception. No visual hierarchy or suggested order was evident from the placement of the icons on the webpage, and users chose their own paths through reviews and unpublished passages. The incidental ordering therefore echoes the chronicle form in which several passages of the novel are written. In the novel, the interspersed sixteenth-century legends, fires, floods, and trials in Early New High German are recounted or invented seemingly incidentally. Though ordered chronologically, the incidents leave readers wondering about their significance, and whether or not the information will return to gain meaning in the course of the novel. Like the icons on the website, many of the episodes never come together as meaningful events shaped into a narrative, but rather give discrete portraits of additional scenes that did not find a place in the novel, or glimpses into the book's reception. The website therefore extends the novel's formal juxtaposition of temporal layers to develop a temporary archive that, like the archive in Fürstenfelde, included a sort of prehistory of the manuscript, as well as its subsequent influence on critics and readers.

To better understand the relevance of the networked structures arising from the novel's print and digital components, I turn to Katherine Hayles's theoretical approach to electronic literature. In *My Mother was a Computer* (2005), Hayles develops the concept of intermediation to reconcile Wolfgang Kittler's notion of a subject that is an effect of media with Marc Hansen's focus on embodied subjects and lifeworlds that necessarily contextualize media and media users. In Hayles's mediatory account, literature becomes an exemplary case of interface and interaction: "As an embodied art form, literature registers the impact of information in its materiality, in the ways in which its physical characteristics are mobilized as resources to create meaning. This entanglement of the bodies of texts and digital subjects is one manifestation of what I call 'intermediation,' that is, complex transactions between bodies and texts as well as between different forms of media."[16] Key to Hayles's description of intermediation is an interrelated system of feedback and feedforward loops that draws substantially from Nicholas Gessler's "dynamic hierarchies." The complex interactions circulating throughout these hierarchies – or through literary and electronic text and reading or writing user – inform and mutually determine elements at all levels of a relational structure.[17] Just as users and programmers invent new ways of navigating and manipulating digital texts, these texts use the help of affordances beyond the medial functionality of print literature to compel reading practices that fundamentally change readers' perception and cognition in turn.

In Stanišić's work, digital technologies mark both the printed novel and its digital complement, thus sending feedback and feedforward loops through multiple registers of the material. The reading practices developed by the website give new, interactive associations to the archive presented in the novel. Once the German village settled on a digital domain, readers were afforded greater flexibility to navigate its documentary-like photographic icons at will. Without titles to mark the images – and lacking the page numbers, chapter divisions, or other paratextual conventions that guide readers through the novel – users selected images idiosyncratically or randomly, perhaps from left to right and top to bottom, or perhaps according to visual appeal and personal interest. A new narrative could thus be pieced together, in which users recombined literary statements and draft fragments without the neat lines of genre to guide them. Playing off the book's thematic occupation with juxtaposing the chronicles and legends that together form the village's textual history – complete with falsified documents and social intrigue – the website formally bound forgeries and imaginaries to cultivate and virtually realize the town of Fürstenfelde through the

---

[16] N. Katherine Hayles, *My Mother Was a Computer: Digital Subjects and Literary Texts* (Chicago: University of Chicago Press, 2005), 70. Hayles' formulation of the "transactions" between texts and readers resonates with Irene Kacandes' seminal notion of literature as "Talk," which takes up fictional texts that emphasize forms of address. In Kacandes' account, texts "talk" insofar as they put forth statements that elicit replies from readers and call for responses in the extratextual world. See *Talk Fiction: Literature and the Talk Explosion* (Lincoln: University of Nebraska Press, 2001).
[17] N. Katherine Hayles, "Intermediation: The Pursuit of a Vision," *New Literary History* 38.1 (Winter 2007): 100.

creation of its "Haus der Heimat" digital archive. Now that the site is inactive, the limits to its increased interactivity are betrayed by the absence of its author-curator, whose attention has refocused to other projects. The digital archive therefore not only facilitates interaction, but also depends upon use and maintenance to exist at all. Without authorial intervention, the page becomes mere information: subject to the obsolescence of a medial existence that is removed when deemed a waste of server space.

Stanišic's website explicitly played with feedback loops between fictional and lived experience that have since expanded into other domains as well. These loops were visible in part through readers' comments and questions to which Stanišić responded, thereby continuing to muse on the work through living exchanges with new interlocutors. Many authors' websites present an entire oeuvre or focus on publicizing finished work. Stanišić's site certainly had the latter function, but what truly distinguished fürstenfelde.de was the author's interest in archiving the otherwise unpublished fragments of a single work, and his documentation of Fürstenwerder's response to his readings.[18] One page on fürstenfelde.de, for example, accessible through the icon of an Uckermark welcome sign on which the book had been placed, explicitly acknowledged the recursive relationship between Stanišić's work and the community on which it is loosely based. On the page was a list of gifts presented to Stanišić in Fürstenwerder that came "from reality through fiction back to reality."[19] Though the literary work reimagines these simple objects – a carton of (Ditzsche's) eggs, a town painting from "Frau Kranz," a publication from the village museum – they have since transformed readers' perceptions to carry their fictional associations as well. Furthermore, the official website for tourism in Fürstenwerder joins this feedback loop by incorporating Stanišić's work into its historical summary. Alongside links to "Fürstenwerder then" and "Fürstenwerder now," website users find a link to "Fürstenfelde." Selecting this link leads them to a short description of Stanišić's project and its acclaim, including a collection of linked

---

18 Other authors have made unpublished material accessible to readers to create a textual conversation exceeding a single publication. Perhaps most famous are the multimedial productions surrounding Art Spiegelman's *Maus*, a two-volume graphic novel based on the author's family history in Nazi-occupied Poland and as prisoners of Auschwitz. Spiegelman has since made additional material both from his research and his creative process available in *The Complete Maus*, a DVD containing interview and documentary footage along with unpublished sketches and notebooks, and an accompanying volume, *MetaMaus* (2011), in which the author reflects on the conception and reception of his work.
19 Saša Stanišić, "Lesung in Fürstenwerder," *Fürstenfelde*, http://fürstenfelde.de/?p=169, (2014–2021), 29 July 2019.

press releases.[20] The fictionalized version of the town therefore takes its place as a complement to past and present in the self-presentation of Fürstenwerder itself. The literary tourism that has ensued since the novel suggests effects on the future of the town as well, which has begun to host "Wortgarten" literary festivals celebrating works and authors connected to the Uckermark region.[21] Though fürstenfelde.de was a temporary project dependent on Stanišić's work to maintain it, the economic and cultural impact of his project reverberates through these continued celebrations and promotions of the region.

The creative feedback loops traced by the intermingling of documentary and imagined textual sources within the novel results in unexpected resonances that connect actual archival material with Stanišić's inventions. These extend beyond the printed novel through the author's relationship to the community that inspired it to reveal the imaginary work required to create, and cultivate, *Heimat* as a social space. Just as the bellringer's apprentice Johann configures continuities between medieval practices and pop culture in the novel, the work as a whole uses the new affordances of its digital presence to reinvigorate the traditional power of print literature, too. While the novel cues readers to proceed in a linear fashion, its digital counterpart at fürstenfelde.de inspired non-hierarchical connections among fictionalized material, actual objects and places, and reader reception not usually considered part of the work itself. The formal implications of the intermedial project as a whole, including its influence on cultural events hosted by the actual Fürstenwerder, trace reciprocal interactions that loop readers into a dynamic, active process co-constructing the village. The collective storytelling that results creates Fürstenfelde as a *Heimat* imbricated in and recursively defining extraliterary lives, too. Stanišić's project therefore musters intermediality as an antidote to the insularity defining conservative trends in *Heimatliteratur*, while making readers all the more aware of the power of narrative in its printed form as well.

---

20 Tourism Association Fürstenwerder Lake Region e.V., "Willkommen in der Fürstenwerder Seenlandschaft," https://fuerstenwerder-seengebiet.de/fuerstenwerder-uebersicht/, 6 May 2021.
21 The Wortgarten festivals took place in 2015 and again in 2019. Programs and photos from the event have been archived at http://www.wortgarten.de/. Olivia Albiero also addresses these feedback loops in her detailed reading of the "Haus der Heimat" webpage, if not in such terms. For Albiero, the website becomes an extension of genre, and its key function to bring additional attention to the town: "the website reinforces the role of the village tale and its author, who uses the technology at his disposal to also introduce the readers to the writing and circulation of the novel and its stories." See "Fürstenfelde and Unterleuten," 151.

Remembering Heimat: "Böhmische Dörfer"

Stanišić's intermedial construction of *Heimat* contrasts productively with a digital-born memory project, "Böhmische Dörfer. Sudeten Germans: Germanophone inhabitants of Bohemia and Moravia," by author and media theorist, Alexandra Saemmer. Though both works suggest the potential of engaging the notion of *Heimat* digitally, Stanišić's work relies more heavily on temporal and multimodal aspects of narration, whereas Saemmer engages the spatial configurations made possible by her chosen platform. For Stanišić, literary narration weaves the contemporary living voices of Fürstenfelde into the musty chronicles housed in the fictional "Haus der Heimat," which becomes in turn a digital presence interfacing with actual users. It thus tests the porosity of temporal layers to play on the social construction of *Heimat* through fact and forgery, history and story. Saemmer also explores the construction of *Heimat*, but foregrounds memory and trauma as they touch collective experience instead. Absent is the humor of Stanišić's work, which involves traumatic ellipses and obliquely-narrated violence but does not focus on them. Gone, too, is the novel's not omniscient, but rather ubiquitous collective we-narrator, which provides a stabilizing, if not entirely reliable, coordinate to guide readers through the story. Instead, Saemmer's work locates readers in the midst of a traumatic recollection of expulsion staged in fragments by a first-person singular lyrical subject. Though *Heimat* is only alluded to in the German version of Saemmer's tri-lingual work, the artist's choice of topic points toward one of the most problematic abuses of the term by Nazi Germany.

Instead of emphasizing temporal aspects of narrative, Saemmer uses the spatial affordances of the online presentation tool Prezi to construct a simultaneity across multiple temporal layers. Her e-poem, "Böhmische Dörfer" (Bohemian villages), constructs the speaker's mother's memory of being expelled from the town of Brno in present-day Czechia in January 1946. Only one year old at the time of expulsion, the mother returns with Saemmer in 2007 to her former home, and the work is based on their interaction and the memories it involves. The work therefore mediates the expulsions as a postmemory, twice removed from the event through the mother's account – impossible as a consciously-lived memory given her young age – and through the interventions of the narrating subject who reconstructs her mother's performed recollection.[22]

---

[22] "Postmemory" is Marianne Hirsch's term for memories passed through generations but perceived as one's own. See Marianne Hirsch, *The Generation of Postmemory: Writing and Visual Culture after the Holocaust* (New York: Columbia University Press, 2012).

Because the expulsions of German-speakers from eastern Europe at the end of World War II were highly politicized in public discourse in Germany, the work may also be understood as an intervention in discourses of German victimhood, which have sought in more and less nuanced ways to acknowledge how non-Jewish Germans were traumatized by war-related acts of aerial bombing, rape, and expulsion. In her now seminal account of cultural memory in Germany, *Shadows of Trauma* (2006), Aleida Assmann interrogates the notion that discussion of war crimes immediately after World War II was taboo, and shows instead the ways that suffering and guilt were perceived to be incompatible.[23] The dichotomous relationship posited between victim and perpetrator thus caused individuals either to appropriate Jewish suffering, or to relativize the six million Jewish people murdered in the Holocaust (as well as Roma, Sinti, queer and disabled victims, forced laborers, and others marked as degenerate) with seven million displaced peoples. In the decades after the war, the discourse of German victimhood was also mustered by far right-leaning groups such as the Federation of Expellees, and West German politicians sought affiliation from a potential electorate during the 1950s and 60s through a now discredited appeal to compensation. Although increasing interest in a shared experience of victimhood was fueled in part by questions of identity in a reunited Germany, more variegated approaches to these contested histories have brought to a head crucial conversations about integrating German-Jewish experience into national frameworks of memory while also acknowledging the wide scope of suffering incited by the war.

Saemmer's work contributes to these negotiations of memory and shared history by using her mother's postmemories of expulsion as a point of departure for a work that more explicitly addresses the collective and continuous work of remembering itself. Using sparse, poetic fragments, the author scatters quotations and impressions from the visit with her mother and brother against a pixelated photograph of a water-washed clearing. Some statements seem attributable to the mother, whereas others invoke an insistent probing that seeks access beyond the scene of recollection. Users gradually orient themselves in the work's deictics as they navigate from the opening lines, "The house. It is

---

23 Aleida Assmann, *Shadows of Trauma: Memory and the Politics of Postwar Identity*, trans. Sarah Clift (New York: Fordham, 2016), esp. 154–173. Assmann resolves the competing memory discourses she addresses by suggesting a "German national framework of memory" in which public discourse foregrounds its acknowledgement of responsibility for the Nazi regime and the Holocaust, but does not obstruct the framework of social memory in which families and communities address their particular suffering, guilt, and trauma. See 173.

there, / there behind. Do you see it?"[24] through a recollection of a grandmother who dies of hunger, a mother who descends from a train, and a brother and father who are simply posited without further description. Insistent assertions of "here" and "I restart" give readers a sense of the speaker's desperation and persistence as she searches to position the figures in memory and in the poem: "and now: Restart / but what / on the left / and on the right / what / but what / January 1946."[25]

The work website is available, though not quite identical, in three languages: French, English, and German. The absence of a Czech version of the poem is significant given the histories that it addresses, and the choice of languages reflects instead the languages in which the Paris-based author is fluent. Saemmer's turn to English is likely based on reaching a wider audience that may include Czech speakers, but is not directed primarily at them with the intention that a Czech translation would have implied. The privileged attention devoted to the English version is suggested by the archived version of the work in the *Electronic Literature Collection*. In this version, a video recording of the English poem in motion is set against an embedded black-and-white video of people walking beside heavily laden horse-drawn carriages in winter. The shifting grayscale pixels moving behind the fragments are difficult to discern as more than shadows until the final minute, in which the presentation zooms out to bring the whole video into focus. Throughout the video a fuzzy audio track suggests the thick thunder of firing tanks.

Except for the archived video, which does not depend on user interaction beyond initiating play, the text in all languages may be viewed in two ways by readers. One path through the text is ordered by the author, and users click on an arrow to be lead through the Prezi canvas by way of a predetermined sequence. Users may also determine their own way through the fragments by holding down a mouse key to drag other parts of the text into view. While doing so, they may zoom in and out to see what view various vantage points yield. In all versions, the text includes a portion that is not part of the pre-programmed path. This brief description, which readers must intentionally drag into view, situates Saemmer's mother's postmemories in two important historical contexts. Because the text is located on a horizontal axis in Prezi just below the work's title, it functions as a likewise paratextual framework that explicitly familiarizes readers with a brief history of the relevant events. This is a stark contrast to the

---

24 Alexandra Saemmer, "Böhmische Dörfer – English Version" (2011) *Electronic Literature Collection* vol. 3 https://prezi.com/m7lq5txsl5qz/bohmische-dorfer-english-version/ Topics 2 & 3. 9 October 2021.
25 Saemmer, "Böhmische Dörfer – English Version," Topics 15–21. 9 October 2021.

rest of the work, which provides only the temporal marker "January 1946"[26] and nondescript signifiers in the text itself such as "the house," "a train" and white fields.[27] The first named historical context is the Brno Death March, which was part of a series of expulsions of Germans from the redrawn borders of Czechoslovakia to Austria and Germany between 1945 and 1946.[28] In this context, the temporal marker provided locates the postmemory at a turning point between the "wild expulsions" unofficially and violently initiated by citizens and vigilante groups, and the state-organized "transfer" of German speakers out of Czechoslovakia. The second context provided moves back in history to Adolf Hitler's declaration in 1938 that Nazi Germany would liberate the Sudeten Germans by annexing Czechoslovakia, which is often considered the impetus for the expulsions.[29]

The work's title elaborates an additional level to this paratextual framework as well. "Bohemian Villages" alludes to the German expression, "Das sind mir böhmische Dörfer" or "It's Bohemian villages to me," a reference to something beyond a speaker's ability to comprehend. Ethnologists root this expression both in difficulties German speakers had pronouncing the Slavic town names in Bohemia, as well as in the destruction of Bohemian villages during the Hussite wars of 1419 to 1434 that rendered them unrecognizable.[30] The designation "Sudeten German," also used in the work's title, is a more recent invention, however. This latter dates to a climate of rising nationalization in the wake of World War I, when borders were redrawn, and Czechoslovakia was created from former Austria-Hungary. The title of Saemmer's work therefore refers both to the long history of co-existence shared by Germans and Slavs in Bohemia, as well as the unfathomability of the experience of expulsion for the lyrical

---

26 Saemmer, "Böhmische Dörfer – English Version," Topics 21 & 66, 20 April 2021.
27 Saemmer, "Böhmische Dörfer – English Version," Topics 2, 36 (house); 54, 95, 112, 119 (train), and 37, 70, 94, 99 (fields), respectively, 20 April 2021.
28 For a short history of the expulsions, see Eagle Glassheim, "The Mechanics of Ethnic Cleansing: The Expulsion of Germans from Czechoslovakia, 1945–1947," in *Redrawing Nations: Ethnic Cleansing in East-Central Europe, 1944–1948*, eds. Philipp Ther and Ana Siljak (Lanham: The Rowman & Littlefield Publishing Group, 2001), 197–220.
29 Other frameworks for analyzing the expulsions include critiques of nation-building projects in Europe, such as Marina Cattaruzza, who argues, "German minorities in Czechoslovakia and Poland were accused not so much of having colluded in the crimes against humanity as having helped to dismantle the Czechoslovak and Polish states." See "'Last stop expulsion' – The minority question and forced migration in East-Central Europe: 1918–49," *Nations and Nationalism* 16.1 (2010), 111.
30 See Rudolf Kubitschek, "Böhmische Dörfer," *Allerlei Bayerisches und Böhmisches*, 1940. https://www.projekt-gutenberg.org/kubitsch/bayboehm/chap019.html, 8 April 2021.

subject and her mother. Similarly, Saemmer's text thematizes the inconceivability of its historical referent. Instead of attempting to write her family's narrative of expulsion, the author creates a performance of recollection staged by reader and text. Facilitated by the spatializing techniques of Prezi, which arrange sweeping paths through the text that zoom in and out and pan sweep right and left, the e-poem refuses linear reading conventions to echo both the disorientation of the journey and the fragmentation of traumatic experience resonating in memory.

This reading is further supported by the author's statement, in which the artist describes creating "a piece about the impossibility of reconstructing the failing memory of the 'March of Death.'"[31] Yet the piece opens additional readings as well. It is not merely about reconstructing memory, but also about the recursive formation of subjectivity among user(s), program, and text. As the lyrical subject stumbles into the knowledge of the unknowable Bohemian villages left behind before her birth, readers join in the frantic movements through insistently reinscribed deictic markers of here, there, and now, as the text reiterates "I restart." These digital techniques make the processual, local, and interrupted formation of subjectivity visible as the lyrical subject becomes conscious of her heritage among the scattered marks and spaces of the mother's recalled words. This personal experience, facilitated by the reader's manipulation of the text, turns on moments of fragmentation and erasure, but also on users who find new paths. Dropped *in media res* into "The house . . . there behind" from which users watch as family members appear only to disappear, the lyrical subject probes "the forbidden space" behind background and décor.[32] The traumatic details of expulsion have largely been bracketed out of the scene as the mother revisits it with her family, yet her repeated insistence that together they "look at it . . . in my décor" points toward a blind spot to which the lyrical subject seeks access.[33]

The subjectivity created by the work is clearly not an individual consciousness unfolding across time, but rather a series of interruptions and initiations calling on users to navigate and bridge the gaps. To do so effectively – that is, to investigate the historical background on which the text rests – they must respond to the work's cues. These are recognizable in both formal aspects of the written text, which is only fully visible as the work's canvas, and implied through the medial affordances of Prezi. Saemmer creates topics (the name for

---

31 Saemmer, "Statement" in "Böhmische Dörfer" (2011) *Electronic Literature Collection* vol. 3 http://collection.eliterature.org/3/work.html?work=bohmische-dorfer, 8 April 2021.
32 Saemmer, "Böhmische Dörfer – English Version," Topics 2–3 and 13, respectively.
33 Saemmer, "Böhmische Dörfer – English Version," Topics 106 and 108.

slides in Prezi) from most, but not all, of the work's full text, which inspires additional user interactivity by affording varying amounts of visual access to the canvas and the otherwise invisible paratextual features located there. Tempted by textual traces they can decipher only by seeking them out and zooming in, users are compelled to manipulate the canvas beyond the predetermined path laid out for them in the presentation. Doing so allows them a greater degree of historical orientation, which counters an understanding of the work as merely the performance of one individual's failing memory and implies the relational quality of subjectivity itself.

Teasing apart the synthesis of textual and medial effects users experience requires a short theoretical detour by way of a return to intermediation. With reference to Daniel C. Dennett's *Consciousness Explained*, N. Katherine Hayles describes the literary subjectivity established through the feedback loops of electronic literature as "not a continuous coherent stream [of consciousness] but rather multilayered shifting strata dynamically in motion relative to one another."[34] Constitutive of these strata are the multiple simultaneous processes running in computers as they translate binary code into interfaces for users. In her reading of electronic works that engage stream-of-consciousness narrative, Hayles demonstrates how digital narratives require a conceptual reworking of subjectivity: "The computer, programmed by the writer and designer, reveals to the human player the mechanisms whereby her interior monologue is (mis)taken as the production of a coherent self . . . Consciousness in this view is disjunctive, emergent, dynamic, and temporally stratified, created through local interactions between diverse agents/processes that together create the illusion of a continuous coherent self."[35] In Hayles's account, computer consciousness does not so much change human cognition as reveal a more fitting model of its function. Electronic literature, a malleable medium that can respond, and even adapt, to user manipulation, extends the feedback loops also observable in print literature so that users may affect the text itself, not merely vice versa. The resulting subjectivity is highly relational due to its heterogenous layers and temporalities. This is the case, as will be relevant for Saemmer's work, not because of ellipses born of inaccessible traumatic experience, but rather because centralized continuity and the coherence of a unified consciousness are not determinate features of subjectivity in the first place.

Saemmer's work, although interactive, does not display the level of adaptability of other digital works that allow user choices to radically change the text

---

[34] Hayles, "Intermediation," 118.
[35] Hayles, "Intermediation," 119.

or code on which it is based. It is however significantly interactive because a user's choices matter. Users decide the speed at which the topics progress, or choose to watch on autoplay, and at any moment they may click and drag the field behind the words designed to appear in order to investigate other clusters of fragments on the canvas. In addition to these medial affordances, the text engages narrative strategies that incorporate users as well. Among these formal cues are a pronominal play which mirrors Prezi's interpellations of users into the text through user manipulation. The second-person pronoun "you" plays on an ambiguity that may be construed to address the speaker's memory of her mother (as spoken by the lyrical subject), the first-person lyrical subject (as spoken by her mother), and readers of the text (addressed by the lyrical subject as well). These pronominal shifts remain throughout the piece and bear different degrees of ambiguity depending largely on the language of the version and whether or not users have navigated through it before.

When the work begins, the context may be construed as the mother pointing out her former house to her visiting family. The "you" in this case refers to the daughter, as spoken by the mother: "The house. It is there, / there behind. Do you see it?" Although first-time readers may imagine the speaker is also addressing them to orient them in the work, the pronouns quickly shift to "your brother" / "ton frère" / "den Bruder meiner Mutter" to resolve this ambiguity and construct a speaker addressing the memory of her mother. The nuanced differences across the versions are also clear in this example, which employs the second-person address in English and French, and thereby maintains ambiguity for first-time readers who assume the same reference as the preceding fragments. The German version resolves the ambiguity, however, and clearly describes the figures' relationship to the first-person narrator. At the conclusion of the poem readers will learn that the speaker visited the mother's former house with her own brother, thus creating a parallel between siblings across two generations. Upon first reading, however, the details of the visit remain to be seen. Even so, readers of the German and French versions will begin to wonder about the changing contexts due to unexplained pronominal shifts between singular and plural forms of address that are not detectable in the English *you*.[36] These shifts differentiate the voices more strongly, but the overall effect in all versions remains the same. In the absence of other markers of direct

---

[36] The pronominal shifts are most clear at different moments in the versions depending on the expressions used. By way of example, here is one such shift in the German version: "ich sende **euch** / mein Szenenbild / erinnert sich konturlos / **schau** mal an: / . . . / kreist **du** herum" (Topics 71–79) and one such shift in the French version: "c'est ici. **Vous** la voyez? / **ton** frère aussi. Se perd / au fond / vois-**tu**?" (Topics 3–6).

speech, the repeated second-person addresses create strong resonances between lines focalized through the mother and those attributable to the narrator. In some fragments the figures may be differentiated, and in others the figures inhabit the same ambivalent referent.

The invocation of multiple addressees into the work's subjectivity allows the fragments to participate in multiple temporalities including the 1946 event, its reconstruction in 2007, and the narrator's recurring attempts to grasp it: "I move around it, since."[37] Readers are also called to participate, both as users manipulating the work, and as its explicit addressees. Three topics in the presentation repeat the phrase "Let me introduce."[38] Out of place in the memory itself, the imperative formulation in English speaks directly to readers. This sense is underscored in the French version, "je vous présente," which explicitly references either a plural audience or formal address, and more subtly implied in the German indicative, "Ich stelle vor."[39] Because Prezi is often used for structuring and delivering presentations, the phrase may furthermore be interpreted as a self-reflexive reference to the platform in which the work is built. The presentational language thematizes the author's choice of a presentational platform, which has been reimagined to serve aesthetic purposes but still leaves its mark in the work. Despite the intimate circumstances of the memory, this reference to the media composing it creates a tension between the act of remembering within the family and the highly political stakes of the memory. Readers are not only called into the presentation, but also addressed as the audience for whom it is being staged. In addition, Saemmer has published her work with a reusable license, which allows users to freely download, share, and manipulate the topics. Given the contested legacy of the expulsions, which continue to raise questions in Czechia, Germany, and Austria about ethical ways to represent and acknowledge past violence,[40] Saemmer highlights the

---

[37] Saemmer, "Böhmische Dörfer – English Version," Topic 122.
[38] Saemmer, "Böhmische Dörfer – English Version," Topics 30, 32, and 42.
[39] Saemmer, "Böhmische Dörfer – English Version," Topic 30, 32, and 42 and "Böhmische Dörfer – German version," Topic 30, 32, and 42.
[40] Public confrontations with this history are extremely difficult to summarize briefly, no less so given the different political pressures during the Cold War on the countries involved. For an ambitious and intriguing discussion of these memory cultures, see Václav Smyčka, *Das Gedächtnis der Vertreibung. Interkulturelle Perspektiven auf deutsche und tschechische Gegenwartsliteratur und Erinnerungskulturen* (Bielefeld: transcript, 2019). According to Smyčka, the Sudeten Germans in West Germany were able to publish and organize freely since 1948, but found diminishing political support, especially by the 1970s due to Willy Brandt's *Ostpolitik*. In East Germany, authors such as Christa Wolf and Franz Fühmann contributed literary representations of ethnic German expulsions to GDR cultural politics, and critiques in Czechoslovakia

fundamentally political connotations of a seemingly personal shared experience. Weaving readers into an already multiple subjectivity constituted by the fits and starts of an incomplete memory suggests the necessity of continuing to contend with this unsettled past collectively.

At the conclusion of the pre-programmed path through the Prezi canvas, which is accessed by clicking arrows at the bottom of the screen, users are brought to the title of the piece and, below it, the author's name. If they choose not to interact with the text, the next topic brings them to the year 2007 with a description of the family's visit. Yet before zooming in on this topic, Prezi zooms out to show the entire canvas with the poem's full text, revealing the pixelated field behind it. While zooming back into the poem, insightful readers will notice additional text beyond the frame of title topic. Thereby encouraged to take advantage of Prezi's interactive capabilities, readers may choose to manipulate the text and, by scrolling around the field, find the aforementioned frameworks that contextualize the mother's memory and the family's visit in a chronology of political events precipitating the expulsion. The work therefore lends access to the historical framework giving rise to the memory, offering a partial answer to users who follow the narrator's searching through her mother's ellipses: "I dig the forbidden space."[41] By adapting their reading technique to the spatial arrangement of the text and the medial affordances of Prezi, users hone the keen attention necessary to detect what is hidden between the lines of the path presented.

Conclusion

Attention to intermediality in Saša Stanišić's novel-based website and Saemmer's digital-born e-poem helps us expand our notion of literary interventions in discourses of *Heimat*. The intermedial features of Stanišić's *Vor dem Fest* and its digital complement allow users to explore additional, self-published features of a fictionalized town, actualized virtually on the fürstenfelde.de domain. By interacting with the author and recombining literary and documentary information while perusing the real – if virtual – "Haus der Heimat," users participate in the

---

began with journalists who criticized the plundering of abandoned German property as early as 1945. The first open critiques of expulsion as such in Czechoslovakian presses were published in the 1960s, and then continued underground during the 1970s due to increased censorship. These discussions resurfaced in various forms after the *Wende*, which brought both opportunities to reevaluate national memory cultures, as well as anxieties about the newly opened borders, see 35–40.

41 Saemmer, "Böhmische Dörfer – English Version," Topic 61.

development of the work and extend its narrative further across time. Following the feedback loop in the opposite direction, fans shape existing geographies to augment reality through literature in the form of cultural events and touristic adventures in Fürstenwerder, on which the novel is based. The result is a notion of *Heimat* that becomes medially uncoupled from territorial associations which might exclude some participants from engaging in its construction.

Alexandra Saemmer's "Böhmische Dörfer," on the other hand, pushes the spatial arrangements of its digital platform to construct a performance of memory while teaching users new ways to read between the lines. In Saemmer's work, a mother's *Heimat* is torn asunder by the experience of expulsion, and recedes into "the background" of her consciousness with the childhood house she is forced to leave.[42] Behind the image of a house, which grounds the memory of postwar expulsions of ethnic Germans from Czech-German borderlands, users discover the historical narrative that contextualizes the mother's experience, even though their reading process is driven by the fragmentary, elliptical performance of remembering itself. The form of intermediation put forth in Saemmer's digitally-born text exceeds mere interaction between reader and text conceived as discrete entities, and brings a dynamic, interrelated subjectivity spanning the lyrical I, addressee, user, and program to the fore. Co-constructing a failing memory allows users to find additional vantage points into a traumatic history and brings attention to a *Heimat* still contested in national public discourse.[43]

Works cited

Adelson, Leslie A. *The Turkish Turn in Contemporary Literature: Toward a New Critical Grammar of Migration* (New York: Palgrave, 2005).

Albiero, Olivia. "Fürstenfelde and Unterleuten: Two Literary German Villages and Their Digital Representation," *Pacific Coast Philology* 54.2 (2019): 135–160.

Bartels, Gerrit. "Die wertvollste Gabe ist die Erfindung," *Tagesspiegel*. 14 March 2014. https://www.tagesspiegel.de/kultur/sasa-stanisics-roman-vor-dem-fest-die-wertvollste-gabe-ist-die-erfindung/9617570.html, 7 September 2019.

---

[42] Saemmer, "Böhmische Dörfer – English Version," Topic 5.
[43] For example, in 2015 a group of Germans and Czechs undertook a 32-kilometer pilgrimage organized by the city of Brno in collective remembrance of the death marches. The commemoration was criticized by Czech resistance fighters who had fought against the Nazis in World War II. See "Czech city remembers expelled ethnic Germans," *Deutsche Welle*. 30 May 2015. https://www.dw.com/en/czech-city-remembers-expelled-ethnic-germans/a-18487935, 7 April 2021.

Böttcher, Philipp. "Fürstenfelde erzählt. Dörflichkeit und narrative Verfahren in Saša Stanišićs "Vor dem Fest," *Zeitschrift für Germanistik* 30.2 (2020): 306–325.

Cattaruzza, Marina. "'Last stop expulsion' – The minority question and forced migration in East-Central Europe: 1918–49," *Nations and Nationalism* 16.1 (2010): 108–126.

"Czech city remembers expelled ethnic Germans," *Deutsche Welle*. 30 May 2015. https://www.dw.com/en/czech-city-remembers-expelled-ethnic-germans/a-18487935. 7 April 2021.

Genette, Gérard. *Paratexts: Thresholds of Interpretation*. Trans. Jane E. Lewin (Cambridge: Cambridge University Press, 1997).

Glassheim, Eagle. "The Mechanics of Ethnic Cleansing: The Expulsion of Germans from Czechoslovakia, 1945–1947," in *Redrawing Nations: Ethnic Cleansing in East-Central Europe, 1944–1948*. Eds. Philipp Ther and Ana Siljak (Lanham: The Rowman & Littlefield Publishing Group, 2001), 197–220.

Hayles, N. Katherine. *My Mother Was a Computer: Digital Subjects and Literary Texts* (Chicago: University of Chicago Press, 2005).

Hayles, N. Katherine. "Intermediation: The Pursuit of a Vision," *New Literary History* 38.1 (Winter 2007): 99–125.

Hirsch, Marianne. *The Generation of Postmemory Writing and Visual Culture after the Holocaust* (New York: Columbia University Press, 2012).

Kacandes, Irene. *Talk Fiction: Literature and the Talk Explosion* (Lincoln: University of Nebraska Press, 2001).

Kubitschek, Rudolf. "Böhmische Dörfer," *Allerlei Bayerisches und Böhmisches*, 1940. https://www.projekt-gutenberg.org/kubitsch/bayboehm/chap019.html. 8April 2021.

Matthes, Frauke. "'Weltliteratur aus der Uckermark': Regionalism and Transnationalism in Saša Stanišić's *Vor dem Fest*," in *German in the World*. Eds. James Hodkinson and Benedict Schofield (Rochester: Camden, 2020), 91–108.

Osborne, Dora. "'Irgendwie wird es gehen': Trauma, Survival, and Creativity in Saša Stanišić's *Vor dem Fest*," *German Life and Letters* 72.4 (2019): 469–483.

Saemmer, Alexandra. "Böhmische Dörfer" (2011) *Electronic Literature Collection* vol. 3 http://collection.eliterature.org/3/work.html?work=bohmische-dorfer. 6 May 2021.

Sandberg, Anna. "Etische Ökokritik der Gegenwartsliteratur: Saša Stanišić *Vor dem Fest* (2014)," in *Ökologischer Wandel in der deutschsprachigen Literatur des 20. und 21. Jahrhunderts*. Eds. Gabriele Dürbeck et al. (Berlin: Peter Lang, 2018), 91–105.

Stanišić, Saša. *Vor dem Fest* (Munich: Luchterhand, 2014).

Stanišić, Saša. *Before the Feast*. Trans. Anthea Bell (Portland: Tin House Books, 2016).

Stanišić, Saša. *Fürstenfelde*. http://fürstenfelde.de/ (2014–2021), 26 January 2021.

Smyčka, Václav. *Das Gedächtnis der Vertreibung. Interkulturelle Perspektiven auf deutsche und tschechische Gegenwartsliteratur und Erinnerungskulturen* (Bielefeld: transcript, 2019).

Spiegelman, Art. *Maus. A Survivor's Tale* (New York: Pantheon Books, 1986).

Spiegelman, Art. *Maus II: And Here My Troubles Began* (New York: Pantheon Books, 1991).

Spiegelman, Art. *MetaMaus* (New York: Pantheon Books, 2011).

Tourism Association Fürstenwerder Lake Region e.V., "Willkommen in der Fürstenwerder Seenlandschaft," https://fuerstenwerder-seengebiet.de/fuerstenwerder-uebersicht/, 6 May 2021.

Communities / Constellations of the Aftermath

Barbara Mennel
Private Precarity and Public Theory in Irene von Alberti's *The Long Summer of Theory*

A unique essay film, Irene von Alberti's *Der lange Sommer der Theorie* [*The Long Summer of Theory*, 2015] stages a search for collective visions of a future for a generation that has come of age in precarious living and working conditions. In the film, a group of young women occupy an empty apartment in the no-man's-land behind the Berlin Central Station (Berlin Hauptbahnhof, opened in 2006). The film's main character Nola, one of three women who share the apartment, interviews scholars and artists in Berlin about utopian visions of solidarity. This article takes up the question the film poses: how are we to imagine the relations among theory, everyday life, artistic production, and sustainable work?

By interrogating the relationship between theory and the public sphere that the film posits, I investigate its presuppositions of precarity and feminism. *The Long Summer of Theory* excites with its experiment to bridge the divide between the public sphere and scholarly production about critical, feminist, artistic, and social theories. It also disappoints with its limitations that reflect premises of dominant scholarly paradigms regarding precarity as an overarching economic and social phenomenon that defines a generation. In instances, theories of precarity reflects the shock to middle-class white citizens, and in other cases, scholars do not differentiate between middle-class interns and refugees from the Global South as members of the precariat. *The Long Summer of Theory* makes an important intervention by searching for the historical legacy of 1968 and the feminism it engendered in the present time of the early twenty-first century. Its blind spots regarding race and class reflect the dominant understanding of precarity and results from ignoring the subtle interventions by the theorists whom the film showcases.

The Long Summer of Theory explores a cinematic language to capture the economic reality for a current generation that has come of age under neoliberalism. The film moves beyond social-realist depictions of the proletarian struggle and melodramatic portraits of the precarious underclass. It challenges its viewers by breaking with familiar aesthetic conventions and rhetorical strategies, typically associated with commentary on social ills or economic struggles. While it reflects the transformation brought on by neoliberalism, it also reproduces pitfalls of the discourses that define precarity, particularly the unacknowledged primacy of the white middle class.

https://doi.org/10.1515/9783110778922-013

The film successfully captures the normalized gig-economy that defines middle-class cultural workers. The film's three main characters, artists Nola (Julia Zange), Katja (Katja Weilandt), and Martina (Martina Schöne-Radunski), struggle to advance in their professions while they work in the gig-economy to survive. Actress Martina practices her lines and auditions for roles in a film, while photographer Katja prepares a portfolio and simultaneously runs an Airbnb in another apartment in the building, in which they live. Work in their middle-class occupations to which they aspire is indistinguishable from leisure activities. As Martina practices lines for a film about the Nazi period, her declaration could be mistaken for a high cultural form of passing time. Katja photographs participants in underground punk culture and performs in a band. The context of leisure obscures the fact that she works. The friends' conversations reveal that neither has a permanent position.

At the heart of the film lies Nola's engagement with critical theory via interviews with scholars and public intellectuals, which expands the film's narrative into a meta-level reflection on contemporary politics, economics, culture, and philosophy. Nola shoots a film with theorists, scholars, public intellectuals, and cultural workers. The diegesis includes versions of her encounters as part of the narrative. She questions students at the Free University (Freie Universität) in Berlin and a range of high-profile German scholars and intellectuals with a focus on what distinguishes 1968 from the early twenty-first century, probing whether collective action is possible for her generation. She interrogates Professor of History and Cultural Studies Philipp Felsch (Humboldt University), Professor of Philosophy Rahel Jaeggi (Humboldt University), feminist theorists Lilly Lent and Andrea Trumann, dramaturge Carl Hegemann (Volksbühne), sociologist Jutta Allmendinger (Humboldt University), and Boris Groys (Professor of Philosophy and Art History at the Karlsruhe University of Arts and Design [Staatliche Hochschule für Gestaltung Karlsruhe] and New York University). *The Long Summer of Theory*'s advertising campaign includes references to scholarly extratextual material, such as full-length interviews on the extra material of the DVD, references to the publications in the final credit sequence, and the availability of the entire interviews on the platform Vimeo. Nola repeatedly compares the generation of 1968 to her own. She wonders whether a mandate to optimize oneself defines her cohort. Her confident walks to her interviewees rhythmically organize the film. These excursions into public spaces interrupt the film's privileging of the interior space of the apartment where the characters discuss the politics of representation in closed circuits of networks in stilted dialogues.

The film astutely explores the postwar history of theory as it displaced philosophy and moved from a left-wing periphery into the core institutions of knowledge and cultural production. *The Long Summer of Theory*'s title quotes Philipp Felsch's book *Der lange Sommer der Theorie: Geschichte einer Revolte 1960–1990* (2018).[1] Nola's interview with Felsch is the first in the film, mobilizing a meta-reflection on the status, practice, and material history of theorizing. In his book, Felsch analyzes Peter Gente's West German Merve publishing house, a small company that emerged from the student movement and that specialized in translating, publishing, and circulating theory in contradistinction to philosophy. Merve authors included Giorgio Agamben, Alain Badiou, Roland Barthes, Jean Baudrillard, Rosi Braidotti, Michel de Certeau, Guy Debord, Gilles Deleuze, Jacques Derrida, Michel Foucault, Felix Guattari, Luce Irigaray, Pierre Klossowski, Bruno Latour, Jean-Francois Lyotard, Jean-Luc Nancy, Jacques Rancière, and Paul Virillio. These theorists engendered a belief in the possibility of societal transformation. Felsch describes the "victory march of theory in the 1960s," as the history of the paperback book, bound up with the transformation of the West German book market.[2] The film posits his study as an intertext that suggests a temporal frame that connects 1968 to 2018. This half-a-century provides the two reference points for the comparative interrogation of theory production, reception, and politics. Felsch explains that 1968 produced a generation of readers who believed in the transformative potential of its practice. In contrast to Merve's high French theory, the scholars that Nola interviews are theatre directors, sociologists, philosophers, and historians. Together, book and film demonstrate the move of theory from outside of traditional institutions to their center as Nola's interview partners are celebrated and well-established scholars and intellectuals.

The film anchors these meta-theoretical reflections int the material reality of the three characters. The acting, however, emphasizes performativity and abandons realism. *The Long Summer of Theory* narrates the three young women artists' last days living in the apartment in an area undergoing gentrification in Berlin. Departing from the familiar conventions of social realism, the film depicts highly educated characters radically distinct from the proletarian underclass of the social critique films of the 1970 and 1980s as in *Das Ende des Regenbogens* [*The End of the Rainbow*, Uwe Frießner, West Germany, 1979], *Nordsee ist Mordsee* [*North Sea Is Dead Sea*, Hark Bohm, West Germany, 1976], or more famously, in the love story of a cleaning lady and a migrant automechanic in *Angst Essen Seele auf* [*Ali: Fear Eats Soul*, Rainer Werner Fassbinder,

---

[1] As Irene von Alberti's film and Felsch's book have the same title, I refer to the book title in German to distinguish it from the film title, to which I will refer in English.
[2] Philipp Felsch, *Der lange Sommer der Theorie: Geschichte einer Revolte 1960–1990* (Munich: CH Beck, 2018), 19, 36.

West Germany, 1974]. The threesome differs from the anarchist aesthetics of squatters, depicted for example in the comedy *Was tun, wenn's brennt?* [*What to Do in Case of Fire*, Gregor Schnitzler, Germany, 2001], in which the punk activist appears as a melancholic and immature figure reminiscent of the pre-Berlin Republic 1980s. *The Long Summer of Theory*'s female characters would also appear more at home in *Vogue*, the global fashion magazine, than in *Emma*, Germany's leading feminist journal. They embrace accoutrements of femininity like flowing dresses, high heels, and frilly blouses that evoke 1950s fashion in some scenes while referencing 1970s design in others.

The characters evoke but are distinct from the heroines of the postfeminist visual culture that emerged in the 1990s. The figure of the single woman working in the creative industry in the city captures its ideological underpinning. Two emblematic films, *Bridget Jones's Diary* and *Sex and the City*, imagine a liberated creative woman who embraces femininity.[3] Immaterial labor consists of leisurely typing on laptops as a pretext for women to indulge in consumption. The "working girls," as Yvonne Tasker labels them, invoke the diminutive, immature heroes of chick lit and chick flicks.[4] Throughout the 1990s, film and television portrayed women retreating from the workforce.[5] Make-over shows rehearse neoliberalism's demand for women's entrepreneurial self-improvement through technologies of the self, offering consumption as reward and self-reclamation.[6] These kinds of postfeminist mainstream films and television series focus on middle-class white women, ignoring the labor that migrant, minority, and working-class women perform. While they offer neoliberal fantasies of cultural immaterial labor, they reproduce the reliance on material invisible labor of others, in the German context, often migrant and postmigrant women.

The Long Summer of Theory's (post)feminist-feminine aesthetic emphasizes costume, mise-en-scène, playfulness, and improvisation and thus animates its subversive potential in contradistinction to its mainstream counterparts. In their embrace of the "pretty image," they depart from the conventions of the art

---

[3] *Bridget Jones's Diary*, dir. Sharon Maguire (Miramax, 2001); *Sex and the City*, dir. Michael Patrick King (New Line Cinema, 2008).
[4] Yvonne Tasker, *Working Girls: Gender and Sexuality in Popular cinema* (New York: Routledge, 1998). See also Diane Negra, *What a Girl Wants? Fantasizing the Reclamation of Self in Postfeminism* (New York: Routledge, 2009). For a critique, see Barbara Mennel, *Women at Work in Twenty-First-Century European Cinema* (Urbana: University of Illinois Press, 2019), 18.
[5] Elizabeth Nathanson, *Television and Postfeminist Housekeeping* (New York: Routledge, 2013).
[6] Angela McRobbie, *The Aftermath of Feminism: Gender, Culture and Social Change* (Washington, DC: Sage, 2009); Mennel, *Women at Work*, 18.

and the essay film.⁷ Intriguingly, the three main characters also drive the narrative forward through their self-confident agency, in contrast to Laura Mulvey's foundational argument about women's-to-be-looked-at-ness (1988), which they invert by depicting men as potential sex objects and turning them into lamps with a snap of a finger. Such absurd action conjures up a postmodern magical realism. In this literalization of objectification, the three women amass a collection of standing lamps. Whimsical design, costume, hair, and make-up define the interior spaces and the main characters. Like the apartment and its residents, Berlin remains under constant construction, creating opportunities of creative remaking. The film situates its narrative explicitly in the capital's urban setting. Historically, cities produced "a new urban imaginary" with "unstable subject positions, the breakup of plot, discontinuous narrative, hallucinatory imaginaries, and fragmented spaces of perceptions."⁸ These characteristics illuminate some of the disorienting features of *The Long Summer of Theory*, for example its lack of offering characters for identification and the absence of a coherent narrative. These features, which it shares with literary modernism, highlight the film's essayistic nature that links it to the literary form of the essay. Yet, place-making occurs primarily in interior spaces and on women's bodies.

Nola, Martina, and Katja look and act like postfeminist characters. Well dressed, well read, and well fed, they appear to live a care-free life despite their declarations to the contrary. The bare apartment with second-hand plush sofas and colorful clothes with soft, flowery fabric, lacy blouses, and hats reflect the third-wave feminist embrace of femininity. But their intellectual conversations distance them from the equivalents in the chick flick. Their theoretically informed and politically astute self-reflexive insights situate them in the genre of the essay film instead. They deliberate on economics, labor, gender, and social, critical, and cultural theory. Consequently, economy appears as discursive phenomenon, not material condition. As a result, alienation, a key term for Jaeggi, taken from Karl Marx and Hannah Arendt, does not affect the characters. Jaeggi explains that "alienation from oneself is inseparably bound up with alienation from the material and social world."⁹ The lack of alienation, on the one hand, and emotions, on the other, disorients spectators who are familiar with genre conventions of social-realist accounts of under- or unemployment, as genre not only creates narrative expectations but also emotional horizons. It is no surprise

---

7 Rosalind Galt, *Pretty: Film and the Decorative Image* (New York: Columbia University Press, 2011).
8 Andreas Huyssen, *Miniature Metropolis: Literature in the Age of Photography and Film* (Cambridge, MA: Harvard University Press, 2015), 10.
9 Rahel Jaeggi, *Alienation* (New York: Columbia University Press, 2014), xxi.

then, that the film evoked negative reviews.[10] The characters' homogeneous whiteness and visually appealing femininity counters expectations associated with political cinema or feminist theory. The invocation of radical politics in the jarring visual register of postfeminist femininity creates a cognitive dissonance for viewers. The theoretical dialogue, the sparse setting, and the sophisticated interviews reveal a fundamentally different attitude than the postfeminist neoliberal chick flick. Yet, middle-class signifiers in the mise-en-scène, such as the plush sofa, frilly blouses, and the group's homogeneous ethnic make-up of white creative workers, contrast with the intellectually critical approach to issues of economy, labor, and solidarity.

Despite its invocation of 1968, the film also does not continue the convention of the cinefeminism of the 1970s, in part because feminism does not occupy a clear oppositional position anymore. Feminist authors Lent and Trumann in their interview with Nola explain that in Germany the state has appropriated feminism. As they eloquently elaborate, the government advances its normative understanding of feminism because of its investment in the education of upper middle-class women. In addition, the generation of young women who viewed the postfeminist cinematic fantasies *Sex and the City* and *Bridget Jones's Diary* a decade ago has come of age in the twenty-first century unable to progress past unpaid internships. Those post-feminist films still advanced a narrative of romance. As the characters in *Summer of Theory* have sex for pleasure without searching for love, the film also does not integrate romance into its political and theoretical narrative. It thus abandons the 1990s romantic (sex) comedy in addition to the 1970s socially conscious realist docudrama.

Instead of following these familiar modes of representation, *The Long Summer of Theory* evokes the genre of the essay film, for example, by French director Jean-Luc Godard. Following its convention, the minimal framing narrative provides the setting for reflective conversations, reducing filmic action to illustration of perspectives instead of inviting viewer identification with characters or creating suspense about the narrative. Splitting the reflecting subject of the essay film onto three young women at the prolonged stage to adulthood departs from traditional essay-film conventions. The film thus importantly appropriates a genre that takes it contemporary roots in the French New Wave and that claims intellectual reflection in a unique cinematic language.

---

10 See Gregor Dotzauer, "Quatschen mit Soße," *Der Tagesspiegel*, 25 November 2017, https://www.tagesspiegel.de/kultur/der-lange-sommer-der-theorie-von-irene-von-alberti-quatschen-mit-sosse/20629068.html and Andreas Fanizadeh, "Die Revolution, ein Roman," *taz*, 23 November 2017, https://taz.de/Kinofilm-Der-lange-Sommer-der-Theorie/!5461704/.

The genre of the essay film has garnered academic attention in the twenty-first century. Film scholars Nora Alter, Timothy Corrigan, Caroline Eades, Elizabeth A. Papazian, and Laura Rascaroli have authored or edited book-length studies that claim that the genre constitutes an important albeit unrecognized contribution to the history of cinema. Corrigan labels the essay film, which he extends back to D. W. Griffith's 1909 *A Corner of Wheat*, "the most vibrant and significant kind of filmmaking in the world today."[11] Essay filmmakers Alexandre Astruc, Peter Greenaway, Chris Marker, and Hans Richter, in Corrigan's words, "hailed the unique critical potentials and powers of this central form of modern filmmaking."[12] Including examples, such as Michael Moore's *Sicko* (2007) or Errol Morris's *Fog of War* (2003), Corrigan proposes that these kinds of films have "the look of a documentary filtered through a more or less personal perspective," which makes them "difficult to classify" as they belong to the "long and varied tradition of the essay."[13]

The personal of the essay film manifests in a position from which to speak; it does not account for the imbrication of the private in economic and political structures, which the feminist slogan "the personal is political" asserts. Yet, the personal of the essay and of the feminist slogan share the "mundane or quotidian," as the essay film defines a mode of contributing to public discourse that differs from documentary or theory, both of which claim impersonal objective knowledge.[14] *The Long Summer of Theory*'s shift to interview as a mode of knowledge transmission foregrounds the personal dimension that shapes scholarship. Instead of reading theory, we see and hear the embodied theorists. Corrigan points out that essay films "have frequently been viewed as a parasitic practice," because they are not original articulations of art, which gives them an "anti-aesthetic status."[15] Therefore the essay film often does not appear cinematic, eschewing both the beautiful image and the melodramatic narrative. As essay films straddle "fiction and nonfiction, news reports and confessional autobiography, documentaries and experimental film" and "lean toward intellectual reflection," they constitute an important claim of mastery and authorship for a female director, here doubled within the diegesis by the filmmaker Nola.[16]

---

11 Timothy Corrigan, *The Essay Film: From Montaigne, After Marker* (Oxford: Oxford University Press, 2011), 3.
12 Corrigan, *The Essay Film*, 3.
13 Corrigan, *The Essay Film*, 4.
14 Corrigan, *The Essay Film*, 4.
15 Corrigan, *The Essay Film*, 4.
16 Corrigan, *The Essay Film*, 5.

Traditionally, the director is present in the essay film or relies on a stand-in for the filmmaker to share opinions, a role that Nola appears to take on as she directs the film-within-the-film. Nola's continuous repeated inquiry into the relationship between the generation of 1968 and of the film's characters opens up questions for audience members. Nola and von Alberti belong to distinctly different generations. Born in 1963, von Alberti is twenty years older than the majority of actors in the film who were born between 1980 and 1987. Nola, her roommates, and their friends, however, are millennials or generation Y, born between 1981 and 1996.[17] The question about the possibility for utopian collectivity concerns Nola's generation but also that of the students whom she interviews at the Freie Universität. *The Long Summer of Theory* does not nostalgically look back at 1968. Instead, Nola turns to established experts in institutions of knowledge and performance. Such activity differs fundamentally from the action of the 1968 generation that proclaimed that the mustiness of a thousand years existed under scholarly robes ("Unter den Talaren, der Muff von 1000 Jahren").

Intriguingly, in this context of the legacy of 1968 and the post-feminist search for utopia, Nola expresses the linkages through her clothing. Scholars of the essay film connect it to its literary predecessor, implying that the cinematic genre eschews filmic qualities. They emphasize the essay film's indebtedness to its literary pendent by including literary critic Georg Lukács's famous reflection on the essay as the first contribution in the book *Essays on the Essay Film*. Literary scholar Leslie A. Adelson points out that Lukács in the early years of World War I captured "'transcendental homelessness' that pivots on modernity's alienated relationship to 'the starry sky' [Sternenhimmel]."[18] *The Long Summer of Theory* cites "the starry sky" when Nola wears a cape with stars and the moon while she interviews students. Nola's search for viable notions of solidarity and futurity implies not only a rupture in Left theory but also produces a radical shift to female embodiment of intellectual and essayistic commentary, which includes sartorial pleasures. Nola wears costumes that literalize her role, including a suit with German, French, and English key words of the film-within-the-film and *The Long Summer of Theory*, such as "Be reasonable," "les femmes" ("the women"), "Bürger" ("the bourgeoisie"), "Lebensformen," ("life forms"),

---

[17] In 2001, German sociologist Heinz Bude defined the "Generation Berlin" in a book published by Merve as those born between 1960 and 1965, who sported "entrepreneurial individualism," which *Der Spiegel* commentator Gunnar Luetzow questioned (June 14, 2001). Some reviewers incorrectly assume that Nola and her friends belong to the Generation Berlin.

[18] Leslie A. Adelson, *Cosmic Miniatures and the Future Sense: Alexander Kluge's 21st-Century Literary Experiments in German Culture and Narrative Form* (Berlin and Boston: De Gruyter, 2017), 8.

"Zukunft" ("future"), and "Berlin." Nola's literal and symbolic costumes emblematize the film's emphasis on mise-en-scène and outfits that exceed realism.

The film captures the many ways that neoliberal labor regimes shape social life for the generation growing up in this new reality. Yet, the collective living in *The Long Summer of Theory* is not motivated by political ideology. Guy Standing's notion of "urban nomads" illuminates the characters' unmoored relationship as they lack anchoring in the past.[19] None of them appears to have other attachments or a backstory that provides insight into their biography. Without attachment to place in the days before they must leave the apartment, they conclude their stay with a party and start a drone from their balcony. Not only are they replaceable at work, but they also appear exchangeable in their social networks as well. Such nomadic subjectivity does not result from social media; the film's diegesis is strangely devoid of any means of electronic communication, such as cell phones, part of the film's unsettling sense of being out of time. Computers only appear in an imaginary office scene when the women fantasize alternative lives for themselves. When they engage in a private form of spoken theatre in the kitchen with their group of friends, Nola hands out index cards, a symbol of an outdated data-organizing-system, while they gather around a shopping cart, reading lines about the political economy of ownership.

Millennials have attracted attention as the burnout generation unable to realize their life goals by their mid-30s. Focusing primarily on the United States, Anne Helen Petersen sums up her generation's experience: "We've been conditioned to precarity," a reality that contrasts to the promise to "particularly white, middle-class millennials," raised on the mandate: "If we worked hard, no matter our current station in life, we would find stability."[20] In particular, she claims that for millennials burnout is "our contemporary condition."[21] She concludes that "the overarching trend of upward mobility has finally reversed itself, smack dab into the prime earning years of our lives."[22] Her assessment echoes Standing's analysis: "overwork became avant-garde, fashionable forward-thinking – while unionized protections for the forty-hour workweek became not only old fashioned and out of touch, but distinctly *uncool*."[23] She argues that consequently, her generation eschews "solidarity for *more work*" in

---

[19] Guy Standing, *The Precariat: The New Dangerous Class* (London: Bloomsbury, 2011), 65.
[20] Anne Helen Petersen, *Can't Even: How Millennials Became the Burnout Generation* (Boston: Houghton Mifflin Harcourt, 2020), viii.
[21] Petersen, *Can't Even*, xvii; the range of birthyears for millennials includes the oldest born in 1981 and the youngest born in 1996.
[22] Petersen, *Can't Even*, xix.
[23] Petersen, *Can't Even*, 74, italics in the original.

attempts to cultivate dream jobs.[24] Her observations pertain especially to creative professions and the art labor market: "Hope labor" constitutes "un- or under-compensated work, often performed in exchange for experience and exposure in hopes that future work will follow."[25] Nola, Martina, and Katja engage in hope labor, the result of which does not occur in the temporal frame of the film. Such work is reminiscent of Lauren Berlant's concept of "cruel optimism," which she defines as "something you desire," which is "actually an obstacle to flourishing."[26] While Berlant focuses on the dynamics of the psychosocial make-up of the individual in the context of neoliberalism's "precarious public sphere," that produce fantasies "that are fraying," and that concern such notions as "upward mobility, job security, political and social equality, and lively, durable intimacy," the notion of "hope labor" more concretely encapsulates the ideological exploitation of the mini-job and gig economy that in Germany is associated with the Hartz reform. In other words, Berlant as well focuses on the affective manifestations of precarity in the individual instead of the structural analysis of the economic and material system that produces the condition in the first place. *The Long Summer of Theory* attempts to escape this dilemma of contemporary theories of precarity but ultimately fails to overcome the split between the emphasis on the private sphere and the theorization in the public sphere.

The film's generation grew up and entered adulthood under the conditions of precarity produced by neoliberal economics. Standing coined the term "the precariat" in his eponymous book, departing from the classic Marxist model of a proletarian revolution, while retaining a class-based imaginary, defining the precariat as "a class-in-the-making."[27] He diagnoses the destructions of the traditional working class, emphasizing instead youth, especially interns, and migrants. The incongruent combination of interns and migrants in the precariat, the class-in-the-making, serves the important function for Standing to map out the distance to historic classic class warfare. However, unfortunately, his model does not account for overlap and distinction between the two categories, which are, after all, not parallel. While migrants can be interns, such a reductive account obscures the increasing class polarization and the ways in which dynamics of traditional social categories still determine access. Fear and insecurity result from the shift by companies from regular to precarious jobs, including flexible labor, which increases inequality. Rahel Jaeggi, one of the interviewees, in her

---

24 Petersen, *Can't Even*, 74, italics in the original.
25 Peterson, *Can't Even*, 78.
26 Lauren Berlant, *Cruel Optimism* (Durham: Duke University Press, 2011), 1.
27 Standing, *The Precariat*, vii.

book *Alienation*, refers to "flexible capitalism," which "threatens the individual identity and social coherence."[28]

The acting style and episodic plot of *The Long Summer of Theory* echoes the theatrical and carnivalesque demonstrations of the early twenty-first century, which Standing references in his account of the precariat. Standing's term "status discord" offers insight into the film's disjuncture between its political discourse about precarity and high level of education and self-confidence of the young women. They indulge in stylish decor in their comfortable and spacious apartment. Their space appears as sets for different narrative units. A communal room with a sofa functions as the backdrop for different episodes. They meet with their friends in the kitchen to discuss the viability of art. Finally, one room serves solely as a place for standing lamps, the objects into which the women transform lovers, sex-partners, and delivery men. As the rooms appear as stages for individual episodes, they subvert the time-space continuum. The characters repeatedly change their feminine costumes. When they imagine themselves in scenarios of their hypothetical lives, they are transferred into different settings: as suburban mothers with their children in a backyard; posing with champagne in high-fashion evening gowns in an elegant old-fashioned apartment; or finally as office workers in a plain office setting.

Camp appropriation of 1970s style sets the tone from the outset. In the film's opening scene, Nola, Martina, and Katja self-confidently stride toward the camera down a wide and empty street in Berlin, unfold their beach chairs, and seemingly relax in the sun in the middle of the urban setting. The opening beat reminiscent of the 1970s and the straight-on long shot of the three women evoke 1970s gestures of feminist camp appropriations of the Western in films such as *Rote Sonne* [*Red Sun*].[29] Similar to *The Long Summer of Theory*, *Red Sun* portrays a female commune with attractive young women, including 1970s pop icon Uschi Obermaier. In *Red Sun*, the women kill men after they have sex with them, while the contemporary female characters in *The Long Summer of Theory* turn them into lamps. The nostalgia for 1970s culture in a film that searches for the possibility of utopian imagination for the millennial generation constitutes another estranging effect. Many of the scholars whom Nola interviews emerged from the 1970s, the point of reference of Felsch's book, but have developed their theoretical apparatus out of the moment of 1968. The film accompanies their presence with a style that nostalgically recycles past periods, providing a pastiche of temporality that defines the contemporary generation.

---

28 Jaeggi, *Alienation*, xix.
29 *Rote Sonne,* dir. Rudolf Thome (Independent Film, 1969).

History appears only in such iconic and aesthetic citations. The film does not endow its characters with biographical pasts. Standing's analysis of the precariat further illuminates the representation of these characters unmoored from their biographies. As a high level of formal education does not prevent people from taking jobs of lower status or income, as temporary workers, dependent contractors or interns, they focus on the present.[30] Reflecting this experience under neoliberalism, Nola, Katja, Martina, and their friends live in the moment. Even though they reflect on the past and search for a perspective for the future, both remain elusive. The narrative neither provides backstories, nor perspectives on the individual or collective futures. The characters occupy only the present in which futurity has become a theoretical question. In other words, the film cinematically and narratively captures a radical presentism, from which it explores futurity in relation to its theoretical possibility.

The film's rational engagement with a broad question of economy and work in intellectual conversations in the apartment and in interviews with scholars contrasts to Standing's claim about precarity's emotional dimension, which one could read as an attempt to overcome it affective state. According to him, "anger, anomie, anxiety and alienation" constitute the defining emotions of the precariat.[31] Anger stems from the lack of "trusting relationships built up in meaningful structures or networks"; anomie reflects "passivity born of despair"; anxiety results from "chronic insecurity" of those "underemployed" and "overemployed"; and alienation remains the "defining feature of the proletariat."[32] Yet, the characters appear as detached intellectuals who theoretically reflect on the material conditions and economic dynamics that create their situation, preventing spectators from identifying with them. Thus, as the film refuses melodramatic conventions of identification, it leaves viewers cold and disoriented. The characters drift through life reflecting Standing's observation that "'[h]anging around' becomes a dominant form of using time."[33] His demand that "[w]ork must be rescued from jobs and labor," evokes Hannah Arendt's distinction between work and labor, which Matthew Tinkcom succinctly summarizes: "Labor is characterized as the ongoing, repetitive, dull task of scratching out a life from the world, but work appears in the acts by which humans create for themselves."[34]

---

[30] Standing, *The Precariat*, 10–16.
[31] Standing, *The Precariat*, 19.
[32] Standing, *The Precariat*, 20.
[33] Standing, *The Precariat*, 129.
[34] Matthew Tinkcom, *Working Like a Homosexual: Camp, Capital, Cinema* (Durham: Duke University Press, 2002), 11.

While Nola, Katja, and Martina experience the precarious working conditions in a neoliberal economy, as intellectuals they engage in a meta-commentary that analyzes without responding emotionally to their circumstances. Like the intellectuals in Godard's *All's Well* [*Tout Va Bien*, 1972], they inhabit a dual role of participants and simultaneous observer-commentators. In other words, their ability to engage solely with an intellectual response reflects their privilege. Not only the conditions of work have changed but also the embodiment of the intellectual who authors the essay film. That comparison highlights the historic shift from Godard's 1970s film, in which the intellectual filmmaker struggled with the distance to the laboring class on strike in *All's Well*. In the twenty-first century, neoliberal conditions of precarity encompass all classes, a fact that scholarship based on Standing's foundational work emphasizes without highlighting the continuation of historical inequities thoroughly anchored in the history of race, class, and gender. The strangeness *of The Long Summer of Theory* results not only from the fact that, per Standing's and other theorists' paradigms, precarity has reached all classes, but also from the lack of the main characters' affective or despairing reaction.

The stylized episodes reference 1968 as point of origin of societal rebellion for a postfeminist critique of the precarious gig-economy and underpaid care work. Gender's deep imbrication with the transformation of work motivates the film's portrait of women's labor. Martina and Katja strive to transform society through their artistic practice. They question the visual representation of gender through their art and confront the ideological pressures of current market forces. For example, when Martina rehearses her role in a film, the three roommates reflect on the seductive fantasy of the Nazi past and its period's appeal for audiences. When she takes photos of men modelling colorful tights in punk underground culture, Katja reverses the roles that Mulvey famously inscribed in her groundbreaking essay of feminist theory of female to-be-looked-at-ness and male carriers of the gaze who advance the narrative. Katja violently rejects the curator who wants to commodify her subversive gaze. The gallerist who looks at her portfolio recognizes her potential but his positive response to her work intends to commodify its transgressive quality into radical chic. He accompanies his compliments with sexual innuendo, which Katja rejects by cursing at him and leaving the meeting. Her refusal to be implicated in his sexist gaze, prevents her from actively participating in the art market.

The Long Summer of Theory insists on the particularity of women. Whereas the action of Godard's *All's Well* takes place in a factory, in *The Long Summer of Theory* it occurs in the home, the traditional scene of domesticity. The home, however, has become a multifunctional space not limited to private activity. The increase in computerized work and telemarketing has eroded the boundary between work and leisure, and between public and private.³⁵ The home, Melissa Gregg has shown in her book *Work's Intimacy* (2011), has become a renewed site for work. Part of the sharing economy, Katja cleans the Airbnb. As service labor, historically rooted in the private sphere, has increased, the invisibility of women's domestic work defines current immaterial labor. The feminization of work not only denotes that more women take up flexible and precarious jobs, but also that men take up insecure and informal low-paying positions previously considered the norm for women.³⁶ The film challenges audiences' perception by depicting what appears as leisurely life of young women who, as a result of feminism, do not perform housework but, as a result of precarity, also do not labor in continuous, reliable professions outside the home.

The Long Summer of Theory keeps its view tightly on the progressive subjects searching to define their politics in regard to their selves, yet not in relation to a public or the state. The characters' artistic professions indicate the creative turn in the urban economies but also continue traditions of artistic work and collective projects. The shared apartment evokes the experimental living forms of 1968 without its political aims. The film's iteration of unreflectively white and middle-class feminism returns to its twin moment in the past. The lack of attention to class, race, and ethnicity frames gender as the singular category that matters, relying on and mobilizing problematic discourses about neoliberalism. The precarious labor conditions that have historically affected working classes now also shape the working experience of middle-class women. While they clean the Airbnb, Katja and Martina discuss how women are overrepresented in care work, the lowest category of labor. They dismiss "neoliberal chatter" ("Gequatsche") as women have to take care of themselves. As tall and blonde Katja cleans for tourists, the film ignores that gendered care work in a German context has an ethnic dimension, as Eastern European women with rotating visas conduct care work in Western European countries.³⁷ Thus, while the feminism of *The Long Summer of Theory* includes men, in contrast to many of the 1970s feminist films, it does not consider the racial and ethnic politics of labor of the Berlin Republic.

The film's artifice rejects sociological readings. Yet, Nola, and by extension the film, invokes an experiential dimension when she interviews established German sociologist Jutta Allmendinger. In her interview, the sociologist paints a fundamentally different picture of the younger generation than Nola implies. Allmendinger's research demonstrates that young people move in multicultural

---

35 Melissa Gregg, *Work's Intimacy* (Cambridge: Polity, 2011).
36 Standing, *The Precariat*, 60.
37 See Anca Parvulescu, *The Traffic in Women's Work: East European Migration and the Making of Europe* (Chicago: University of Chicago Press, 2014).

and multinational circles of friends that offer collective possibilities beyond the limitations of past generations of Germans like herself. For an observant spectator, Allmendinger's empirical claims unsettle Nola's presupposition. The scholar's sociological approach not only counters Nola's repeated argument that she implies in her interviews. It advances a counterpoint to the film's homogeneous representations of characters in terms of race, class, nationality, and ethnicity. Finally, it also demonstrates that theory itself exceeds both essayistic narrative and cinematic closure.

The interview format does not encapsulate the complexity of the scholars' theoretical elaboration. For example, in their 2015 book *Kritik des Staatsfeminismus, Oder: Kinder, Küche, Kapitalismus* [Critique of State Feminism, Or: Children, Kitchen, Capitalism], Lent and Trumann analyze the ideology of idealized motherhood, which increased just as the number of working women rose. They highlight the tension of this development, which expects working women to perform the majority of childcare.[38] In the interview, however, they are able only to point toward symptoms in the current moment, while their book advances a differentiated account how motherhood took center stage in the women's movement. There, they explain that the women's movement aimed to dissolve the division between productive and reproductive labor.[39] Interviews are limited in their capacity to present complex phenomena. *The Long Summer of Theory* popularizes theory, but in that process reveals its limitations of a vision of how theory could engage the public. Inadvertently, it illustrates what it tries to overcome: the self-referentiality of public conversation in an age of social media, which relies on immediacy and lacks communication beyond closed social networks.

The film inscribes blonde, white, middle-class women as representative of the new-class-in-the-making. Its fails to investigate the social and economic consequences of race, ethnicity, and class in line with dominant scholarship on precarity, i.e., by Standing and Petersen. Even though migrants make an entrance, for example in Standing's account of the precariat, *The Long Summer of Theory* reduces them to minor appearances that reproduce their marginal status. The film neither interrogates how migration and race position subjects

---

[38] Lilly Lent and Andrea Trumann, *Kritik des Staatsfeminismus. Oder: Kinder, Küche, Kapitalismus* (Berlin: Bertz + Fischer, 2015), 13. The book title references and revises the motto that the place for women is with children, kitchen, and in the church (Kinder, Küche, Kirche), the so-called three K's, which defined the attitude of the German Empire about women. Instead, Lent and Trumann's book inserts capitalism as the undergirding mechanism that has substituted for religion.

[39] Lent and Trumann, *Kritik des Staatsfeminismus*, 19.

differently vis-à-vis precarity nor takes serious Allmendinger's claim that networks have become diverse and multicultural. The only two scenes that include non-white characters reduce them to transactional relations with Nola, Martina, and Katja. A group of darker-skin men with dark beards lie in the bed in the Airbnb, and, at a later point, a realtor guides them and their dog through the apartment as if they are inspecting it for rent or purchase. In another scene in their kitchen at the last dinner before they must leave the apartment, while friends sit around the kitchen table, the character Hasan makes his one-time appearance to clean the dishes and speak to the camera, breaking the fourth wall and declaring that he does not want to be typecast as an actor for criminal minority roles. This occurs in an obvious contradiction to his sole appearance in the film. While making an ironic gesture, the film does not move beyond pointing to the potential and reduces Hasan to a position of negation. These characters function in the economic but not in the emotional circuits. As the only characters who are "other," are also male, they are evocative of a much earlier turning point in feminist theory, marked by the book title, *All the Women Are White, All the Blacks Are Men, But Some of Us Are Brave*, originally published in 1982 and initiating a rethinking of feminist theory.[40] Thus, the film's mapping of ethnicity onto gender reproduces an outdated paradigmatic axis of the imbrication of race and gender in the cultural imaginary. More importantly, those characters do not participate in intellectual networks of the film that establish its discourse community.

The film's own representational politics thus fall behind the theories it endorses. For example, in their published conversations, Nancy Fraser and Rahel Jaeggi point out that they "bring key ideas from the critique of political economy back into critical theory," in the case of Fraser "crisis" and in the case of Jaeggi "alienation."[41] They point out that "the pressures of paid work and debt are altering the conditions of child-rearing, eldercare, household relations, and community bonds – in short, the entire organization of social reproduction," in a crisis that is "not only economic" but rather also affects "de-democratization."[42] They agree about the productivity of not subordinating issues, such as gender race, sexuality, and identity to economics, as was the case in 1968-inspired Marxism, advocating for a "both/and" approach: "both class *and* status, redistribution

---

40 Akasha (Gloria T.) Hull, Patricia Bell-Scott, Barbara Smith, eds., *All the Women are White, All the Blacks Are Men, But Some of Us Are Brave* (New York: The Feminist Press, 2015).
41 Nancy Fraser and Rahel Jaeggi, *Capitalism: A Conversation in Critical Theory* (Cambridge: Polity, 2018), 2.
42 Fraser and Jaeggi, *Capitalism*, 3.

and recognition."[43] Yet, in the cinematic language of *The Long Summer of Theory*, the latter categories have displaced the former, as status and recognition marginalize notions of class and redistribution.

The Long Summer of Theory implies that the legacy of Left theory, particularly regarding solidarity, utopia, and futurity, has been disrupted. However, as Adelson has shown, essayist, theorist, and filmmaker Alexander Kluge offers a lineage from Max Horkheimer and Theodor Adorno's critical theory to a contemporary vision of futurity, which overlaps with concepts that continue to define Left thinking, such as alienation – a central topic of scholars, including for political philosopher and author Rahel Jaeggi whom Nola interviews on a roof top. According to Adelson, Kluge orients literary and filmic creative expression and theoretical work toward "hope for human survival and unalienated life in the face of catastrophic destruction," which he associates with "war, genocide, fascism, dictatorship, and capitalist exploitation of life, labor, and time."[44] Adelson proposes that Kluge cultivates "a new sensorium of time, notably in differential but conjunctive relation to futurity."[45] Further, she sees futurity "as constitutive of modern society, politics, philosophy, economy, and culture," promising progress.[46] As the search for futurity motivates Nola and by implication director von Alberti, the film purports that the current economic, social, and political situation has led a generation that has come of age under neoliberalism to give up a utopian sense of the future. The scholars who appear in the film repeatedly debunk mythical memories of 1968, for example by pointing out, so Felsch, that its generation in West Germany was not one of theorists but of readers.

In several instances, then, the film's mode of irreverent postfeminist and postmodern ironic pastiche is seemingly at odds with the theoretical contributions of the interviewees. More than once, the setting ironizes the theorists' work. For example, when Nola interviews Lent and Trumann, they sit on small children's chairs in a daycare facility surrounded by toys. While the mise-en-scène could invite a reading of the setting as gesturing toward the double burden of women or the connection of theory and practice, posing Lent and Trumann on children's stools infantilizes them. Lent, a teacher in Berlin, and Trumann, a youth social worker, have published important feminist works, including *Kritik des Staatsfeminismus* (Critique of State Feminism), which takes as its reference point the 1968 student movement and its development into 1970s feminist theory. The

---

43 Fraser and Jaeggi, *Capitalism*, 7.
44 Adelson, *Cosmic Miniatures*, 20.
45 Adelson, *Cosmic Miniatures*, 21.
46 Adelson, *Cosmic Miniatures*, Koselleck 46.

scene in the Kindergarten captures the film's intentional confusion about verisimilitude as the fictional character Nola interviews actual public intellectuals, cultural workers, and scholars. Their conversation captures only part of the analysis and argument of *Kritik des Staatsfeminismus*. In the film, Lent and Trumann explain how the state requires educated women to have more children and return to work quickly. Feminists did not demand the double burden of paid and unpaid labor. The state changed laws and social welfare, such as *Hartz IV*.[47] With the emergence of mini jobs, more women work. These mini jobs demonstrate that the state mobilized feminism in order to increase women's productivity to fulfill capitalism's imperative. Simultaneously, expectations for parents have increased as well.

Such a theoretical context frames the refusal of work as a political act. Katja tells a story of working as a corpse on stage in a play where she failed because she got up during the performance to go to the bathroom. Her demand to be lazy enacts Kathi Weeks's anti-work politics as she declares the refusal to work to be political resistance to the neoliberal labor regime. She proposes to substitute labor for the category of class in contemporary Marxist analysis (2011). Katja's resistance to working invokes its own history, for example West Berlin's Tunix event, which Michel Foucault visited at the invitation of Merve publishing house.

The film aims to popularize theory and criticizes the Right-wing dominance of the public sphere. Whereas the theorists primarily appear in interior spaces, the new Right and nationalists dominate the public space in demonstrations, having appropriated protest from the Left. While the film captures that public space is not the rational public sphere that Jürgen Habermas had declared it to be, the film also reproduces the hope for rational discourse through its turn to theory. Martina stands among right-wing nationalists in the public without interacting with them. Instead of engaging or confronting, her generation turns to theory in search of a direction and a position. In the feminist classics of the 1970s, such as *Redupers – The Allround Reduced Personality* [*Die allseitig reduzierte Persönlichkeit*, West Germany, Helke Sander, 1978], the members of the artistic collective took their photographs into the city to create a public sphere through their mobile bodies. Here and now, intellectuals have retreated to the domestic space where they congregate with like-minded interlocutors.

---

[47] Hartz IV was part of comprehensive restructuring of labor, named after Peter Hartz, personnel director of VW and head of the committee that developed the plan. Hartz I created job services agencies; Hartz II institutionalized mini-jobs and jobcenters; Hartz III restructured the Federal Labor Agency; and Hartz IV, instituted 1 January 2005, reorganized unemployment and welfare benefits as social assistance.

A greater-than-life-size poster of Black activist Angela Davis hangs in the kitchen – another figure that connects Adorno's critical theory to post-1968 political activism – overlooking intellectual conversations. Whereas the political activism of Davis once commanded attention in the public sphere, her image is now frozen, fossilized in the interior of the young women's apartment, while a nationalist demonstration dominates the public sphere. *The Long Summer of Theory* centers on theory but is unable to mobilize it for a future-oriented perspective and practice to overcome the conditions it lays bare for its audiences. While it points beyond its own diegesis and its own film text toward the selected books, intending to turn viewers into readers, if we read Felsch's book, we understand that the moment of 1968 is irretrievably lost as a moment of reading that turned philosophy into theory, which, however, has now transformed again into academic disciplines and the culture industry.

In sum, *The Long Summer of Theory* articulates the dilemma of the post-Left and post-feminist precarious class-in-the-making as a loss of political position, orientation, and lack of outlook to the future. It thus critically explores the conditions for critical cultural engagement with the current moment in its historical context of the social liberation movements of the late twentieth century. It's reliance on the convention of the essay films situates itself in that critical tradition. The film successfully captures the characters who describe their provisional life with short term goals and confront the demand of self-optimization of the neoliberal labor regime. It also makes abundantly clear how these artistic women, as stand-ins for progressive members of their generation, find themselves at a loss when the Right has appropriated the anti-state position previously held by the Left. The state, however, is absent. Instead, we observe an inward-looking generation that turns to theorists for insight. This representation of young, white middle-class women reflects the postfeminist embrace of sexual liberation and of femininity. Adhering to key theorists of precarity, the film captures the prolonged insecurity of laboring in the gig-economy without roots in a place, but ignores the intersectionality of race, class, gender, ethnicity, and migration in lived precarity. The content of the interviews by the scholars and theorists Allmendinger, Felsch, Jaeggi, Lent, and Trumann portray a different picture of sociability among the young generations and of the role of the state. The film offers an important contribution to the reflection of precarity, cultural production, and theory, without moving beyond the limitations of existing theoretical paradigms. Following the breadcrumbs of theories, it lays out for its viewers and offering an essay film on the intersection of lived experiences and theoretical reflection, it makes an important contribution to the theoretical discourse of political economy, the history of social movements, and the questions of utopia they engendered, a contribution that is not without its limitations.

Works cited

Print sources

Adelson, Leslie A. *Cosmic Miniatures and the Future Sense: Alexander Kluge's 21st-Century Literary Experiments in German Culture and Narrative Form* (Berlin and Boston: De Gruyter, 2017).

Alter, Nora M. *The Essay Film After Fact and Fiction* (New York: Columbia University Press, 2018).

Alter, Nora M. and Timothy Corrigan, eds. *Essays on the Essay Film* (New York: Columbia University Press, 2017).

Arendt, Hannah. *The Human Condition* (Chicago: University of Chicago Press, 1998).

Bude, Heinz. *Generation Berlin* (Berlin: Merve, 2001).

Corrigan, Timothy. *The Essay Film: From Montaigne, After Marker* (Oxford: Oxford University Press, 2011).

Dotzauer, Gregor. "Quatschen mit Soße," *Der Tagesspiegel*, 25 November 2017.

Fanizadeh, Andreas. "Die Revolution, ein Roman," *taz*, 23 November 2017.

Felsch, Philipp. *Der lange Sommer der Theorie: Geschichte einer Revolte 1960–1990* (Munich: CH Beck, 2015).

Fraser, Nancy and Rahel Jaeggi. *Capitalism: A Conversation in Critical Theory* (Cambridge: Polity, 2018).

Galt, Rosalind. *Pretty: Film and the Decorative Image* (New York: Columbia University Press, 2011).

Gregg, Melissa. *Work's Intimacy* (Cambridge: Polity, 2011).

Hull, Akasha (Gloria T.), Patricia Bell-Scott, and Barbara Smith, eds. *All the Women are White, All the Blacks Are Men, But Some of Us Are Brave* (New York: The Feminist Press, 2015).

Huyssen, Andreas. *Miniature Metropolis: Literature in the Age of Photography and Film* (Cambridge, MA: Harvard University Press, 2015).

Jaeggi, Rahel. *Alienation* (New York: Columbia University Press, 2014).

Lent, Lilly and Andrea Trumann. *Kritik des Staatsfeminismus. Oder: Kinder, Küche, Kapitalismus* (Berlin: Bertz + Fischer, 2015).

Luetzow, Gunnar. "Frische Munition für die Faulheitsdebatte," *Der Spiegel*, 14 June 2001.

Lukács, Georg. "On the Nature and Form of the Essay," in *Essays on the Essay Film*. Eds. Nora M. Alter and Timothy Corrigan (New York: Columbia University Press, 2017), 21–41.

McRobbie, Angela. *The Aftermath of Feminism: Gender, Culture and Social Change* (Washington, DC: Sage, 2009).

Mennel, Barbara. *Women at Work in Twenty-First-Century European Cinema* (Urbana: University of Illinois Press, 2019).

Mulvey, Laura. "Visual Pleasure and Narrative Cinema," in *Feminism and Film Theory*. Ed. Constance Penley (New York: Routledge, 1988), 57–68.

Nathanson, Elizabeth. *Television and Postfeminist Housekeeping* (New York: Routledge, 2013).

Negra, Diane. *What a Girl Wants? Fantasizing the Reclamation of Self in Postfeminism* (New York: Routledge, 2009).

Papazian, Elizabeth A. and Caroline Eades, eds. *The Essay Film: Dialogue, Politics, Utopia* (London: Wallflower Press, 2016).

Parvulescu, Anca. *The Traffic in Women's Work: East European Migration and the Making of Europe* (Chicago: University of Chicago Press, 2014).
Petersen, Anne Helen. *Can't Even: How Millennials Became the Burnout Generation* (Boston: Houghton Mifflin Harcourt, 2020).
Rascaroli, Laura. *The Personal Camera: Subjective Cinema and the Essay Film* (London: Wallflower, 2009).
Standing, Guy. *The Precariat: The New Dangerous Class* (London: Bloomsbury, 2011).
Tasker, Yvonne. *Working Girls: Gender and Sexuality in Popular Cinema* (New York: Routledge, 1998).
Tinkcom, Matthew. *Working Like a Homosexual: Camp, Capital, Cinema* (Durham: Duke University Press, 2002).
Weeks, Kathi. *The Problem with Work: Feminism, Marxism, Antiwork Politics, and Postwork Imaginaries* (Durham, NC: Duke University Press, 2011).

Films

Alberti, Irene von. *Der lange Sommer der Theorie* (*The Long Summer of Theory*). 2015.
Bohm, Hark. *Nordsee ist Mordsee* (*North Sea Is Dead Sea*). 1976.
Fassbinder, Rainer Werner. *Angst essen Seele auf* (Ali: Fear Eats Soul). 1974.
Frießner, Uwe. *Das Ende des Regenbogens* (*The End of the Rainbow*). 1979.
Godard, Jean-Luc. *Tout Va Bien* (*All's Well*). 1972.
Griffith, David Wark. *A Corner of Wheat.* 1909.
Maguire, Sharon. *Bridget Jones's Diary.* 2001.
Moore, Michael. *Sicko.* 2007.
Morris, Errol. *Fog of War.* 2003.
King, Michael Patrick. *Sex and the City.* 2008.
Sander, Helke. *Die allseitig reduzierte Persönlichkeit* (*Redupers – The Allround Reduced Personality*). 1978.
Schnitzler, Gregor. *Was tun, wenn's brennt?* (*What to Do in Case of Fire*). 2001.
Thome, Rudolf. *Rote Sonne* (*Red Sun*). 1969.

Brett de Bary
Unnatural Disaster as Chronotope: "Lines" of Connection and Language as the "Flesh" of Time in Yoko Tawada's *The Emissary*

> "Do you like milk?"
> Without skipping a beat Mumei replied, "I like worms better." Unable to see the line that connected milk to worms, Yoshirō let his eyes wander out the window.
>
> Yoko Tawada, The Emissary

Introduction

In the "unnatural" island world of Yoko Tawada's 2014 novel, *The Emissary*, it is often difficult for the characters, not to mention the readers, to see "lines" of connection. The only maps have been rendered anachronistic by an earthquake that pushed the archipelago further from the continent to which it had originally been joined. Unable to "feel the roundness of the earth," many believe it to be flat, and cannot gauge the distance between one spot and another.[1] From the flat map, one must imagine a "spherical world."

Moreover, the greater distance, a teacher instructs his students, is "not just the result of natural disasters."[2] What else produced the disaster, we are never told directly. Thus if through a modern homonym from the characters that, in

---

[1] Yoko Tawada, *The Emissary*, trans. Margaret Mitsutani (New York: New Directions, 2018), 25. Henceforth I will use Mitsutani's translations from the Japanese text by Tawada Yōko, *Kentōshi* (Tokyo: Kodansha, 2014). In this essay I use the Japanese word order, with the last name first, for Japanese names other than the author's, but refer to the author as Yoko Tawada, when referring to her German language and English language publications.

[2] Tawada, *The Emissary*, 123.

Notes: This essay is a slightly revised version of the text of a lecture I was invited to deliver at the international workshop "The Event as Remembrance and Oblivion: The Dynamics of Collective Memory" (*Dekigoto wa ikani kiokusare, ika ni bōkyaku sareruka – shūgōteki kioku no dōtai o kangaeru*), scheduled to be convened on 1–2 March 2020, at Tokyo University of Foreign Studies, but cancelled due to Covid-19. I warmly thank my valued colleagues over many years, Professors Iwasaki Minoru and Narita Ryūichi for their invitation. Thanks also to Professor Kimura Saeko, and to Iwakawa Arisa, for sharing their powerfully insightful papers with me. My lecture is written in dialogue with them.

https://doi.org/10.1515/9783110778922-014

her unorthodox orthography, comprise Tawada's title we were to make a pun, the "votive lantern" literally referred to by its first two Japanese characters (*kentō* or 献灯) could also refer to the reader who must constantly "guess" (*kentō* or 見当) at riddles, at connections obliquely visible in the text.

In her essay, "Rusty Rails and Parallel Tracks: *Trans-Latio* in Yoko Tawada's *Das Nackte Auge*," Leslie A. Adelson highlights the figure of "lines" in the novel as it extends an engagement by Tawada with the writings of Walter Benjamin on translation. Reading the railroad tracks as an evocation of parallel lines, Adelson offers a most subtle commentary on the German critic Irving Wohlfarth's discussion of "lines" in the "Task of the Translator." In what she suggests should be properly seen as a "translational turn," she notes that Wohlfarth replaces one German word by another in explicating Benjamin's oft-cited notion of "inter-linear translation."[3] For Benjamin's "zwischen den Zeilen," Wohlfarth instead uses "zwischen den Linien," substituting for Benjamin's allusion to lines of print or text ("Zeilen") the geometrical term for "line" ("Linien") as a vector path, a line or curve, defined by two points. Adelson suggests that through this slight re-inflection towards the geometrical, Wohlfarth is able to argue that for Benjamin reading between the lines is actually a means of "disrupting a linear 'continuum,' and allowing something else to happen, by reading in the space between the lines." Emphasizing how Benjamin's "Task" addresses the "task" of the reader, Wohlfarth also, for Adelson, finds in the notion of the "inter-linear" a characteristic Benjaminian emphasis on language itself as a "medium," one allowing for what she calls "encounters between disjunctive temporalities." Through this "turn," Adelson adds, "inter-linearity" is expanded, even bringing out connotations that would link it more strikingly to "many allusions to things planetary and cosmic" in Benjamin's work.[4] Such allusions are certainly pertinent for a consideration how of Tawada asks her literary characters, and her readers, to "connect the lines" among questions of shifting planetary time, life, and language in *The Emissary*.

A consistent effort across Adelson's writings on Tawada, it seems to me, has been to identify the "newness" of its language as a mode of addressing history. In this sense, Adelson's reading of *Das Nackte Auge* [*The Naked Eye*] may

---

[3] Leslie A. Adelson, "Parallel Tracks and Rusty Rails: *Trans-Latio* in Yoko Tawada's *Das Nackte Auge*," in *Un/Translatables: New Maps for Germanic Literatures*, eds. Bethany Wiggin and Catriona MacLeod (Evanston, IL: Northwestern University Press, 2004), 281–298. Adelson draws on Irving Wohlfarth, "'Was nie geschreiben wurde, lesen': Walter Benjamins Theorie des Lesens," in *Walter Benjamin 1892–1940 zum 100. Geburtstag*, ed. Uwe Steiner (Bern: Peter Lang, 1992), 297–344.

[4] Adelson, "Parallel Tracks," 286.

be brought together with broader reflections that open her "Literary Imagination and the Future of Literary Studies," an essay that also touches on Tawada's work. The "structural stakes of imagination are both exceptionally high and structurally shifting at the turn of the 21st century," she asserts.[5] While Adelson cites destabilization of the nation state and "delocalization of the world," climate change, and the "tectonic" struggle between the expropriative regimes of global capital and an ethics of equitable redistribution as factors in such structural shifts, crucial to an understanding of Tawada's aesthetics, for me, is Adelson's depiction of imagination in this context as a "quotidian labor," as well as her proposal that a foremost challenge to imaginative labor after the turn of the century has been a shift in human perceptions of "dimensionality."[6] Surely readers have noted that a conspicuous aspect of the strangeness produced by Tawada's texts lies in their insistent focus on defamiliarizing "quotidian" objects from everyday life, while questions of "dimensionality" are posed as they repeatedly present us with translational puzzles regarding measure words for volume, distance, and time.

Returning to Adelson's discussion of *Das Nackte Auge*, we see that here, as well, she grapples with the problem of how to name the writing style through which Tawada confronts a shift, the "changing historical relations between the text and reader." Adelson eventually settles for Tsvetan Todorov's "fantastic marvelous," with some qualifications. This further elaboration on Tawada's style seems especially significant for *The Emissary* for two reasons. First, because Todorov himself distinguishes between a "fantastic uncanny" where "the laws of reality remain intact," and Adelson's preferred "fantastic marvelous," where, she says, "readers must confront new laws of nature." But more salient in Tawada's case, insofar as for Todorov the fantastic in general can be recognized through the impact it makes on the reader, might be the reader's "hesitation" before the new, the ambiguous, the seemingly inexplicable.[7] One might say that throughout her writings Tawada has sought to elicit this "hesitation" as a quality of the new reading subject. It is a willingness to tarry in a moment of surprise, to accept the unknown precisely as that which cannot yet be mastered cognitively. Her writings offer readers an open-ended invitation to imaginatively "connect the lines." As we shall see, in the "fantastic marvelous"

---

5 Leslie A. Adelson, "Literary Imagination and the Future of Literary Studies," *Deutsche Vierteljahrsschrift für Literaturwissenschaft und Geistesgeschichte* 89 (2015): 675. Adelson takes the term "quotidian labor of imagination" from Arjun Appadurai, *The Future As Cultural Fact. Essays on the Global Condition* (London: Verso Books, 2013), 287.
6 Adelson, "Literary Imagination," 678.
7 Adelson, "Parallel Tracks," 285.

world of *The Emissary*, where the same characters who walk dogs, push baby carriages, bake bread, and take children to the dentist register on their bodies the mutating effects of invisible substances with "life" spans extending incalculably beyond human perceptions of "dimensionality," these acts of "quotidian" imagination can be not only literary, but political.

Lines of literary imagination

In the passage above, a dentist is speaking to a boy called Mumei (literally named "Nameless"), the great grandson of Yoshirō, the protagonist of the novel. While, in a major conceit of the novel, humans of Yoshirō's generation cannot grow old and die, the body of the young Mumei, born after an unnamed disaster, is rapidly growing more fragile, and he is already losing his teeth. The dentist asks Mumei whether he likes milk, since calcium is thought to be an essential element in teeth and bones. Here Tawada's text presents "teeth" as indicators of both time and contamination. Getting calcium from cows' milk has become dangerous. A better source, the dentist recommends, is "the bones of fish and animals." Since the earth has become "irreversibly contaminated," however, "some people say we should dig way, way down underground to find dinosaur bones."[8]

But what is the "line" connecting milk with earthworms that Yoshirō cannot fathom? With an ironic touch typical of Tawada's writing, Yoshirō's puzzlement becomes an occasion to highlight Yoshirō's status as a writer, a role emphasized in Kimura Saeko's analysis of the novel.[9] Dentists, Yoshirō reflects, are apt to be loquacious, perhaps because they want to show off their beautiful teeth. And maybe this dentist, rivalrous with Yoshirō because he knows he is a wordsmith, is making a show of his way with words. Indeed, the reader is told the words of the dentist and Mumei may be flying in a future direction Yoshirō cannot grasp.

A consideration of literary rhetoric, however, allows us to perceive a logic of literary connections in the conversation between the dentist and the young boy. Linking the two points after hearing Mumei say he likes earthworms, the

---

8 Tawada, *The Emissary*, 22–23.
9 Kimura Saeko, "Imagining Radiation Disaster: Tawada Yōko's *The Emissary* and its Tale" (Hōshanōsai no sōzōryoku: Tawada Yōko no *Kentōshi* o kataru koto), https://ferris.repo.nii.ac.jp/?action=pages_view_main&active_action=repository_view_main_item_detail&item_id=2425&item_no=1&page_id=13&block_id=21 (Yokohama: Ferris University, 2019), December 2020.

dentist says, "So this means you are a baby bird rather than a calf. While calves drink their mother's milk, baby birds eat the worms their parents bring them."[10] Through his figurative reference to Mumei as a "baby bird," the dentist also precisely conveys something essential about the relationship between Yoshirō and Mumei. The great-grandfather Yoshirō has been the primary provider of care for Mumei since his birth, but one who has never been able to provide him with "mother's milk."[11] The relationship does not conform to a dominant gendered binary used to organize human sociality, nor to the system of classification designating the class of animals called "mammalian." Moreover, that Mumei seeks nourishment from earthworms situates this young boy, with extremely fragile teeth and bones, on the very border of another fundamental zoological categorization: that between vertebrate and invertebrate life. Mumei's and the dentist's "flying" words make organizing categories of modern knowledge overlap and cut across each other, exposing confusions and unexpected commonalities. Hierarchies instituted in and through language are subverted. What, then, do we call life? And what of bones and teeth, which long outlast the span of a human life in their material existence in time, are they a kind of life? What about the life of words themselves?

Language, writing, time

In the novel's chronotope, Mikhail Bakhtin proposed, "Time, as it were, thickens, takes on flesh, becomes artistically visible; likewise, space becomes charged and responsive to the movements of time, plot, and history."[12] Near the beginning of *The Emissary*, Yoshirō raises the question of how we perceive the passage of time in the human body by considering it in relation to wood. In wood, the passage of time is traced by the growth rings in trees – as if it were a kind of "flesh" in plant, if not animal, life. Traces of time in human flesh are not so easy to organize.

---

10 Tawada, *The Emissary*, 22.
11 Iwakawa Arisa calls attention to Tawada's emphasis on the bond of care, rather than biological motherhood, between Yoshirō and Mumei in her essay, "'Metamorphose, Nameless Ones!': On Tawada Yōko" (Kawarimi seyo, mumei no mono: Tawada Yōkoron), *Subaru*, April 2018, 164–173.
12 Mikhail Bakhtin, "Forms of Time and of the Chronotope in the Novel," in *The Dialogic Imagination: Four Essays by MM. Bakhtin*, ed. Michael Holquist, trans. Caryl Emerson and Michael Holquist (Austin, TX: University of Texas Press, 1981), 84.

> Stumbling as he took his shoes off, Yoshirō rested a hand on the wooden pillar to steady himself, feeling the grain of wood under his fingers. The years are recorded in rings inside the trunk of a tree, but how was time recorded in his own body? Time didn't spread out neatly in a row; could it just be a disorderly pile, like the inside of a drawer no one ever bothers to straighten?[13]

Bakhtin's own figuration of words of the novel as a "flesh" of time, and of how words provide a site where "space responds to the movements of time" are broadly resonant for the language of Tawada's writing, where considerations of the ineluctably spatialized nature of writing are regularly foregrounded. A work like *Nur da wo du bist da ist nichts* [*Anata no iru tokoro dake nani mo nai*, 1987, Nothing Only Where You Are], whose typography features linear, horizontal, and diagonal patterns of words, for example, makes us aware of how time is marked by writing, and how writing itself involves spatial arrangements. Different possible shapes of time–spherical rather than linear, for example – are explored in her 2002 *Kyūkei Jikan* (Spherical Time).[14]

But it is also true that time *exceeds* writing. In *A Brother-in-Law in Bordeaux*, Tawada's protagonist, who keeps a small notebook filled with single Chinese characters, raises a question about writing and time: "I wish I could write down everything that happens to me. But too many things happen at once. So I just record each event by jotting down a single character."[15] By invoking an endless, unrepresentable simultaneity, this passage indicates the inadequacy of writing to record time. But how else do we know time? If, as many scholars have suggested, time is difference and difference is what constitutes our perception of time, how do we understand "time difference"? Yoshirō's words above raise this question. If there is a time that somehow exists apart from our spatialized markings and signs that, like drawers, measure and categorize time, time must be fundamentally without order, a "disorderly pile."

Similarly, *The Emissary* calls attention to the question of how we represent space. In Mumei's classroom, fellow students are incredulous about his statement, "The earth's round, you know." The physical sensation of the roundness of the earth exceeds the experiential knowledge of these students – although the text hypothesizes that such a sensation of roundness must have been available, like the teeth and bones of dinosaurs, in a remote time. It was a time, the

---

13 Tawada, *The Emissary*, 6.
14 The novel has been translated as *Time Differences* by Jeffrey Angles (Norwich, UK: UEA Publishing Project, 2017).
15 My English translation from Tawada Yōko, *Borudō no gikei* (Tokyo, Kodansha 2009), 77. The novella was published in German as *Schwager in Bordeaux* (Tübingen: konkursbuch Verlag Claudia Gehrke, 2008).

novel states, when people could physically traverse the space between the Asian continent and the Japanese archipelago. A map is two-dimensional, inscribed on a flat surface. But, as is the case with time and language, the map is a system of symbols that needs translation; it is only through a process of translation that the flat surface can be understood to represent a sphere. When the teacher, Mr. Yonatani, tells the disbelieving students that they will do an exercise where they "fold cardboard into a globe," he seems to be seeking to endow them with a bodily sensation that will help to translate the flat into the spherical. It is thus perhaps not surprising that after Yonatani suggests that touch may convey roundness, a student pursues this logic of sensation by asking him, "How many glasses of water are there in the Pacific Ocean?" During this conversation, however, Mumei develops a fierce headache, as he alone looks into himself and finds the entire world map inscribed inside his body. The "overlapping" of map and body causes him immense pain, and he loses consciousness. But it is perhaps by undertaking a process of translation as bodily transformation that Mumei's body becomes capable of the translational role of "emissary," bearing light ahead. For the next time the reader encounters Mumei, he will have become the emissary of the novel's title.[16]

The life of words

The Emissary thus engages questions about how different types of sign systems represent time and space. But at the same time, in this work, words are also shown to have their own temporality *as words*. It is a temporality shown, from the beginning of the novel, to be connected to questions of usage, politics, and identity. Yoshirō rents a dog each day when he goes jogging. But when he uses the familiar Japanese word to refer to a "walk" with a dog, the clerk laughs at him for using a "dead word," while the narrator observes "The lifespan of words is getting shorter and shorter."[17] Indeed, numerous words in the world of *The Emissary* have become "dead words." Yonatani teaches his students that an expression like "putting people to a lot of trouble" is a "dead word." It was once linked to undemocratic distinctions between the "useful" and "useless"

---

16 Tawada, *The Emissary*, 123–124.
17 Tawada, *The Emissary*, 4. In the Japanese text, it is *sanpo* that is termed a *shigo*, literally meaning "dead" (shi) "word" (go) in Japanese. I've used my own translation of the narrator's observation in the next sentence, using "life-span" instead of "shelf-life" for the Japanese "*jūmei*," to bring out the association of "words" with time, as well as "life."

members of society, but that was "long ago before civilization had advanced."[18] Another reason for the death of words is that a secretive and barely visible authority has outlawed "foreign words," as well as the study of English, and the reading of translated novels. These prohibitions cannot be separated from the authorities' enforcement of an isolation policy which absolutely forbids travel abroad. This drawing of a strict distinction between what is "inside," and a forbidden "outside," also comprises the basis for the authorities' attempt to purify language. We see throughout the text, however, that such a purification is impossible, even laughable. Inscriptions in the Japanese phonetic syllabary, *katakana*, for words as basic as "table" (*teeburu*) or "bread" (*pan*) prove to be indispensable for the depiction and practices of everyday life. When the imported word for "dry cleaning" (*kuriiningu*) is on the verge of extinction, a permissible substitute has to be found: "someone got the idea of writing it in "Chinese characters that approximate its sounds," although their meaning is "chestnut-person-tool."[19] While this form of writing is not marked as "foreign" by the authorities, the word's pronunciation depends on replacing *katakana* with "Chinese" characters.

The rate of time's passing also poses a crisis of language in *The Emissary*. Words are not dying slowly, but at a rapid rate. Some word-deaths are associated with the policy prohibiting the use of foreign words. In other cases, words are replaced by politically euphemistic expressions. Post-disaster, dandelions have developed enlarged petals that make them look like the chrysanthemums on the imperial crest. The population is told these must not be referred to with the more scientific term "mutation," but rather as products of "environmental assimilation" (*kankyō dōka*), a euphemism that brazenly rehabilitates Imperial Japan's name for its colonial assimilation policies (*dōka*).[20] While old words are dying, the many new things that appear, whether through mutation or "assimilation," require constant invention of words to replace old words that no longer fit. Gender categories associated with biological traits have become irrelevant, as the younger generation begins to manifest both "male" and "female" physical attributes – indeed, many boys become women. The rate of change in human bodies, as a process of maturation, has led to the emergence of new time-related adjectives – words like "young elderly" (若い老人) for those in their seventies, "middle elderly" (中年の老人), and so forth.[21] In the characters' bodies, the

---

18 Tawada, *The Emissary*, 118.
19 Tawada, *The Emissary*, 51. The characters are "栗人具" in the Japanese text, 63.
20 Tawada, *The Emissary*, 8–9.
21 Tawada, *The Emissary*, 11.

relation of time to human life is thus reversed: children are those who will meet an early death while the older generation are quite literally "death-less."

Facing this situation, Mr. Yonatani loses confidence in his ability to find new words for new developments. "All he could do was feel his way forward, unsure of the way, thinking carefully about each new thing he encountered . . ."[22] Yet the figurative language of the text also depicts language as something that nourishes and sustains human life, while censorship of words is an attempt to exert power over the never-ending change that is "life," often by controlling the very words used to describe and inevitably hierarchize various forms of "life." Of his students, Yonatani thinks: "All he could teach them was how to cultivate language. He was hoping they would plant, cultivate, harvest, and grow fat on words."[23]

Such passages demonstrate how, by contrast to the highly naturalized binary that opposes death/extinction to immortality, Tawada's text posits an endless motion of words fostering the life and growth of language. Figuratively, it endows words with the power to bestow life. After the dentist suggests Mumei be given calcium from a powder ground out of the bones of a prehistoric animal, Hokkaido's Naumann Mammoth, Mumei becomes entranced with the animal's name. "To Mumei, the words themselves were an animal that would start moving if only he stared at it long enough." Similarly, with words like "heron" or "sea turtle," he became "unable to take his eyes off the name from which he believed a living creature might emerge."[24] Mumei knows that wild animals in Japan have all been extinct for many years. But for him it is possible that a word can bring forth life. Tawada's texts are sometimes linked by commentators with the "pantheism" of the indigenous practices of Shinto, according to which the world is filled with innumerable human and inhuman deities. But we should be careful to note that in her texts it is *words* that animate non-human life, and the choice of words that often make humans the object of a non-human gaze. Plant life and inanimate objects are given voice, capable of both addressing and being addressed by human interlocutors. Thus Yoshirō can think of plants as "placid" but "stubborn," and of the kitchen knife he uses to cut an orange for Mumei as "never hesitating," never "wasting time on needless anxiety."[25] When Yoshirō jogs with a rented German shepherd who runs at precisely the same speed that Yoshirō does, he becomes the object of the animal's

---

22 Tawada, *The Emissary*, 119.
23 Tawada, *The Emissary*, 121.
24 Tawada, *The Emissary*, 23.
25 Tawada, *The Emissary*, 32.

gaze: "the dog would flash back a glance as if to say, 'How am I doing? Perfect, wouldn't you say?'"[26]

Walter Benjamin's figurative use, in "The Task of the Translator," of plant life to refer to language and its growth is well-known and bears a resemblance to the figurations we see here. For Benjamin, the language of the "original" work is given new life through translation, which involves the work's encounter with linguistic difference. In Benjamin's text, the original is figuratively an "embryo" that "matures" and "flowers" in translation. However, Benjamin is at pains to stress to the reader that he does not mean that linguistic expression is a form of *organic* life. As Benjamin writes,

> The idea of life and after-life in works of art should be regarded with an entirely unmetaphorical objectivity. Even in times of narrowly prejudiced thought, there was an inkling that life was not limited to organic corporeality . . . In the final analysis, the range of life must be determined from the standpoint of history rather than the standpoint of nature.[27]

It is precisely in this sense that for Benjamin, the life of words, as they move from one context to another, must be an "after-life." As Benjamin stressed, a text never carries the same message as it passes through different temporal contexts, languages, and media. The often-invoked "loss" in translation refers to this process. For Benjamin, the original must die, must survive an inevitable discontinuity, in order to enjoy its after-life. This discontinuity is also taken up extensively in Naoki Sakai's writings on translation.[28]

In his reflections on Benjamin, Paul De Man pushed Benjamin's logic of the temporality of language further. He asserted that, insofar as it is language that we must use to inscribe history, language must be seen as something that can only be *both* "human" and "inhuman." Language crosses the border of the distinction between human and inhuman. As De Man argued, there is a "constant problem about the nature of language as being human or non-human" and this is because "language does things that are out of our control." In order for us to produce a historical account "of good or bad things, not only catastrophes, but felicities also," De Man insisted, "a certain initial discrepancy in language must be examined."[29] In other words, as we have seen one of Tawada's characters

---

26 Tawada, *The Emissary*, 5.
27 Walter Benjamin, "The Task of the Translator," in *Walter Benjamin: Selected Writings: Volume 1 1913–1926*, trans. Bullock and Jennings (Cambridge, MA: Harvard University Press, 1996), 255.
28 See Naoki Sakai, *Translation and Subjectivity* (Minneapolis: University of Minnesota Press, 1997).
29 Paul De Man, "Conclusions: Walter Benjamin's 'The Task of the Translator,'" in *Resistance to Theory* (Minneapolis: University of Minnesota Press, 7th ed., 2006), 101. This comment can be found in the Q&A after the last essay in the book.

say, language will never be fully adequate to depicting all that happens with the passage of time. These reflections return us to our earlier observation that, in Tawada's texts, time and space exceed writing and language in such a way that makes language escape human control.

The "Absent Cause"

In the landscape of *The Emissary* there are streets that have been paved over with transparent sheets of glass: "The street was made of glass sheeting. Below it was a seemingly bottomless cavern." We learn that contamination from soil had seeped into the asphalt of the older streets. The government had refused to conduct an investigation to determine responsibility. Instead, local officials hired people to dig up and dispose of the contaminated earth. After the glass sheets had been installed, to keep people from "falling into the depths of hell," people preferred not to pursue the question of where the waste had been hauled.

> The public reacted to a dodgy explanation offered by an official from the Ministry of Environmental Pollution – that it had been carried outside of the solar system by a private spaceship where it had been duly discarded – with derision. For many nights, the sky was full of stars laughing coldly down at them.[30]

In this scene, and many others that tell of the earth's contamination, the reader is never informed of the actual cause. Similarly, during Yonatani's geography class, the students are told that after some "natural" and "unnatural" disasters, Japan has drifted farther from the Asian continent. Aside from a student's response that, "My great-grandpa says Japan did something really bad so now the continent hates us," we are not told what that "unnatural disaster"– Japan's colonialism and its wars of imperial aggression – might be.[31] But we can link this gap in narration as a formal feature of *The Emissary* to the structure of another memorable image of Yoshirō passing through a Shinjuku that has become deserted by humans, but where traffic signals, and other automated systems, continue to function. There Yoshirō sees "Traffic lights that change regularly from red to green on streets without a single car; automatic doors opening and closing for nonexistent employees, reacting perhaps, to big branches on the trees that lined the streets, bending down in the wind."[32] Here the novel's

---

30 Tawada, *The Emissary*, 125–126.
31 Tawada, *The Emissary*, 122.
32 Tawada, *The Emissary*, 25.

chronotope itself seems to represent visible movement as something produced by what we cannot see directly. It is a passage that allows us to vividly understand how *The Emissary*'s pervasive demonstrations of the ways in which space and time "exceed" language can be grasped as an aspect of the "absent cause" articulated in psychoanalytic and Marxist theory.

In *The Political Unconscious: Narrative as a Socially Symbolic Act*, Fredric Jameson grounds his formulation of "absent cause" in observations about language, text, and history. History, according to Jameson, "is *not* a text," because "history is fundamentally non-narrative and non-representational." But it is also true that "history is inaccessible to us except in textual form." Of pertinence to Tawada's style in *The Emissary*, I think, is Jameson's explanation that by presenting this paradox as a "necessity" he hopes to escape two common problems of literary interpretation. One is to *overemphasize* the activity of the text in organizing what it draws in from history, in such a way that the text seems completely autonomous from history. The other problem would be to approach the text as if it "passively reflects . . . some inert given" and thus reflects a reified social context, an interpretive move that, for Jameson, will simply produce "sheer ideology"[33] that often passes for common sense, can never be expressed in its totality by language or a text, yet the text is affected by the force of history. These conflicting forces, which always produce social contradictions, are better exposed in the text's form (let us define form here using Jameson's words as the "*activity through which the text organizes itself*") than in what is traditionally seen as its "content," or explicit "message," according to Jameson. Thus history, which must always take the *form* of narrative (organizing elements into a beginning, middle, and end), encounters the formal contradiction of bringing together two incompatibles. That is, what is *diachronic* (history) must be organized into the *synchronic*, "flat" form of narrative. Maria Elisa Cevasco sees the problems Jameson raises here as ones of "cognitive mapping," which entail "location in time and space." Cognitive mapping is what "also clears a site in which thought can be set in motion by answering two fundamental questions of dialectics: where are we and what time is it? It is no coincidence that these are the very questions ideologues try to avoid."[34] Keeping in mind the problem of representing spherical space with a flat map in *The Emissary*, I

---

[33] Fredric Jameson, *The Political Unconscious: Narrative As a Socially Symbolic Act* (Ithaca: Cornell University Press, 1981), 81.
[34] Maria Elisa Cevasco, "The Scandal of Theory," a review of *A Singular Modernity: Essay on the Ontology of the Present* by Fredric Jameson (London: Verso, 2002) in *Historical Materialism*, Volume 134 (Leiden, NL: Koninklijke Brill NV, 2005), 349.

propose that these ideas open up a fruitful way of discussing the representation of the "absent cause" in Tawada's novel and its relation to literary imagination.

For example, in yet another humorously sardonic passage related to changes in language, *The Emissary* narrates how holidays have increased in Japan, raising the problem of how new names for holidays are to be produced. These names are described by the narrator as "perfectly democratic," since they are "decided by popular elections." Apparently, popular opinion presents the following impeccable logic:

> The stream of voices calling for abolition of "National Founding Day" grew into a deluge, washing this holiday away so completely it was never heard from again. The main objection was that a splendid country like Japan could not possibly have been founded in a single day.[35]

Tawada's satire here evokes a comparison of *The Emissary*'s time-warped island chronotope with that of fantastic islands depicted by Jonathan Swift in *Gulliver's Travels*. In a discussion that resonates with Adelson's designation of Tawada's fiction as "fantastic," Abigail Williams and Kate O'Connor write that, as an "allegory" of British eighteenth-century politics, it is precisely the nature of Swift's text as fantasy fiction that allows for what his characters named "Hounynyms" call "telling the thing that is not." I suggest that this "thing that is not" is something similar to an "absent cause." Such allegory, however, can never be taken to mean a strict "equation" of elements in the text with a "true set of values," or fixed historical context, Williams and O'Connor caution, because, as with Tawada's fiction, *Gulliver's Travels'* frame of reference is constantly changing. Rather, the "very fictionality of the account makes it possible to reveal what it is not possible to articulate."[36]

It is also true of *The Emissary* that "its frame of reference is constantly changing." Such formal shifting is an effect produced by the constant destabilization of measurements for time and space in Tawada's text. The reader can never be assured of whether time goes forward or backward. Thinking of his grandson's bones, which are weak yet flexible as the tentacles of an octopus, Yoshirō wonders if humans are experiencing "evolution," or "devolution" to the level of molluscan life. On one level, the narration seems to present a recollection of past events (of past natural and unnatural disasters). But it also draws on the ability of the literary imagination to envision a future. Most importantly, the text not only constantly alludes to the way language changes, but

---

35 Tawada, *The Emissary*, 44.
36 Abigail Williams, Kate O'Connor, "Jonathan Swift and 'Gulliver's Travels,'" http://writersinspire.org/content/jonathan-swift-gullivers-travels, 22 February 2020.

presents us with a narration that is full of new and invented words. Tawada's word-play, as many critics have observed, thereby detaches words and the texts from a stable reference. I find Adelson's phrase, "riddles of referentiality," more appropriate.[37] Presenting a narrative as a "riddle of referentiality" may be a way of preventing the text from being read in a manner that reifies context and, as Jameson puts it, will "surely produce sheer ideology."

Eric Cazdyn's study of Japanese film, *The Flash of Capital*, foregrounds the question of "absent cause" and maintains that it is the form, not the content, of a film text that exposes social contradictions as an "absent cause." His book treats each film as a "problem cinema," linking the problems of the films to "three moments of Japanese modernity": 1. Japan's pre-World War II sense of being colonized as well as being a colonizer nation; 2. the contradiction between the individual and collective in the postwar moment and 3. between the national and transnational in the contemporary moment.[38] Like Jameson, Cazdyn's analyses hold to the idea that a text can never represent a totality, yet both Cazdyn and Jameson maintain that the text indirectly bears the traces of "social forces" in a way a reader can decipher. These are the "absent causes" Cazdyn specifies above, or that Jameson analyzes as the traces of imperialism manifested in the British nineteenth-century novel.

Conclusion

How then do we discuss the "absent cause" of Tawada's narrative in *The Emissary*? Let me suggest, as I have at the outset, that through their "riddles," Tawada's texts seek to offer a maximum of imaginative and interpretive flexibility to readers. They strive to produce a kind of "linguistic anarchy," and this anarchy itself can be deeply political. Given the focus on "contamination" and "mutation," fallout from radiation quickly suggests itself as possible "absent cause," while Yonatani's "map discussion" of earthquakes and tsunami produce hard-to-miss associations with the accompanying "unnatural disaster" of the meltdown at the Fukushima nuclear reactor. Most strikingly, though, and as incisively discussed by Kimura, is the way the invisibility of radiation is enacted by its *invisibility in the text*. She proposes that the text itself mimics the way Japanese state's censorship policy, promulgated on December 2013 in the wake of the Fukushima disaster as

---

[37] Leslie A. Adelson, *The Turkish Turn in Contemporary German Literature: Toward a New Critical Grammar* (New York: Palgrave, 2005), 2–5.
[38] Eric Cazdyn, *The Flash of Capital* (Durham: Duke University Press, 2002), 5.

the State Secrecy Law or Act on the Protection of Specially Designated Secrets, silences the narration of "secrets." Kimura's formal analysis of *The Emissary* with its hidden secrets as absent causes resonates powerfully with Adelson's notion of the formal organization of the text as a "riddle."[39]

In the moving conclusion of her essay on *The Emissary* and "care," Iwakawa Arisa proposes yet another line of connection, linking the unpredictability of the changes experienced in Mumei's (and other characters') bodies to Mumei's ability to face the future with "hope." Iwakawa cites words from Tawada's reading of "Metamorphosis: A Late Autumn Ballet" in a 2011, post-disaster, performance with pianist Takase Akiko:

> One morning, no matter what body I wake up to, one morning, because it's morning, it's lovely to open my eyes. Because any body will do, because I can open my eyes, I'll throw open the window. Because, when I open the window the sunshine floods through it, I'll put on my shoes and open the door. I don't need to carry a thing. Just run through that dark corridor and open the door. Open it and walk outside. Everybody's out there! I don't know your names. But because you woke up one morning, yes, one morning that was everybody's morning, you woke up and the world changed just a little bit.[40]

Here, Iwakawa's interpretation can be seen to connect the text's formal qualities of unpredictability, in both the bodies of the characters and in the rapid temporal shifts in the narrative itself, to what Iwakawa sees as the quality of hope. I would further link Iwakawa's "hope" to "imagination," as the "quotidian labor" Adelson sees as necessary to envision a future time, a task this novel, as fiction, indeed takes on.

Bearing in mind that Tawada's writings can have multiple interpretations, I will add a few more interpretive thoughts in dialogue with both the essays above, further extending the ideas of censorship of language, and of metamorphosis as an unpredictable change perceived as arising from oneself, from within oneself. In other words, I propose that if we take the question of language, in its "human" and "inhuman" aspects, as the problem, in Jameson's sense, that *The Emissary* grapples with through its form, we can see how the most prominent feature of its language, word play, creates tensions between language's classificatory, hierarchizing, and discriminatory potential and its anarchic potential. The text's shadowy government's isolation policy, the policy of making the geopolitical boundaries of Japan absolutely impermeable to penetration either by foreigners coming "in" from without or by residents travelling

---

39 Kimura, "Imagining Radiation Disaster," 103.
40 Iwakawa, "Transform, Nameless Ones," 172. In my translation, I have opted to use a singular subject for the verb forms *akeyō* and *deyō*, although the implication that others are called on to join in the action is also present in Japanese.

"inside" from "outside," overlaps precisely with the goals of its policy towards language. For the goals of the language policy are to purify, to purge both written and spoken language in Japan from the "foreign."

In a lecture entitled, "Fascism as a Transhistorical Phenomenon," Enzo Traverso presented the idea of political developments in our contemporary moment, not as simple repetition of the history of the 1930s, but as "post-fascism." A notable difference, for example, is that while fascism in 1930s Germany and Italy elaborated a vision of the future, "post-fascism" that emerged in Donald Trump's United States has only advocated a return to the past. It is a past of ethnic purity. On the other hand, "post-fascism," for Traverso, also resembles fascism of the 1930s in its phantasm of the dangers posed by the outside. But, in fact, fascism emerges from within, where it can coexist with what appears to be "democracy."[41]

Whenever Yoshirō reads the newspapers, words written with characters like "regulation" (規制), "standards" (規準), "bring into conformity with" (適合), "counter- measure" (対策) and "self-restraint" (慎重, frequently used for citizens' expected behavior with respect to funerals, accession ceremonies, and other rituals related to the imperial family), are said to "leap out" from the pages at him. The irony, of course, is that in order to communicate its policies, even to go so far as to make policy a matter of "self-restraint" on the part of the population, it is unavoidable for the government to deploy script still referred to as "Chinese" writing (漢字). In fact, countless puns featured on every page of Tawada's narrative expose how writing systems carry traces of difference and violate boundaries. While the loan word "jogging" is presumably a "dead word" because it has been outlawed, the loan word for "bread" (*pan*) is so necessary and ubiquitous it cannot be so prohibited. Even the bakery Yoshirō is fond of is covered with signs featuring the *katakana* phonetic script used for loan words. Because of the language policy, the baker has had to replace the reference to Germany on his rye bread with a Japanese place name (calling it *Sanuki-pan*); he shares with Yoshirō that no one seemed to care that the word *pan* has been retained because they had "forgotten it was a foreign word."[42] Parodying the difficulty of identifying origins through names, this character has absurdly travelled to the island of Shikoku to search for the "roots" of the rye bread he has renamed *Sanuki-pan*.[43]

The significance of this kind of word-play as formal element in the text is underscored by the feature Kimura Saeko has highlighted. Yoshirō is a writer,

---

41 Enzo Traverso, "Fascism as a Trans-Historical Concept," Institute for Comparative Modernities Invitational Lecture, Cornell University, 12 February 2020.
42 Tawada, *The Emissary*, 14.
43 Tawada, *The Emissary*, 31.

and midway through the narrative we learn that he had been writing a book also called *The Emissary*. The title is a homonym for Tawada's novel's title, but written with a more standard orthography that conveys its historical reference to an emissary sent from Japan to the T'ang court in China: 遣唐使. As Kimura notes, because of the policy of banning foreign words, Yoshirō has buried this book.[44] Could the novel by Yoko Tawada we are reading simply be a copy, a rewriting, or translation of this book? The sounds of the title, at least, have been preserved and transmitted through writing.

Moreover, the important homonym (*kentō* meaning "votive lantern," 献灯, or emissary to the T'ang, 遣唐) names the mission of Mumei, one of the two central characters in the novel. While the Chinese character for T'ang (or China, a place from which the Japanese archipelago has been distanced) has been replaced by the Chinese character for "lantern," there is no doubt that the secret task of the emissary is to violate the prohibition on moving out, across the territorial and linguistic boundaries of Japan. We could also say it is a defiance of the "post-fascism" that seeks a future only by returning to a false past of "origins" or ethnic purity, and a defiance of the complicity between authoritarianism and enfeebled democracy that is complicit with it. In the aftermath of the unnatural disasters at Fukushima, it is remarkable that Yoko Tawada has prepared a tale that does not limit itself to relating the traumas of individual survivors. Nor does *The Emissary* only constitute critique of Japanese government policy. In addition to that trenchant critique, literary imagination is also deployed to envision something more broad, profound, and systemic: the emergence of post-fascism.

Because language itself is a system of differences, it can be wielded by human subjects to inflict violence. But against this, Tawada sets the anarchic potential of language, its "inhuman" aspect, by which it can constantly escape our control. If Mumei is an emissary, he has a suitable name. We must recall the line from Iwakawa Arisa's citation: its address to the "everybody" whose names we do not yet know. Mumei, as literally one who has no name, can perhaps not be classified by the "human" language we use. Neither male nor female, he slips out of gendered categories. Literally, one with "no name" in the formal structure of Tawada's text, Mumei's position is one the text itself cannot name or refuses to name. Or perhaps, in a text whose word play invents countless new words, his namelessness is that which can inspire us to draw on the resource of literature, the imagination, to invent a new language, and languages, to come.

---

[44] Kimura, "Imagining Radiation Disaster," 103–104.

Works cited

Adelson, Leslie A. *The Turkish Turn in Contemporary German Literature: Toward a New Critical Grammar* (New York: Palgrave, 2005).
Adelson, Leslie A. "Rusty Rails and Parallel Tracks: *Trans-Latio* in Yoko Tawada's *Das Nackte Auge*," in *Un/Translatables: New Maps for Germanic Literatures*. Ed. Bethany Wiggin and Catriona MacLeod (Evanston, IL: Northwestern University Press, 2004), 281–298.
Adelson, Leslie A. "Literary Imagination and the Future of Literary Studies," in *Deutsche Vierteljahrsschrift für Literaturwissenschaft und Geistesgeschichte* 89 (2015), 675–683.
Appadurai, Arjun. *The Future As Cultural Fact. Essays on the Global Condition* (London: Verso Books, 2013).
Bakhtin, Mikhail. "Forms of Time and of the Chronotope in the Novel," in *The Dialogic Imagination: Four Essays by MM. Bakhtin*. Ed. Michael Holquist. Trans. Caryl Emerson and Michael Holquist (Austin, TX: University of Texas Press, 1981), 84–259.
Benjamin, Walter. "The Task of the Translator," in *Walter Benjamin: Selected Writings: Volume 1 1913–1926*. Trans. Bullock and Jennings (Cambridge, MA: Harvard University Press, 1996), 253–262.
Cazdyn, Eric. *The Flash of Capital* (Durham: Duke University Press, 2002).
Cevasco, Maria Elisa. "The Scandal of Theory." A review of *A Singular Modernity: Essay on the Ontology of the Present* by Fredric Jameson (London: Verso, 2002) in *Historical Materialism*, Volume 134 (Leiden, NL: Koninklijke Brill NV, 2005).
De Man, Paul. *Resistance to Theory* (Minneapolis: University of Minnesota Press, 7th ed., 2006).
Iwakawa, Arisa. "'Transform, Nameless Ones!': On Tawada Yōko" (Henshin seyo, mumei no mono: Tawada Yōkoron), *Subaru* (April 2018): 164–173.
Jameson, Fredric. *The Political Unconscious: Narrative as a Socially Symbolic Act* (Ithaca: Cornell University Press, 1981).
Kimura, Saeko. "Imagining Radiation Disaster: Tawada Yōko's *The Emissary* and its Tale" (Hōshanōsai no sōzōryoku: Tawada Yōko no *Kentōshi* o kataru koto). https://ferris.repo.nii.ac.jp/?action=pages_view_main&active_action=repository_view_main_item_detail&item_id=2425&item_no=1&page_id=13&block_id=21 (Yokohama: Ferris University, 2019), December 2020.
Sakai, Naoki. *Translation and Subjectivity* (Minneapolis: University of Minnesota Press, 1997).
Tawada, Yoko. *Borudō no gikei*. (Tokyo: Kodansha, 2009).
Tawada, Yoko. *The Emissary*. Trans. Margaret Mitsutani (New York: New Directions, 2018).
Tawada, Yoko. *Kentōshi* (Tokyo: Kodansha, 2014).
Tawada, Yoko. *Schwager in Bordeaux* (Tübingen: konkursbuch Verlag Claudia Gehrke, 2008)
Traverso, Enzo. "Fascism as a Trans-Historical Concept." Institute for Comparative Modernities Invitational Lecture, Cornell University, 12 February 2020.
Williams, Abigail and Kate O'Connor. "Jonathan Swift and 'Gulliver's Travels.'" http://writersinspire.org/content/jonathan-swift-gullivers-travels, 22 February 2020.
Wohlfarth, Irving. "'Was nie geschrieben wurde, lesen': Walter Benjamins Theorie des Lesens," in *Walter Benjamin 1892–1940 zum 100. Geburtstag*. Ed. Uwe Steiner (Bern: Peter Lang, 1992), 297–344.

Gizem Arslan
Writing *Heimat*: José F. A. Oliver at *Heim* with Paul Celan

Introduction: Poetry's unrootedness in Paul Celan and José F. A. Oliver

> Der Dichter, der mitten im Wort wohnt, verläßt das Land. Celan war selten an der Geburtsstätte seiner Wörter. Seine Wörter waren fern von ihren Wurzeln. Deutsch ist eine Sprache, doch was ist Deutschland? Ein Land ohne seine Sprache? Für Celan ist Deutsch eine Sprache, seine Sprache ohne Land.
> (. . .) Der Sprachgebundene ist der Bodenständigste auf schwankendem Boden.
> Sprache ist die unverträgliche Landschaft. Man schlägt dort keine Wurzeln. Man kommt in der Sprache auf den Weg. Man staunt über die Blüten an den abgeschnittenen Wurzeln. Celans abgeschnittene Wurzeln berührten meine abgeschnittenen Wurzeln.[1]

> The poet, who resides within the word, leaves the land. Rarely was Celan at the place where his words were born. His words were far away from their roots. German is a language, but what is Germany? A land without its language? For Celan, German is a language, his language without land.
> (. . .) He who is bound to language is the most firmly rooted of all on shaky ground.
> (. . .)
> Language is the irreconcilable landscape. One puts no roots down there. In language one enters a path. One marvels at the blossoms on the roots that have been hacked off. Celan's hacked-off roots touched my hacked-off roots.[2]

Turkish-German author Zafer Şenocak's reflections on Paul Celan, one of the greatest German-language poets of the post-World War II era, indicate the inexorable paradoxes that underlie any space that lays claim to language: The exclusionary language of "Blut und Boden" (blood and soil) was part and parcel of nationalistic claims on German as a national language bound to a "Land" (country, but also land or soil) and shared by its people. This very claim to the groundedness of language and identity *dis*placed the German language from the many lands where it resided. Celan's birthplace Czernowitz, once a vibrant German-speaking city and the birthplace of many other writers such as Rose

---

[1] Zafer Şenocak, *Zungenentfernung: Bericht aus der Quarantänestation: Essays*, 1st ed. (Munich: Babel, 2001), 95, https://hdl.handle.net/2027/mdp.39015054158111?urlappend=%3Bsignon=swle:https://shibidp.cit.cornell.edu/idp/shibboleth.
[2] Zafer Şenocak, "Paul Celan," in *Atlas of a Tropical Germany: Essays on Politics and Culture, 1990–1998*, trans. Leslie A. Adelson (Lincoln: University of Nebraska Press, 2000), 70–71.

Ausländer, Alfred Margul-Sperber, and Immanuel Weissglas, is largely purged of German today.³ This cleaving of language and land went hand in hand with the loss of "shared universe or world" after the Holocaust. Indeed, poetry after the Holocaust sought to "account for an experience that seems to have no proper setting."⁴ For the remainder of his life after World War II, Celan lived in and on translation, teaching literature and translation in Paris and translating poets such as Charles Baudelaire, Emily Dickinson, Osip Mandelstam and William Shakespeare into German. Beyond the biographic, however, and in Şenocak's adroit formulation, Celan's rootlessness of language splinters words such as "Deutschland" and "Landessprache" (vernacular or national language), uprooting "Deutsch" and "Sprache" (language) from "Land." What remains is "Sprache ohne Land" (language without land or language without country).

Be it due to migration (as in Şenocak's case) or persecution (as in Celan's), the poet's displacement yields a language of severed roots and shaky ground – in Şenocak's tellurian imagery – which in turn raises the expectation that the poetry of displacement be one of isolation. Contrary to this expectation, Celan's and Şenocak's severed roots come in contact with one another. In fact, for both Şenocak's and Celan's literary output, contact and encounter are key preoccupations, as both authors contend with gaps in horizons of experience, in the wake of transnational labor migration for Şenocak, and the Holocaust for Celan. It should then come as no surprise that Paul Celan is a literary muse for prominent German-language authors who write under the sign of migration and translation, and like Şenocak, reflect intensively on multigenerational experiences of migration and multidirectional histories of genocide.⁵ In addition to Şenocak, some of Celan's key influences in German-language literatures of migration include the 2009 Nobel Prize winner Herta Müller, the title of whose 2009 novel *Atemschaukel* (translated into English as *The Hunger Angel*, whereas the literal translation would be "Breathswing") strongly resembles Celan's 1967 poetry collection *Atemwende* (*Breathturn*) and tells of the persecution of ethnic

---

3 Czernowitz appeared under numerous names within the borders of many powers over the centuries. Since Celan's birth, the city has changed hands between the Kingdom of Romania, the Soviet Union (Ukranian SSR) and Ukraine, appearing under the names Чернівці (Černivci), Cernăuți, and in Celan and Oliver's poetry, Czernowitz.
4 Ulrich Baer, *Remnants of Song: Trauma and the Experience of Modernity in Charles Baudelaire and Paul Celan*, Cultural Memory in the Present (Stanford: Stanford University Press, 2000), 222, 227.
5 Michael Rothberg opposes what he views as a zero-sum-game of thinking Holocaust memory as in competition with other histories of colonialism, slavery and racism. In response, he defines multidirectional memory as "a productive, intercultural dynamic" that arises from interaction between different historical memories (Stanford: Stanford University Press 2009), 3.

Germans in Romania by Stalin's regime and their life in labor camps. Japanese-German Yoko Tawada, equally renowned in her literary languages of Japanese and German for her writings on travel, translation and catastrophe, has published numerous essays on Celan as well as the 2020 novel *Paul Celan und der chinesische Engel* [Paul Celan and the Chinese Angel] about a young Celan-researcher. The Spanish-Andalusian-German-Allemanic poet José F. A. Oliver stands out in this literary landscape for the stark co-presence in his poetry of rootlessness in language on the one hand, and the strength of his connection to regional language and identity on the other. Like Celan's, Oliver's literary output is comprised largely of lyric poetry and relatively few prose works. Oliver's poetry, like Celan's, presents interlaced histories of displacement and persecution and seeks to alienate its readers from their own language through plurilingual juxtaposition, neologistic composite nouns, as well as experimental typography that includes but is not limited to line breaks that split words in unexpected ways and reveal new lexical possibilities. Like Celan's, Oliver's relationship to language and space is fraught and his biography marked by displacement (his parents migrated from Spain to Germany as workers).[6] It should then come as no surprise that for Oliver, Celan is a literary muse, and that some of Oliver's most pointed interventions into the concepts of home and homeland are formulated as responses to Celan's poetry. Particularly in his poems about visiting Paul Celan and Rose Ausländer's birthplace Czernowitz, Oliver reveals homeland (*Heimat*) as mediated space, and subjects it to displacement in mediation.

Oliver's critique of the concept of *Heimat* through experimentation with the medium of writing constitutes the core of this contribution. I propose that Oliver – via Celan and to a lesser degree Ausländer – disorients his readers with respect to spaces that can be identified as *Heimat*. That Oliver does so through wordplay with the words "Heim" and "Heimat," as well as by critiquing unitary conceptions of space, language and geography has been addressed in existing scholarship.[7]

---

[6] Unlike Celan, Oliver does enjoy a lasting connection to Hausach, a small town in Baden-Württemberg that remains his adopted home. Some of Oliver's poetry is in Allemanic, the dialect spoken there. Despite his enduring affinity to this rural German town and its language, Oliver's poetry and prose reveal a critical attitude towards the unity of languages and their boundedness to spaces that can be designated "home" or "homeland".

[7] Joseph Jurt, "La double patrie: A propos de la poésie lyrique de José F. A. Oliver," in *Heimat: La petite patrie dans les pays de langue allemande*, ed. Marc Beghin et al., 13 (Grenoble, France: Centre d'Etudes et de Recherches Allemandes et Autrichiennes Contemporaines (CERAAC), Université Stendhal-Grenoble 3, 2009), 179; Hannelore van Ryneveld, "Lyrik im Dialog: Ein Interpretationsversuch zu José Olivers Lyrikband Duende (1997)," *Acta Germanica: Jahrbuch des Germanistenverbandes im südlichen Afrika* 30–31 (2002–2003): 127–138; Marc James Mueller, "Zwischen 'Heimatt' und 'Fremdw:Ort': Über poetische identitäts-Mobilität in der deutsch-

Distinct from previous scholarly accounts, however, I argue that Oliver critiques *Heimat* through experimentation with the medium of writing, in that he disrupts unidirectional reading practices on the typo-topographic space of the page in favor of multilingual lexical possibilities and unexpected directions of reading. Moreover, Oliver's unusual punctuation, italicization and capitalization draw attention to his poems' writtenness in ways that exceed meaning and highlight the poems' mediation in print. In Oliver's poems about *Heimat* in general, but particularly in those about Celan's troubled *Heimat* Czernowitz, Oliver not only subjects *Heimat* to doubling and slippage, but more fundamentally reveals processes of mediation that underwrite – and undermine – *Heimat* in the print medium.

This contribution's focus on Oliver's written experimentation with *Heimat* has two key implications for scholarship on *Heimat* and migration. First, while *Heimat* is often associated with unmediated experience, it has been shown to rely on processes of mediation and to have an enduring appeal in numerous media.[8] While most existing studies deal with mediation processes in film and multimedia, this study focuses on *Heimat*'s reliance on mediation in the print medium. Another key intervention of this study is its broader urging for more sustained attention to minoritarian rethinking of media in German-speaking contexts. Scholarship on migration and media deals extensively with representations of minorities in literature, media, film, and theater. What has received less critical attention to date are minoritarian interventions into the key concepts that govern our thinking about media, which in turn influence the ways in which we receive and produce texts of various modalities.[9] This study, by contrast, pays sustained attention to experimentation

---

spanischen Lyrik José F. A. Olivers," *Glossen: Eine internationale zweisprachige Publikation zu Literatur, Film, und Kunst in den Deutschsprachigen Ländern Nach 1945* (2007), 26; Áine McMurtry, "Sea Journeys to Fortress Europe: Lyric Deterritorializations in Texts by Caroline Bergvall and José F. A. Oliver," *The Modern Language Review* 113.4 (2018): 811–845, https://doi.org/10.5699/modelangrevi.113.4.0811; Horst Fassel, "Kultureinintegration in der deutschen Literatur: Zwei Autoren: Rafik Schami und José F. A. Oliver," *Estudios Filológicos Alemanes* 21 (2010): 201–223.

8 Kurt Beals, "High-Tech Heimat: Mountains and Mediation in Literature, Film and Digital Art," *The German Quarterly* 92.2 (2019): 166–186. https://doi.org/10.1111/gequ.12101; Johannes von Moltke, *No Place Like Home: Locations of Heimat in German Cinema* (Berkeley: University of California Press, 2005), 36; Anton Kaes, *From Hitler to Heimat: The Return of History as Film* (Cambridge, MA: Harvard University Press, 1989); Christopher J. Wickham, "Representation and Mediation in Edgar Reitz's Heimat," *The German Quarterly* 64.1 (1991): 35–45. https://doi.org/10.2307/407303.

9 Jocelyn Aksin and Gizem Arslan, "Migration and Media: Reenvisioning Media Representations of Migration to and around Europe," *Seminar Proposals, American Comparative Literature Association 2020 Annual Meeting*, 2019.

with the print medium as it relates to mediation processes underlying *Heimat*, a term often launched as a weapon for the exclusion of minorities. In addition, it observes the processes by which Oliver's typography makes all words – regardless of language – appear foreign to their readers and draws attention to the displacement of languages and people. This is displacement not only in the sense of travel and migration, but also the severing of language from geographies and onto the printed page. This literary strategy of multilingual alienation subverts customary publishing practices by which typography serves to mark foreign words as foreign (e.g. through italicization) or where foreign words are otherwise purged (e.g. through translation) in the service of a global Anglophone readership.[10] Oliver publishes his poetry with Suhrkamp Verlag, one of the leading publishing houses in Europe, and the most prominent publisher of twentieth- and twenty-first-century literature in Germany. His deliberate choices of typography, capitalization and layout favor literary multilingualism from the center of the German-language publishing landscape.

Heimat: Definitions, history, and critique

Histories of – at times violent – sociopolitical exclusion and memories of migration are spoken in Oliver's poetry in the same breath as the word *Heimat*. Indeed, numerous Oliver poems capture *Heimat*'s troubled history. The poem "heimatt" from the 1989 collection *HEIMATT und andere FOSSILE TRÄUME* (*Homelan(d) guid and other Fossil Dreams*), for instance, enumerates fragments of a Spanish migrant's memories of life in Germany. Among these are glimpses of home life, but also of men calling her "doña" or "señorita," both objectifying her and marking her as non-German: "und die augen die stechenden/ der herren/ die sie leichtzüngig doña nannten/ manchmal señorita" ("and eyes gimleting/ of men/ who lighttongued called her doña/ sometimes señorita"). This othering takes on more sinister contours as the poem later recounts election posters for the NPD (Nationaldemokratische Partei Deutschland/National Democratic Party of Germany), a small extreme right-wing party modeled on Hitler's NSDAP.[11] Although

---

10 For a detailed analysis of Anglo-American publishing practices that favor monolingualism, see Brian Lennon, *In Babel's Shadow: Multilingual Literatures, Monolingual States* (Minneapolis: University of Minnesota Press, 2010).
11 José F. A. Oliver, *Sandscript: Selected Poetry 1987–2018*, trans. Marc James Mueller (Buffalo: White Pine Press, 2018), 52–53. All translations of Oliver's poetry are Marc James Mueller's unless indicated otherwise.

Oliver foregrounds memory rather than history in this poem, both his poetry and prose respond to *Heimat* as historical term. That Oliver's "heimatt" is a "fossil dream," a petrified delusion, is reflected in scholarship on the historical development of the term leading up to current debates.

Heimat has become shorthand for "regressive, narrow, or nostalgic notions of place" and "has assisted in more than mere exclusions."[12] Its imprecise English translation is often accepted as "homeland," but it is often left untranslated. The traditional understanding of *Heimat* emerged in response to dizzying technological advances, noise pollution, invasion of private space by infrastructural channels (electricity, telephone, water, sewage) associated with modernity, and in their wake, "the perceived or real loss of social stability and transparency, and of a sense of community, all tied to a specific locale."[13] In this narrower conception, *Heimat* evokes a pure, idyllic space in a stable world. *Heimat* is often contrasted to the city as a nostalgic construction, allies itself to tradition over modernity, and presents itself as an image of the past.[14] At best, *Heimat* offers visions of stability in an idealized world in which everyone has a clearly defined place, combining belonging and identity with an attachment to a specific place.[15] At worst, *Heimat* has been weaponized in the political realm for the exclusion and at times violent persecution of minorities.[16]

In recent years, *Heimat* has resurged in German public discourse in the wake of Europe's numerous crises, as mainstream politicians, right-wing groups and left-wing resistance alike have sought to reclaim the term. Horst Seehofer renamed his interior ministry "Federal Ministry of the Interior, Building and Community (Heimat)," thus institutionalizing *Heimat* on a national level. For right-wing political movements such as Alternative for Germany and Pegida, *Heimat* encapsulates a longing for a white, Christian, western community that excludes non-Christian others such as migrants, refugees and Muslims. In response, left-wing parties such as the Greens seek to imbue the term with anti-exclusionary resistance. President Frank Walter Steinmeier too attempted to reclaim *Heimat* away from the far-right by echoing the term's reimagination

---

12 Friederike Ursula Eigler, *Heimat, Space, Narrative: Toward a Transnational Approach to Flight and Expulsion* (Woodbridge: Camden House, 2014), 22; Peter Blickle, *Heimat: A Critical Theory of the German Idea of Homeland*, (Rochester, NY: Camden House, 2002), x.
13 Eigler, *Heimat, Space, Narrative*, 2.
14 Celia Applegate, *A Nation of Provincials: The German Idea of Heimat* (Berkeley: University of California Press, 1990), 9; von Moltke, *No Place Like Home*, 227–228.
15 Caroline Bland, Catherine Smale, and Godela Weiss-Sussex, "Women Writing Heimat in Imperial and Weimar Germany: Introduction" *German Life and Letters* 72.1 (2019): 1–13. https://doi.org/10.1111/glal.12213; Eigler, *Heimat, Space, Narrative*, 13.
16 Blickle, *Heimat*, x.

by hyphenated German journalists and intellectuals as *Haymat*, a term that accords more visibility to previously excluded communities and includes their voices in defining in *Heimat* for contemporary Germany.[17]

As tenacious as the term *Heimat* have proved its related genres in cultural production, such as *Heimatliteratur* and *Heimatfilm*, in which *Heimat* is typically associated with rootedness in an idyllic setting, belonging to a community, and unmediated experience. All three associations have been deconstructed in existing scholarship. Although *Heimat* in these genres is presented as "the place beyond alienation and displacement," scholars have revealed that displacement is inherent to the very structure of *Heimat* (as evident both in the historical circumstances that yielded *Heimat*-genres and the fictional circumstances presented in them).[18] The displacement of reality into the idyllic fantasy world is a doubling that renders home and away difficult to distinguish, but more fundamentally suggests that home itself is ontologically unstable.[19] In print as in film, *Heimat* evokes an unmediated "realm of innocence and immediacy," yet mediation plays a key role in imagining that purportedly unmediated *Heimat*.[20] Indeed, thematizing mediation processes is a "self-reflexive technique" that draws attention to the craft of producing fictional accounts of *Heimat* and calls upon the "audience to consider his own position relative to the broader context represented by that craft."[21] In short, turning critical attention to *Heimat's* mediation in literary and visual arts reveals *Heimat* to be anything but immediate and stable. Artistic treatments of the intersection between *Heimat* and mediation processes additionally reveal media literacy as a key component of critical reflection on *Heimat*.[22] To date, however, the intersection between *Heimat* and mediation processes has been explored primarily in film and visual arts. One recent notable study is Kurt Beals's investigation of mediation processes in *Heimatliteratur* and *Heimatfilm* alike, in which he examines short stories by the Swiss writer Regina

---

[17] For a more detailed discussion of the resurgence of *Heimat* in recent years, see Claudia Breger's contribution in this volume, as well as Annika Orich, "Archival Resistance," *German Politics and Society* 38.2 (2020): 1–34, https://doi.org/10.3167/gps.2020.380201.
[18] Kaes, *From Hitler to Heimat*; von Moltke, *No Place Like Home*; Wickham, "Representation and Mediation."
[19] Von Moltke, *No Place Like Home*, 3–6.
[20] Von Moltke, *No Place Like Home*, 37; Beals, "High-Tech Heimat," 167.
[21] Wickham, "Representation and Mediation," 35–38.
[22] In referring to German filmmaker Edgar Reitz's *Heimat*-trilogy, Christopher Wickham concludes: "The ultimate 'success' of Heimat as a text that takes a position on filmmaking, historiography, or 'Heimat' thinking depends on the media literacy of the spectator, which necessarily must differ from one viewer to the next. Media literacy itself, as I have shown, is a topic of Heimat" ("Representation and Mediation," 44).

Ullmann. However, Beals discusses mediation as presented *in* those texts (for instance, the stories' prominent thematization of media such as letters and telegrams), and not these texts' self-reflexive treatment *of* themselves as medium. The question of mediation, then, requires scrutiny in the print medium beyond literary analysis's traditional focus on reference and meaning. This study adds to its interpretive arsenal material effects of Oliver's typography in order to pay sustained attention not only to Oliver's conceptual and thematic critique of *Heimat*, but also his typographic experimentation that highlights the writtenness of his poems, and by extension, the reliance of *Heimat* on mediation in print.

José F. A. Oliver's critique of Heimat

José F. A. Oliver's critique of *Heimat* takes several forms. First, Oliver critiques *Heimat* in his essays through explicit discussions of home and cultures of migration alike, and in his poetic work via representations of people whose persecution stems from exclusionary notions of identity. These peoples are not limited to Oliver's personal experiences as the child of Andalusian migrants in Germany. In fact, Oliver frequently thematizes displacement and persecution more generally, referring to Sinti and Roma in and beyond Spain, refugees from North Africa and the Middle East in Europe, and Jews, the last primarily through Oliver's preoccupation with the poetry of Paul Celan as one of his prime literary muses.[23] Other strategies through which Oliver critiques *Heimat* can be characterized as plurilingual juxtaposition and typographic experimentation. One of many poems that feature these is "kompaß & dämmerung" ("compass & twilight") from the poetry collection *nachtrandspuren* (*nightfringetraces*):

für Harald Weinrich[24]

kompaß & dämmerung
Da ist der osten weit hinter meiner stirn. Da
ist der westen ein pfandaug *hei*
matt. Da ist der süden würfel
becher dem hunger. Da ist NORDEN. *No*
pierdas el norte. Da ist ostwest
laibung der sonne. Da ist der mond

---

[23] Oliver's 2015 essay collection *fremdenzimmer* (Guestrooms), for instance, includes numerous references to homelands and nationalism. The essay "Wider die Vereinsamung" ["Against Isolation"] in particular weaves together the histories of Andalusia, Flamenco, and Sinti and Roma. José F. A. Oliver, *Fremdenzimmer: Essays* (Frankfurt am Main: weissbooks, 2015), 71–83.
[24] José F. A. Oliver, *nachtrandspuren: Gedichte* (Frankfurt am Main: Suhrkamp, 2002), 12.

auf seiner suche nach dem zwiegeschlecht. Da ist
die SPRACHZEITLOSE licht
verzweigung der vogelunruh. Da ist tau
brotwärme im verlegten w:ort
ist stille noch. Da ist der tag
so reichbar nah

compass & twilight
There is the east far behind my brow. There
is the west a pawn gaze *homelan(d)*
guid. There is the south dice
box for the hunger. There is the NORTH. *No
pierdas el norte*. There is eastwest
loafing of the sun. There is the moon
on his search for the twi-gender. There is
SPEECH TIME LESS light
branching of the birds disquiet. There is dew
bread-warmth in the displaced wor(l)d
is silence still. There is the day
so reachable close[25]

The plurilingual juxtaposition of German and Spanish is not specific to "kompaß & dämmerung." It constitutes a key strategy through which Oliver challenges unitary correspondences between a space one could call *Heimat* and the language(s) spoken in it. Of particular significance here is not only the bilingual juxtaposition of German and Spanish as national languages but also of regional ones in other poems and essays: the Alemannic dialect of the Black Forest region where Oliver grew up, as well as the Andalusian and Castilian of his family. As his English translator Marc James Mueller observes, Oliver is not a poet of only two languages, but his "*linguistic* 'worlds' are rather composed of two times two languages."[26] Indeed, dialects do not only offer an expanded lexical field for Oliver's poetry, but constitute loci of resistance against structures of repression perceptible in the German and Spanish languages' relationships to nationalism. Oliver's stance with respect to the politics of language is clear. In the essay collection *fremdenzimmer*, for instance, Oliver narrates the pedagogical repression of Alemannic dialect by one of his "dialect-orphaned" ("dialektverwaist") teachers in the local *Gymnasium*, as well as the imposition of prayer and the Spanish national anthem by a Franco-worshipping Spanish teacher in the Spanish School, an afternoon school for the children of guest workers.[27] Here and elsewhere, Oliver proves

---

25 Oliver, *Sandscript*, 169.
26 Oliver, *Sandscript*, 9; Emphasis in original.
27 Oliver, *Fremdenzimmer*, 28, 19 ft.1.

fully cognizant of nationalism's history of weaponizing language – and particularly language education – in the service of homogenization.

"kompaß & dämmerung" is also thematically representative of Oliver's oeuvre in that it interlaces the concepts of homeland and (dis)orientation in a context of mobility. Many of Oliver's texts tell of migration or feature his extensive travels to various corners of the world, including Australia, Eastern Europe, Egypt, and the United States.[28] The theme of travel also relates seamlessly to migration, featuring many instances of arrival, departure, and displacement. Instead of familiarizing his readers with the world of the nomad-traveler, however, Oliver's texts seek rather to defamiliarize the world as his readers know it.[29] They do so in three main ways. First, as Marc James Mueller observes, Oliver generates alienation effects in his texts by self-foreignizing its languages (proper names in particular) in order to disrupt the linguistic and referential flow of his texts for an "audience already on foreign ground."[30] Second, Oliver inserts his own multiplicity of identities into his language, telling extensively of his identity as Spanish-German-Andalusian-Black Forester, including poetry and prose in dialect as well as words and phrases in multiple languages. Finally, Oliver places foreignness and familiarity "into a dynamic, temporary, and thus unstable dialogue, deconstructing fixed expectations and stereotypes for and about what it means to be a foreigner – anywhere."[31] Questions of orientation are foregrounded by "kompaß & dämmerung"'s title and thematization of cardinal directions. While the poem does not feature travel, its narrator does muse soberly about what lies beyond – and in one case, "far behind" – the speaker's field of vision along any

---

[28] "kompaß & dämmerung" appears as the second poem in *nachtrandspuren*, the later sections of which feature Oliver's travels to Australia.

[29] For a more thorough analysis of Gilles Deleuze and Félix Guattari's critical term "deterritorialization" as it relates to Oliver's poetry, see Áine McMurtry, "Sea Journeys to Fortress Europe: Lyric Deterritorializations in Texts by Caroline Bergvall and José F. A. Oliver," *The Modern Language Review* 113.4 (2018): 811–845. https://doi.org/10.5699/modelangrevi.113.4.0811.

[30] Oliver, *Sandscript*, 23; The term "alienation effect" is often used to refer to Bertolt Brecht's works for the theater. Literatures of migration often launch such effects and modernist strategies of defamiliarization modified for their contexts. Through these effects, these texts seek to break through established, dulled modes of perception and allow their readers to experience the world of language anew. Oliver's key strategy of "self-foreignization" has similar objectives. Mueller notes this as a sustained strategy for inserting the foreign into the referential and material world of text, by means of which, ultimately, "foreignness and familiarity enter into a dynamic, temporary, and thus unstable dialogue, deconstructing fixed expectations and stereotypes for and about what it means to be a foreigner – anywhere" (Buffalo: White Pine Press, 2018), 23.

[31] Oliver, *Sandscript*, 22–23.

of the four main points of the compass. Oliver's compass operates by means of conspicuous absences and gaps, however. The north is presented with the phrase in Spanish "No pierdas el norte" (literally, "do not lose the north"), which not only escapes immediate comprehension by most German-speaking readers, but also questions the very permanence and discoverability of the north. In an extended sense, "no pierdas el norte" can also mean "don't lose your direction," or "don't lose sight of your goal," again suggesting that orientation is in peril even as one is tasked with keeping it.[32] The south, too, is not a space in any positive sense, but rather a container in which hunger, another term of lack, rattles like dice. West and East are symbolically suggestive as indicating Oliver's two homelands Spain and Germany, but also longstanding oppositional relationships posited between the East and West. Marc James Mueller merges these two dimensions of association by suggesting that one could understand East and West as Spain and Germany, the poet's two homelands, one associated with rationality and grounded in the poet's mind, and one as representing a faded homeland that the narrator nonetheless carries with him.[33] The poem complicates any possibility of claiming either direction as leading home, however. Instead, the west is "far behind" the narrator's head and outside his field of vision, and the east is a "Pfandaug," a neologistic composite noun comprised of "Pfand" (security, deposit, pawn, mortgage) and "Aug(e)" (eye), translated here as "pawn gaze." As suggested by the word "matt" (matte, faded), *Heimat* is already in the process of fading, and comprises more lack: The organ of sight has been left as security, and the home that it might have seen is already fading. Both East and West, then, are associated not with what is discoverable, but rather that which is inaccessible or removed from sight, nevertheless always hearkening back to the seeable, as though to highlight this very lack. Symbolically, too, Oliver plays with Germany's self-conception as "the West," since Germany in this context is an unseeable, unknowable East, subject to a similar orientalist dismissal to that which it has long subjected the cultures of the "East." The sense of disorientation, or rather, loss of orientation intensifies in the suggestive uses of "hei-/ matt" (translated by Mueller as "homelan(d)/guid") and

---

[32] Many thanks to Victor Herrera for clarifying the extended meanings of this phrase.
[33] "Ost und West können hier als Verweise auf Deutschland und Spanien gelesen werden: Deutschland, das 'rationalere' Land, das tief im Denken des Lyrischen Ichs verankert ist, und Spanien als nicht gegenwärtige, aber 'mitgegebene' Heimat," Marc James Mueller "Zwischen 'Heimatt' und 'Fremdw:Ort': Über poetische Identitäts-Mobilität in der deutsch-spanischen Lyrik José F. A. Olivers," *Glossen: Eine internationale zweisprachige Publikation zu Literatur, Film, und Kunst in den deutschsprachigen Ländern nach 1945* 26 (2007).

"w:ort" (wor(l)d), two words that appear time and again in Oliver's poetry in the distinct spelling reproduced here.

These unusual spellings are my point of entry into the third, and for this study, most significant aspect of Oliver's third strategy of *Heimat*-critique: typographic experimentation, which in turn draws attention to the written dimensions of language. Oliver often splits words in order to reveal unexpected lexical possibilities, while also highlighting their writtenness. A "w:ort," for instance, is a word ("Wort") opened up to reveal the "place" (ort) hidden from view when customary modes of reading are left intact. Existing scholarship and commentaries on Oliver note that he foregrounds material dimensions of language, thereby achieving an effect of "self-foreignness," but the role of mediation for his work has not been addressed explicitly to date.[34] In his laudatory speech on the occasion of Oliver's receiving the Basler Lyrikpreis in 2015, Rolf Hermann draws attention to the "Sprachsensorium" (language-sensorium) of Oliver's poetry, through which Oliver discovers unusual aural and semantic connections between words and creates unusual words.[35] Ulrich Schäfer-Newiger notes Oliver's use of punctuation in "de-automatizing our perception of language" and of page justification in decentering and discomfiting the reading eye.[36] Marc James Mueller observes that Oliver shifts his readers' attention from meaning to material character of words by temporarily overwriting the referential dimension of language.[37] In addition to Mueller, Ilija Trojanow and Rolf Hermann too observe that Oliver approaches language materially: Trojanow portrays Oliver as a language-tinkerer, whereas Hermann draws attention to the corporeal dimensions of Oliver's texts, referring to them as "Körper-Texte" (body-texts).[38] By and large, these critics view typographic experimentation as a means of rendering the German language other to itself and confronting Oliver's readers with foreignness.

Without contesting the dimension of literary multilingualism in Oliver's texts and their key role in disrupting the purported homogeneity of language and identity, I argue that attention to writtenness in Oliver's poetry uncovers

---

[34] Oliver, *Sandscript*, 23–24.

[35] Rolf Hermann, "'pendelschreiben.' Laudatio auf José F.A. Oliver zur Verleihung des Basler Lyrikpreises 2015," 2015, http://oliverjose.com/wp-content/uploads/2016/12/Laudatio-Basler-Lyrikpreis-2015.pdf, 3–6.

[36] Ulrich Schäfer-Newiger, "Sprache, Tod, Verwandlung," *Signaturen* (n.d.).

[37] Oliver, *Sandscript*, 23–24.

[38] Hermann, "pendelschreiben," 5; Ilija Trojanow, "Laudatio auf José F.A. Oliver zur Verleihung des Thaddäus Troll Preises," 2009, http://oliverjose.com/wp-content/uploads/2016/12/Harald-Weinrich-Rede-zur-Verleihung-des-Chamisso-Preises-an-Jose%CC%81-F.A.-Oliver-1997.pdf, 5.

processes through which any place that can be called *Heimat* is displaced in a concrete sense beyond reference and metaphor. Unquestionably, the words "Heimat" and "Ort" (place) in "kompaß & dämmerung" have meaning-based associations. *Heimat* is associated with "matt" (faint, dull, dim) and "wort" (word) with "Ort" (place, location). The homeland is already receding from view, while any "place" to which one might want to navigate is to be found not in the world of things, but in the world of words. More pointedly, however, Oliver literally rends *Heimat* in transformatively rewriting it as "hei-/matt."

The word is interrupted with a hyphen, separated into syllables by a line break, the syllables then written as their homophones "hei" (hey) and "matt" (faint, matt, languid). This typographic experimentation ferries the spatial disorientation thematized in "kompaß & dämmerung" onto the typo-topographic space of the page. Oliver achieves this effect additionally through his typographic manipulation of the words "Wort" (word) and "Ort" (place) into an uncapitalized "w:ort," which Marcus James Mueller savvily translates into English as "wor(l)d." In Oliver's rewriting, "w:ort" indicates simultaneously a place in the word, the word as place, but also the word's emplacement on the page. This last possibility is supported by the text's most overt reference to mediation, in the phrase "im verlegten w:ort/ ist stille noch" (in the displaced wor(l)d/ is silence still). The "wor(l)d" is "verlegt," which can mean "displaced" as in Marc James Mueller's translation, but also "transferred" or more important yet, "published." The modifier "verlegt" indicates the simultaneous status of "w:ort" as word-space subject to displacement, as a "wor(l)d" that is transferred to another language or space, and as published artifact. The statement "im verlegten w:ort/ ist stille noch" ("in the displaced wor(l)d/ is silence still") could simply mean that there is stillness in the world, but the combination of the word "verlegt" and the colon that divides "w:ort" suggests another possibility, namely that the colon *is* that stillness. The "wor(l)d" has been "transferred" to the space of a written page. The reading eye stumbles upon the punctuation symbol, which introduces a moment of hesitation into "word" and thus becomes stillness. In short, "kompaß & dämmerung" continually brings up orientation, both in its reference to cardinal directions and repetitions of the word "da" (there). Oliver opens up the words "Heimat" and "Wort" in transformatively rewriting them in ways that highlight their writtenness on the page, while his play on the word "verlegt" interweaves displacement and the medium of print. In doing so, he enacts disorientation on the space of the page, disrupting both automatized reading practices and the notion of immediacy associated with *Heimat* as space that evades mediation.

José F. A. Oliver at Heim with Rose Ausländer and Paul Celan

In his poems about traveling to the Bukovina region, where Paul Celan had been born in the city of Czernowitz, Oliver reveals the conceptual slipperiness of terms such as *Heim* and *Heimat*. In *fahrtenschreiber* [tripwriter], Oliver's poems about Czernowitz, he recalls literary strategies by both Paul Celan and to a lesser degree by Rose Ausländer, who lost their *Heimat* of Czernowitz and who relied on the tainted German language for poetic expression. Oliver's poems take up Ausländer and Celan's approach to poetry as embodied practice and the materiality of the written page.

The poem that best encapsulates the influence of literary figures associated with the diverse and thriving cultural hub Bukovina, and one that remembers the displaced who once called it home, is perhaps "zu Rose Ausländer" [to Rose Ausländer] from a group of Czernowitz poems in *fahrtenschreiber*.[39] Rose Ausländer (1901–1988) was a Jewish poet from Czernowitz who wrote in German and English, and for whose poetry *Heimat* and home were common motifs. Her sparse yet musical poetic style was deeply influenced by Celan, whom she met after the war and who urged her to modernize her style. Recognizable in Oliver's poem are references to themes, motifs, wordplay in both Celan's and Ausländer's poetry as well as explicit references to home and dwelling, but with an attention to the materiality of language that is also reminiscent of Celan.

> **zu Rose Ausländer**
> ihr lichtalphabet, wo?
> das flügelleere dichterzimmer/ ich hab es
> nicht gefunden/ I w:ort
>
> im buchenland vom buchenblatt
> der reim eine Fußnote weiter
> ihr zeitmaß. Sie ging
>
> die kellerstufen ins exil
> dann folgte den Asseln
> das niemandhaus

---

[39] All but one of the Czernowitz-poems in *fahrtenschreiber* appear in the section "im ungeschliffenen grün" (in uncut green). The exception is "Czernowitz," which is the first poem in the collection.

& war fortan nachbewohnt
& jemand sagt: "Rück-
schmerz der Verse." Sie

knien ins wandergebet
aus mutter & sprache & geben
der nacht vielleicht einen tag

: die nächste "heimatlosigkeit"
die wohnt im menschenw:ort
& füllt die koffer mit namen[40]

to Rose Ausländer
her gleam-alphabet, where?
the wing void room of the poet/ I haven't
found it/ I wor(l)d

in the beech land from the beech leaf
the rhyme one footnote further
her meter of time. She took

the basement steps into exile
later cellar beetles
followed by a no man's home

& from here on re-occupied
& someone says: "Back-
lash pain of verses." They

kneel into the wandering prayer
out of mother & tongue & giving
maybe a day to the night

: the next "heimatlessness"
dwells in the human wor)l(d
& fills the baggage with names[41]

The poem contains several particularly stark markers of Celan and Ausländer as literary interlocutors. The first is the word "niemandhaus," which recalls both Celan's poetry collection *Die Niemandsrose* (*The No-One's-Rose*, 1963) and the poem "Psalm" that carries this collection's titular neologism. The themes of travel, flight and migration in Oliver's poetry collection also resonate with that

---

[40] José F. A. Oliver, *fahrtenschreiber: Gedichte* (Berlin: Suhrkamp, 2010), 67.
[41] Oliver, *Sandscript*, 249.

of itinerancy and rootlessness in Ausländer's poems "Unendlich" and "Niemand." Oliver's "niemandhaus" echoes the word "Niemandsland," a word that appears prominently in Ausländer's poems, both of which "focus on an absence of place, revealing Ausländer's concerns with the viability of poetic language in the aftermath of the Shoah."[42] The second is the separation of "Mutterspache" (mother tongue) into "Mutter" (mother) and "Sprache" (language). As Zafer Şenocak observes in the Celan-essay quoted in the introduction to this essay, poetic language is a landscape in which one may not put down roots but always be on the way. Celan's is a language without a country, as Oliver's is a language in which the fusion of mother and tongue is not a given. In Yasemin Yildiz's words, "the manufactured proximity between 'mother' and 'language' stages the fantasy behind the modern notion of the mother tongue (. . .). This notion indicates that, within the monolingual paradigm, 'mother tongue' is more than a metaphor. Instead, it constitutes a condensed narrative about origin and identity."[43] Critical of such myths of origin and identity encapsulated in the word "mother tongue" (Muttersprache), Oliver decomposes this composite in a context of travel. In doing so, he cleaves language from the bloodlines that the word "mother" evokes and that contribute to the genocidal politics of identity and belonging that wrested Celan from Czernowitz. The third and starker marker is Oliver's wordplay with "buchenland" (beech land, also the German name for Bukovina) and "buchenblatt" (beech leaf). "Buchenblatt" is the title of a 1981 poem by Ausländer, in which a beech leaf that has flown into the speaker's room prompts homesick musings about her hometown and the beech forests surrounding it. The "heimatlosigkeit" (translated as "heimatlessness") that is the subject of the concluding sentence of Oliver's poem is a prominent theme in the poem "Buchenblatt" and in Ausländer's poetry more broadly. Beyond the thematic, however, for Ausländer, the "Buchenblatt" (beech leaf) also refers to the material of writing and books. "Blatt" (leaf) is the word not for the leaf of the beech tree but also a book leaf. As Aurora Romero observes, "[t]he leaf is also the empty page, sent out by the forest to her in its rawest form. It is a remembrance

---

[42] Leslie Morris, "Mutterland / Niemandsland: Diaspora and Displacement in the Poetry of Rose Ausländer," *Religion & Literature* 30.3 (1998): 58.
[43] Yasemin Yildiz, *Beyond the Mother Tongue: The Postmonolingual Condition*, 1st ed. (New York: Fordham University Press, 2012), 10; Yildiz defines the "monolingual paradigm" thus: "According to this paradigm, individuals and social formations are imagined to possess one "true" language only, their "mother tongue," and through this possession to be organically linked to an exclusive, clearly demarcated ethnicity, culture, and nation" (New York: Fordham University Press, 2012), 2.

of her origins and an invitation to write."⁴⁴ Celan also frequently played with the words "Buchenland," "Buch" (book) and "Buche" (beech). The word "Buche" appears frequently in Celan's poetry. The fragment "buk" is also found in "Bukowina," the region Celan identifies as "meine Heimat" (my homeland) in his letters. "Buche," on the other hand, means both the beech tree and "Buch" (book).⁴⁵ The "wandering particles" "Buche" and "buk" attest to Ausländer and Celan's preoccupation with poetry as embodied practice and with the materiality of writing.

Celan often conveys textual-material fragmentation in spatial terms, as in the poem "Deine Augen im Arm" from the 1968 poetry collection *Fadensonnen* [*Threadsuns*]: "Wo?/ Mach den Ort aus, machs Wort aus. /[. ..] /Vermessen, entmessen, verortet, entwortet,/ entwo."⁴⁶ The opening up of place – or world – here is uttered in the same breath as the opening up of the word, a move Oliver takes up in his poetry. Increasingly disorienting is also the progression of the words "verortet" (located *and* mislocated),"entwortet" (a neologism that can mean de-worded, also sounds like the word "entwertet" (voided or devalued)), and "entwo" (a neologism that can mean de-where, sounds like "entzwei" or "entzwo" (apart, asunder)).⁴⁷ In his consistent use of "w:ort" in his poetry, Oliver appears to heed the call of these Celan verses. He fragments his words and reveals other worlds – of meaning and spaces, fragmenting language in order to make perceptible fissures in the world of language.

In *fahrtenschreiber* too, references to the material of text is couched in spatial terms. The poem "kurische dreizeiler" (curonian three-liners), for instance, depicts landscape-elements around the Curonian Lagoon in Latvia in terms of writing and writing systems. Oliver makes references to "1 grenzalphabet" ("1 borderline alphabet") in depicting the coast, and to an undecipherable ("nicht zu entschlüsseln") "sandschrift" (sandscript) in reference to the sand dunes in the area. He also refers to a "ziffernblatt der see."⁴⁸ Marc James Mueller's translation reads "current page to the sea," which addresses the word "Blatt" (tree leaf or book leaf) in "Ziffernblatt" (dial, clock-face), the literal translation of

---

44 Aurora Belle Romero, "Heute hat ein Gedicht mich wieder erschaffen: Origins of Poetic Identity in Rose Ausländer," PhD diss. (Vanderbilt University, 2016), 92.
45 Thomas Schestag, *buk: Paul Celan* (Munich: Boer, 1994), 3.
46 Paul Celan, *Die Gedichte: Kommentierte Gesamtausgabe*, vol. 1, 1st ed. (Frankfurt am Main: Suhrkamp, 2003): 225–226.
47 For an extensive analysis of the word "Buche" and the fragment "buk" in Celan's poetry including in "Deine Augen im Arm," see Schestag, *buk*.
48 Oliver, *fahrtenschreiber*, 64.

which would be, in turn, "numeral leaf."[49] In the Czernowitz poems, the written page becomes another space in which *Heimat* is set, often with reference to the material on which words are written ("Blatt"), writing systems, and decipherment. Oliver's page-justification too draws attention to printed matter, as all but a handful of poems in *fahrtenschreiber* are right-justified, a somewhat unusual layout choice that the bilingual English-German edition of Oliver's selected poems preserves. Rolf Hermann notes that this line justification recalls Arabic writing. He also surmises that this unusual choice changes the reading eye, requires another type of readerly orientation, and has the effect of unsettling the gaze and making it wander.[50] For *fahrtenschreiber* and particularly for the Czernowitz poems, Hebrew constitutes another point of reference as a language that has been shown to infuse Celan's poetry in significant ways.[51] Anna Glazova shows, for instance, that Celan inverts syllables and changes the direction of writing in German in order to change the direction of writing from right to left. This move makes perceptible "the Hebrew alphabet's countermovement" in German, staging an encounter between words, writing systems and languages on the space of the page.[52] Responding to these important yet understudied features of Celan's poetry, Oliver foregrounds the materiality of the representing: of the page, printed letters, letters of the alphabet, and word-segments that can be disassembled and reassembled.[53]

Oliver launches this textual materiality, like Celan, in the service of spatial and linguistic disorientation. Oliver intertwines language and place in "Czernowitz" by juxtaposing verses with the sounds of nature, and by presenting their intertwining as a question of orientation: "vom silber der dächer/ kraucht

---

49 Oliver, *Sandscript*, 247.
50 Hermann, "Pendelschreiben," 5.
51 For a detailed morphological overview of Hebrew's influence on Celan's poetic language, see Klaus Reichert, "Hebräische Züge in der Sprache Paul Celans," in *Paul Celan*, eds. Winfried Menninghaus and Werner Hamacher (Frankfurt am Main: Suhrkamp, 1988).
52 For examples of Celan's word- and word-fragment inversions informed by the direction of Hebrew writing, see Anna Glazova, "Paul Celan's Improper Names," in *Messianic Thought Outside Theology*, eds. Anna Glazova and Paul North (New York: Fordham University Press, 2014), 139–154.
53 Several studies have examined ways in which Celan manipulates elements and mechanics of writing, as well as his poems' self-presentation as fragmented textual-material artifacts. One of the most influential yet contested readings in this regard is Peter Szondi's *Celan Studies*, in which Szondi reads Celan's poem "Engführung" (Stretto) as landscape (Szondi). Matthew Handelman argues that the poem "Engführung" (Stretto) presents parentheses as the textual likenesses of geologic crevices, and that the intensified verticality of the text's flow presents the poem's title optically, literally leading the text and reader into a tight space and highlighting the vastness of its unprinted, white margins (Handelman, "Text is Landschaft", 2012).

lärm / ein laut-// fall der Spatzen & verse / die sind // biographische lotsen" (from the silver of the roofs/ creeps noise / a sound-// fall of sparrows & verses / that are//biographical pilots").[54] In this semi-urban landscape, sounds of sparrows and verses, that is, sounds of nature and poetry entwine and fall together. Ainé McMurtry observes the manner in which the projected homeland of Czernowitz loses its spatial contours through this move: "The lyric figuration of the verses as sparrows guiding the lyric speaker's biography takes on further metamorphic character as the speaker claims their own bird's-eye view of a merging land- and sea-scape that (. . .) relinquishes exclusive claims on any defined territorial space." McMurtry notes further that line breaks and forward slashes in the poem disrupt the geographic and textual cohesion of this text.[55] Oliver's typography and line breaks are indeed reminiscent of Celan's own stuttering rhythm, heightened by his use of dashes, parentheses, line breaks and empty space on his textual surfaces.

The Czernowitz-poems in *fahrtenschreiber* recall their own status as written material by continually referring to writing and the written page. The poem "Lemberg – Czernowitz, zufallsbilder" ("Lemberg – Czernowitz, chance-images"), for instance, likens mowed meadows to opened books ("aufgeschlagen wie bücher/ die umgemähten wiesen"), notes "das kuhwerk der bauern ist ebenfalls schrift" ("the cow work of the farmers is likewise writing") and contains the phrase "kyrillischer sommer" ("cyrillic summer") in reference to the Cyrillic script.[56] Space in "Lemberg – Czernowitz, zufallsbilder" is relayed into the realm of language, but more particularly to that of script. "zu Rose Ausländer" makes a similar move, but in a more private – yet elusive – space in contrast to the open spaces in the former poem: "ihr lichtalphabet, wo?/ das flügelleere dichterzimmer/ ich hab es/ nicht gefunden/ I w:ort//im buchenland vom buchenblatt" ("her gleam alphabet, where?/ the wingvoid room of the poet/ I haven't/ found it/ I wor(l)d//in the beechland from the beechleaf").[57] The relative stability of the pastoral landscape in the previous cited poem "Lemberg – Czernowitz, zufallsbilder" yields here to an untraceable room that is presumably the scene of the poet's writing practice. This "dichterzimmer" (poet's room) and references to "buchenland and buchenblatt" (beechland and beech leaf) recall the setting of the Ausländer poem "Buchenblatt" (1981), in which a beech leaf

---

54 Oliver, *fahrtenschreiber*, 13–14; Oliver, *Sandscript*, 243.
55 Áine McMurtry, "'Ruf's, das Schibboleth, Hinaus | in die Fremde der Heimat': Gebietscelan in the Poetry of José F. A. Oliver," in *Paul Celan Today: A Companion*, eds. Michael Eskin, Karen Jane Leeder and Marko Pajević (Berlin and Boston: De Gruyter), 121–142.
56 Oliver, *fahrtenschreiber*, 65–66.
57 Oliver, *Sandscript*, 248–249.

flies into the lyric speaker's room. Like many Czernowitz-poems in *fahrtenschreiber*, however, "zu Rose Ausländer" refrains from providing clearer geographic information or making its allusions more explicit. More explicit is the setting of this scene as one of writing, both as the act of writing in the poet's room, and as words and letters set on a page, as reference to "gleamalphabet," "wor(l)d" and "Buchenblatt" (beech leaf or book leaf) suggest. Both by direct reference and by foregrounding typography, the poems achieve a level of opacity. They are not transparent windows into the spaces and geographic locations they depict, but rather force their readers to contend with the written page and the elements of writing that allow that mediation to take place.

This textual opacity helps obscure the contours of *Heim* and *Heimat* as depicted in the Czernowitz poems. Oliver's attention to writtenness and mediation processes additionally inverts the spaces he depicts as *Heimat*. Oliver achieves this partly through neologisms, which are not only means to constructing new words from the ground up, but also inverting words, readerly expectations and his poetic spaces. Another Czernowitz-poem in *fahrtenschreiber*, "Czernowitz, 5km," for example, coins the suggestive compound "gebietscelan:" "[dämmerhunde, dunkel-/ licht & wortankunft, gebietscelan]" ([duskhounds, dark- / light & wordarrival, areacelan]).[58] The poem begins with a street scene, but space is soon transported to the realm of language, as the poem announcing a "wortankunft" (wordarrival): "gebietscelan" (area-Celan or territory-Celan). This neologism subverts the expectations set up in the poem's title with the name Czernowitz, which is, if anything, "Celansgebiet," that is, the place of Celan's birth and early life, which is associated today with his name as well as those of other major literary figures. "gebietscelan," on the other hand, can be read as space inverted and made into language. Ainé McMurtry reads "gebietscelan" "as a liminal space, intuitively known by the lyric speaker, in which a form of ambivalent epiphany suggested in the declaration of simultaneous light and darkness enables a coming of words," and asserts that the poem's words "offer a deterritorialized form of *Heimat*, closely connected with the writing process itself."[59] While *Heimat* is certainly displaced and "gebietscelan" is liminal in that it relates to a sensory threshold for the poem and its readers, the neologism in inverted form does not indicate a space but a person.[60] Indeed, even the inversion

---

[58] Adapted from Ainé McMurtry's translation (Berlin and Boston: De Gruyter, 2020).
[59] McMurtry, "'Ruf's.'".
[60] Inversion itself is a key term for Celan's poetry. According to Werner Hamacher, inversion in Celan reveals the instability of language's referential functions and its conditions of possibility, when language withdraws from its representative function and interrupts itself. See Werner Hamacher, "The Second of Inversion: Movements of a Figure through Celan's Poetry,"

is implied, as "Celansgebiet," which might indicate Czernowitz, is an admissible German word but itself a neologism. The implied inversion of the neologisms, however, subjects *Heimat* not so much to deterritorialization, as McMurtry suggests, than a doubling. "gebietscelan" conjures up its absent counterpart "Celansgebiet," which is lost to history. Oliver at *Heim* with Paul Celan has crafted this word and announced its arrival, only to present an "unheimlich," inverted double of *Heim*, thus revealing its instability in language and writing.

Conclusion: Sensory and medial dimensions of Heimat

In concluding his glowing review of José F. A. Oliver's 2005 poetry collection *finnischer wintervorrat [finnish winter reservoir]*, the critic Joachim Sartorius suggests a literary lineage from Celan to Oliver, but insists on privileging understanding and decipherment over sensory perception:

> Wer im heutigen Gedicht nach Musik, nach Lust am sprachlichen und formalen Experiment, nach Übereinstimmung von Atem und Bild, nach Lautkristallen sucht, wird hier reichlich belohnt. Dabei überwiegt bei der Lektüre die Anstrengung zu entschlüsseln, zu verstehen, nie die unmittelbare sinnliche Anschauung. Deshalb sind diese Gedichte sehr gute Gedichte.

> Whoever seeks music, pleasure in linguistic and formal experimentation, correspondence of breath and image, sound crystals in today's poetry will be richly rewarded here. And yet in reading it the effort to decipher, to understand, prevails over sensory perception. That is why these poems are good poems.[61]

For Sartorius, good poems are cerebral above all else, even though he observes earlier in the review that through Oliver's unusual typography, his poems appeal to sensory perception. Sartorius's emphatic declaration of decipherment and comprehension's victory over sensory perception omit the significance of disorientation for Oliver's poetry, as central theme, literary strategy and unmistakable effect of typographic experimentation. An understudied yet key strategy

---

in *Premises: Essays on Philosophy and Literature from Kant to Celan* (Cambridge, MA: Harvard University Press, 1996), 337–387.

61 Joachim Sartorius, "Das schlanke Brustweiß einer Möwendame Lichtblattschatten zwischen Schwarzwald und Andalusien: José F. A. Oliver und sein Gedichtband 'finnischer wintervorrat,'" *Süddeutsche Zeitung*, 14 November 2005, http://oliverjose.com/wp-content/uploads/2016/12/S%C3%BCddeutsche-Zeitung-14.11.2005-Kritik-Finnischer-Wintervorrat.pdf. Translation by the author.

of Oliver's *Heimat*-destabilization is his experimental typography through which he rewrites key concepts, rends words to reveal unexpected constellations of meaning, manipulates the direction and rhythm of reading, offers multiple recombinatory possibilities for his lexemes, and linguistically disorients his readers.

This disorientation constitutes a key dimension of an encounter with otherness. Oliver renders the German language other to itself. In launching his critique of *Heimat*, Oliver's literary language renders *Heimat* strange, or rather, uncovers the otherness and displacement that is inherent to the very structure of *Heimat*. As Johannes von Moltke illustrates in his study on *Heimatfilme*, the concept of *Heimat* emerges in moments when there is a perceived threat to what one considers to be home, or when what one considers to be home is already lost. Drawing a parallel to Sigmund Freud's exposition of the the uncanny (das Unheimliche) as always building on the familiar (*Heim, heimelich* or *heimatlich*) and carrying it in itself like a kernel, Moltke reveals loss, rootlessness and the foreign as likewise constitutive of *Heimat*.[62] *Heimat*-genres, then, reveal the unrootedness of *Heim* in the very act of representing it as idyll. Fully cognizant of this unrootedness, authors like Şenocak and Oliver – via Celan – shift emphasis from a yearning for rootedness towards literary encounters with the ontological instability of home. Şenocak's term of choice is "Berührung" (touching), no doubt indebted to Celan's "Begegnung" (encounter) as touchstone term. Instead of relying on *Heimat*'s claims to stability and wholeness even when they are no longer possible, Şenocak foregrounds rootlessness over *Heimat*'s claims to mythic roots. Şenocak's is a rootlessness that seek encounters, however, with other ethnic and linguistic groups, with fraught transnational histories of genocide, and with any audience he seeks to reach. Şenocak's work in general but his essay on Celan in particular posit a "kind of Berührungsgeschichte, a history of 'touch' among Germans, Turks, and Jews," in Leslie A. Adelson's words.[63] Ultimately, Oliver's readerly attention to the materiality of writing in Paul Celan is a literary encounter with the otherness of language and home. Oliver relays this encounter to his readers by presenting and urging textual-material encounters with the foreignness of *Heimat*.

---

62 von Moltke, *No Place Like Home*, 3–6.
63 Leslie A. Adelson, "Coordinates of Orientation: An Introduction," in *Atlas of a Tropical Germany: Essays on Politics and Culture, 1990–1998, Texts and Contexts* (Lincoln: University of Nebraska Press, 2000), xxx.

Works cited

Adelson, Leslie A. "Coordinates of Orientation: An Introduction," in *Atlas of a Tropical Germany: Essays on Politics and Culture, 1990–1998 Texts and Contexts* (Lincoln: University of Nebraska Press, 2000), xi–xxxvii.

Aksin, Jocelyn and Gizem Arslan. "Migration and Media: Reenvisioning Media Representations of Migration to and around Europe." Seminar Proposals. *American Comparative Literature Association 2020 Annual Meeting* (blog), n.d. https://www.acla.org/sites/default/files/files/2020%20ACLA%20Conference%20Guide.pdf.

Applegate, Celia. *A Nation of Provincials: The German Idea of Heimat* (Berkeley: University of California Press, 1990).

Baer, Ulrich. *Remnants of Song: Trauma and the Experience of Modernity in Charles Baudelaire and Paul Celan* (Stanford: Stanford University Press, 2000).

Baldick, Chris. "Poetry," in *The Oxford Dictionary of Literary Terms*, 3rd ed. Oxford Paperback Reference (Oxford: Oxford University Press, 2008), 206.

Beals, Kurt. "High-Tech Heimat: Mountains and Mediation in Literature, Film, and Digital Art," *The German Quarterly* 92.2 (2019): 166–86. https://doi.org/10.1111/gequ.12101.

Bland, Caroline, Catherine Smale, and Godela Weiss-Sussex. "Women Writing Heimat in Imperial and Weimar Germany: Introduction," *German Life and Letters* 72.1 (2019): 1–13. https://doi.org/10.1111/glal.12213.

Blickle, Peter. *Heimat: A Critical Theory of the German Idea of Homeland* (Rochester: Camden House, 2002).

Boa, Elizabeth. *Heimat: A German Dream: Regional Loyalties and National Identity in German Culture, 1890–1990* (Oxford: Oxford University Press, 2000).

Celan, Paul. *Die Gedichte: Kommentierte Gesamtausgabe*. Vol. 1, 1st ed. (Frankfurt am Main: Suhrkamp, 2003).

Culler, Jonathan D. *Theory of the Lyric* (Cambridge, MA: Harvard University Press, 2015).

Eigler, Friederike Ursula. *Heimat, Space, Narrative: Toward a Transnational Approach to Flight and Expulsion* (Woodbridge: Camden House, 2014).

Fassel, Horst. "Kulturenintegration in der deutschen Literatur: Zwei Autoren: Rafik Schami und José F. A. Oliver," *Estudios Filológicos Alemanes* 21 (2010): 201–223.

Glazova, Anna. "Paul Celan's Improper Names," in *Messianic Thought Outside Theology*. Eds. Anna Glazova and Paul North (New York: Fordham University Press, 2014), 139–154.

Hamacher, Werner. "The Second of Inversion: Movements of a Figure through Celan's Poetry," in *Premises: Essays on Philosophy and Literature from Kant to Celan* (Cambridge, MA: Harvard University Press, 1996), 337–387.

Handelman, Matthew. "Der Text ist Landschaft: Marginalität in Paul Celans 'Engführung,'" in *Am Rand; Grenzen und Peripherien in der europäisch-jüdischen Literatur*. Eds. Sylvia Jaworski and Vivian Liska (Munich: Edition Text+Kritik, 2012), 224–237.

Hermann, Rolf. "'pendelschreiben'. Laudatio auf José F. A. Oliver zur Verleihung des Basler Lyrikpreises 2015." Basel (2015).

Jurt, Joseph. "La double patrie: a propos de la poésie lyrique de José F. A. Oliver," in *Heimat: la petite patrie dans les pays de langue allemande*. Eds., Marc Beghin, Ursula Bernard, Christian Eggers, Sophie Lorrain, Herta Luise Ott, Gaëlle Vassogne, François Genton ed. and foreword, and Alfred Grosser intro. *Chroniques Allemandes* (ChroniquesA): 13.

Grenoble, France: Centre d'Etudes et de Recherches Allemandes et Autrichiennes Contemporaines (CERAAC), Université Stendhal-Grenoble 3, 2009, 179.

Kaes, Anton. *From Hitler to Heimat: The Return of History as Film* (Cambridge, MA: Harvard University Press, 1989).

McMurtry, Áine. "Sea Journeys to Fortress Europe: Lyric Deterritorializations in Texts by Caroline Bergvall and José F. A. Oliver," *The Modern Language Review* 113.4 (2018): 811–845. https://doi.org/10.5699/modelangrevi.113.4.0811.

McMurtry, Áine. "'Ruf's, Das Schibboleth, Hinaus | in Die Fremde Der Heimat': Gebietscelan in the Poetry of José F. A. Oliver," in *Paul Celan Today: A Companion*. Eds. Michael Eskin, Karen Jane Leeder, and Marko Pajević (Berlin and Boston: De Gruyter, 2021), 121–142.

Morris, Leslie. "Mutterland / Niemandsland: Diaspora and Displacement in the Poetry of Rose Ausländer," *Religion & Literature* 30.3 (1998): 47–65.

Mueller, Marc James. "Zwischen 'Heimatt' und 'Fremdw: Ort':Über poetische Identitäts-Mobilität in der deutsch-spanischen Lyrik José F. A. Olivers," in *Glossen: Eine internationale zweisprachige Publikation zu Literatur, Film, und Kunst in den deutschsprachigen Ländern nach 1945* 26 (2007).

Oliver, José F. A. *nachtrandspuren: Gedichte* (Frankfurt am Main: Suhrkamp, 2002). http://hdl.handle.net/2027/[u]:mdp.39015056163465.

Oliver, José F. A. *fahrtenschreiber: Gedichte* (Berlin: Suhrkamp, 2010). http://mirlyn.lib.umich.edu/Record/007553877.

Oliver, José F. A. *Fremdenzimmer: Essays* (Frankfurt am Main: weissbooks.w., 2015).

Oliver, José F. A. *Sandscript: Selected Poetry 1987–2018*. Trans. Marc James Mueller (Buffalo, New York: White Pine Press, 2018).

Oxford English Dictionary. "'analysis, n.'," n.d. http://www.oed.com/view/Entry/7046.

Reichert, Klaus. "Hebräische Züge in der Sprache Paul Celans," in *Paul Celan*. Eds. Winfried Menninghaus and Werner Hamacher, 1st ed. (Frankfurt am Main: Suhrkamp, 1988), 156–169.

Romero, Aurora Belle. "Heute hat ein Gedicht mich wieder erschaffen: Origins of Poetic Identity in Rose Ausländer." PhD diss. (Vanderbilt University, 2016).

Rothberg, Michael. *Multidirectional Memory: Remembering the Holocaust in the Age of Decolonization* (Stanford: Stanford University Press, 2009).

Ryneveld, Hannelore van. "Lyrik im Dialog: Ein Interpretationsversuch zu José Olivers Lyrikband *Duende* (1997)," *Acta Germanica: Jahrbuch des Germanistenverbandes im Südlichen Afrika* 30–31 (2002–2003): 127–138.

Sartorius, Joachim. "Das schlanke Brustweiß einer Möwendame Lichtblattschatten zwischen Schwarzwald und Andalusien: José F. A. Oliver und sein Gedichtband 'finnischer wintervorrat,'" *Süddeutsche Zeitung*, 14 November 2005. http://oliverjose.com/wp-content/uploads/2016/12/S%C3%BCddeutsche-Zeitung-14.11.2005-Kritik-Finnischer-Wintervorrat.pdf.

Schäfer-Newiger, Ulrich. "Sprache, Tod, Verwandlung," *Signaturen*. n.d.

Schestag, Thomas. *buk: Paul Celan* (Munich: Boer, 1994).

Şenocak, Zafer. *Zungenentfernung: Bericht aus der Quarantänestation: Essays*. 1st ed. (Munich: Babel, 2001). https://hdl.handle.net/2027/mdp.39015054158111?urlappend=%3Bsignon=swle:https://shibidp.cit.cornell.edu/idp/shibboleth.

Şenocak, Zafer. "Paul Celan," in *Atlas of a Tropical Germany: Essays on Politics and Culture, 1990–1998*. Trans. Leslie A. Adelson. (Lincoln: University of Nebraska Press, 2000), 69–71.

Trojanow, Ilija. "Laudatio auf José F. A. Oliver zur Verleihung des Thaddäus Troll Preises," 2009. http://oliverjose.com/wp-content/uploads/2016/12/Harald-Weinrich-Rede-zur-Verleihung-des-Chamisso-Preises-an-Jose%CC%81-F.A.-Oliver-1997.pdf.

von Moltke, Johannes. *No Place like Home: Locations of Heimat in German Cinema* (Berkeley: University of California Press, 2005).

Wickham, Christopher J. "Representation and Mediation in Edgar Reitz's *Heimat*," *The German Quarterly* 64.1 (1991): 35–45. https://doi.org/10.2307/407303.

Yildiz, Yasemin. *Beyond the Mother Tongue: The Postmonolingual Condition*. 1st ed (New York: Fordham University Press, 2012).

Damani J. Partridge
Comparison Limits – "Touching Tales" of Atrocity: An Anthropologist's Reflections

Moved by Palestinian- and Turkish/Turkish-German youth responses to Auschwitz, to the smell of the major collection of hair violently cut off by the Nazis, suitcases left over from the unknowing death trip, a shooting wall where both the young and old were repeatedly murdered at close range, and flakes of bone still left on the surfaces commemorating the lives of those exposed to genocide, in 2010, I noted: "The relationships between distance, 'being touched' (in the sense of being both physically and emotionally moved),[1] Holocaust memorialization, and contemporary racism are not just German problems, but transnational ones."[2] In other words, an analysis of touch helps us to better understand experiences that might be relatable if not equivalent. Even if I have not been subjected to genocide directly, even if it was not directed at people to whom I am related, stories and evidence of it make me upset and even bring me to tears. They also call me to action in the midst of contemporary atrocities. Beyond the language of comparison, an analytic that often causes fights and evokes zero sum games (in spite of Rothberg's-2009-warning[3]), touch allows us to see and potentially feel closer to events, experiences, and histories we, ourselves, have not experienced.

We had spent months preparing for the trip, learning about German history, visiting the Memorial to the Murdered Jews of Europe in Berlin, the *Reichstag*, watching documentary films, and going to another memorial that traced the everydayness of the Shoah by recounting the gradual worsening of laws and lives under the Nazis. As an anthropologist accompanying a youth center project from Berlin to Auschwitz, I witnessed youth in tears, trying to make sense of contemporary and past events, being stared at by guards with other youth flying Israeli flags, being made conscious by these same guards about their Palestinian scarves. As Palestinians, Turks, Palestinian- and Turkish-Germans, their experiences in the world and in Germany had led them to an

---

[1] Leslie A. Adelson, *The Turkish Turn in Contemporary German Literature: Towards a New Critical Grammar of Migration* (New York: Palgrave Macmillan, 2005).
[2] Damani J. Partridge, "Holocaust Mahnmal (Memorial): Monumental Memory amidst Contemporary Race," *Comparative Studies in Society and History* 52.4 (2010): 838.
[3] Michael Rothberg, *Multidirectional Memory: Remembering the Holocaust in the Age of Decolonization* (Stanford: Stanford University Press, 2009).

existence that fit only with difficulty into the transnational politics of memory and contemporary analyses of everyday life in the Federal Republic. They were implicitly held responsible for crimes whose history they and their parents had entered. Of course, in Germany, comparisons to Auschwitz are taboo, and they knew this. They didn't try to say that their experience was worse or to deny the atrocities. One young member of the group, though, talked about "Jews then and Jews now," reflecting a modification of some of the sentiment that likely led to the workshop in the first place – the charge that these youth were antisemitic and needed to learn about German history in order to be better integrated (or integrated at all) into German democracy.

One might think of touch as a methodology that is opposed to comparison. Comparison, as we know, often assumes bounded units and often neglects the ways in which seemingly closed systems or things overlap and influence each other, and the extent to which they may be partially or entirely part of the same system.

In this essay, I would like to problematize comparison. I would like to think further about comparison as methodology versus comparison as social fact. What do we mean by comparison? What are the potential problems with comparison, particularly as it relates to social memory and memory of atrocity, and what alternative methods to relating atrocity might exist? What potential social benefits come out of finding other ways to think about and relate the past, present, and future, particularly with regard to mass murder and social death?

According to literary theorist and memory scholar Michael Rothberg, "Comparison of colonial violence to Nazi genocide has a tradition that stretches back to the early postwar years – as I have demonstrated in my book *Multidirectional Memory* – but activism by Namibian and Black German activists, among others, has now made it an unavoidable, if still frequently marginalized, reference in mainstream German debates."[4] As Rothberg's note suggests, comparison weaves in, with, and between academic debates, global atrocities, and popular sentiment. The question is not only what can be compared, but who can compare, and then whether or not a comparison is warranted at all. Rothberg wants us to resist the temptation to avoid comparison, arguing that memory relies on association. Hearing about atrocity reminds one of one's own experience with atrocity, whether or not one is familiar with the one being mentioned. But memory of atrocity is not a zero-sum game, Rothberg goes on. Comparison, for Rothberg,

---

4 Michael Rothberg, "Comparing Comparisons: From the '*Historikerstreit*' to the Mbembe Affair," *Geschichte der Gegenwart* (2020), https://geschichtedergegenwart.ch/comparing-comparisons-from-the-historikerstreit-to-the-mbembe-affair/, 23 June 2021.

has the potential to create more social space for more memories, whether or not these memories can be proven to be related.

The stakes here, however, become tied to a fear that some memories will lead to the blocking out of others. They will draw false equivalences and thus reduce the significance. This will lead to another kind of erasure scholars, politicians and activists argue.

I worry about comparison for different reasons. I worry that comparisons may fail to actively see and cultivate connections, and connections are where I see the greatest potential for memory work to impact the present and the future. What I would like to read as Leslie A. Adelson's method of touch allows the viewer, reader, analyst, the affected, and the witness to relate without erasing, to potentially see mutual accountability and collective action in the present and for the future.

As I note above, Rothberg argues that "Comparison of colonial violence to Nazi genocide has a tradition that stretches back to the early postwar years."[5] I would now ask how an analysis of continuity, here, might work in relation to comparison? If there is continuity and if there are direct links, to what extent can we really compare? If memory is not a zero-sum game, as Rothberg argues in *Multidirectional Memory*, then saying that global atrocity is incomparable does not mean that one cannot draw links between it and other atrocities. Even if one cannot, touch offers a different possibility for thinking about the relationships. Who and how one can be moved by the memory, by the recounting of atrocity, suggests a different possibility for what one does with it in the present. Erasure seems a more serious problem than establishing its significance once and for all "in comparison." Relating is essential. The extent to which one uses one horror to forget another seems inexcusable.

Leslie A. Adelson sums up the dynamic with two words: "postnational intimacy."[6] In other words, the nation-states should not be at the center of the methodological imaginary. It is also not necessarily at the center of everyday life. Diaspora is not either. Origins do not necessarily reflect aspirations and perhaps that is not yet any place at which one can feel totally at home, particularly if one is constantly displaced, in this case, in both Turkey and Germany. This, however, also does not mean that one does not or cannot find affiliation.

Transnational memory exceeds the logic of comparison.

---

5 Rothberg, "Comparing Comparisons."
6 Adelson, *The Turkish Turn*, 20.

While I worry about comparison as a potentially totalizing (and in this way reductive) practice,[7] I do think that Adelson's idea of "touching tales" gets us beyond the "impossibility of translation."[8] It is the possibility of relation that Adelson encourages us to access. Incommensurability is a key problematic linked to a critique of comparison, particularly as it concerns the comparison of atrocity, which often seeks recognition, a problematic that is linked also to a demand for a redistribution of resources – e.g., land, money (via reparations), or political power.

While Adelson focuses on literature, as an anthropologist, my research has attended to how touch and how "touching tales" work in everyday life.[9] In particular, I have been concerned with Holocaust memory and its relation to processes of democratization in contemporary Germany. How must one participate in the memory of atrocity in order to participate in German democracy? To what extent must one understand oneself as a perpetrator if one is to take part in this discussion? If being a perpetrator or the descendant of perpetrators then also requires taking responsibility in order to proceed justly into the future, what happens when one has no familial connection to the particularity of European atrocity?

For Muslim and Arab subjects, German state institutions persistently tie the possibility for "democratic participation" to acknowledging past anti-Jewish atrocities and their potential link to the contemporary persistence, often via mainstream accusations of antisemitism.

Antisemitism is also present (and must be fought against), but it does not go without saying. Non-Arab-, non-Turkish-, and non-Muslim-German teachers should also not assume a superior position in their work to challenge antisemitic persistence.

On the one hand, the extent to which one can discuss Israel/Palestine as a Muslim or Arab subject in Germany, and the extent to which one can talk about one's own experiences of racism, are potentially curtailed by the impossibility of comparing atrocity now and then (although Rothberg's account of *Multidirectional Memory*) is significant here, as is his understanding of "implication," as

---

7 See Duster, Troy, "Comparative Perspectives and Competing Explanations: Taking on the Newly Configured Reductionist Challenge to Sociology," *American Sociological Review* 71.1 (2006): 1–15, cited in Jörg Niewöhner and Thomas Scheffer, "Thickening Comparison: On The Multiple Facets Of Comparability," in *Thick Comparison*, eds. Jörg Niewöhner and Thomas Scheffer (Boston: Brill, 2010), 1–15.
8 Lyotard 1988, cited in Niewöhner and Scheffer, "Thickening Comparison," 6.
9 Adelson, *The Turkish Turn*.

in the *Implicated Subject*). On the other hand, thinking through *touch* might be much more productive for thinking and working through possibility.

While I continued to be concerned about the colonial links and those who persist and insist on anthropology as the study of the Other, as an anthropologist thinking through Adelson's text, it also makes sense to think through ethnography and what relating atrocity might potentially do for an understanding of a possible future.

While comparison, here, has a long tradition, again, Adelson's notion of touch and "touching tales," offers another path forward for relating everyday lives and also relating the histories and figures remembering and memorializing atrocity. To what end should comparisons of atrocity work? From its early beginnings, ethnography has been a comparative enterprise that contrasted foreign culture with home culture, the other with the familiar, the exotic with the common. This difference "'helped to make discoveries through different ways of seeing things – by drawing forth new, unique and possibly odd implications that bear on what is being compared'".[10] In a short piece on "Comparison: The Impossible Method," anthropologist Matei Candei argues that, "These familiar difficulties [with comparison] mean that while we, necessarily, compare all the time, many of us feel that if we really thought about it, comparison would be impossible – so best not think about it too much."[11] In his longer book, Candei continues, quoting a phrase from Evans Prichard: "Anthropological comparison was born impossible." Candei argues further, "The politically unsavory implications of such accounts – in which concreteness lies with informants and abstraction with the anthropologist – have come to seem obvious." The language of "informant" is, of course, problematic, but perhaps appropriate to the kind of anthropology Candei describes. Within this context, those who challenge the absolute "truth" of anthropological writing, James Clifford and George Marcus (1986), seem reduced to straw men. Why we compare becomes a question that seems never resolved. Again, the possibility of touch suggests an alternative route that allows even anthropologists studying atrocity to build on and forge new relations in contexts that then may forthrightly exceed the paradigm of the nation-state.

---

10 Aram A. Yengoyan, "Introduction," in *Modes of Comparison. Theory & Practice*, ed. Aram A. Yengoyan (Ann Arbor: University of Michigan Press, 2006), 4, cited in Niewöhner and Scheffer, "Thickening Comparison," 7.
11 Matei Candei, "Comparison: The Impossible Method?," *Where Have All the Comparisons Gone?* https://culanth.org/fieldsights/comparison-the-impossible-method (2019), 1 July 2021.

Detroit touching Berlin

Between Detroit and Berlin, techno is one of the most obvious ways the cities and their people find connection, but there is also the experience of gentrification, speculation, displacement, of being pushed out of the center of one's neighborhood, of no longer being able to play with one's friends, of being forced to the outskirts of the city, of finding out (in the case of Berlin) that one is now in the center of the city even though one used to be on the margins. Residents are now being punished for having kept this (now) center vibrant and attractive.

How might this touch lead to a strategy for undoing the present, to redo it for those who have been at the center, but for whom the focus on them has meant a new concerted effort to decenter our focal point?

It is not that the decentering is explicit or conscious, but when they raise issues with this decentering, they get ignored on behalf of other objectives, development, tourism, new ideas.

The methodologies of touch allow us to decenter. They also help us to think more critically about efficacy. If touch means to love, e.g., where touch means that I have also grown close to you, then this feeling too will focus on changing the dynamics.

Touch also implies something deeper than pity. It means physical and emotional movement simultaneously. Touch means exceeding egocentric logics. Touch means connection outside one's own initial experience; it also means a new kind of relation to experience.

It simultaneously becomes a method for activism and for research. It is very different from the logic of recognition. Recognition holds the expectation of conforming to an existing system or (at the very least) for those who dominate that system to find space for you within it.

Touch means potential reorientation. It makes the necessity for a new form of social organization visible.

The Mediterranean and the child who washed up

In the late summer of 2015, Alan Kurdi's lifeless body washed up on a Turkish shore near Bodrum. The death of a three-year-old Syrian child fleeing unlivable conditions changed both the narrative and the stakes of a so-called "summer of migration." One could not deny this death. One could not help but be moved. The fact that it was a child who died demanded feeling, an affective response.

Even if this political accounting was not universal, it did lead to a reprieve in the border logic of insiders and outsiders.

Writing about Merkel's decision to change her refugee policy (particularly in relation to the Syrian crisis), *Spiegel Online* reports:

> Others believe it was an emotional decision, and that Merkel, normally such a composed politician, was moved by images like that of a truck found on the autobahn in Austria on August 27, filled with dead refugees or, three days later, the photo of Alan, a three-year-old boy who died en route and whose body washed up on the beach at Bodrum, Turkey.[12]

Whether or not it was Alan Kurdi's body washing up that led to Merkel's ultimate decision to allow Germany to accept more refugees and to promote Germany's role in shaping their futures, his death and the persistent images of this death in the national, International, and transnational media were definitely part of the discussion with which politicians would also have to contend.

The world-famous artist Ai Weiwei also chose to pose as the boy in an image he created as an act of memorialization, recalling the initial touch, even if some saw the re-creation as an act that seemed be in poor taste. On May 26, 2016, the *Süddeutsche Zeitung Magazin*, reported: "Clearly, Ai Weiwei wants to make us feel uncomfortable. He sees it as his job. Ai against the system: it used to be the dictatorship back home, now it is Europe's refugee policy."[13]

Here, Adelson's analysis of touch is helpful. While one cannot plan this kind of touch, it nevertheless speaks to Adelson's understanding of postnational intimacy. Wherever one is situated, one has the potential and chance to feel close to these images. The death of a child trying to find safety moves.

For once, one does not need to be a citizen to be mourned. On the other hand, the lack of citizenship leads to the death in the first place. If one were a European citizen, then one wouldn't need to use such desperate measures in order to arrive in Europe.

---

12 "The Makings of Merkel's Decision to Accept Refugees," *Spiegel International*, https://www.spiegel.de/international/germany/a-look-back-at-the-refugee-crisis-one-year-later-a-1107986.html, 10 October 2021.

13 "Essential or impudent? The debate about art and refugees," *DW*, https://www.dw.com/en/essential-or-impudent-the-debate-about-art-and-refugees/a-39177781?maca=en-EMail-sharing, 10 October 2021.

Mutual struggle as a touching tale: "Detroit, the intersection: Arab and Black Mutual Struggles between 1967 and 2020"

The film, "Arab and Black Mutual Struggles," was created as part of a collective filmmaking endeavor, entitled "Filming the Future of Detroit." It thinks through touch in a different context. Quotes from this film follow:

> "Detroit is the intersection for a lot of people to engage with each other." [Activist Ras Jah-T, TRIBE organizer, former organizer for Detroit Will Breath.] Detroit has the largest Black and Arab populations in the United States. [my voice]

> Filmmaker: "Rather than understanding 1967 as the start of the decline, we can focus, instead, on how 1967 was the starting point for activists and organizers who stayed in the city."

> The film pictures images from the 1967 Arab-Israeli War, including images of bombing in Israel/Palestine. Archival footage from The South End by Michael J. Zeko: "Over the past 13 years when the Middle East conflict was at its greatest, Dearborn experienced its largest influx of Arab immigrants and refugees. . ."

> Thinking about how Arab and Black communities can work together, Ras Jah-T concludes that work in Detroit offers space for:

> "Not just solidarity, but mutual struggle between allies. You know what I mean? Because I am not really for lip service or reform. I'm not for being, like you know, 'I feel your pain.' I'm for 'Where are our enemies? Let us mutually destroy, so that we can survive.'"[14]

The project I direct in Detroit and in Berlin that seeks to offer young people's perspectives on the future of each city, offers a perspective on the city that links Palestinian and Black struggle via simultaneous histories of violation. Here the filmmaker and his interlocutors note the link between 1967 in Detroit and Israel/Palestine, a moment when hundreds of Palestinians were forced to flee the Middle East (many ultimately arriving in Detroit and the neighboring city of Dearborn), and also a moment in which Black residents faced military occupation and mass arrest after protesting police violence in Detroit.

While often characterized in terms of the era of "White Flight," the filmmaker asks the viewer what it would mean to think of 1967 not as an end but also as the beginning of a different kind of possibility. Here, Black and Arab

---

[14] Basil Alsubee, "Detroit, the Intersection," in *Filming the Future of Detroit* film series at the University of Michigan in Ann Arbor, MI, curated by Damani Partridge, 2021.

stories touch. Through the Black Lives Matter moment, the film then asks us to think not simply about parallel, but about "mutual struggle."

Adelson's method of touch is generative not only for social analysis but also for social and political possibility. Ultimate success should not be assumed, but the possibility for new feeling should continue to be fostered. Beyond the nation state, remembering atrocity can be generative for a new kind of connection in unexpected places and along unexpected lines.

In the end, as Adelson teaches us, if we are touched, we will be moved. Thus, the politics of touch might lead to a different kind of political possibility. While one cannot structure all of ones political efforts along the lines of touch, it does seem that touch will be a necessary component of political movement. It also allows us to think beyond the constraints of the nation-state.

Works cited

Adelson, Leslie A. *The Turkish Turn in Contemporary German Literature: Towards a New Critical Grammar of Migration* (New York: Palgrave Macmillan, 2005).

Alsubee, Basil. "Detroit, the Intersection," in *Filming the Future of Detroit* film series at the University of Michigan in Ann Arbor, MI. Curated by Damani Partridge, 2021.

Candea, Matei. *Comparison in Anthropology: The Impossible Method. New Departures in Anthropology* (Cambridge, UK and New York, NY: Cambridge University Press, 2019).

Candea, Matei. "Comparison: The Impossible Method?," *Where Have All the Comparisons Gone?* https://culanth.org/fieldsights/comparison-the-impossible-method (2019), 1 July 2021.

Clifford, James and George E. Marcus. *Writing Culture: The Poetics and Politics of Ethnography: a School of American Research Advanced Seminar* (Berkeley: University of California Press, 1986).

Duster, Troy. "Comparative Perspectives and Competing Explanations: Taking on the Newly Configured Reductionist Challenge to Sociology," *American Sociological Review* 71.1 (2006): 1–15.

Niewöhner, Jörg and Thomas Scheffer. "Thickening Comparison: On The Multiple Facets Of Comparability," in *Thick Comparison*. Eds. Jörg Niewöhner and Thomas Scheffer (Boston: Brill, 2010), 1–15.

Partridge, Damani J. "Holocaust Mahnmal (Memorial): Monumental Memory amidst Contemporary Race," *Comparative Studies in Society and History* 52.4 (2010): 820–850. https://doi.org/10.1017/S0010417510000472.

Rothberg, Michael. *Multidirectional Memory: Remembering the Holocaust in the Age of Decolonization* (Stanford, CA: Stanford University Press, 2009).

Rothberg, Michael. *The Implicated Subject: Beyond Victims and Perpetrators. Cultural Memory in the Present* (Stanford, CA: Stanford University Press, 2019).

Rothberg, Michael. "Comparing Comparisons: From the '*Historikerstreit*' to the Mbembe Affair," *Geschichte der Gegenwart* https://geschichtedergegenwart.ch/comparing-comparisonsfrom-the-historikerstreit-to-the-mbembe-affair/ (2020), 23 June 2021.

Yengoyan, Aram A. "Introduction," in *Modes of Comparison. Theory & Practice*. Ed. Aram A. Yengoyan (Ann Arbor: University of Michigan Press, 2006), 1–30.

Envoi

Zafer Şenocak
Ausreisen oder Reißaus nehmen

Für Leslie

ich stehe am Vorhang meines vorhanglosen Fensters
graue Zeit zwischen mir und den chemischen Bildern
die von uns übrig bleiben werden
es regnet es regnet auf alte Filme
die graue Zeit ist im Hinterhof einer fernen Stadt
zwischen mir und der Stadt eine Schleiermauer
hinter meinem Haus Hofszenen bei den Trödlern
erwarb ich meine erste Lederhose
mein erstes Messer schnitt Muster in die nicht vorhandenen
Gardinen vor meinem Fenster
es heißt der Regiemann drehe einen Film der nicht enden wolle
ich sah ihn auf seinem nicht vorhandenen Regiestuhl stehend
waghalsig der Mann
ich höre Stimmen hinter dem Vorhang die es nicht geben würde
wenn es den Vorhang gäbe
ein Regen den es nicht gäbe wenn es den Film nicht geben würde
es regnet auf alte Filme
das Zimmer wird immer kleiner
je weiter ich zurückschauen kann
umso mehr Regen
an grauen Tagen rostige Regentropfen
machen Musik auf dem Blech der Dächer
der Hinterhofhimmel über den Trödlern
dort erwarb ich eines Tages den Roman eines Stadtromantikers
setzte mich in eine Regenpfütze und spürte die ferne große Stadt
in meinen Gliedern
der Roman zerschlissen vom Regen hatte den Regen erfunden
die graue Zeit auf den Vorhang geworfen
es regnet auf alte Filme
die Pfützen auf dem Pflaster sind kaputte Spiegel
wie eine Geschichte aus Glas
wieder ganz wird
darüber nachdenken sollte der Stadtromantiker
bevor er schreibt so ein dickes Buch während der Regiemann für
seinen Film der nicht enden will den Regen aufnimmt
er zog in diese Stadt um sie zu verlassen zog es ihn zu den Frauen
er zog um sein Geschlecht zu verlassen zog es ihn zum Ewigen Nein
Ausreisen oder Reißaus nehmen
er wollte den Regen anhalten und aus einem neuen Glas trinken

https://doi.org/10.1515/9783110778922-017

aus der versiegten Quelle die Buchstaben zerbröckelter Sprachen
sie schütteln sich unter dem Mikroskop
werden träge in der ewigen Suppe
werden zum Fossil im Gestein
frieren das Unverstandene ein
Verstehen ist Versehrung
Unvollendeter Brief
Abgebrochene Reise

To Exit or To Escape

For Leslie

I am standing at the curtain of my curtainless window
grey time between me and the chemical images
that will remain of us
it is raining, it is raining on old films
the grey time takes place in the courtyard of a distant city
between me and the city a veil wall
behind my house court scenes with the junk dealers
where I acquired my first Lederhosen
my first knife cut patterns in the non-existent
curtains outside my window
they say the director is making a movie that won't end
I saw him standing on his non-existent director's chair
reckless the man
I hear voices behind the curtain that would not exist
if the curtain existed
a rain that would not exist if the film did not exist
it is raining on old films
the room becomes smaller and smaller
the further back I can see
the more rain
rusty raindrops on grey days
make music on the tin of the roofs
the courtyard sky above the junk dealers
that is where one day I acquired the novel of an urban romantic
sat down in a puddle of rain and felt the distant big city
in my limbs
the novel tattered by the rain had invented the rain
the grey time projected on the curtain
it is raining on old films
the puddles on the pavement are broken mirrors
like a story made of glass
becomes whole again
that is what the urban romantic should be thinking about
before writing such a thick book while the director
is recording the rain for his movie that won't end
he moved to the city to leave her he was drawn to women
he moved to leave his gender he was drawn to the Eternal No
to exit or to escape
he wanted to stop the rain and drink from a new glass

from the dried-up source the letters of shattered languages
they shudder under the microscope
become sluggish in the eternal soup
become fossils in the rock
freeze the unintelligible
To understand is to feel pain
Unfinished letter
Interrupted journey

Translation Bettina Brandt

Notes on Authors

Gizem Arslan is Assistant Teaching Professor of German in the Humanities and Arts Department at Worcester Polytech Institute (WPI). She publishes primarily on migration studies and translation studies. Her recent publications include "Tracing the Continual Present: Yoko Tawada and Vilém Flusser" (*German Quarterly*, 2021) and "Making Senses: Translation and the Materiality of Written Signs in Yoko Tawada" (*Translation Studies*, 2019). She is currently finishing her book project titled *Illegibility in Translation: Writing Alterity into German*.

Brett de Bary is Professor Emerita of Asian Studies and Comparative Literature at Cornell University. Her recent publications have dealt with women writers and artists such as Tawada Yōko, Morisaki Kazue, and Soni Kum. Her newest book entitled, *Tawada Yōko's The Brother-in-Law in Bordeaux: Translation As Method*, is forthcoming with Columbia University Press. In 2020, her chapter on the topic, "Fiction, Theory, and the Lightness of Translation in Tawada Yōko's *Schwager in Bordeaux*/ボルドーの義兄" was published in *Tawada Yōko: Writing and Rewriting*, edited by Doug Slaymaker (Lexington Books, 2020). The volume *Still Hear the Wound* (co-edited by Brett de Bary and Rebecca Jennison), a series of translated essays on the work of video, performance, and installation artists Ito Tari, Oh Haji, Soni Kum, Yamashiro Chikako and others was published by the Cornell East Asia Series, 2015. Earlier publications and translations have been in the area of Japanese fiction and film, Japanese literary theory, and gender studies.

Bettina Brandt is Teaching Professor of German and Jewish Studies at Penn State University. She obtained MA degrees from the University of Utrecht and a PhD in Comparative Literature from Harvard University. Before joining the German faculty at Penn State she taught at MIT, Columbia University, and Montclair State. Her recent publications include "Nelly and Trudie: Deciphering a Transatlantic Holocaust Correspondence" (*On Being Adjacent to Historical Violence*, ed. Irene Kacances, De Gruyter, 2021), "From Vienna to the Midwest: Austrian Refugees and Quaker Rescue Efforts after 1938," (*Germany from the Outside. Rethinking German Cultural History in an Age of Displacement*, ed. Laurie Johnson, Bloomsbury Press, 2022) and "Taming Foreign Speech: Language Politics in Shadow Plays around 1800," in *The German Studies Review* (2018.2.) for which she won the 2019 essay prize from the Goethe Society of North America. Brandt is co-editor of *China in the German Enlightenment* (with D. Purdy, University of Toronto Press, 2016) and of *Herta Müller. Politics and Aesthetics* (with V. Glajar, University of Nebraska Press, 2013.) With D. Schyns, Brandt is Dutch translator of Yoko Tawada's *De Berghollander* (Amsterdam: Voetnoot, 2010.) Most recently, Brandt translated Yoko Tawada's German Fukushima poems into English in *Out of Sight* (Marseille: Le bec-en-l'air, 2020).

Claudia Breger is the Villard Professor of German and Comparative Literature at Columbia University. Having received her PhD and Habilitation from Humboldt University, Berlin, she taught at the University of Paderborn, Germany, and Indiana University, Bloomington, before joining Columbia in 2017. Her research and teaching focus on modern and contemporary culture, with emphases on film, performance, literature, and literary and cultural theory, as well as the intersections of gender, sexuality, and race. Her most recent book, *Making Worlds:*

Affect and Collectivity in Contemporary European Cinema, was published by Columbia University Press in 2020.

John Namjun Kim is Associate Professor of Comparative Literature, German and Japanese at the University of California, Riverside, where he also serves as the Director of Graduate Studies of Comparative Literature. He is the co-editor of *The Politics of Culture: Around the Work of Naoki Sakai* (Routledge, 2010). His publications on Yoko Tawada include, "Ethnic Irony: The Poetic Parabasis of the Promiscuous Personal Pronoun in Yoko Tawada's 'Eine leere Flasche'" (*The German Quarterly*, 83.3), "Writing the Cleft: Tawada Translates Celan" (Stauffenburg, 2010), and "Die Poetik einer transzendentalen Deduktion: Das Ich bei Tawada und Kant" (*Text + Kritik*, 191/192).

Yuliya Komska is an Associate Professor of German Studies at Dartmouth College. She is the author of *The Icon Curtain: The Cold War's Quiet Border* (University of Chicago Press, 2015) and co-author (with Michelle Moyd and David Gramling) of *Linguistic Disobedience: Restoring Power to Civic Language* (Palgrave, 2018). With Irene Kacandes, she co-edited *Eastern Europe Unmapped: Beyond Borders and Peripheries* (Berghahn Books, 2017). She is currently completing a biography of Margret and H. A. Rey, the creators of Curious George.

Paul Michael Lützeler is Rosa May Distinguished University Professor in the Humanities at Washington University and Director of the Max Kade Center for Contemporary German Literature in St. Louis. For twenty years Lützeler has been President of the International Research Circle Hermann Broch. He is also the founder of the German Studies yearbook *Gegenwartsiteratur*, which he edited for two decades. In his research he focuses on the literary discourse on Europe; exile literature, with an emphasis on Hermann Broch; and contemporary German literature. His publications include an award-winning biography of Hermann Broch, three books on the idea of Europe in German and European Literature, and seven books on other topics of nineteenth- and twentieth-century German literature.

B. Venkat Mani is Professor of German and World Literature and Race, Ethnicity and Indigeneity Senior Fellow at the Institute for Research in the Humanities at the University of Wisconsin-Madison. He is the author or editor of seven works including *Cosmopolitical Claims: Turkish German Literatures from Nadolny to Pamuk* (University of Iowa Press, 2007) and *Recoding World Literature: Libraries, Print Culture, and Germany's Pact with Books* (Fordham UP, 2017; winner of GSA's DAAD Prize and MLA's Aldo and Jeanne Scaglione Prize for Best Book in German Studies 2018). He's the co-editor of *A Companion to World Literature* (Wiley Blackwell 2020), and editor of *German Quarterly*'s Forum "World Literature: Against Isolationist Readings" (2021). His public humanities essays can be read in *Inside Higher Ed*, *TeloScope*, *The Wire* (Hindi), and *The Hindustan Times*.

Barbara Mennel is the Rothman Chair and Director for the Center for the Humanities and the Public Sphere at the University of Florida. She is Professor of Film Studies with a joint appointment in the Departments of English and of Languages, Literatures, and Cultures. Her research interests are feminist and queer theory, city films, labor and film, and European cinema. Her recent books include *Women at Work in Twenty-First-Century European Cinema* (2019) and the second and revised edition of *Cities and Cinema* (2019). She is completing an auteur study of experimental filmmaker Su Friedrich. With Angelica Fenner she is co-editing a special volume for *Feminist German Studies*, titled *Feminist Filmmaking in the Twenty-First Century: Continuation and Innovation* (forthcoming 2022).

Dr. Katrina L. Nousek is Visiting Assistant Professor of German Studies at the University of Richmond. Her current research focuses on postsocialism and globalization in German-language culture. Recent articles address the intersection of ecology and postsocialist literature, and literary futurity in German-language depictions of Eastern Europe. Her wider teaching and research interests include visual culture and new media, migration, and narrative studies. She is currently working on *The Vanishing Point of the Future*, a book that analyzes postsocialist migration narratives to show how transnational texts construct European futures beyond rubrics of nostalgia and trauma. Her research-in-progress turns to intermediality and new media to investigate commemorative projects and monumentality that reestablish cultural ideas of Europe after the Cold War. Her close readings of digital narratives and intermedial art demonstrate artistic critiques of neoliberalism, excavate alternative political projects, and interrogate a politics of erasure giving rise to populism in contemporary Europe.

Anna Parkinson is Associate Professor in German at Northwestern University as well as a member of the Critical Theory Cluster, the Jewish and Israel Studies Program, and Gender and Sexuality Studies. She has published a monograph entitled *An Emotional State: The Politics of Emotion in Postwar West German Culture* (University of Michigan Press, 2015); other publications include articles on psychoanalysis, exile and cosmopolitanism, German women film makers and, of late, on the interdisciplinary writings by Jewish-German exile, author and psychoanalyst Hans Keilson in edited collections and journals, including *New German Critique*, *Exilforschung*, and *Psychoanalysis and History*. During 2021–2022 she was a Faculty Member at the Alice Kaplan Institute for the Humanities at Northwestern, where she worked on a book titled *Contrapuntal Humanism*. In 2019–2020 an Andrew W. Mellon New Directions Fellowship allowed her to pursue formal training in the fields of forensic science, criminal justice, and forensic and cultural anthropology towards her next project on modalities of evidence.

Damani J. Partridge is a Professor of Anthropology and Afroamerican and African Studies at the University of Michigan. He is also an affiliate with the Department of Germanic Languages and Literatures and has published broadly on questions of citizenship, affect, urban space, sexuality, post-Cold War "freedom," Holocaust memorialization, African-American military occupation, Blackness and embodiment, the production of noncitizens, the culture and politics of "fair trade," and the Obama moment in Berlin. He has also made and worked on documentaries for private and public broadcasters in the United States and Canada, and currently directs the Filming Future Cities Project in Detroit and Berlin (see filmingfuturecities.org). His first book, *Hypersexuality and Headscarves: Race, Sex, and Citizenship in the New Germany*, was published in the New Anthropologies of Europe series with Indiana University Press in 2012. His forthcoming book, *Blackness as a Universal Claim: Holocaust Heritage, Noncitizen Futures, and Black Power in Berlin* will be published with the University of California Press in 2022.

Erik Porath is a philosopher, media scholar and visual artist based in Berlin. He received his Ph.D. from the University of Basel in 2004 with a dissertation entitled *Gedächtnis des*

Unerinnerbaren. Philosophische und medientheoretische Untersuchungen zur Freudschen Psychoanalyse (Bielefeld: transcript 2005). His research interests include theories of expression, memory theory, media theory, history of concepts and science, psychoanalysis, contemporary art. Porath is on the editorial board of *RISS. Zeitschrift für Psychoanalyse* and co-founder of the *Assoziation für die Freudsche Psychoanalyse* (AFP.) His publications include: *Kinästhetik und Kommunikation: Ränder und Interferenzen des Ausdrucks*, Berlin: Kadmos 2013 (Ed. with Tobias Robert Klein); *Arbeit (in) der Psychoanalyse*, Bielefeld: transcript 2012 (Ed. with Anna Tuschling); *Figuren des Ausdrucks. Formation einer Wissenskategorie zwischen 1700 und 1850*, Munich: Fink 2012 (Ed. with Tobias Robert Klein); *Ränder der Enzyklopädie*, Berlin: Merve-Verlag 2012 (with Christine Blättler). His most recent publication is entitled "Im Zusammenhang: Auge, Bild, Wort, Geschichte. Zu Alexander Kluges Einsatz der Bilder im Text", in: Richard Langston/Leslie Adelson/N. D. Jones/Leonie Wilms, eds.: *The Poetic Power of Theory. Alexander Kluge Jahrbuch 6/2019*.

Zafer Şenocak is a widely published German poet, essayist, journalist, literary translator and editor, who has won several prestigious literary awards in Germany. He is a leading voice in the German discussions on multiculturalism, national and cultural identity, and a mediator between Turkish and German culture. His writings have been translated into Turkish, English, French, Dutch, and Hebrew. Translations into English include *Atlas of a Tropical Germany: Essays on Politics and Culture, 1990–1998*. Translated and edited by Leslie Adelson (University of Nebraska Press, 2000) and the poetry collection *Door Languages*, translated by Elizabeth Oehlkers Wright (Brookline, MA: Zephyr Press, 2008).

Yoko Tawada is a bilingual poet residing in Berlin. Tawada was born in Japan and educated at Tokyo's Waseda University and the universities of Hamburg and Zurich. Major awards for her writing including the Akutagawa Prize, the Tanizaki Prize, and the Kleist Prize. Tawada has published 24 book titles in German and 30 book titles in Japanese. Her work has been also translated into more than two dozen languages including English. Her most recent novels in English translation, all published with New Directions publishers, include *The Emissary* (from the Japanese), *Memoirs of a Polar Bear* (from the German), *The Naked Eye* (from the German), and *The Bridegroom was a Dog* (from the Japanese.) Her story collections in English translation include *Where Europe Begins* (from the German and the Japanese) *Facing the Bridge* (from the Japanese and the German) and *Three Streets* (from the Japanese.)

Jamie H. Trnka is Professor of German and Chair of Classics and Modern Languages at Xavier University (Cincinnati, OH, USA). Her comparative research addresses literatures of migration and exile, documentary and paraliterary writing, theatre and performance studies, translation studies, international artistic collaboration, and cultural history. She is the author of *Revolutionary Subjects: German Literatures, Geoculture, and the Limits of Aesthetic Solidarity with Latin America* (2015). Her current project is in the evolving field of Critical European Studies and examines collective translation and transnational, multimedial authorship as key forms of advancing new political and aesthetic agendas in twenty-first century Europe. She has published numerous articles in such journals as *Critical Stages, Internationales Archiv für Sozialgeschichte der Literatur, The German Quarterly, German Studies Review*, and *New German Critique*.

Ulrike Vedder is Professor of German at the Institute for German Literature at the Humboldt-University in Berlin and co-editor of the *Zeitschrift für Germanistik*. Her research areas include literary gender studies; narrations on the threshold of death; literature and material culture; genealogy, heritage, generation. Recent publications include: *Gegenwart schreiben. Zur deutschsprachigen Literatur 2000–2015* (Ed. with C. Caduff, 2017); *Handbuch Literatur & Materielle Kultur* (Ed. with S. Scholz, 2018, Paperback 2019); *Herausforderungen des Realismus. Theodor Fontanes Gesellschaftsromane* (Ed. with P. U. Hohendahl, 2018); *Alter und Geschlecht. Soziale Verhältnisse und kulturelle Repräsentationen* (Ed. with E. Reitinger, P. Chiangong, 2018); *Grenzen des Humanen. Biotechnologie und Medizin in der Gegenwartsliteratur* (Ed. with A.-K. Reulecke, Issue 3/2018 of *Zeitschrift für Germanistik*); *Das moderne Haus. Bau- und Wohnformen in der (Sach-)Literatur* (Ed. with C. Holm, Issue 1/2020 of *Zeitschrift für Germanistik*); and *Museales Erzählen. Dinge, Räume, Narrative* (Ed. with J. Stapelfeldt, K. Wiehl, 2020).

Yasemin Yildiz is Associate Professor of German and Comparative Literature at UCLA. Prof. Yildiz's first book, *Beyond the Mother Tongue: The Postmonolingual Condition* (New York: Fordham University Press, 2012) won the MLA's Scaglione Prize in Germanic Languages and Literatures in 2012 and received Honorable Mention for the Laura Shannon Prize for Contemporary European Studies in 2014. She has translated Turkish-German literature into English and published essays on topics ranging from multilingualism, literature of migration, Berlin literature, Holocaust testimonies, and minority discourse to Islam and gender in Europe. In 2016, she was awarded the DAAD Prize for Distinguished Scholarship in German and European Studies for her work to date. Currently, she is working on the book project *Memory Citizenship*: *Migrant Archives of Holocaust Remembrance*, co-authored with Michael Rothberg.

Index

Abasıyanık, Sait Faik 157, 160
Adelson, Leslie A.
– as translator 16, 139
– critique of betweenness 3–4, 15, 119–121, 136
– critique of positivism 3, 5n15, 120
– on affect 4–5, 234n3
– on Alexander Kluge 4–6, 17, 19, 78–80, 273
– on bodies 80, 101–102
– on German literature of Turkish migration 2, 4, 6, 9, 139
– on futurity 6, 17, 19, 273
– on quotidian labor 281–282, 293
– on referentiality 3–4, 5n15, 7, 18, 19, 120, 292
– on touching tales 1–5, 9, 16, 18–19, 90, 116, 139, 234n3, 318, 325–327, 329, 331
– on Yoko Tawada 6, 8, 19, 121, 127, 280–281, 291
– on Zafer Şenocak 5n16, 6, 16n45, 19, 139–140
– Works
– "Against Between" 2, 119–121
– *Cosmic Miniatures and Future Sense* 4, 6, 16, 75, 79, 90, 264, 273
– *Crisis of Subjectivity* 17n48
– "Experiment Mars" 6
– "Future Narrative" 10
– "Literary Imagination and the Future of Literary Studies" 6, 14, 16, 195, 208, 281
– *Making Bodies, Making History* 4, 48–49, 101–102
– "Opposing Oppositions" 1, 2
– "Touching Tales" 2–5, 7–9, 14–16, 18–19, 90, 114–116, 139, 147n27, 234, 318, 323–33
– *The Turkish Turn* 2, 4, 140n5, 234n3, 292, 323–326
Adler, H. G. 57–58, 68
Adorno, Theodor W. 57n15, 210, 273, 275
affect
– and belonging 191–192
– and precarity 266–269
– connection to the world 202
– in structure of hatred 14, 62–69
– of touching tales 4–5, 116, 234n3
Afrofuturism 8
Agamben, Giorgio 259
Akhanlı, Doğan 155n59
Ali, Sabahattin 158–160
alienation
– alienation effect 306n30
– Jaeggi on 261, 272–273
– multilingual 301, 306
– of the proletariat 268
animality 168, 183
animals
– anthropomorphization of 170, 172n27, 174
– as commodities 170
– displaced 173
– H. A. Rey's depictions of 12, 165–168, 174–184
– humans as 169
– in *The Emissary* 282–283
– Jewish representations of 184–185
Armenian genocide 5, 146, 153
Anna O. *see*: Pappenheim, Bertha
antifascism
– aesthetics of 35, 44–47
– literature of 14, 31, 35–47
– memory in 34, 40–42, 44, 48
antisemitism
– affective structure of 14, 62–69
– animalization as 169
– in Chile 40
– Muslim and Arab subjects accused of 326
Appadurai, Arjun 6, 195n21, 281n5
Apter, Emily 156, 161
Arendt, Hannah 261, 268
Asian-German Studies 8–9
Assmann, Aleida 244
Auerbach, Erich 156–157
Ausländer, Rose 18, 297–299, 310–313, 315
Ausländerliteratur 2n3, 145n19
– *see also*: German literature of Turkish migration

autobiography
- autobiographical contract (Lejeune) 192n7
- in Holocaust literature 57–58, 60
- elements of in Stanišić 192–194, 201, 204, 210
autofiction 16, 192n8, 193n9, 200n51, 212n138
Arslan, Gizem 11, 18, 50, 133
Avellaneda, Andrés 44
Aydemir, Fatma and Hengameh Yaghoobifarah 11

Bachmann, Ingeborg 142–143
Bakhtin, Mikhail 283–284
Barthes, Roland 41n38, 259
Bartolini, Paulo 45n51, 46n54, 48n58
Baudelaire, Charles 298
Baudrillard, Jean 259
belonging
- and identity 302–303, 312
- as product of critical fabulation 194–199, 202–205
- "De-Heimatize Belonging" 191
- in relation to *Heimat* 191, 238, 302–303
- in Stanišić 191–192, 194, 199, 202, 204–205, 211
- in Oliver 18, 302–303, 312
Benjamin, Walter
- inter-linear translation 280
- on 'after-life' of art 288
- on 'art of being off center' 90
- on 'homogenous, empty time' 53
- on literary imagination 157
- on order and chaos 110–111
- on translatability 141–142, 160
Benveniste, Émile 125–127, 131, 132n39
Berger, John 167
Berlant, Lauren 266
betweenness
- Adelson's critique of 3–4, 15, 119–121, 136
- and ethnicity 130–132, 136
- in Tawada 119–136
bilingualism *see: multilingualism*
blackness 131, 199, 209
Black Germans 8n27, 10, 324
bodies
- Adelson on 80, 101–102

- body-texts (Körper-Texte) 308
- entanglement of texts and 240
- in *The Emissary* 282–285, 286, 293
- in *The Long Summer of Theory* 261, 274
- hystericized 101–102
- *see also: corpses*
Bosnian genocide 199, 202, 207
Brandt, Bettina 9, 19, 44, 124
Brecht, Bertolt 209, 231, 306n30
Breger, Claudia 10n33, 10n34, 11, 16, 18, 303n17
Breuer, Josef 95–106, 112
Büchner, Georg 218–219

Cazdyn, Eric 292
Celan, Paul
- as translator 298
- Hebrew language in 314
- influence on Oliver 18, 299–300, 304, 310, 312–318
- influence on Şenocak 140, 142, 297, 312, 318
- influence on Tawada 120–121, 127, 299
- rootlessness of 298
Cerda, Carlos
- antifascist politics of 14, 31, 34–48
- as exilic author 13–14, 31–32, 34–37, 44, 47
- connection to Communist Party of Chile 31, 43
- multidirectional memory in 34, 36, 39, 41–42, 48–49
- multilingualism in 14
- suspended time in 14, 34–35, 41, 46, 49
- Works
- *An Empty House* ("Una casa vacía") 38
- "Balconies with Flags" ("Balkons mit Fahnen" / "Balcones con banderas") 35, 37n21, 47
- "Dialectic of the Persecuted" ("Dialektik des Verfolgten") 36, 40n33
- *Explorations II* 37
- "Manola" 36, 37n20
- "The Poet's Trip to the Heart of Time" ("Reise des Dichters zum Herzen der Zeit") 36
- "The Poster" ("Das Plakat") 37–48, 50

Index — 347

– "The Student in Leipzig" ("Der Student in Leipzig") 36, 37n20
– *Written with L* ("Escrito con L") 37
Chandler, Nahum Dimitri 130–132, 136
chronotope 184, 279–295
cinema *see: film*
Cold War, the 5, 55, 250n40
collective identity 139, 160, 192, 194
collective memory *see: memory*
colonialism
– in Brazil, legacy of 12, 168, 176
– Japanese 289
– neocolonialism 176, 182
– settler 12, 168–169, 181n58
comparison
– limits of 198, 323–327
– Pappenheim on 108
– Rothberg on 49, 323, 325
corpses
– corpse-poem (Fuss) 64–65, 68
– illegal (Adelson) 59, 63
– poetics of 65–66, 68
cosmopolitanism
– Apter on 161
– German as language of 106
– in *Baumgarter's Bombay* 85–86
– in Brazil 184
COVID-19 78, 279
cultural fable
– touching tales as alternative 2–4
Culler, Jonathan 33n6, 132
Czernowitz 140, 297, 298n30, 299–300, 310–317

dazwischen see: betweenness
de Man, Paul 288
de Bary, Brett 13, 18, 127n26
decolonization 12n40, 19, 83
defamiliarization 140, 148–149, 161, 306
Deleuze, Gilles 105, 209, 259, 306n29
denazification 59
Desai, Anita 14, 73–90
– multilingualism in 15
Dickinson, Kristin 5, 21, 144, 159, 162, 298

digital media
– affordances of 233, 240, 242–243, 247, 249, 251
– born-digital texts 17, 233, 243, 251
– e-poems 243, 247, 251
– electronic literature (Haynes) 239–240, 248
– reading practices developed by 240
– Prezi, literary use of 243–251
disorientation
– deliberate production of 35–36, 47, 247, 309, 314, 317
– semantic 104
– spatial 309, 314
– temporal, of torture 40–41
displacement
– as structuring *Heimat* 299, 301, 303, 318
– collective experiences of 48
– forgotten histories of 1
– poetry of 298
– *see also: exile*
Du Bois, W. E. B. 131–132

East Germany *see: German Democratic Republic*
ecocriticism 237
El-Tayeb, Fatima 3n6, 10n32
electronic literature *see: digital media*
enunciation 125–127, 131–132
ethnicized subjects 119–121
– *see also: race and ethnicity*
ethno-nationalism 1, 75
ethnography 19, 111, 327
exile
– and refugeedom 12, 14
– and translation 13, 45–47, 49
– as mode of literary circulation 33
– as process 33–34
– experience of 32, 34, 36
– literature of 13–14, 31–34, 44, 46, 55–56, 75–76
– memory in 34, 47
– of Chilean leftists in GDR 14, 31–32, 37–43, 48
– relationship to time 13–14, 34, 46, 49
– *see also: forced migration, refugees*

fabulation
- Afro-fabulation 10n33, 199, 200n52–53, 209
- critical fabulation 10n33, 194, 198–199, 209–211
- reflexive 200, 212
- relationship to truth 194, 200–201, 206, 208
- reparative potential of 16, 194, 198, 202–203

fascism
- aesthetics of 47
- aftermaths of 13
- contemporary resurgence of 40, 50
- in Austria 114
- in Pinochet's Chile 14, 39
- memory of 41, 45
- post-fascism 18, 41, 294–295
- *see also: Nazism*

feminism
- and femininity 260–262
- in 1970s cinema 262
- in *The Long Summer of Theory* 257–258, 260, 262–264, 267, 269–275
- postfeminism 260–262, 269, 273, 275
- third wave 261

fictionality 16, 193, 195–199, 203

film
- cinematic language of 257, 262, 273
- French New Wave 262
- postfeminist 260–262, 269, 273, 275
- social critique 259

forced migration
- of ethnic German expellees from Czechoslovakia 234, 243–246, 250n40, 252
- of Kurds within Turkey 7
- *see also: exile, refugees*

form, elements of
- experimentation in 8, 12, 33, 206, 299–300, 304, 308–309, 317–318
- focalization 63, 105, 126–127, 131, 136, 234–236, 243, 249
- imagery 102, 134–135, 180, 225, 252, 289, 298, 315
- narration 8n28, 57, 86, 148, 194, 199, 200, 211, 236, 243

- prosody 125, 133, 135
- rhythm 113, 121, 130–136, 315

fragmentation 9, 57, 68, 148, 196, 211n129, 243–244, 247, 313

Fraser, Nancy 272

Freud, Sigmund
- Keilson's interest in 54, 61–62, 66–67
- in Wolf 106, 112–114
- on the uncanny 318
- treatment of Bertha Pappenheim 95–103, 109n48

Fukushima meltdown 292, 295

Fürstenfelde (Fürstenwerder) 234–243, 251

future sense 6, 14, 73–90

futurity 6, 10n32, 17, 19, 83, 264, 268, 273

Gadamer, Hans-Georg 149

Ganguly, Debjai 80–81, 86

gaps (conceptual motif)
- in Oliver 307
- in Pappenheim 15, 95, 100–104, 107–108, 110, 114–115
- in Şenocak 148, 298
- in Stanišić 199
- in Wolf 15, 112–113

Gastarbeiterliteratur 2n3
- *see also: German literature of Turkish migration*

generational identity
- effect of 1970s student protest movement on 217–219, 222
- 'generation of 1968,' memory of 17, 257–259, 264, 269–270
- of millennials 264–265, 267

genre
- and fictionality 193, 195–196, 201, 212
- choose-your-own-adventure 205
- corpse-poem (Fuss) 64–65, 68
- epistolary novel 223
- essay film 261
- *Heimat*-genres 17, 192, 237–238, 303
- object biography 110–111
- of Holocaust literature 57, 58n16

German Cultural Studies 1, 31

German Democratic Republic 14, 31–50, 235, 250n40

German-Jewish authors 7, 14, 15, 18, 53–54, 57–59, 60, 95, 104, 140, 169, 184, 310
German Jewish Studies 7n24, 90
– see also: Jews
German literature of Turkish migration see: Adelson
Gezen, Ela 5, 11n36
global novel, the 15, 73–90
Godard, Jean-Luc 262, 269
Goethe, Johann Wolfgang 17, 34n9, 115, 143, 153, 218–220, 223, 227–228
Gordon, Avery F. 53, 69
Göktürk, Deniz 5n15, 15, 17, 203n71
Götting, Michael 9, 10n31, 19
Gramling, David 13n43, 160, 203n71

Haraway, Donna 199
Hartman, Saidiya 10n33, 16, 194n15, 198–199, 202, 209
Hayles, Katherine 239–240, 24817–18, 79
Heimat
– and migration 10–11
– as touching tale 18
– association with nationalism 18, 191, 243
– "De-Heimatize Belonging" 191
– digital engagement with 17, 233–234, 239, 241–243, 251–252
– genres of 17, 192, 237–238, 303
– "Haus der Heimat" 238–239, 241–243, 251
– intermedial engagements with 242–243, 251
– José F. A. Oliver's critique of 299–309, 317–318
– Paul Celan's Czernowitz as 300, 310, 315
– reclamation of 18, 191
– resurgence in contemporary German discourse of 10–11, 191, 303n17
– Saša Stanišić on 191–213
– sensory and medial dimensions of 317–318
– social construction of 238, 243
Heimatliteratur 17, 192–194, 237–238, 242, 303
Heller, Agnes 48–49
Hilsenrath, Edgar 58
Hirsch, Marianne 41n38, 243n22
history of Turkish-German cultural exchange 143–144, 147–149

Hoffman, E. T. A. 226–232
Holocaust
– aftermath of, co-incidence with partition of India and Pakistan 74, 83, 89
– and anti-fascist memory 40
– appropriation, Desai accused of 74–77
– comparisons to 40–41
– Holocaust piety (Rose) 60
– memory of 5, 60, 244n23
– memorialization of 41, 323–326
– relativization of 244
– literary representations of 18, 57–58, 60–61, 68–69, 298
hope
– Adelson on 6, 17–18, 79, 83, 90, 273, 293
– counterfactual (Adelson) 6, 17, 79
– countertemporality of 41
– in Cerda 41–42, 44, 45–47
– labor of 266
Hoyos, Hector 32, 43

identity 7n25, 9, 42, 44, 77, 126, 153, 202, 204, 244, 267, 285, 297, 299, 302, 304
– see also: collective identity
imagination see: literary imagination
immigration see: migration
imperialism 87, 134, 289, 292
Interkulturelle Literatur 2n3
intermediality 1, 17, 133, 233, 242–243, 251
intertextuality
– and multilingualism 15, 112
– in Oliver 18
– in Şenocak 157–161
– in Schneider 17, 218, 223, 227
– post-modern 149
irony 15, 140–141, 145, 148–149, 153, 294

Jaeggi, Rahel 258, 261–262, 267, 272–273, 275
Jameson, Fredric 290, 292–293
Jews
– as refugees from Nazism 14, 73–75, 83, 85–88, 158
– hystericized bodies of 100–102
– immigration of 168, 170, 177
– in colonial India 14, 73, 76, 78n12, 86, 90
– in touching tales 5, 140, 318

- purported zoophobia of 169
- see also: German-Jewish

Kafka, Franz 34n9, 143, 169, 224, 226
Keilson, Hans
- and psychoanalysis 14, 61, 66, 68–69
- Jewish identity of 14, 53, 57
- publication history 14, 54, 56, 58–59
- spectral modernism of 14, 68–69
- uncanniness in 61, 68
- untimeliness in 14, 53–55
- Works
- *Comedy in a Minor Key* (*Komödie in Moll*) 54, 56, 59–60, 63
- *The Death of the Adversary* (*Der Tod des Widersachers*) 14, 54–56, 60–64, 67
- *Life Goes On* (*Das Leben geht weiter*) 54
- *There my House Stands* (*Da steht mein Haus*) 53, 69
Kim, John Namjun 3n6, 15, 18
Kluge, Alexander 4–6, 17, 19, 78–80, 273
Klüger, Ruth 60–61, 69
Komska, Yuliya 12, 16
Konuk, Kader 5n16, 156
Kurdi, Alan 19, 328–329

labor
- craftwork, as women's 107–109
- cultural 3, 9
- exploitation of 79, 170
- hope labor 266
- migrants', invisibility of 260
- neoliberal regimes of 265, 274–275
- quotidian (Adelson) 281–282, 293
- women's, invisibility of 269–270, 274
landscape (place) 185, 238–239, 289, 313, 315
language
- crossings 8n26, 15, 48, 140
- materiality of 15, 18, 124–125, 128, 132–133, 308, 310
- politics of 293–294, 305–306
- referential function of 15, 132, 135, 308, 316n60
- relationship to land/place 297–299, 301, 312, 314–316
- sensorium of 308

- tropological dimension of 121
- see also: multilingualism
- see also: translation
Latour, Bruno 196
Layne, Priscilla 8n27
Leitkultur 203, 236
linguistic anarchy 292–293, 295
literary figuration 3, 120, 315
Lowe, Lisa 199
Lützeler, Paul Michael 17

Mani, B. Venkat 2n3, 14
materiality *see: language*
materialism
- New Materialism 43
- transcultural 32, 43
McLennan, Sophia 46
mediation
- imprecise sites of (Adelson) 79, 86
- of Heimat 18, 299–301, 303–304, 309
- writing as 152, 300, 316
memory
- antifascist 34, 40–42, 44, 48
- and migration 5, 18, 60, 147n27, 237, 298, 301
- co-memory 42
- cultural 41n38, 115, 147, 160, 244
- collective 147
- global circulation of 32, 81, 86
- global politics of 40, 42, 60, 139, 160
- in exile 13, 14, 34, 46–48
- *lieux de mémoire* 184
- multidirectional 34, 36, 39, 41–42, 48–49, 298, 324–326
- postmemory 41n38, 243, 246
- remembrance 4, 39, 40, 41n38, 86, 160, 234, 252n43
Mennel, Barbara 17–18
migration
- between Germany and Turkey 2n3, 4, 11, 36, 156, 203n71
- conceptions of 2, 5–6, 10–12, 78, 157, 169, 209, 238, 298, 300, 304, 306n30
- multigenerational experience of 298
- literature of 2, 4, 6, 11, 18, 82, 192, 238, 298, 306

Migrantenliteratur 2n3
– see also: German literature of Turkish migration
– see also: migration
modernism
– contrast with aesthetics of Brazilianness 175
– formal techniques of 57
– spectral 14, 68–69
modernity
– Benjamin on 53
– feminine Jewish 100, 101n23
monolingualism 13n43, 160, 301n10
Morris, Leslie 7n24, 90, 312
multilingualism
– Adelson on 1, 12–13, 31
– as code-stitching 82, 84
– as cultural norm 106
– in the global novel 82, 90
– of German Studies 1, 8–9, 12–13
– subjectivity of 160
Mulvey, Laura 261, 269

Nadolny, Sten 19
narration *see: form*
narrative
– Adelson on 4–6, 10, 79, 82, 87, 292–293
– destabilizations of 35, 44, 47, 61, 148, 200, 211, 261
– in Asian-German studies 9–10
– medial affordances of 233, 248–249
– see also: time
narratology 6, 16–17, 195–199, 200n51, 237n11
nation-state
– history in service of 136
– Japan, concept of 136
– Japan, nineteenth-century "opening" of 132, 134, 135
– partition of India/Pakistan 74, 83, 89
– sovereignty of 135–136
– Turkey's emergence as 151, 155, 158
nationalism
– contemporary resurgence of 161
– Serbian 208
– Turkish 149, 153
– relationship of Spanish and German to 305

Nazism
– annexation of Czechoslovakia under 246
– comparisons to Chilean fascism 14, 34
– flight of Jews from 14, 54, 87, 155, 156, 184
– German-Turkish relationship under 149–156
neoliberalism 18, 260, 262, 265–266, 269–270, 274–275
Nousek, Katrina L. 10n34, 11, 17–18, 192n6
Nyong'o, Tavia 10n33, 198–199, 200n52, 201, 209–210

Oliver, José F. A.
– and Şenocak 18, 297, 298, 312, 318
– critique of *Heimat* 299–309, 317–318
– on Paul Celan 18, 299–300, 304, 310, 312–318
– on Rose Ausländer 18, 297–299, 310–313, 315
– Works
– "compass & twilight" ("kompaß & dämmerung") 304–306, 309
– "Czernowitz" 314–315
– *finnish winter reservoir* (*finnischer wintervorrat*) 317
– *guestrooms* (*fremdenzimmer*) 304n23, 305
– *HOMELAND/LANGUID and other FOSSIL DREAMS* (*HEIMATT und andere FOSSILE TRÄUME*) 18, 301–302, 307n33
– "Lemberg – Czernowitz, chance-images" ("Lemberg – Czernowitz, zufallsbilder") 315
– *nightfringetraces* (*nachtrandspuren*) 304–305, 306n28
– *sandscript* (*sandschrift*) 306n30, 313
– *tripwriter* (*fahrtenschreiber*) 310, 313–316
Ören, Aras 11n36, 16, 19, 145n19
Otoo, Sharon Dodua 7–8
Özdamar, Emine Sevgi 4, 9–10, 11n36, 19

Pamuk, Orhan 144
Pappenheim, Bertha (Anna O.)
– aphasia of 15, 99, 103–104, 106
– as translator 95–96, 100, 106–107
– Jewish identity of 96, 100–102, 104, 106, 114–115

- lace collection and lacework of 96–98, 107–110
- multilingualism 15, 96, 103–107
- Works
- "The Tale of the Old Lace" 109–110
paratextuality 238n14, 240, 245–246, 248
Parkinson, Anna 13, 14, 15, 56n9, 59n20
Partridge, Damani J. 4n13, 18–19
poetics
- ironic 160–161
- of citation 148–149
- of the uncanny 59
- of torture 7
pop culture 236, 242
Porath, Erik 15
post-fascism *see: fascism*
post-feminism *see: feminism*
posthumanism 8, 169
postmemory *see: memory*
postnational intimacy (Adelson) 325, 329
precarity 18, 257, 265–272, 275
psychoanalysis 15, 66, 68n44, 69, 95, 99–104, 202

race and ethnicity 120–121, 130–131, 159, 169, 257, 269–273, 275, 312n43
- *see also: blackness, whiteness*
Rancière, Jacques 196–197, 259
reading publics
- global 35, 48
- global Anglophone 56, 301
- postwar German 14, 55–56
- postwar Turkish 151
referentiality
- definition of 3–4
- riddle of referentiality (Adelson) 4, 18–19, 292–293
- within fictional discourse 199, 203
Rey, Margret 166–167, 170–179, 185
Reyersbach, Hans Anderson (H. A. Rey)
- Jewish identity of 12, 165, 168, 170
- work in advertising 12, 168–179
- Works
- *Cecily G. and the Nine Monkeys* 172
- *Curious George* series 12, 167n8, 171–173, 185

- *Nonsense ABCs* 173, 174n30
- *The Story of a Boy who Became an Anteater* (*História do menino que verou tamanduá*) 181–183
reunification of Germany 139, 153, 227, 244
Ricoeur, Paul 149, 196n30
refugees
- and the novel form 75–80
- creation of 73
- German Jewish refugees in India 73, 90
- refugee literature 75, 82
- temporality of experience 14, 82
- *see also: exile, forced migration*
Rothberg, Michael 39n30, 58n16, 199, 298n5, 323–326

Saeko, Kimura 282, 294
Saemmer, Alexandra
- expulsion as theme in 234, 243–244, 246–247, 251
- Works
- "Böhmische Dörfer" 233, 243, 245–247, 250
- *see also: digital media*
Şahin, Cemile 7
Salomon, Ernst von 58–59
Sanyal, Mithu 7n25
script
- Arabic, as private language 145–146
- *kanji* 121, 129n32, 133–134
- *katakana* 286, 294
- Latin, Turkish transition to 149–156
Sedgwick, Eve Kosofsky 194n18, 202–203
Schneider, Peter
- influence of student protest movement on 17, 217, 219, 222
- intertextuality in 17, 218, 223, 227
- *Sturm und Drang* 17, 218, 222
- Works
- *... Already You Are An Enemy of the Constitution* (*... Schon bist du ein Verfassungsfeind*) 218, 223–225
- *Couplings* (*Paarungen*) 227–231
- *Lenz* 17, 218–223, 227–228
- *The Wall Jumper* (*Der Mauerspringer*) 226, 228

Şenocak, Zafer
- Adelson on 5n15–16, 6, 16, 19, 139–140, 147n27
- as translator 141–143
- connections to Oliver 18, 297, 298, 312, 318
- irony in 15, 140–141, 145, 148–149, 153
- on 'black whites' 143, 145
- poetics of 148–149, 161
- translation in 139–142, 145, 148–149, 152, 156, 161
- Works
- "Ausreisen oder Reißaus nehmen" ("To Exit or To Escape") 19
- *The Foreign Dwells in Everyone* (*Das Fremde, das in jedem wohnt*) 140–142
- *German Education* (*Alman Terbiyesi / Deutsche Schule*) 147, 149–155, 157–158, 160–161
- *Perilous Kinship* (*Gefährliche Verwandtschaft*) 5n16, 146–147, 149, 152, 161
- *The Perpendicular Sea* (*Das senkrechte Meer*) 142
- *Rituals of the Youth* (*Rituale der Jugend*) 142
- *Wanderlust Institutions* (*Fernwehanstalten*) 142
settler colonialism *see*: colonialism
Shemoelof, Mati 7
Sherman, Cindy 125
Spiegelman, Art 241n18
solidarity 17, 31, 37, 43–45, 47, 149, 222, 257, 262, 264–265, 273
spatiality 132, 247, 284
Spivak, Gayatri 139, 142–145
Stanišić, Saša
- fabulation in 16, 194–195, 198–203, 205–206, 209–212
- inter/mediation in 17, 239–240
- narratological dimensions of 17, 233–237, 239–240, 242
- reparative project of 16, 194, 202–203, 205, 208, 210
- Works
- *Before the Feast* (*Vor dem Fest*) 17, 192, 233–237, 251–252
- "Fürstenfelde" 234–243, 251

- *Herkunft* (*Where You Come From*) 10n33, 16–17, 191–194, 197–212, 233n2, 238
- *How the Soldier Repairs the Gramophone* (*Wie der Soldat das Grammofon repariert*) 192
storytelling 33, 79, 81–82, 90, 96, 180, 198, 209, 211, 236, 242
Strauss, Botho 17n48, 19
synchronicity 13, 38, 44, 290

Tawada, Yoko
- "absent cause" in 18, 289–293
- Adelson on 6, 8, 19
- and Asian-German Studies 8–9
- betweenness in 3n6, 15, 119–136
- influence of Paul Celan on 120–121, 127, 299
- referentiality in 18, 120–121, 132, 135, 136, 292
- time in 127–128, 132, 280–287, 289–293
- writing disaster 18, 282, 286, 289, 291–293, 295
- writing systems in 121, 129n32, 133–134, 286, 294
- Works
- *A Brother-in-Law in Bordeaux* (*Schwager in Bordeaux / Borudō no gikei*) 284
- *The Emissary* (*Kentōshi*) 18, 279–295
- *Nothing Only Where You Are* (Nur da wo du bist da ist nichts / Anata no iru tokoro dake nani mo nai) 284
- *Paul Celan and the Chinese Angel* (*Paul Celan und der chinesische Engel*) 299
- "A Poem for a Book" ("Ein Gedicht für ein Buch") 121–127, 132–134
- "The Name and the Time" ("Der Name und die Zeit") 19
- *Time Differences* (*Kyūkei Jikan*) 284
- "The Translator's Gate or Celan Reads Japanese" ("Tor des Übersetzers oder Celan liest Japanisch") 120–121
- "Yokohama" (よこはま) 121, 128–129, 130–135
temporality *see also*: time
- Adelson on 6, 13, 82
- of antifascism 34–35, 46
- of exile 14, 34, 59

- of fascism 36, 47
- of language 125–126, 285, 288
- of translation (Walkowitz) 49
thing theory 109
time see also: temporality
- and narrative 35, 57
- calendrical time 14, 78, 82
- refugee time 14, 73–90
- sensorium of (Adelson) 6, 273
- suspended time 14, 31–50
- untimeliness 14, 53–56
touching tales 2–5, 7–9, 14–16, 18–19, 90, 114–116, 139, 147n27, 234, 318, 323–33
Transnational German Studies 1, 10–11, 13, 16
transnationalism 1, 5n15, 14, 32, 40, 44, 156, 209, 237n11, 323–325
translatability 120, 141–142
translation
- Benjamin on 141, 288
- "born translated" 45
- cultural contact through 144
- ethics of 160
- in world literary study 32–33
- politics of 46, 160
- Spivak on 142
translation studies 44
translative reading 48–50
translators
- as double agents 149, 153–157
- invisibility of 160
- labor of 139
- outsider/insider 140, 148, 161
trauma 40, 41n37, 42, 57, 69, 101, 103, 235, 243–244, 247–248, 252, 295
Trnka, Jamie 9, 13, 14–15
"Turkish archive" 5n15
Turkish literature 141–149, 158, 160
Turkish-German literature 2n3, 5n15, 7, 9–10, 11n36–38, 15, 147n27, 158, 297
- see also: German literature of Turkish migration

typography, experimental
- in Oliver 301, 304, 309, 315–318
- in Tawada 299
- in Uljana Wolf 111–112

uncanny, the (das Unheimliche) 54, 59–68, 318

Vedder, Ulrike 15, 17
ventriloquism 65, 140, 148–149, 152, 154, 161
Vergangenheitsbewältigung 13
von Alberti, Irene 17, 257–275

Walkowitz, Rebecca 45–46, 49
Wenzel, Olivia 8n27, 8n28
whiteness 12n40, 17–18, 257, 260, 262, 265, 270–272, 275, 302, 330
witnessing 42n41, 43, 325
work see: labor
Wolf, Uljana
- intertexts 103–104, 106, 112–113
- multilingualism in the work of 12n42, 15, 103–104, 111
- Works
- Method Acting with Anna O. 104, 111
- "tatting" 112–133
- "Annalogue on Flowers" 104
- "Annalogue on Oranges" 104–106
world literature
- circulation of 31–33, 49, 75, 143, 242n21
- debates in 32, 145
- translation in 32, 45, 143, 145, 158
writing systems see: script

Yildiz, Yasemin 5n16, 12n41, 13n43, 50, 136, 312

Zweig, Stefan 184

www.ingramcontent.com/pod-product-compliance
Lightning Source LLC
Chambersburg PA
CBHW020218170426
43201CB00007B/254